HOW TO REACH & TEACH
ALL STUDENTS
in the INCLUSIVE
CLASSROOM

*Ready-to-Use Strategies, Lessons
and Activities for Teaching Students
with Diverse Learning Needs*

SANDRA F. RIEF • JULIE A. HEIMBURGE

**THE CENTER FOR APPLIED
RESEARCH IN EDUCATION**
West Nyack, New York 10994

Library of Congress Cataloging-in-Publication Data

Rief, Sandra F.
    How to reach & teach all children in the inclusive classroom : ready-to-use strategies, lessons, and activities for teaching students with diverse learning needs / Sandra F. Rief, Julie A. Heimburge.
        p. cm.
    Includes bibliographical references (p.   ).
    ISBN 0-87628-385-7 (spiral-wire/paper)—ISBN 0-87628-399-7 (pbk.)
    1. Mainstreaming in education—United States.   2. Elementary school teaching—United States.   3. Cognitive styles in children—United States.   4. Lesson Planning—United States.   5. Motivation in education—United States.   6. Learning disabled children—Education—United States.   I. Heimburge, Julie A.   II. Title.
LC3981.R54   1996   96-26633
371.9′046—dc20   CIP

Printed in the United States of America

10   9   8   7   6   5   4   3   2   1   10   9   8   7   6   5   4   3

ISBN 0-87628-385-7   ISBN 0-87628-399-7

ATTENTION: CORPORATIONS AND SCHOOLS

The Center for Applied Research in Education books are available at quantity discounts with bulk purchase for educational, business, or sales promotional use. For information, please write to: Prentice Hall Special Sales, 240 Frisch Court, Paramus, New Jersey 07652. Please supply: title of book, ISBN number, quantity, how the book will be used, date needed.

**THE CENTER FOR APPLIED RESEARCH
IN EDUCATION**
West Nyack, NY 10994
A Simon & Schuster Company

On the World Wide Web at http://www.phdirect.com

Prentice-Hall International (UK) Limited, *London*
Prentice-Hall of Australia Pty. Limited, *Sydney*
Prentice-Hall Canada Inc., *Toronto*
Prentice-Hall Hispanoamericana, S.A., *Mexico*
Prentice-Hall of India Private Limited, *New Delhi*
Prentice-Hall of Japan, Inc., *Tokyo*
Simon & Schuster Asia Pte. Ltd., *Singapore*
Editora Prentice-Hall do Brasil, Ltda., *Rio de Janeiro*

DEDICATION

This book is dedicated to all of our children—the many, many students we have been privileged to teach, and, of course, our own. They have all inspired and challenged us to keep learning, growing and developing as teachers.

ACKNOWLEDGMENTS

We wish to thank the following individuals:

- Those administrators, teachers, and district counselors from San Diego City and County Schools who shared with us regarding some positive programs and practices that are taking place in their schools: Carroll Jean Anderson, Eileen-Marie Moore, Barbra Balser, Mike Giafaglione, Ann Van Sickle, Dr. Jeannie Steeg (and team), Mary Gilliland, Fran Greene, Jeanette Lisiak, Steve Kaplan, Todd Morano, Jacqueline Montague, Tommie Lenox, Pat John, and Michael Calamar

- Our dear friends and colleagues, the wonderful staff and 'family' of Benchley-Weinberger Elementary School, San Diego Unified School District

- Ruth DeCarie, our creative and talented illustrator

- Dr. Carol Pearson Donahue, for her contribution to Section 8

- Our husbands for their computer and technical assistance, encouragement, and loving support

- Susan Kolwicz, our editor at Prentice-Hall/Simon & Schuster

- Sue Sachs, Jim Solo, and Kathy Aufsesser for being the best, most dynamic teaching partners we could hope for

- Those students who allowed us to showcase their work samples throughout this book: Laura, Sarah, Breanna, Bryan, Andy, Johnny, and James.

ABOUT THE AUTHORS

Sandra Rief, M.A., is a resource specialist and mentor teacher emeritus in San Diego Unified School District. She was the California Resource Specialist of the Year (1995). Sandra has been teaching full-time in public schools for over 20 years. She presents numerous workshops and conferences; and lectures nationally and internationally on the topic of effective instruction, strategies and school interventions for meeting the needs of students with learning and attention difficulties. Sandra is the author of several publications including the books *How to Reach and Teach ADD/ADHD Children* (The Center for Applied Research in Education, 1993), *Simply Phonics* (EBSCO Curriculum Materials, 1993), as well as the videos she developed and presented, *ADHD: Inclusive Instruction & Collaborative Practices* (National Professional Resources, 1995) and *How Can I Help My Child Succeed in School?* (Educational Resource Specialists, 1996).

Julie Heimburge has taught at the upper elementary level in San Diego Unified School District for the past twenty-five years. As a mentor teacher, she has been involved with curriculum writing, staff development, demonstration lessons, and inservice training throughout San Diego County. Her workshops focus on developmental learning, thematic teaching, language arts, and multiple intelligences. Julie received her Bachelor of Arts Degree and teaching credential from San Diego State University, and her Master of Arts Degree in Person-Centered Studies from the United States International University.

INTRODUCTION

As an educator you are in a position of great privilege. Every day you have the opportunity to make a positive difference in the lives of children. The manner in which you interact with your students, the environment you create, and the curriculum and methods you use to teach greatly affect how motivated and successful your students will be in the classroom. It also affects how willing your students will be to take risks, work together and accept others. Not only do you teach our students countless academic skills and behaviors, but you also have great influence on how your children accept and appreciate the differences among all of us. A vital role of your job as a teacher is to ensure that each of your students feels that he/she is vital to the "community," valued and respected for their individuality. You need to make the connection with your students, stimulate in them the desire to learn and participate, and do everything in your power to build their confidence and trust.

This philosophy and our strong belief are the underlying theme of this book. As colleagues and friends for a number of years, we have worked together and taught many of the same students. We are very fortunate to be teachers at an elementary school (Benchley-Weinberger Elementary) that has a strong commitment to the individual child. Our school of about 520 students is one of the magnet schools of San Diego Unified School District. We are located in a middle-class neighborhood of San Diego; however, the majority of our students are bussed from all parts of the city. We draw a very diverse population, with close to 50 percent non-white students. Our school has recently refocused as a "communications magnet," and we are in the process of enhancing our instructional program in this direction.

We have a reputation for high achievement and a very caring, nurturing, child-centered program with a great deal of parental support and involvement. Our staff has historically been on the cutting edge of innovative teaching practices including learning styles, multiple intelligences, cooperative learning, developmental learning, alternative assessment, whole language, hands-on instruction for math and science, thematic teaching, and collaborative teaching models. We have a supportive administration that allows us to become current in technology and updated innovative programs. Our teachers are always eager to participate in training to update and build their skills, and teamwork forms the foundation of how we operate.

At our school we have always had a firm commitment to heterogeneous groupings of students in every classroom. When we form our classrooms they are carefully structured to be multiethnic, multicultural/multi-racial, with the full spectrum of high and low achievers, and those with challenging behaviors. We make every effort to balance each classroom so that students identified as gifted and talented (GATE) as well as special education students are integrated throughout. Our upper-grade teachers have all been certified or are in the process of being certified to teach students identified as GATE.

Within a classroom of 33 students, for example, it is possible to find a cluster of 12 GATE students, 8 or 9 special needs students (including those with learning disabilities, ADHD, health impairments, language disorders, etc.), students who are limited English proficient, as well as children who have significant issues in their personal/home lives. Observers would have a difficult time distinguishing children with special needs from the other children in the class; and will typically find that students are working together cooperatively, are happy and comfortable in their learning environment, and are achieving success.

Our school has always had an inclusive philosophy, even though "the inclusive classroom" is a relatively new emphasis in education. Some of our classes are combination grades (e.g. K–1, 1–2, 3–4, 5–6). Our staff often opts to combine grade levels for developmental purposes or teacher preference; and others are formed because of enrollment needs. The majority of teachers at our site team teach by choice for some portion of the school day.

One of the main purposes of a magnet school is to integrate students. We are proud of how successfully we do integrate our diverse student population, and maintain a highly successful educational program that is recognized not only by the district, but at the state level (as a California Distinguished School) and nationally.

The U.S. Department of Education conducted a nationwide search for promising practices in the education of students with attention deficit disorders. Our elementary school was one of seven schools in the country to be recognized for our promising practices in teaching students with ADD/ADHD, and participated in an intensive study for the U.S. Department of Education on effective educational practices of children with ADD.

Cumulatively, the two of us have over 45 years of experience teaching in public schools in both general and special education. It is our intent to share lessons, activities, and successful teaching practices that have been proven to be effective in an inclusive school setting. The focus of this book will be on how **all** students can learn and be successful if the proper techniques are employed, and when instruction is presented in a way that is motivating and relevant. The specific lessons included in this book are carefully structured to provide active, high-interest learning and address the multiple intelligences and wide range of learning styles of all students. For teachers, the lessons are designed to be used for instruction within the inclusive classroom. The developmental activities provide choices that will meet the needs of your individual students. For parents, these activities become an extension or reinforcement of the classroom at home.

We wish to clarify one very important point in our reference to "reaching and teaching all children in inclusive classrooms," as we do not want to mislead any readers. It is not our intent to imply that all children—including those with more severe disabilities—are able to be taught effectively in the general education classroom. We believe in a *full spectrum* of service and placement options to students in need of special education. Not every student is able to function in a regular classroom, even with a maximum amount of support from special education. The regular classroom setting is not the best or most appropriate placement for every student. Children with various handicapping conditions are entitled to appropriate placements and supports that will provide them with the most effective educational program to meet their needs.

What we will be addressing throughout this book is how school personnel can effectively reach and teach *all of the children who are generally placed within the mainstream classroom*. This may include students with learning disabilities, attention deficit disorders, speech and language needs, various social, emotional and/or health impairments, and those who are "at risk" due to any number of factors. This also includes children who are linguistically diverse and may be limited in English proficiency. Inclusive classrooms are respectful of and take into account the wide range of background experience, ability, and developmental levels of students placed in the classroom. We firmly believe that **most** students with mild to moderate disabilities and various learning differences can be successful in general education classrooms through the collaborative efforts and partnership of the classroom teacher, special education staff, other student support personnel, and parents.

It is our hope that this book will provide the necessary information and specific techniques to ensure the success of every child in the classroom. It is designed to provide complete guidance for educators, parents, administrators, school counselors and other school personnel seeking to create a school truly inclusive of all children. The specific lessons and activities across the curriculum are designed to be adaptable for grades 3–8. Other chapters will focus on creating learning environments and instruction that build upon the strengths, learning modalities, developmental levels, and multiple intelligences of all students. In addition, we will address topics such as: increasing home/school communication, getting students organized for success, positive discipline and behavior management, making provisions and adaptations for students in need of support, numerous resources to address the challenges and specific needs of individual children, schoolwide programs designed to enhance students' self-esteem and achievement; and a variety of other strategies, techniques, topics, and ready-to-use materials.

Sandra F. Rief and Julie A. Heimburge

CONTENTS

Section 3
INCREASING HOME/SCHOOL
COMMUNICATION AND PARENT INVOLVEMENT—105

Section 4
BEHAVIOR MANAGEMENT AND POSITIVE DISCIPLINE—119

Section 5
GETTING STUDENTS ORGANIZED FOR SUCCESS: HOME AND SCHOOL STRATEGIES—147

Section 6
PROGRAMS AND STRATEGIES FOR FOSTERING STUDENTS' SELF-ESTEEM—157

Section 7
REACHING ALL STUDENTS WITH SPECIAL NEEDS—167

Section 8
INTERVENTIONS AND ADAPTATIONS
FOR ACCOMMODATING SPECIAL NEEDS—197

For Students Having the Following Difficulties and Needs—197

Section 9
PROGRAMS FOR BUILDING POSITIVE RELATIONSHIPS, SOCIAL SKILLS, AND CONFLICT-RESOLUTION SKILLS—213

Section 10
TEAM EFFORTS—221

Section 11
EFFECTIVE QUESTIONING TECHNIQUES FOR THE CLASSROOM—235

Section 12
MOTIVATING TECHNIQUES FOR
TEACHING SPELLING AND VOCABULARY—243

Section 13
HOOKING IN RELUCTANT READERS/WRITERS—257

Section 14
STRATEGIES FOR HELPING STUDENTS WITH READING AND WRITING DIFFICULTIES—319

Section 15
MAKING ORAL LANGUAGE COME ALIVE IN YOUR CLASSROOM—335

Section 16
MOTIVATING STUDENTS TO BE SUCCESSFUL MATHEMATICIANS—357

Section 17
REVVING UP THOSE RESEARCH SKILLS—417

Section 18
GETTING THE MOST OUT OF STUDENTS THROUGH SCIENTIFIC INVESTIGATION—437

Section 19
MAKING THE MOST OF MUSIC IN THE CLASSROOM—445

Section 20
REACHING STUDENTS THROUGH THE ARTS—451

Section 21
A FEW FINAL WORDS—459

REACHING ALL STUDENTS THROUGH THEIR MULTIPLE INTELLIGENCES AND LEARNING STYLES

How do children learn that it is all right to be different—to learn, think, approach problems—in different ways? How do children come to accept others and recognize that we all have strengths in some areas, weaknesses in others? Children learn that we all have our differences—which are to be respected and appreciated—by our *teaching* them from as soon as they enter school, all the way up through the grades. This may indeed be one of the most important lessons we ever teach children—if we hope they will grow up to be adults with tolerance and empathy for others, individuals capable of developing positive relationships in their lives and working successfully in a global society. One of the greatest ways to instill this understanding in our students is to teach them that we each have our own uniqueness, comprised of various learning styles and multiple intelligences.

LEARNING STYLES

"Learning styles" affect our way of thinking, how we behave and approach learning, and the way we process information. Recognizing our own learning styles and preferences is the first step teachers need to take in order to be most effective in working with students of diversity; and this should be a staff development priority in schools. Teachers first need to take a close look at their own functioning as learners: their own propensities, strengths, weaknesses and preferences, and how that is transferred into the classrooms they teach. It is quite an eye-opener at a teacher workshop for staff to be administered learning style instruments (of which there are a number of different kinds), and then share and compare our own learning styles with those of our colleagues. Of course, this leads to more awareness of our own *teaching* styles and how we may need to learn new strategies and techniques, and provide more choices in order to reach *all* of our students.

1

Students need to be developing understanding that we all learn differently, that there is no right or wrong way to learn. It is helpful if, starting from the first week of school, teachers communicate to their students something like, "Each of us is different, has our own unique way of learning, and our own special needs; and, therefore, I'm probably going to treat each of you differently throughout the year—to make sure you all can be successful in this class."

WHAT IS LEARNING STYLE?

"Learning style is a biologically and developmentally imposed set of personal characteristics that make the same teaching method effective for some and ineffective for others. Every person has a learning style—it's as individual as a signature. Knowing students' learning styles, we can organize classrooms to respond to their individual needs for quiet or sound, bright or soft illumination, warm or cool room temperatures, seating arrangements, mobility, or grouping preferences. We can recognize the patterns in which people tend to concentrate best—alone, with others, with certain types of teachers, or in a combination thereof. We become aware of the senses through which people remember difficult information most easily—by hearing, speaking, seeing, manipulating, writing or notetaking, experiencing, or again, a combination of these. Learning style also encompasses motivation, on-task persistence, the kind and amount of structure required, and conformity versus nonconformity."

(Rita Dunn, Jeffrey Beaudry, and Angela Klavas, "Survey of Research on Learning Styles," *Educational Leadership*. Vol. 46, No. 6. March, 1989.)

Modality Preferences and Instructional Strategies

Most of us tend to have strengths and preferences for learning and processing information through different modalities or channels (hearing, seeing, touching and doing). The following descriptions of modality preferences (and those characteristics that signal strengths in that area) are accompanied by *teaching strategies* that address those areas of strength and allow students to learn more effectively.

Auditiory Learners These students learn through verbal instruction from others, self or oral reading, lecture, discussion, brainstorming, oral reports, speeches, TV, radio, music, verbal games, paraphrasing, repetition, spelling bees, audiotapes, books on tape, creative dramatics, phonics, reader's theatre (dialogue), poetry, and verse. They remember through language and use self-talk or verbalizations to help themselves get through large- and small-muscle motor movements, organization of tasks, and steps in problem solving. They are typically very verbal and can memorize easily. Usually they do well with rhyming and blending and word games. They learn well when information is reinforced through melodies, beats, and rhythms. It is helpful to give directions and questions orally and have children repeat them, let students answer questions orally, and practice spelling words orally. Phonetic approaches are to be utilized in reading/decoding. Allow and encourage the use of tape recorders for this type of learner, and provide many opportunities to use listening centers, books on tape, and participation in discussions. These are the students who should always be involved in small- and large-group discussions, partner talk, and oral activities prior to independent work (i.e., silent reading, projects, writing assignments). During silent reading, they are often observed to subvocalize (read aloud to themselves). They may need the auditory input to hold their attention or get meaning, so it should be permitted if not loud and distracting to others.

Visual Learners These students learn by seeing, watching, and observing, and are strong in remembering visual detail. They often learn to read best through recognition of visual patterns in words (i.e., *word families* such as date, fate, grate, state, equate; or ink, pink, wink, clink, shrink, blink), structurally, and through the configuration (shape) of words. Color cues are very helpful, and when these students need to recall information and the salient, most important points, the use of color highlighting, framing with a heavy line/boxing in, or using any visual symbols near or around that information you want them to attend to is very helpful. For assisting these students with word recognition and spelling, draw lines around the configuration or shape of words and then color-code structural elements such as prefixes, syllables, suffixes, vowels.

These students remember best through pictures and images. Information should be written for them to refer to, and graphics, pictures, key words or phrases in writing should accompany verbal presentations and directions. Use the overhead projector with colored pens, and dry-erase whiteboards with colored pens. Visual learners *need* instruction to include many graphic organizers (charts, clusters, webs, outlines, story maps, diagrams, etc.). They would benefit from writing things down, circling information, underlining, color highlighting their texts, notetaking, and practicing with flashcards. Use maps, films, visual samples and models, puzzles, matching activities, videos, clustering, demonstrating, graphics, and computers. Provide many books with pictures that accompany text—even at the secondary level (i.e., reference books with pictures). Word searches, using sentence strips with information to sequence appropriately, word cards to arrange into sentences, and letter cards to arrange into words are all good techniques to use with visual learners.

Tactile–Kinesthetic Learners These learners learn by doing, touching, and direct involvement. They are hands-on learners who need to be involved physically with projects and activities. These students need to use manipulatives and have many objects to touch and utilize to help lock in learning through their sense of touch. These students need many opportunities to participate in learning games, laboratory experiences, performance/acting out experiences, crafts, drawing, various arts, construction, and use of computers and other technology. Teach concepts with concrete examples that students can act out in the classroom. For example, the concept of conflict between protagonists and antagonists in literature can be demonstrated through arm wrestling. The symbols of greater than (>) and less than (<) can be demonstrated through use of a crocodile puppet or similar animal with a big mouth that opens up wide to face the larger number because it only "eats" the larger number.

Tactile–kinesthetic learners do well when they can tap out or clap out the sounds and/or syllables they hear in words. This often assists them through decoding and spelling. Use of number lines; a variety of different writing materials; tracing with their fingers on sandpaper, carpet, and other textures/surfaces are all useful with these types of learners to help them to remember. Kinesthetic learners do best when information to be learned is tied to a motion. Even having them listen with headphones to a tape-recorded lecture, or practice reciting information to be remembered while *walking* is helpful.

Analytic and Global Learners The terms *left brain* or *left hemisphere dominant/right brain or right hemisphere dominant, analytic/global*, and *inductive/deductive* have been used in the literature to describe individuals' learning styles. Basically, left hemisphere dominant, analytic, and inductive learners are *the same type* of learner. Their characteristics are summarized below and they learn step by step, parts to whole.

Characteristics of analytic learners:
- learn best through sequential processing
- work from parts to whole
- are logical
- are time conscious
- like to plan ahead
- are rational
- enjoy writing, reading, talking
- like to follow written directions
- make lists
- need to follow steps in a process
- like closure on projects
- tend to need quiet to concentrate
- pay attention to a series of facts that build up to concept
- process information linearly
- have linguistic/verbal strength
- are reflective

In most cases the left hemisphere of the brain controls the functions of: language, sequential thinking, literal thinking, logical thinking, mathematical thinking, reasoning, and analysis. This is the hemisphere that generally takes care of reading, writing, and speaking.

Right hemisphere dominant, global or deductive learners have the following characteristics. They more easily learn by obtaining meaning from a broad concept and then focusing on details.

Characteristics of global learners:
- utilize holistic thinking (like to look at the whole first or the overall picture)
- are simultaneous processors of information
- see resemblances and analogies
- are intuitive
- tend to need background noise or music to be able to concentrate
- are artistic
- are creative
- are fantasy oriented
- can have several projects going at once
- are not very time conscious
- grasp large concepts, then tackle details
- need to see the big picture
- find it helpful to see an example of the end product
- need to discuss the relevance and make a connection
- find clustering/mind mapping very helpful

In most cases the right hemisphere controls the following functions: simultaneous processing, imagination, sense of color, musical abilities, pattern thinking, spatial tasks, intuition, metaphorical thinking (difference between what is said and what is meant). This is the creative and emotional side of the brain. These individuals tend to have visual, tactile–kinesthetic learning styles and process information in chunks. They tend to be spontaneous, impulsive, intuitive, creative, and random.

Learning Style Elements

According to Drs. Rita and Kenneth Dunn, authors of *Teaching Students Through Their Individual Learning Styles: A Practical Approach* (Prentice Hall, 1978), there are a number of specific elements that comprise a person's learning style, including:

- Environmental elements (sound, light, temperature, and design)
- Sociological elements (pair-oriented, peer-oriented, team-oriented, self-oriented, and authority-oriented)
- Emotional elements (motivation, persistence, responsibility, and structure)
- Physical elements (perceptual/modality strengths, time of day, need for intake—eating/drinking, and need for mobility)

For some students certain elements are critical to their success, and teachers need to be aware of these factors. For example, the elements of sound, structure, need for mobility, and time of day need to be addressed with students who have attention deficit hyperactivity disorder (ADHD). For an ADHD student it is necessary to provide a great deal of structure, and allow for frequent opportunities to move and be active. Some of these children may be so distracted by noise in the environment, that they do much better during seatwork time or taking tests with earphones that block out and reduce environmental sounds. Some do much better when instrumental music (or white noise) is played in the background during seatwork time. If a child with ADHD is on medication, certainly the time of day is a major factor. There are optimal times to expect the student to be able to focus and times that are far more difficult, depending on when the medication was administered.

A classroom designed for a diversity of learning styles might have some of the following:

- areas with more illumination/areas with less lighting
- listening posts with headsets/earphones and books, music
- carpet areas
- beanbag chairs, couches, large pillows, other informal/comfort areas as well as tables, desks, and formal areas
- opportunities for students to work alone, in groups, with partners throughout the day
- places for individual, small-group and large-group activities
- lots of hands-on materials
- active and quiet areas
- variation in instructional methods
- many opportunities for exploring, experimenting, and choices

Many teachers are incorporating *centers* in their classrooms to expand choices of activities that interest and motivate students. Centers are created and used in a variety of ways and are highly recommended. (Section 2, *Learning Developmentally*, provides detailed information regarding the utilization of centers within the classroom.)

MULTIPLE INTELLIGENCES

"Multiple Intelligence (MI) theory proposes that people use at least seven relatively autonomous intellectual capacities—each with its own distinctive mode of thinking—to approach problems and create products. Every normal individual possesses varying degrees of each of these intelligences, but the ways in which intelligences combine and blend are as varied as the faces and the personalities of individuals."

(Howard Gardner and Tina Blythe, "A School for All Intelligences," *Educational Leadership*, April, 1990.)

Types of Intelligences

Dr. Howard Gardner, Professor of Education at Harvard University, developed the theory of Multiple Intelligences (MI). In his book *Frames of Mind* (1983), he posed the theory that there are at least seven distinct intelligences and corresponding styles of learning.

Linguistic Learner Word smart: These individuals are adept in verbal and language skills (reading, writing, speaking). Lawyers, journalists, broadcasters, and novelists are some professions that require this aptitude. Linguistic learners are able to appreciate and use metaphors, analogies, various forms of humor; and play with language (word games, tongue twisters, jokes, puns). People with strength in this intelligence are often good at playing games such as Scrabble®, Wheel of Fortune®, hangman, and crossword puzzles. They generally do well in school, as they learn and can express themselves best through oral and written language.

Logical Mathematical Learner Number smart: These individuals are skilled at manipulating numbers, problem solving, and analytical reasoning; are good at interpreting data, figuring things out, exploring abstract patterns and relationships; and are strong in math and science. These individuals learn best through the opportunity to experiment, search for patterns, and make their own discoveries. They typically enjoy games of strategy such as: various card games, Rummicube®, Battleship®, and so forth.

Spatial Leaner Art smart: These individuals are skilled at visualizing, perceiving, and recreating aspects of the spatial world. They use their mind's eye making mental pictures, and are adept with drawing, constructing, designing, creating, building, painting, and imagining. These individuals learn best through visual presentation (use of images, color, pictures, graphics) and opportunity to engage in artistic activities. Games such as Pictionary® address this intelligence.

Bodily-Kinesthetic Learner Body smart: These individuals are adept in physical activities and executing goal-oriented movements with their bodies (i.e., surgeons, athletes, dancers, actors, crafts people, mechanics). They learn best by *doing*—through active learning, movement, and hands-on activities. Bodily-kinesthetic learners often report that they need to be in movement to process new information (walking/pacing, acting out a concept, manipulating objects, etc.). The various sports, crafts and games such as charades and Twister® address this intelligence.

Musical Learner Music smart: These individuals appreciate, recognize, and are attuned to rhythm, melody, pitch, tone. They should have the opportunity to listen and respond to, produce, and express through music. They learn best through music (i.e., melody, rhythm, and songs that teach). They often seek background music when they work.

Interpersonal Learner People smart: These individuals are sensitive and attuned to others' feelings, moods, and desires and motivations. They are empathetic and understanding of other people's needs, and often are the mediators of conflicts and leaders. These individuals are frequently very social, but not necessarily so. They enjoy and learn best through interaction with others (i.e., cooperative learning and games with partners/groups).

Intrapersonal Learner Self smart: These individuals understand and know themselves well. They are introspective, often dreamers, and are able to recognize and pursue their own interests and goals. This important intelligence allows an individual to utilize self knowledge to guide actions and make decisions. These people often like to work alone, independently; and often learn best working at their own pace, in their own space, on individualized projects.

Throughout this book in all of the activities and lessons provided, there is a strong emphasis on teaching to the seven intelligences. First, we need to introduce students to the concept of multiple intelligences and then reinforce throughout the year.

Activities to Teach About Multiple Intelligences

- **The 100% Smart Activity (See the end of this section.)** This activity is very effective with upper-grade students. The teacher first needs to spend time discussing Gardner's theory of the seven different intelligences (in terms that children of that level can understand). The students are taught what it means to be math smart, art smart, word smart, music smart, body smart, self smart, and people smart. Then they are taught that we all possess a degree of "smartness" in each of the seven areas and are 100% smart. However, because we are all different, we have more skill and strength in certain areas than others.

  Everyone in the class (including the teacher) makes a pie/circle graph using a paper plate to show the degrees of aptitude/strength they feel they have in each of the seven areas to make up the whole. *WE ARE 100% SMART* makes a fascinating bulletin board display for the classroom.

  Schools that are teaching students about multiple intelligences need to bring in the parents and teach them about MI theory, as well. At a Back to School parent meeting, it is helpful to present some information about learning styles and multiple intelligences, and to have parents also participate in the *100% Smart* activity. Parents can make their own profile, and they can make one for their child—how they perceive their child's areas of strength/weakness. This can then be compared with the one the child made of him-/herself.

- Throughout the school year have discussions about being smart/skilled in different areas. To give students this awareness, provide a sheet that asks them to list a person in class whom they think is "logical–mathematical smart." They have to write why they think that person is number smart and to give evidence. Do the same for the other intelligences.

- On a chart have each child put a self-stick note sheet with their name under the specific intelligence they think is their major area of strength or "smartness." Then students write paragraphs about why they think they are strong in that intelligence and give examples. "I think I am best at . . . ."

- Use pictures of the students instead of self-stick notes to place on the graph. These types of graphs can and should change throughout the year. For example, one graph could be "My Primary Intelligence"; another could be "Which Smartness Do I Want to Gain More of This Year?"

- Giving students many choices of activities and projects, rather than requiring everybody to do the same, is one very important way to address the multiple intelligences of children. This will be illustrated throughout the book in the activities and lessons presented.

- Collect games that address the different intelligences. One day a week a designated amount of time can be devoted to having students select a game to play at different stations. Games can be purchased and often they can be donated by parents. One child in each group needs to understand how to play the game and be able to teach it to the group. Students rotate among the stations/centers so that over the course of a few months every child is exposed to each of the games. These games can also be shared with other teachers. For example, one teacher can use the games on Wednesday afternoons; another teacher, on Fridays. By teachers sharing, it is another way to expand the number and types of games available at a nominal cost.

It is important that during this game time the teacher is actively involved in observing, watching how students are interacting, and informally assessing the specific skills they have in understanding/playing the game. At the end of the game (approximately 30 minutes), allow five to ten minutes for the students to evaluate. Upper graders can evaluate in writing. For example, "Today I played chess with Bobby. I learned the names of the players and how each one can move on the board. Next time I play this game I want to learn some strategies on how to protect my king, and expose my opponent's king for attack." *Note:* During this game time, all students are utilizing their interpersonal intelligence/skill; and when they self-evaluate, they are each tapping their intrapersonal intelligence.

How Choices Make a Difference Reaching Individual Students

In Section 13 *Hooking Reluctant Readers/Writers*, you will find a unit on World War II, and the vast array of choices students are given to select a project from. The following are three examples of students with special needs and/or challenges who experienced great motivation and success last school year when given this assignment.

Josh, a sixth grader with ADHD and learning disabilities, had a passion for music. In fact, he ran his own little business as a disc jockey at children's parties. Josh always struggled significantly with any written project. He wisely chose to do a project that tapped right into his area of strength. He selected the activity where he had to go looking for songs of that time period (around 1940) and compare with songs of today. Building on his strong interest in music, Josh eagerly and actively participated in the project. He made meaningful connections between the music of the decades. Josh brought in music for the class to listen to together. He became the class "expert" of the musical period of World War II.

Peter generally took little pride in his classroom work. He rarely turned his work in; and when it was turned in, it was generally sloppy or done with little effort. His attitude was often one of "Why do I need to do this?" For the World War II project, however, Peter selected the activity to draw aircraft of that particular time period and tell about each of the aircraft. Peter was a child who had never finished any of the numerous art projects that were worked on that school year or previous years. He wasn't particularly strong in art, but he was so *interested* in this particular project that he executed it with very high quality, and great pride in his accomplishment.

Amy was a resource student with learning disabilities. She was also a very popular, social young lady with strong interpersonal and intrapersonal abilities. Even though she had difficulty in a lot of the academics in the classroom, when given a choice to engage in a project that capitalized on her strengths, she participated fully and eagerly. Amy chose to do an interview with a neighbor who was a participant in WW II. In spite of her aversion to writing, she was able to produce a 2-page interview that she shared very introspectively with the class. One of her statements was, "Being Jewish, I wouldn't have wanted to live during that time period."

As will be illustrated throughout this book, *choices, options, variety in instructional strategies and techniques* are all critical elements in classrooms that are inclusive of all students. Attention to learning styles, multiple intelligences, and developmental levels of students all need to be addressed and practiced if we are to reach and teach ALL of our students effectively.

BIBLIOGRAPHY AND RECOMMENDED RESOURCES

Armstrong, Thomas. *Awakening Your Child's Natural Genius.* Los Angeles: Jeremy Tarcher, Inc., 1991.

Armstrong, Thomas. *In Their Own Way.* New York: St. Martin's Press, 1987.

Barrett, Susan. *It's All in Your Head—A Guide to Understanding Your Brain and Boosting Your Brain Power.* Minneapolis: Free Spirit Publishing, Inc., 1992.

Botroff-Hawes, Sally. "Understanding Learning/Teaching Styles," *Thrust*, September 1988.

Chapman, Carolyn. *If the Show Fits . . . How to Develop Multiple Intelligences in the Classroom.* Palatine, IL: IRI/Skylight Publishing, Inc., 1993.

Dunn, R.; Dunn, K.; and Price, G.E., *Learning Style Inventory* (revised 1985), Price Systems, Box 1818, Lawrence, KS 66044-0067.

Dunn, Rita. "Introduction to Learning Styles and Brain Behavior: Suggestions for Practitioners," *The Association for the Advancement of International Education*, Vol. 15, No. 46, Winter (1988).

Dunn, R., and Griggs, S.A. *Learning Styles: Quiet Revolution in American Secondary Schools.* Reston, VA: NASSP, 1988.

Dunn, Rita; Beaudry, Jeffrey; and Klavas, Angela. "Survey of Research on Learning Styles," *Educational Leadership*, Vol. 46, No. 6, March 1989.

Dunn, Rita and Kenneth. *Teaching Students Through Their Individual Learning Styles: A Practical Approach.* Englewood Cliffs, NJ: Prentice Hall, 1978.

Gardner, Howard. (VIDEO) *How Are Kids Smart? Multiple Intelligences in the Classroom,* 1995. Available from National Professional Resources, Inc., 25 South Regent St., Port Chester, NY 10573. Phone: 1-800-453-7461.

Gardner, Howard. *Frames of Mind. The Theory of Multiple Intelligences.* New York: Basic Books, 1983.

Gardner, Howard. *Multiple Intelligences: The Theory in Practice.* New York: Basic Books, 1993.

Gardner, Howard. *The Unschooled Mind: How Children Think and How Schools Should Teach,* Port Chester, NY: National Professional Resources, 1991.

Haggerty, Brian A. *Nurturing Intelligences—A Guide to Multiple Intelligences Theory and Teaching.* Menlo Park, CA: Innovative Learning Publications/Addison-Wesley Publishing Co., Inc., 1995.

Lazear, David. *Multiple Intelligence Approaches to Assessment—Solving the Assessment Conundrum.* Tucson: Zephyr Press, 1994.

Lazear, David. *Seven Pathways of Learning—Teaching Students and Parents about Multiple Intelligences.* Tucson: Zephyr Press, 1994.

Lazear, David. *Teaching for Multiple Intelligences.* Palatine, IL: IRI/Skylight Publishing, Inc., 1991.

Learning Styles Network (co-sponsored by National Association of Secondary School Principals and St. John's University, NY) produces a newsletter (editor is Rita Dunn). Write: St. John's University's Center for the Study of Learning and Teaching Styles, Utopia Parkway, Jamaica, NY 11439. Phone: 718-990-6335

Rief, Sandra. *How to Reach & Teach ADD/ADHD Children.* West Nyack, NY: The Center for Applied Research in Education, 1993.

"Suggestions for Starting with Style." *Learning Styles Network*, Vol. 7, Issue 2, Spring 1986.

"Teaching through Learning Channels." Performance Learning Systems, Inc., Emerson, NJ. 1983.

Vitale, Barbara Meister. *Unicorns Are Real: A Right Brained Approach to Learning.* Rolling Hills Estates, CA: Jaler Press, 1982.

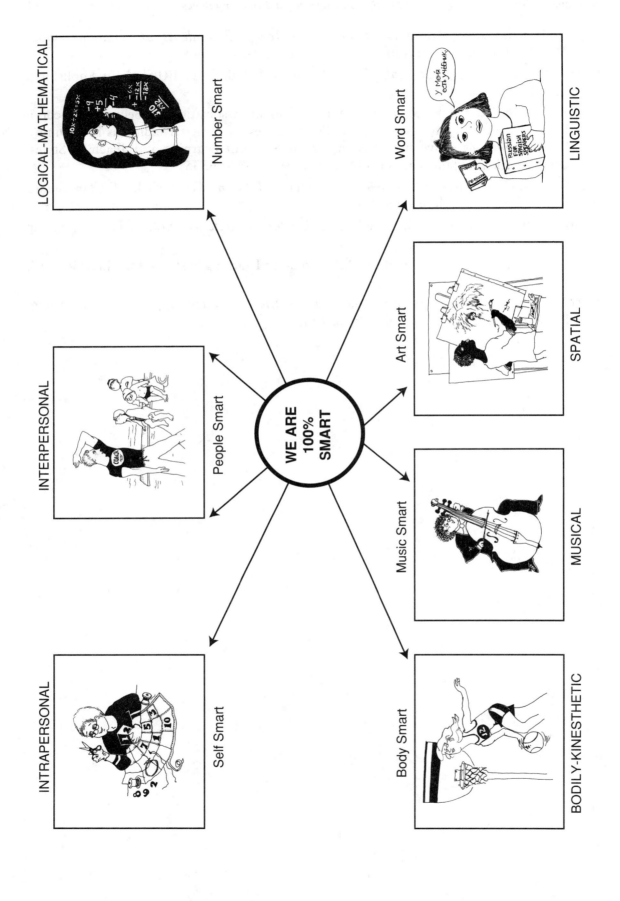

THE 100% SMART ACTIVITY

In class we have been discussing the ideas of a man named Dr. Howard Gardner of Harvard University. He believes that every person is smart, but that the smartness is different in each one of us. Although we are each 100% smart, our total intelligence is made up of seven different areas of intelligence. Each one of us possesses a degree of "smartness" in each of those areas.

The seven intelligences or multiple intelligences are:

logical-mathematical (*math smart*)

spatial (*art smart*)

linguistic (*word smart*)

musical (*music smart*)

bodily-kinesthetic (*body smart*)

intrapersonal (*self smart*)

interpersonal (*people smart*)

Here are two circles. Each is divided into segments of seven. They are examples of how two different people look at their own intelligences using Howard Gardner's theory.

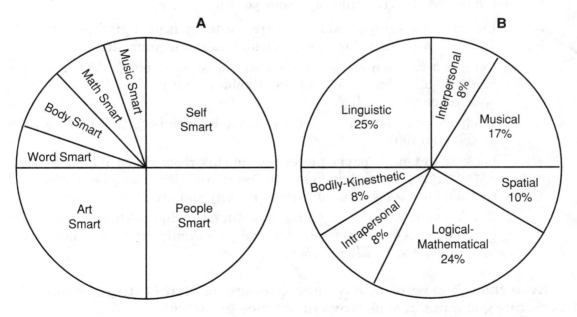

WHAT ARE YOU GOING TO DO?

1. Your job is to **TALK** with your parents and come to some understanding and agreement as to how much of each intelligence you possess. Sometimes your parents see you differently from how you see yourself.

2. Version A: you will be given a white paper plate in class. You are to decide how large each of your seven intelligences is. Then you should shade in each segment using colored pencils, and label each in thin, black marker with the names of the seven intelligences.

3. Version B: Those of you who understand percentage will want to be more exact by using a protractor and ruler with your paper plate. Show precisely the percentage of each of your intelligences. Using your protractor you will end up with degrees. Make a ratio using 360 as your bottom number because there are 360° in a circle. Then use your calculator to figure out what percent of 360 your individual intelligences are. Your percents should add up to 100%. Shade in each area with colored pencils, label your intelligences, and then tell what percent each of them is.

4. Have at least one member of your family design a multiple intelligence paper plate of his or her own. Discuss the similarities and differences between yours and theirs.

5. When you have completed your research about your own multiple intelligences, you are going to write a paper explaining why and how you came up with your conclusions about yourself. After talking these things over with your parents, you should be able to write fluently about your findings.

   a. Include a paragraph about your area (intelligence) of greatest strength. Tell how you think this strength will help you in your life.

   b. Comment on your area (intelligence) of least strength. Tell how this might be a hindrance in your life. Explain what you think you can do to strengthen this intelligence.

   c. Compare your paper plate with your family member's. Tell how they are alike and different.

   d. Look at the other paper plates on the classroom board *WE ARE 100% SMART*. Try to explain how you compare with your classmates and teacher. Discuss your uniqueness and why you are glad to be you.

   6. Display your paper plate on the bulletin board in the *student section* for everyone to see. You may also include your family member's plate in the section labeled *family members*.

Even though most of us have one intelligence that is stronger than the others, our goal should seek ways to balance ourselves.

We should enjoy our uniqueness and appreciate other people's differences.

LEARNING DEVELOPMENTALLY

If we were to ask a thousand teachers to describe the perfect classroom, there would be a thousand different responses. Among those comments, though, would be some common or universal characteristics that would be mentioned. To make things more simple, let's eliminate the money factor, and concentrate on the students and the learning.

- **Children would want to come to school** to learn because their parents and the school worked harmoniously together and each respected and supported each other for the benefit of the students.

- **Children would be motivated to learn** because they knew the instruction was meaningful and relevant to them.

- **Children would be successful** and feel good about themselves knowing that they were doing the best they could at their own level.

- **Children would learn** because teachers would teach in a variety of ways to reach the unique modalities of each individual child.

- **Children and teachers would be respectful towards each other** because they valued each other's diversity and capabilities for learning.

- **Children would be active participants** in their classrooms because they enjoyed learning.

- **All children would perform well** because they could show what they learned through other means of assessment besides tests.

THE DEVELOPMENTAL CLASSROOM

Using these few characteristics, the perfect, or close-to-perfect classroom, *does* exist. It is called the Developmental Classroom. Let's dig deeper to discover just what else this classroom is and how it operates.

Characteristics of a Developmental Classroom

The Developmental Classroom works on the premise that children develop skills at their own unique period of time. Although there are predictable expectations for growth and change in children, not all children progress at the same rate. Expecting all children to learn how to read or write just because they are in the same grade or because they are the same age, does not mean that they will meet with success. In the developmental classroom, teachers meet this challenge head on by providing a variety of techniques and strategies that tap into the child's knowledge and experiences and address his/her learning style by providing opportunities for auditory, visual, and kinesthetic learning.

The developmental approach is comprised of these basic components:

- Children participate in their environment through *active learning*.
- Children are encouraged to make *choices* and learn from their successes and mistakes.
- *Teachers plan and facilitate* the curriculum.
- *Parents are involved* and welcomed in their child's education.
- *Alternative assessment* techniques are used to evaluate children's progress.
- *Children grow and learn at their own unique pace.*
- *The learning environment* is child-centered, nurturing, and success-oriented.

Our staff at Benchley-Weinberger is currently involved in a three-year program to implement a Developmental Program in our classrooms. We have been chosen as a pilot school for developmental learning where other teachers can visit to see the developmental process in action. Because each of our teachers is developmentally at a different stage of implementing this process in his/her classroom, we are working as a staff to see what we already have that is developmentally working, and what else we need to make it work better. As we have a supportive principal who has allowed us to grow at our own pace—but who also nudges us to try new programs and strategies, and to stretch our educational wings—our implementation will be easier than at some schools. Every teacher has had some degree of developmental training and is in the process of putting the program in motion in his/her own classroom. Our three-year plan will evolve in the following manner:

Year 1
- Develop a definition for developmental learning that works for our school.
- Create an environment that allows students to:

use problem-solving strategies

experience active learning

collaborate with their peers

become independent learners

develop a reading continuum for the entire K-5 program

provide opportunities for teacher visitations within the school
to share ideas and strategies

Year 2:

- Create a site continuum for writing, oral language, and listening.

Year 3:

- Create a site continuum for math.

As a staff, we assembled ourselves by multi-age groupings of our students. In other words, we did not meet by grade level. Instead, we grouped ourselves as teachers of the primary, middle, and upper grades. This gave us a wider age span of children to work with while we were discussing our total program in small groups. Although the middle- and upper-grade classrooms would look uniquely different than the primary, teachers were in agreement that the same elements of developmental learning occur in the K-6 classrooms.

The following questions and responses were formulated by the staff. This developmental program in its first year of existence provides the baseline for building upon in the future.

WHAT DO YOU SEE IN A DEVELOPMENTAL CLASSROOM?

- a large variety of activity and materials
- many hands-on materials
- easily accessible materials
- movement
- parent volunteers and involvement
- varied groupings
- good use of space
- children actively engaged in learning
- motivated and excited learners
- students learning and having fun
- students exploring their environment
- students on-task
- students involved in center activities
- students working together
- students working on activities where they have had choice
- alternative furniture (beanbags, round tables, kidney-shaped tables, individual tables, sofas, comfortable chairs)
- alternative assessment files, student portfolios

WHAT DO YOU HEAR IN A DEVELOPMENTAL CLASSROOM?

- children communicating with each other:
    - questioning
    - discussing
    - responding
    - problem solving
    - negotiating
    - peer learning
    - idea sharing
- constructive noise
- background music
- students moving around

WHAT (OR HOW) DO YOU FEEL IN A DEVELOPMENTAL CLASSROOM?

- excitement
- comfortable
- safe
- happy
- welcomed
- invited
- positive
- energy
- relaxed
- happiness
- respect
- enthusiasm
- freedom to explore, observe, and interact

WHAT DO TEACHERS DO IN A DEVELOPMENTAL CLASSROOM?

- facilitate learning
- confer
- guide
- encourage
- organize
- demonstrate
- reflect
- help
- create materials and centers
- assess anecdotal records
- plan and prepare
- interact
- observe
- direct, if needed
- offer opinions
- encourage
- pose problems

WHAT DO CHILDREN DO IN A DEVELOPMENTAL CLASSROOM?

- choose
- plan
- implement
- set goals
- explore
- learn from experiences

- learn to think
- communicate

- participate
- enjoy learning
- evaluate

- help one another
- take responsibility for choices, clean-up, learning
- learn actively
- cooperate
- become independent

In our second session, our staff again broke up into smaller groups and concentrated on our environment. What did we already have that was developmental and where could we put our energy in the future?

WHAT DOES OUR ENVIRONMENT LOOK LIKE NOW?

- center areas
- flexible groupings
- labeling, print rich
- lots of manipulatives
- comfortable, safe and happy
- diversity—everyone at different levels

- students working together
- relaxed atmosphere
- parent volunteers
- children making choices
- children actively involved
- students on-task

WHAT DO WE WANT IT TO LOOK LIKE?

- more alternative-type furniture
- easily accessible materials
- child-centered

- spacious
- efficient use of materials and space

WHAT DO WE NEED?

- space organizers

- more uniform storage bins
- more shelves

- materials for centers

- time to plan, investigate, and build
- alternative furniture

- ziplock baggies for center activities

- cameras and film for taking pictures of students
- computer consultant for troubleshooting
- televisions mounted on walls instead of on stands
- parent workshop for assisting in making center activities
- more hands-on materials for math and science
- workable headphones and tape recorders for centers

From this session, we definitely agreed that we all wanted our rooms to look less cluttered and more spacious. We realized our rooms were getting overloaded and there didn't seem to be enough room to move around. With many manipulatives, centers, and technology, our upper-grade rooms were crowded. Our first goal was to gather together a team of parents to build standard-size shelves that would fit underneath our chalkboards. These would act as storage spaces for our containers of manipulatives and materials. It would also give uniformity to the classrooms, providing even new teachers moving into the school rooms equipped with the same standard shelving. Some money was provided by our principal, and other materials were donated by parents. It was a small step in the developmental ladder, but we were on our way.

Looking ahead to the next rung of the ladder, our wish is to order a large supply of uniform-size and color containers to use for storage bins for our materials. Since this whole process must be done in stages, we look forward to our future goals; and hope that with the help of a supportive principal, a dedicated staff, and a generous group of parents, our developmental process will forge ahead.

If your staff is in the formulating stages of a similar program, we wish you luck and hope that you too forge ahead, taking in the needs of your own staff.

Shared Responsibility

In a developmental program children are educated through shared responsibility. Parents, teachers, administrators, and the child him-/herself must function as a team, with the mutual goal being the successful development of the whole child. Teachers are key players with the responsibility for planning and providing a meaningful and relevant learning environment. They also are the encouragers and supporters who help the children to become successful learners. By providing opportunities for students to build self-esteem and to feel intrinsic rewards, the teacher facilitates learning.

Parents must also realize their importance in the developmental process. As the school and the family work in partnership towards common goals children realize how important their education is. There are many ways parents can show their support and be involved with the school. (See Section 30) When we are fortunate enough to have parent volunteers in the upper-grade and middle school classrooms, we should make sure their time is used wisely. A folder with their materials and clear instructions for what the teacher wants them to do should be easily accessible. The *Parent Volunteer Assistance Form* helps us in our classrooms.

PARENT VOLUNTEER ASSISTANCE FORM

Volunteer's Name _____   Date _____

Today you will be assisting in the classroom by helping the student(s) in the following activities:

_____Measurement ($\frac{1}{8}$", $\frac{1}{16}$", $\frac{1}{4}$", $\frac{1}{2}$")

_____Counting change

_____Telling time

_____Using a protractor or compass

_____Tape-recording student reading

_____Reading orally with _____

_____Reading his/her story to you

_____Rewriting, extending, or editing his/her story or writing assignment

_____Completing an unfinished assignment_____

_____Helping with the understanding of a concept in math

_____Reviewing the basic facts (flash cards)

_____Helping to figure out his/her spelling average

_____Checking individual student three-ring binders

_____Other _____

The child/children you will be working with is/are _____

_____

_____

Assessment in the Developmental Classroom

Many teachers see great similarity between the individualized classroom of the 1970s and the developmental classroom of the 1990s. The one element that seemed to be missing in the individualized classroom was assessment. In the developmental classroom, we must use both formal and informal assessment to evaluate where our students are on the educational continuum, and make sure that parents understand their children's developing skills, abilities, and competencies.

Because the way we are teaching is changing, our way of assessing children's progress must change along with it. Children must continue to understand and respect the importance of tests in their educational lives; but teachers must find new and innovative ways to assess the individual performance of students that coincide with the freshness of whole language, the hands-on approach, and cooperative learning.

Teachers must use a variety of ways to assess children's progress, including :

- teacher observations
- parent evaluation of student's work
- peer evaluation
- student self-evaluations
- videotapes of student's oral language experiences
- audiotapes of student's reading
- portfolios of children's work
- tests that are appropriate to the child's level of development

Teachers must become the investigators who observe their students and find out how and what they are learning. Discovering a particular student's learning style(s) and making teaching adjustments so that all children can learn in their own way, builds stronger creative teaching skills. It is always a source of fascination when we can discover a new teaching method that helps more students remember a new concept or skill more fully. Through "kid watching" and recording, teachers can become more aware of how children process information and how their creativity enters into their learning.

These *observational* notes can be taken in several forms:

- Some teachers keep a notebook with a page with each child's name on it. As they observe the child in different situations, they make a notation on the page and date it.
- Other teachers carry Post-It™ Notes and stick them onto the inside of student folders at the end of the day.

Due to the fact that a teacher's day is extremely filled with activity, this might just seem like another thing to do that is time-consuming. As teachers get proficient at doing this type of notetaking, they will feel the rewards of their efforts. For use in parent and child conferences, this is a method that will ease the mind of having to remember everything about everybody. Instead, the information has been noted and is recorded, and real growth can be indicated, and retrieved instantly.

Teachers at our school use two methods of taking *anecdotal* records:

- Some teachers target five or six students per day, and watch them specifically. This assures the teacher that there will be a record taken for each child each week.
- Other teachers watch and record instances as they happen. This is a bit more informal and must be monitored so that everyone is covered at least several times during the reporting period.

These notations are invaluable during the time teachers are evaluating students for their report cards or progress reports. They are excellent resources to review before a parent conference. They are extremely helpful in letting the parent know you truly know who their child is. Parents like the feeling that you "know" their child. Because all notations are dated, you also can see just how far a child has progressed.

Anecdotal records (dated, informal observations and notations that describe development) can be composed of many items, some of them being:

- interview notes and more extensive summaries that are taken during and after reading, writing and portfolio conferences with the child
- informal and formal interviews
- comprehension checks, during class periods
- observations of group participation, work habits, study skills, learning styles

History of a portfolio Four years ago, our staff decided we would like to begin the portfolio assessment process. It was our decision to begin with a language arts portfolio. Every child would accumulate samples of his/her work and at the end of the year the portfolio would be sent to the next teacher. Each teacher was given the opportunity to collect information he/she deemed important, but certain components were informally agreed upon:

- quick writes
- journal entries
- one writing assignment taken through the entire writing process
- an audiotape of each child with at least two reading samples
- writing samples throughout the year
- illustrations from reading
- graphic organizers showing reading connections and writing organization
- reading comprehension checks

Each teacher was given a class set of accordion-type portfolio file folders for collection of information, an audiotape for each child, and one class videotape to get the program started.

As upper-grade teachers, we now have four years of portfolio assessment housed in our classroom. What a wonderful tool to assess progress and growth in our children! At the beginning of the year, teachers can peruse each child's portfolio and see from where the child has come in educational skill, and how he/she has developed over time. No test scores or cumulative file can give such a complete picture of a child's background and educational history. Students, too, love to look through their portfolios and see their growth.

Where are portfolios kept? As the wealth of materials contained in the yearly portfolio collection accumulate, the problem seems to arise as to where they should be kept. In a developmental classroom, the portfolio is kept in full sight where children and parents can find them easily. Four years of portfolios are kept in easily accessible and visible file boxes that are labeled **PORTFOLIOS** so that anyone who walks in the classroom can see them. Some schools use scanners and the portfolios are less cumbersome.

Many teachers keep two types of portfolios in the room:

- The *working portfolio* is an accumulation of almost all student work during a short period of time, usually a report card or progress report period. The teacher files materials in this folder that will be saved to review for a later date. When this type of portfolio is used, parents become concerned because much of their child's completed work is not sent home. As upper-grade teachers, we must emphasize with parents that student work is always available to review and that they may have access to the portfolio at any time. We must be diligent in sending home completed assignments not contained in this folder. As we accumulate pieces of student work, our parents must not feel we are hiding anything from them. It is essential that parents understand the purpose of portfolios and, when they do, they will also support the fact that not all completed work will be sent home right away for them to look over.

- The *showcase portfolio* is selected from the working portfolio. Before each report card period, the student and the teacher review the working portfolio and the student selects the three to four items he/she wants to be evaluated, and that will be permanently contained in the showcase portfolio. A student/teacher portfolio conference is the most preferred way of portfolio sample selection. Because it is difficult to find time during the instructional part of the day to have a one-to-one conference, teachers must make time to free themselves for this important evaluation process. They might try these ideas:

  1. Start early. Target one or two students per day during the quiet reading time.
  2. Have the entire class look through their portfolios together during a period of the day. Have each child tentatively select his/her choices, so that when you see students individually, you will have a shorter period of time with each.
  3. Schedule a portfolio conference with a child during the first ten minutes of lunch time. Make it a "Let's do lunch" experience. Children enjoy this quiet and personal time with their teacher.
  4. Schedule a 10- to 15-minute before- or after-school "snack-attack" conference. Share cookies and milk, or popcorn and soda.
  5. Have another teacher "watch" your class for a film or physical education to free you for this conference. You, in turn, take that teacher's class on another day.
  6. Ask your principal or vice principal to take over your class for a "principal's special lesson." You do the conferences, while he/she treats your class to a special activity.

- In our fifth and sixth combination room, student portfolios become more than just a collection of work. They become a history of the whole child during the course of one full year. The following pages are collected and stapled into the file folder. (*Note:* Some of these pages are offered here as reproducibles.)

  Student Portfolio in Language Arts

  Student/Parent/Teacher Item Evaluations

  Taping My Reading

  Books I Have Read in Room _____ (**Note:** This is found at the end of Section 13)

  Language Arts Attitude Survey

  A student sample of the report card; students fill out their assessment of themselves before the first report card period

  All About Me (interest inventory)

  A handwriting sample for each reporting period:

This is a sample of my very neatest handwriting on _____ (date). I am in grade _____ in Room _____. My teacher's name is _____. I attend _____ (school). At this time of the year, I would like you to know how I feel about my handwriting: _____
_____

I think I could improve by _____
My goal for the next reporting period is to _____
_____

  Partners in Learning Student-Parent-Teacher-Administrator Agreement (see Section 10)

  Reading Writing Conference sheet (see Section 13)

  Three to four student-selected samples of student work for each reporting period (included with one parent, teacher, and student item evaluation form)

If you have not yet begun a portfolio assessment program at your school, the time to begin is now!

Remember, one very important element that is present in all developmental classrooms is *choice*. When students are given the opportunities to choose learning experiences patterned for their interests and styles of learning, they become much more actively involved in their education. The next area covering planning, doing, and reflecting will open your eyes to the importance of choice in upper-grade classrooms.

STUDENT PORTFOLIO
IN LANGUAGE ARTS

Your Name _____

My teacher and I have selected the following items
for my portfolio. They reflect the work that I have
done in _____ grade.

SELECTIONS FOR THE FIRST TRIMESTER

_____
_____
_____
_____

The reason I have made these selections is because _____
_____
_____

SELECTIONS FOR THE SECOND TRIMESTER

_____
_____
_____

The reason I have made these selections is because _____
_____
_____

SELECTIONS FOR THE THIRD TRIMESTER

_____
_____
_____

The reason I have made these selections is because _____
_____
_____

STUDENT PORTFOLIO ITEM EVALUATION

Student's Name _____

Title of Work _____

Date Written _____

Date of Evaluation _____

One thing I really like about this piece is . . .

_____

_____

_____

It would be even better if . . .

_____

_____

_____

Student's Signature

_____

PARENT PORTFOLIO ITEM EVALUATION

Student's Name _____

Title of Work _____

Date Written _____

Date of Evaluation _____

One thing I really like about what you wrote is . . .

_____

_____

_____

One suggestion I would make is . . .

_____

_____

_____

Parent's Signature

_____

TEACHER PORTFOLIO ITEM REFLECTION

Student's Name _____   Title of Work _____

The special strengths of this piece are . . . _____

_____

I would like to see . . . _____

_____

Teacher's Signature

_____

Name _____

TAPING MY READING

1. Select a part of a book that you are currently reading that you would like to read out loud.
2. Record your oral reading for approximately 3 minutes.
3. Rewind the tape.
4. Listen to your voice reading out loud.
5. Fill out the following information.

Date _____ Time _____ Page # _____

Today I read a segment of a book entitled _____
_____

I chose this part because _____
_____

When I played back the tape and listened to myself, I _____
_____

I think I read _____

I liked/disliked what I heard. (Circle one)

I could improve my oral reading by _____
- -

Date _____ Time _____ Page # _____

Today I read a segment of a book entitled _____
_____

I chose this part because _____
_____

When I played back the tape and listened to myself, I _____
_____

I think I read _____

I liked/disliked what I heard. (Circle one)

I could improve my oral reading by _____

Name _____

LANGUAGE ARTS ATTITUDE SURVEY

1. How do you feel about reading a book when you're at home and have some free time?

2. How do you feel when you receive a book for a gift?

3. How do you feel when your parent reads you a book before going to bed?

4. How do you feel when you have to read in front of your classmates?

5. How do you feel when you read a book to a younger boy or girl?

6. How do you feel about reading the newspaper?

7. How do you feel when you are asked to have a Book Talk with a friend?

8. How do you feel about going to the library?

9. How do you feel when your teacher assigns you a book to read?

10. How do you feel when you have to read out loud with a partner?

11. How do you feel when you don't know a new word in a book?

12. How do you feel when someone asks you to give an oral book report?

13. How do you feel when your teacher calls on you to answer a question in class?

14. How do you feel when you have to speak in front of your classmates?

15. How do you feel when you have to ask your teacher a question?

Name _____

ALL ABOUT ME

MY FAVORITE:

Sport _____

Hobby _____

Food _____

T.V. Show _____

Book _____

Music Group _____

Animal _____

I have lived in: _____

I have visited: _____

Lessons I have taken: _____

Clubs, groups, activities I am involved in: _____

_____

My family and I enjoy: _____

I don't like to: _____

My favorite subject in school: _____

I fear: _____

When I am alone I like to: _____

PLANNING—DOING—REFLECTING

As students progress through the grade levels, the teacher sees a greater span in their developmental level. In an upper-grade classroom, the teacher may have students reading at high school level, while some might still be reading on the primary or intermediate level. Each child is developing, but at an individual speed. The student who encounters difficulty in the academic areas often becomes apathetic, experiences frustration and a decrease in self-esteem, and is dissatisfied with school. Each child should feel successful every day. One way of achieving this goal is through the Planning—Doing—Reflecting process.

WHAT IS PLANNING—DOING—REFLECTING?

Planning-Doing-Reflecting is the time of day in a developmental classroom when students can select their own learning experiences without direct instruction from the teacher. The teacher's role is to provide centers richly supplied with books, manipulatives, equipment, and other hands-on materials that the students choose from and use to investigate their environments. In the upper-grade classroom during center time, students work on various activities, and are engaged in self-initiated learning experiences. The teacher becomes the facilitator, supporter, and observer.

WHY DO WE CALL THE PDR PROCESS "PLANNING—DOING—REFLECTING" IN THE UPPER GRADES?

For upper-grade teachers in the San Diego area, the basic High-Scope model of Plan-Do-Review (PDR) has been modified to accommodate the diverse needs and interests of the upper-grade students. Desiring to keep a similar basic philosophy, while acknowledging that children's needs change as they progress through the grades, the San Diego City Schools uses the term Planning—Doing—Reflecting to describe the PDR process.

As the students develop skills and interests, Planning—Doing—Reflecting in many classrooms will usually differ from the primary Plan—Do—Review. Although the need for exploration, discovery, and creativity are paramount to the developmental process, upper-grade teachers provide student choices in a variety of ways, including individual and group projects, thematic centers, and hands-on activities. A combination of centers that includes free choice, teacher-initiated, exploratory, and instructional activities provides a balance for upper-grade students that promotes progress, while establishing responsibility for the transitional years ahead.

The First Step: Planning

The first step in this process is "planning time," when students are responsible for selecting their own learning experiences from the variety of centers and materials that have been provided. The students make choices and plan how they will structure their own time. There are a variety of ways to do this:

- Use a prepared form for students to actually fill out.
- Use full or half size composition books.

- Use the oral language process. Students may discuss their intentions for the period with a partner or in cooperative groups, or may relay their plan to an adult in the classroom.

Whatever method the teacher uses in this planning stage, students will write down or discuss what they plan to accomplish during the work period. The student might also describe materials they will be using, who they plan to work with, their initial feelings about the center, whether they have used this center before, and what they think they will learn. If the plan is in written form, each entry in the composition book or on the PDR form should have the student's name, the date, and the name of the center at the top of the page.

How Long Is the Planning Period and When Should It Take Place?

Usually the planning segment takes from five to ten minutes. Teachers should choose an approach to planning that is efficient and practical for their particular classroom.

- Students may write their plans directly before the "doing" part of the day.
- Children may plan early in the morning when they first come into class.
- Students may plan *after* the REVIEW time for the next day. After listening to their classmates share their day's experiences, many students are motivated to plan what they want to do for the next day.

What Part Does the Teacher Play During the Planning Session?

Most upper-grade students are capable of writing their own plans. The teacher should be available to review the plans to assure that they are realistic and practical. If during the "doing" period the child is not participating fully in the activity, the teacher might ask the child to review his/her plan. Redirection, motivation, or resetting of the personal plan might need to be done at this point.

Teachers should model the behaviors that are desired from the students:

- Use the overhead projector to write a model plan to show students how entries should be made in their composition book.
- Through role playing, model an oral planning session between a student and a teacher, or other adult, or between two students.
- Use a cooperative group of students who discuss their plans orally in front of the entire class. This, too, provides the necessary modeling students need to approach the planning part of the day with more understanding.

The Second Step: Doing

After planning, the students are ready to begin their center activities. They begin to carry out their plans. Usually the centers have been initiated and introduced by the individual teacher whose goal is to actively involve his/her students. A center should occupy the child's full participation for the extent of the "doing" period. PDR enables students to make individual and responsible choices. The activities should be enjoyable and rich in opportunities to explore, investigate, enrich, and enlighten students. At the end of the period, students should return materials to their original locations in the room and place their completed work in an appropriate spot such as a center folder, or in a special section for center activities in their own three-ring binder.

During the "doing" time, the teacher is an active participant. It is essential that the teacher becomes an observer, enabler, and facilitator. Teachers may assist students in problem-solving techniques, answer questions, find materials, and clarify confusing questions. This is an important time for the teacher to observe and take notes about individual children and their needs, behaviors, learning styles, cooperative interaction, and ability to use higher level thinking skills. There are few times in a teacher's day that allow for observing students. These moments become the foundation for understanding students and how they function in a less-structured environment with minimal teacher direction. Teacher observational notes facilitate communication during parent conferences and in individual interactions with students.

How Much Time Should the "Doing" Part of the Process Take and How Often Should It Be Done?

The "doing" part of the period is again dependent on the individual teacher and the students. Usually in the upper-grade classroom, a period of approximately 30 to 40 minutes is appropriate. This gives the children enough time to be fully involved in the activity, and to gain a sense of completion.

With the many pull-out programs, prep periods, library sessions, assemblies, computer lab times, buddy programs, and responsibilities and programs set up for upper-grade students, teachers must realize that PDR will look different in every classroom. If teachers are incorporating all the elements of developmental learning in their classrooms, PDR may not need to be done on a daily basis. There are other strategies to meet the individual needs and interests of upper-grade students. These include:

- projects
- hands-on activities throughout the curriculum
- thematic teaching
- cooperative learning
- opportunities for "choosing" on daily assignments (For instance, during spelling, students may choose six of the ten activity choices the teacher assigns. On a writing assignment, the teacher may give four choices, and the student must select one.)
- child-initiated enrichment activities

A workable PDR program can be scheduled from one to five days a week based on the teacher's discretion and teaching style. When introducing PDR, one day a week might feel the most comfortable. In team teaching situations, scheduling problems may arise that infringe on PDR. Teachers should feel satisfied knowing that they are providing an exciting opportunity for their students whether PDR is offered on a one-, two-, three-, four-, or five-day program.

WHAT DOES THE TEACHER DO DURING THE "DOING" TIME?

As is the case during "planning," the teacher is an involved observer and communicator during the "doing" part of the period, circulating around the room, answering questions, and responding to concerns. This is a time when the students might need assistance in problem solving, finding materials, or extending their plan because they have finished what they wanted to do. It is important for the teacher to support and guide the students and to show interest in their work. The teacher has opportunities to observe such things as:

- social interaction
- peer cooperation
- how children approach learning tasks
- children's abilities to take risks
- children who are hesitant to participate
- leadership qualities

As the teacher observes, anecdotal records can be taken on Post-it™ Notes, on index cards, or in a record book for future reference. These records are helpful in assessing students' needs, and act as a reference for parent and student conferences. It is essential that teachers write down their observations and use them to better understand their children, their learning styles, and their unique ways of approaching the world around them.

WHAT SHOULD THE TEACHER EXPECT DURING CLEAN-UP AT THE END OF THE "DOING" TIME?

Upper-grade students tend to be less motivated to participate in the clean-up process. It is the responsibility of the teacher to establish the desired expectations and procedures early in the year. The clean-up part of the period is important because it teaches children how to be problem solvers, how to sort and put order to things, and how to classify items. All set-up and clean-up is done by the students. This gives students a sense of ownership in their classroom.

WHAT ABOUT THE NOISE LEVEL AND PROBLEMS THAT MIGHT ARISE?

When students are actively participating in hands-on, stimulating activities, the noise level can become a consideration. Although the activity is very productive, teachers must use a signal of some type such as switching off the light, or ringing a bell to keep the noise level appropriate. Individual teaching styles determine the look and sound of the classroom. The teacher must communicate expectations to the students, so that they quickly learn to adjust the noise level to class standards.

Teachers might use a "three strikes, it's over policy." This means that if the bell or lights signal is given three times, everyone cleans up. The privilege of the PDR period may be taken away if the class is not adhering to the agreed-upon parameters.

If the students are experiencing difficulties getting along at one of the centers, they should solve matters by themselves, with very little negotiation by the teacher. If they are unable to settle differences, or to follow class standards of noise, neatness, staying in the center for the period, and being courteous to the group members, the center may be closed for the day. Those children may be asked to sit quietly at their own desks for a "time out" period, or to read a book of their choice. This discourages disharmony.

In many classrooms, the noise level is busy-sounding, but tolerable. Constructive noise is productive. Music played in the background can have a calming effect during the "doing" time of the day.

How Should Students Behave During the "Doing" Part of the Day?

Discipline problems during the period are kept to a minimum because student self-control is built into the program. When the students are actively participating and enjoying what they are doing, they tend to behave better. Even with the academic, social and cultural diversity of students in individual classrooms, it is very difficult to distinguish the students who have special needs during this period. Students who have learning disabilities blend effectively into the class during the "Doing" segment of PDR and the differences between GATE (Gifted and Talented) and special needs students become less obvious, while their strengths emerge. Everyone becomes an integral part of the class.

How Should We Guide Students Who Lack Self-Discipline?

Every classroom has its share of students who pose a challenge to the teacher. Not every child has developed self-control. Self-discipline is a skill that is developed over time. It is the teacher's responsibility to assist those students. When a child continually has difficulty making good decisions, the teacher must intervene and offer alternatives that limit the child's choices. Instead of ten choices for centers, for example, possibly the children exhibiting inappropriate behavior might be given two choices at the beginning of the year, and then add choices as his/her responsibility grows. The teacher may need to give more individual assistance in the planning stage to those children who are in need of more direction and clarification of expectations.

The Third Step: Reflecting

The last part of the PDR process is "reflecting." Students communicate in written or oral form what they have done and their feelings about their accomplishments during the "doing" part of PDR. At "reflecting" time, the students learn from each other, become motivated to try another center, evaluate their products and learning, and share their enthusiasm about their successes. The children learn how to explain their work and express themselves and take pride in their accomplishments.

In some classrooms, students write their ideas in their PDR folders or on their PDR sheets, while in other rooms students share their ideas with their classmates in pairs, cooperative groups, or with the total class. After the "doing" is completed, students are excited about what they have done, and usually are eager to share their revelations. Teachers should capitalize on this nonthreatening oral language opportunity.

HOW MUCH TIME SHOULD BE GIVEN TO THE "REFLECTING" PART OF THE PDR PROCESS?

Depending on the number of days spent on PDR, the teacher may adjust the length of the "reflecting" time. If PDR is scheduled one day a week, the students may spend twenty minutes "reflecting." If PDR is five days a week, a shorter, five-minute or ten-minute segment may be adequate. The time varies with the needs of the students, type of projects, and the centers used.

Bringing the entire class together outside under the tree or inside on the rug provides an informal setting where they may listen more carefully to each other.

Not every child has to share with the entire group during each PDR session. Students may:

- Review orally with an adult.
- Share with the person who sits next to them, or with their table members in oral communication.
- Write their reviews in composition books.

A combination of these ideas may be used so that students do not get tired of doing the same things each day. Variety of "reflecting" methods gives students a break from routine and helps to rejuvenate them during this part of the PDR session.

WHAT PART DOES THE TEACHER PLAY IN THE "REFLECTING" SEGMENT OF PDR?

The upper-grade teacher is a facilitator in this process. Making sure that each child is given an opportunity to share in some manner what he/she has done is extremely important. Students who usually do not converse or like to be called upon may feel more relaxed when sharing during "reflecting." The students feel less intimidated about making mistakes and are, therefore, happier and more willing to share their achievements. Because much of the time students work cooperatively at a center, some students feel more like participating orally because they are part of a group.

The teacher needs to provide a supportive attitude that makes students feel worthwhile and feel that their activities and projects are valued.

Periodically, the teacher might want to collect the PDR journals or composition books to review choices the students have made and appraise the way students view themselves as learners.

WHAT DO WE WANT UPPER-GRADE STUDENTS TO LEARN FROM REFLECTING?

One teacher goal should be to train students to look carefully at their own learning and progress. Self-evaluation is a skill students develop over the course of time. The PDR process allows children to review their learning and to see what they might have done differently on a second try. If the centers have been geared to the seven intelligences, the students should be able to distinguish which of the intelligences they used during the "doing" period. They should be able to grow in their problem-solving and risk-taking abilities. They may notice the way they approach an activity is different from other children, sometimes being more efficient, sometimes being less efficient. When they view things the other children do, they should be able to evaluate their success or failure as compared with their peers.

The process of self-evaluation develops in each individual at different rates. During the "reflecting" part of the day, students are observing the manner in which their peers approach activities and learning to appreciate diverse ways of doing things.

What Is the Student's Part in the "Reflecting" Process?

Students are often asked to write reviews of what occurred at their center. A good review initially must be modeled by the teacher. They can include:

- how closely they followed their original plan
- what materials they used
- who they worked with
- how they felt about their activity
- how they might extend their ideas in the future
- what processes they followed
- what product they created

Sharing individual plans and reviews can be very time consuming, so a variety of sharing strategies are needed. The children may:

- partner or table share
- volunteer to share with the whole class
- nominate a good plan or review for the class to hear

Other Things to Know About PDR

Because each child is developing at his/her own unique pace, upper-grade teachers need to continue to provide a variety of learning experiences that give students opportunities to make choices and explore their own areas or strengths and weaknesses. Through the PDR process, students tend to choose their own areas of strength first until they are ready or willing to move into their less-developed areas.

PDR allows diverse students to work together. By sharing activities with students who differ from one another culturally, ethnically, by gender, by academic ability, by primary language, by competency in the English language, by physical ability or disability, or any other diversity, students truly come to appreciate and honor one another as individuals, as well as members of groups.

During PDR:

- Students feel empowered as they take responsibility for their own learning. They can choose a center and then choose what they do when they get there. They learn to make choices and the consequences of choices.
- Students develop a sense of ownership and pride for the classroom and materials, and build independence as they structure their environment to accomplish their chosen activity.
- Students are confident in their choices.
- Students are more apt to be willing to share activities and ideas with peers and other adults. They know they are accepted and valued.
- In programs that include PDR, students are eager to come to school and know there will be success built into each day.

With the incredible diversity in our schools today, teachers must provide a variety of methods and instructional strategies that engage student's interests. The process of PLAN-NING, DOING, and REFLECTING is the key that unlocks the door of success. Every child can experience what it is like to be successful during the special part of the day called PDR. Teachers who continue to expand and enrich programs through use of this process will capture and hold the attention of children as they forge ahead in their developmental growth.

Creating and Implementing PDR Centers

HOW DOES THE TEACHER GET STARTED WITH CENTERS?

The upper-grade teacher has a great deal to do before the actual PDR process begins. Most important is the need to generate ideas for centers.

Getting started with center activities sometimes seems overwhelming, costly, and time consuming. Concerns can be minimized when the teacher takes a mental inventory of items already in the classroom, and things that are readily available at no or low cost.

Use the Seven Intelligences to Originate Centers It is important for teachers to incorporate activities into the centers that specifically address the unique intelligences of each child. Having choices during PDR that are keyed to Howard Gardner's seven intelligences helps children to diversify and strengthen all parts of their intellect.

This may be accomplished by providing one center with a number of activities focused on logical/mathematical skills (calculator activities, math tricks and teasers, decks of cards to play educational card games, graphing design sheets, flash cards, computer math games, etc.). Students will have a choice of several activities to tax their logical/mathematical intelligence. Centers using activities that are keyed to the other six intelligences (linguistics, musical, spatial, interpersonal, intrapersonal, and bodily-kinesthetic) can also be an excellent beginning point for PDR.

One day might be set up as a Game Day based on the seven intelligences. Six to ten different games the children already know or could learn quickly could be set out on tables. The children would select the center where they would like to go. The games listed below are just a few contained on Gardner's Key School list which are based on the seven intelligences.

Stations 1 and 2: Twister®, Labyrinths® (*bodily-kinesthetic*)

Stations 3 and 4: Dominoes, Uno® (*logical-mathematical*)

Stations 5 and 6: Connect 4, Chinese Checkers (*spatial*)

Stations 7 and 8 : Scrabble®, Boggle® (*linguistics*)

Station 9: The Ungame® (*intrapersonal*)

Station 10: Music Bingo (*musical*)

Teachers should use all available resources. Asking students to bring games from home, or borrowing or trading materials with other teachers at their site keep the cost of these types of centers to a minimum.

Using a Combination of Student- and Teacher-Initiated Interest and Instructional Centers

Another starting point might be to use materials that are easy-to-obtain, duplicate, or create to develop a combination of open-ended interest centers, and academic or instructional centers. A few ideas are listed below:

Station 1: Computer/Technology Center (writing and math activities)

Station 2: Listening/Viewing Center (obtain materials from the media center)

Station 3: Pattern Block Activity Center

Station 4: Drawing Center with a wealth of "how to draw" books

Station 5: Poetry Center (writing and reading poetry)

Station 6: Newspaper Center (activities to do using the newspaper)

Station 7: Drama Center (students create a puppet and write a script for a performance; a final performance may be given to the class)

Station 8: Coding, Decoding Center (students have copies of Morse Code, Braille, and the Greek alphabet, and then create their own codes and messages for their classmates)

Station 9: Wordsearch Center (students have a large number of word searches to choose from; they use highlighters to find the words they are searching for)

Station 10: The Restaurant Center (students choose a meal from a variety of menus from authentic restaurants, and figure tax and tip)

Station 11: The Department Store Center (students choose items from a store catalog, add up the price, and figure out sales tax)

Station 12: The Grocery Store (Students use food ads to select breakfast, lunch, and dinner food for a day)

Station 13: Music Center (a wide variety of musical activities and a keyboard are available)

Station 14: The Construction Center (students create structures with Legos™, toothpicks, straws, K'Nex®, Lincoln Logs™, and cards)

Station 15: The Comic Gallery (students create their own comic strips)

Station 16: The Travel Agency (students make a travel poster, create a map, and research a country)

Station 17: The Yellow Pages Center (students use the Yellow Pages to locate familiar businesses and agencies)

Station 18: The Drama Center (students create and use puppets, make up their own scripts, etc.)

Station 19: GeoSafari® Center

Station 20: The Research Center (students use the almanac and other research books such as *The Guinness Book of Records*, and write their own top ten questions to stump their classmates; the answers are placed on the back of the questions and partners play a trivia game with each other)

Use Student-Initiated Centers PDR Centers can be set up in an open-ended fashion with materials children may then select from in a more self-initiated manner. Having the materials available allows for student creativity and freedom to choose their own projects, instead of depending on more teacher direction.

Reading Center (classroom library books, magazines, cartoons from the newspaper, comic books, encyclopedias, poetry collections, *The Guinness Book of Records*, riddles, joke books for kids, beanbag chairs, listening post, reader's theater scripts, etc.)

Career Center (employment applications, time cards, calendars, play money, checks, receipts, restaurant order forms, department store order forms, menus, ATM cards, etc.)

Geography Center (wall maps, atlases, table maps, Thomas Brothers maps, trip planner, books, travel brochures, the travel section of the newspaper, GeoSafari®, globe, task cards and activity sheets, almanacs, etc.)

Art Center (paint, watercolors, markers, crayons, brushes, scissors, tape, construction paper, chalk, tissue paper, waxed paper, foil, wrapping paper, colored pencils, paste, glue, stapler, hole punch, sponges, cardboard, wallpaper, paper cups, paper bags, tongue depressors, pipe cleaners, yarn, buttons, spools, paper towels, recyclables—egg cartons, shoe boxes, paper towel tubes, styrofoam, meat trays, etc.)

Drama Center (pantomime cards, tongue twisters, riddles, plays, reader's theater scripts, charades, puppets, unfinished plays, etc.)

Writing Center (whiteboards, stories, poems, book of lists, addresses of famous celebrities to write letters to, personal stationery designs, examples of post cards, letters, similes, alliteration, etc., *The Jolly Postman*, story starters, pictures from magazines to motivate writing, writing prompts, jokes, riddles, comic strips, etc.)

Listening/Viewing Center (headsets, cassette player, record player, tapes, sound strips, short stories on audiotape, CDs, educational videos, TV, VCR, filmstrips, blank cassettes for students to tape their own reading or speaking, electrical outlet, simple screen, etc.)

Puzzles and Games Center (Monopoly®, Outburst®, Life®, Clue®, Battleship®, checkers, chess, tic-tac-toe, dominoes, crossword puzzles, jigsaw puzzles, Connect Four®, Parcheesi®, etc.)

Music Center (keyboard and earphones, almanac, cassette player and cassettes, materials to make musical instruments, books about instruments, music paper, sheet music, a rain stick, metronome, an area that is outside or away from the rest of the class)

Computer Center (a variety of educational games including *Oregon Trail*, *Carmen San Diego*, math and word games, a printer)

Science Center (mystery powders, pulleys, measurement tools, small skeleton, bones book, magnets, microscope and slides, book of simple experiments, old science kits from the district, balance, hand lenses, prisms, thermometer, plastic tubes, droppers, materials used in Foss kits, Aims lesson sheets, pendulums, shell collection and books, etc.)

Math Center (pattern blocks, geoboards, yard-sticks, measuring tools, dominoes, pentominoes, flash cards, graphing projects with designs, calculators and calculator activity cards, dice, decks of cards, spinners, play money, tangrams, protractors, compasses, books about geometry designs, string art, math games, department store catalogs, books of math games, tricks, adding machine with tape, etc.)

Construction Center (Legos®, Unifix® Cubes, Lincoln Logs™, Erector® set, straws, toothpicks, white glue, Tinker Toys™, K'Nex®)

WHAT SHOULD A CENTER LOOK LIKE?

Simplicity is important to remember in starting centers. Although teacher-made, eye-catching display boards may look impressive, students also enjoy a simple, less elaborate center that is easily accessible and looks interesting.

Teachers can use the following ideas when creating centers:

- Tape two pieces of self-stick adhesive covered chipboard together to form a back-board. In front of the boards are the materials and books. Attached to the board are the activity cards or ideas of what to do at the center. Because teachers might want to change these activities frequently, they are not permanently attached to the board.
- Instead of display boards, use totes, baskets, storage boxes or containers on which you have taped or pasted instructions. A print-rich, labeled environment is important. These containers are easy to store and move.

WHAT KIND OF INSTRUCTIONS SHOULD BE WRITTEN TO THE STUDENTS?

Upper-grade students do not like to be bogged down by too many instructions, so they should be short, clear, and to the point. Students are eager to get started. If the centers have been explained clearly early in the year, students already know what to do at the center. Here are some examples.

Writing Center

At this center you may . . .

1. Make a postcard and mail it to someone in the room or to someone who lives in another city.
2. Look in the address book of famous celebrities, and choose someone to write a letter to.
3. Create a poem and illustrate it. Share it with the teacher, class, or a friend.
4. Create a birthday card or thank-you note. Mail it or hand-deliver it to someone.
5. Create your own piece of stationery. Put it in the folder provided. You will receive 10 copies of the stationery for your personal use.
6. Make up your own activity.

Comic Center

At this center you may . . .

1. Look through the comic strips and comic books that are available.
2. Create a comic strip of your own with at least two main characters.
3. Create different shapes of bubbles for the dialogue to fit into.
4. Use colored pencils to make a finished product.
5. Name the comic strip. (Don't forget to capitalize the title.)
6. Create your own activity.

Restaurant World Center

At this center you may . . .

1. Select one of the many menus that are available.
2. Pretend you have $25 to spend for dinner for you and a friend of your choice.
3. Select your food and write what you want in the waitress/waiter order book.
4. Add the cost of both meals.
5. Use your calculator to figure out sales tax for your state.
6. Figure out a 15% tip.
7. How much money do you receive back from your $25?
8. Create your own activity.

Construction Center:

At this center you may . . .

1. Construct a Lego™ structure alone or with a friend.
2. Construct a toothpick structure.
3. Construct a structure with straws.
4. Construct a playing card structure.
5. Look at the books about building bridges and building structures. Use the architecture stamp kit to construct your own building.

Note: Further ready-to-use instructions for creating centers are given later in this section.

HOW SHOULD THE CENTERS BE INTRODUCED TO THE STUDENTS?

-   Set all of the centers on the tables and allow the students to look at the possible choices they have.
-   Introduce one center at a time to the entire class and let each student try one of the activities available in the center. If this method is used, students will not be able to begin the process of PDR until all the centers are introduced.

- Have the centers placed around the perimeter of the room from the first day of school. Let students look at them, gather interest, and then begin PDR. With this method, centers may be used as students complete class assignments throughout the day.

Whatever method is used, the students should be excited about starting the activities. Colorful boards or center cards and the teacher's enthusiasm enhance the PDR process.

HOW MANY CENTERS SHOULD BE SET UP AT ONE TIME?

The number of centers varies with the individual classroom. Six to eight centers allow about four students in each center at a time. Having a variety of centers gives students more choice and helps insure their continued interest and involvement. As the teacher becomes more comfortable with the PDR process, additional centers may be added. Increasing the number of available centers reduces the numbers of students at each center and allows more individual participation. This encourages children to make choices with limited selections. Not all centers have to be available every day. If there are twenty centers in the classroom, the teacher may decide only to open ten each day. Teachers should reserve the right to add or delete centers, but have enough centers so no student ever has to take "what is left."

HOW MANY STUDENTS SHOULD BE ALLOWED AT EACH CENTER?

Since the goal in creating centers is to have everyone participate successfully, having a workable number of students in each center is essential. Usually a center activity can accommodate two to four students in active participation without problems. The teacher decides the appropriate number and modifies as needs arise. Teachers may wish to allow four students at certain centers, or two at other centers. The number of students permitted at each center may either be posted on the center or on the PDR board.

WHAT KIND OF MANAGEMENT SYSTEM SHOULD BE USED?

The teacher needs to establish a management system so students know what centers are available and the maximum number of students who are allowed to participate. A PDR chart with a list of available centers should be accessible.

When planning begins, students choose their centers in a variety of ways:

- Each student could have a colored, laminated card with his/her name on it to be placed in a pocket of the PLANNING—DOING—REFLECTING chart.
- Students could have clothespins with their names or numbers on them. These are placed on the PDR chart, or are actually clamped onto the center itself.
- Post-it™ Notes or stickies with the students' names on them could be placed on the actual center.

Within each classroom, there must be a fair rotational system that allows students to take turns choosing which center they would like to participate in for the day. This can be accomplished in a variety of ways:

- a table rotation system (Table 1 goes first today; Table 2 goes first tomorrow)
- an alphabetical list
- first to line up at the door after recess before PDR time
- any other method the teacher is comfortable with fairly allocates rotational sequence in the way children are allowed to select their centers

SHOULD PDR ALWAYS BE AT THE SAME TIME AND ON THE SAME DAY(S) OF THE WEEK?

In classrooms that have PDR once or twice a week, it is helpful to determine a specific day and time each week and write it on the weekly schedule. This becomes part of the program that students look forward to; they like the consistency of knowing what to expect.

WHAT DOES THE TEACHER NEED TO EXPLAIN TO THE STUDENTS BEFORE PDR BEGINS?

Teachers need to explain each of the centers, and to let the children know activities available within each center, and the expected standards and rules. Center rules should coincide with classroom rules that have already been established. Since this may be the child's first exposure to centers, the teacher needs to set the parameters for the working period. Questions such as "What do I do if I get finished with the activity? "May I go to another center if I don't like what I am doing?" "What can I do if I don't get along with whom I am working?" These need to have answers before the PDR period begins.

The use of task cards, games, and activities needs to be explained thoroughly to the students by the teacher so that the PDR period can run smoothly.

Clean-up time should be modeled by the teacher. Students need to know:

- specific responsibilities during clean-up period
- where materials need to be placed
- where to return the centers and store materials

A good modeling session at the initial stages of PDR will set the tone for the remainder of the year.

WHERE ARE THE CENTERS KEPT DURING THE DAY?

- Keep the centers on tables in the room where the students may easily access the materials. In an upper-grade classroom of 30 to 35 students, space is somewhat limited.
- Provide storage around the perimeter of the room or under the chalkboard areas where students can carry them to the work area when needed. Storage boxes become part of the center and are labeled so that students can easily locate them.
- Students carry the various centers to their own desks, and return them to the storage place when the PDR period is completed.

WHAT WORKS? CORE CURRICULUM CENTERS OR OPEN-ENDED, EXPLORATORY CENTERS?

A balanced approach is essential. Centers should evolve from the curriculum. Some are teacher-initiated and directed; others are student-initiated, allowing students to problem solve through exploration and discovery. While teacher ideas for centers often include the basic instructional program, task cards, activity sheets and directions to follow, children can also learn a great deal from investigating things on their own. Legos™, K'Nex®, straw and toothpick construction, and Erector® sets offer a freer form of creativity and learning.

In an art center, for example, a teacher might:

- Ask the students to draw people, objects, and/or animals by looking at how-to-draw books. This is more directed and less creative because everyone is trying to make their picture look like one that someone else has drawn.

- Provide a large variety of art paper, books, and art materials that invite the students to explore and create in whichever media they choose to use. This is more student-directed and creative.

Both types of centers are worthwhile, and provide students with rich learning experiences. Teachers should establish a balance in the centers to accommodate a variety of learning styles.

HOW IS A PDR CENTER DIFFERENT FROM A THEMATIC CENTER?

A PDR center is an interest center that involves individual choice and student responsibility for learning. Students need opportunities to make decisions on their own; when children make poor choices, they must learn to deal with them, discover how to make them better the next time, and feel the consequences of making an unsuccessful decision. When children have made good choices, they should feel the positive consequences of their decisions.

During PDR, students are not forced to go to any center they do not choose themselves. This is the time of day when independent learning experiences are provided. Students are responsible to plan, follow through during working time, and evaluate their efforts.

The PDR center is different from the thematic center. At a thematic center, teachers direct students' learning activities. Students are usually responsible for rotating into each center to be sure that essential curriculum experiences are covered. For example, in the mystery thematic unit, students rotate through the ten curriculum-based centers, usually one center per day. (See the thematic teaching unit of Mystery later in this section.)

The PDR center time is child-centered. Children choose activities with very little teacher direction. Enough centers are provided to give students choices that tap their intellectual and creative potential.

WHERE SHOULD THE TEACHER OBTAIN MATERIALS FOR THE CENTER?

An upper-grade teacher who is in the initial stages of creating centers should search the materials he/she already has. It is amazing how many items that haven't been used in years now open a door for creation of a center. Experiments and activities from children's science and math magazines sometimes lend themselves to centers. The newspaper offers a wealth of materials, such as ads where children can learn to advertise and create their own ads for things they would like to sell. The movie and television sections of the newspaper can be used to provide students with opportunities to select movies and programs they would like to watch. Food ads can be the basis of a center where students actually have to buy groceries for their families. *Auto Trader* and *Home Buying Guides* may be helpful in showing students how to use math in their everyday life. Each child can be responsible for buying a car and home of his/her dreams. The list is endless!

At some schools, teachers at a particular grade level hand out a *WISH LIST* to the parents early in the year to let parents know what they can offer to enhance the PDR program. Making parents aware of center ideas and how they can help gather materials makes them feel they are involved in their children's education. The collecting of catalogs for the Department Store Center, menus for the Mini-Market Center, and comic strips for the Cartoon Center are small ways in which parents can feel involved.

WHAT ELSE CAN BE DONE TO ENHANCE PARENT INVOLVEMENT IN PDR?

Parents need to have a clear understanding of the value of the PDR process. Many parents feel upper-grade students need formal instruction. The upper-grade teacher must help parents understand the importance of PDR center time for their children. Welcoming parents to visit before PDR actually begins helps avoid any misinformation about what is happening in the classroom. Inviting parents to participate in PDR with their children is also beneficial. Establishing good communication about the benefits of PDR makes parents more assured and confident about their child's experience.

When parents "buy in" to the program, they will be more likely to assist in planning ideas for centers, offering their help, and even wanting to come in to class to create a center of their own. For instance, a parent might:

- Plan a Cooking Center and volunteer his/her time and the materials to get it started.
- Provide expertise about a musical instrument, give instruction on how to play the instrument, and provide opportunities for the students to play it, too.
- Give instruction on origami. Take the students through a series of paper-folding activities.

HOW CAN THE UPPER-GRADE STUDENTS HELP WITH THE CENTERS?

Although most teachers like to develop their own centers, they soon realize that students are among their best resources. After the initial PDR centers have been used by the students, teachers may want the students to brainstorm new ideas that can be implemented. The students suggest ideas and should be able to explain its importance in the classroom and what can be learned from the center proposal.

Students in cooperative groups may be asked to build their own centers as a mid-year project. These may be added to the rest of the centers or used for a period of a month or two; this will need some teacher supervision and direction. The actual construction of the centers by the students may take several PDR sessions. Materials and books for the center should be generated by the students.

The creation of centers is a major undertaking, but with teamwork and resourcefulness, PDR can be successfully operating in a short amount of time. Additional centers may be created as needed throughout the year.

CENTER RECORD SHEET
PLAN—DO—REFLECT

Name _____

Keep a record of each of the centers you visit. You are to place the date that you went to that center inside the box. Use an abbreviated date such as 3/5 for March 5. Your teacher will collect your folders at the end of the fifth day of PDR.

	Day 1	Day 2	Day 3	Day 4	Day 5
Aerodynamics					
Calculator					
Calligraphy					
Card Games					
Checkers/Chess					
Coding/Decoding					
Comics Galore					
Computer					
Construction					
Department Store					
Drama					
Drawing					
GeoSafari					
Graphing					
Mapping					
Mazes					
Mini-Market					
Music					
Observation					
Origami					
Poetry					
Puzzle/Game					
Reader's Theater					
Reading					
Research					
Restaurant					
Science					
Stationery/Letter Writing					
Technology					
Writing					
Word Search					
Yellow Pages					
Other					

Note to the teacher: This form and the PDR Recording Sheet are stapled in a construction paper folder for each student. The child fills out the forms each day and places any activities he/she has completed in the folder. After the fifth day, the teacher collects the folders and evaluates informally what the child has accomplished.

This is a sample form that is used in our classrooms. Each teacher will have his/her own individual form.

PLAN—DO—REFLECT RECORDING SHEET

Student's Name _____

    To get you started with the PDR process, you will be keeping track of your progress on this sheet. Each day you will have a few minutes to plan what you are going to do (*Planning*), to actually get involved in your activity (*Doing*), and then to sum up what you think you learned and accomplished (*Reflecting*). Initially, you will use this page to help you gather your thoughts. As time passes, you will receive a half-size composition book in which to keep your records. Your teacher will collect this sheet at the end of five days to evaluate your progress.

DAY 1:

What do you plan to do? _____

_____

What did you actually do? _____

_____

_____

What did you learn, find new or interesting, or accomplish? _____

_____

_____

DAY 2:

What do you plan to do? _____

_____

What did you actually do? _____

_____

_____

What did you learn, find new or interesting, or accomplish? _____

_____

DAY 3:

What do you plan to do? _____

_____

What did you actually do? _____

_____

_____

What did you learn, find new or interesting, or accomplish? _____

_____

_____

DAY 4:

What do you plan to do? _____

_____

What did you actually do? _____

_____

_____

What did you learn, find new or interesting, or accomplish? _____

_____

_____

DAY 5:

What do you plan to do? _____

_____

What did you actually do? _____

_____

_____

What did you learn, find new or interesting, or accomplish? _____

_____

_____

_____

CARD GAME CENTER

At this center you may . . .

1. Select a game from the books provided, such as Crazy Eight, Concentration, Snap, etc.

2. Read the rules very carefully. Make sure everyone understands the rules before you begin.

3. Play the game with one or two other friends.

4. When you are finished, place all the cards back in the correct baggie.

5. Record the game you played on your PDR sheet.

CALCULATOR CENTER

At this center you may . . .

1. Look through the activity sheets available.

2. Choose to do one activity by yourself or one with a partner.

3. Follow the directions on the activity sheet.

4. Remember to use the eraser-end of your pencil when pushing the buttons on your calculator.

MUSIC CENTER

At this center you may . . .

1. Listen to a tape, CD, or a story that is provided, or one that you bring from home. If you have your own earphones you may use them. Make sure what you bring from home is appropriate and is approved by your teacher.

2. Use the keyboard to create a new melody or play something you already know.

3. Write some new words to a familiar tune you already know. Put the words on an overhead transparency and present it to the class.

4. Write your own rap and be willing to present it in front of the class.

5. Ask for assistance. Have someone videotape you while you sing or dance for the video camera.

6. Lip-sync a song. Make sure you provide movement to go along with it. Present it to the class. You may even want to dress the part.

7. Make a list of your favorite female singers and your favorite male singers.

8. Make a list of as many musical groups you can think of, past and present.

9. Look up the music awards in the almanac. List the songs that won the American Music Awards last year.

10. Make a list of the different kinds of music that exist.

11. Use the music books provided. Draw pictures of the different instruments and label each.

12. Write a report about one of the famous musicians listed on the paper.

13. Write a poem or paragraph about how music effects our lives. Think of how our world would be different if there was no music.

14. The letters used to name the musical notes are **A B C D E F G**. Make a list of all the musical words you can think of that have only those letters in them. After you have about twenty words, use the bells or the keyboard to spell the words musically. (bead, bed, deaf, etc.). Write some musical words using the correct notes on music paper.

15. At home create your own musical instrument. Share it with the class.

16. Use the metronome to try different rhythms. Clap out the sound with your hands.

DRAMA CENTER

At this center you may . . .

1. Choose one or two of the puppets and create a short play. Create your own dialogue.

2. Create your own puppet using the simple construction paper model provided. Use the supplies in the box or bring your own from home.

3. Create a shadow puppet using the instructions provided. Make up your own show.

4. Pretend you are a famous talkshow host or hostess. Interview a celebrity who everyone will know. Dress up with interesting clothing.

5. Invent a new product and create a commercial to advertise it.

6. Write a script with a partner. Perform it for the class.

7. Pretend you are a newsreporter on the scene or in the studio. Report the news as you see it.

8. Prepare a performance that you would like to videotape.

THE CONSTRUCTION CENTER

At this center you may . . .

1. Construct a Lego™ structure along or with a friend.

2. Try making a toothpick structure. Use white glue and a piece of tagboard.

3. Make a structure with straws.

4. Use other forms of math manipulatives to form a creative structure.

5. Make a card structure.

6. Look at the bridge construction book. Using toothpicks try to assemble a bridge that can stand by itself.

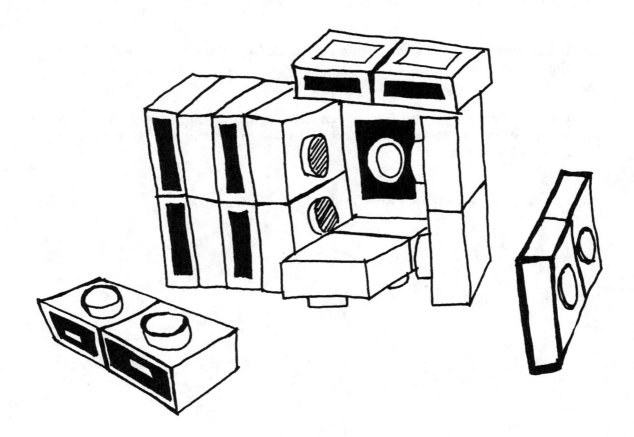

THE NEWSPAPER CENTER

At this center you may . . .

1. Locate words in the newspaper that would describe the following people:

    a. You

    b. Your mom

    c. Your dad

    d. Your best friend

    e. Your teacher

    f. Your brother and/or sister

2. Locate an item in the ad section of the newspaper that you would like to buy. Cut it out and paste it to an index card. On the back side of the card, tell why you chose that item.

3. Create your own ad for something you would like to sell using the classified section of the newspaper.

4. Cut out words from the newspaper. Send a note to someone with newspaper words. Write at least two sentences. Don't sign your name. Have that person guess who sent it.

5. Create a mini-newspaper of your own. Sketch it out first.

READER'S THEATER CENTER

At this center you may . . .

1. Choose a reader's theater script that you would like to work on.

2. Have a partner read it with you.

3. You may need to take several parts.

4. Try to make your voice sound different for each part you take.

5. During "Reflecting," present a one-minute part of the reading you really liked.

PAPER AIRPLANE CENTER

At this center you may . . .

1. Look through all the paper airplane books that are provided at this center.

2. Select a design you would like to try.

3. Make the plane using the white paper in the box. Try not to waste paper.

4. Label your plane:

   a. Name your plane.

   b. Don't forget to put your name on your plane.

5. Before you fly them, predict which plane you think will fly the farthest, the longest, the highest, the "trickiest."

6. Ask your teacher for permission to test-fly your plane. Make sure you aren't near a building or trees where it may get stuck.

7. During the "Reflecting" you may show your classmates your designs and test them out again.

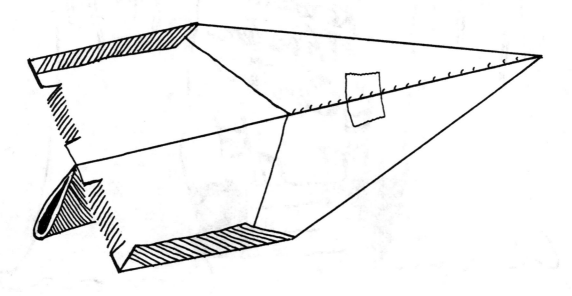

CALLIGRAPHY CENTER

At this center you may . . .

1. Look through the calligraphy books that are at this center.

2. Use the special calligraphy pens that your teacher has purchased. Be careful not to press too hard on the pens.

3. Take a piece of wide-lined primary writing paper. Use the model examples that show calligraphy writing. Copy the letters as carefully as you can. Try to make them look like the samples.

4. Write all the letters of the alphabet and then attempt to write some words and sentences.

5. Practice makes perfect, so have fun practicing.

6 Keep your paper to share with your classmates during the "Reflecting" period of the day.

THE SCIENCE CENTER

At this center you may . . .

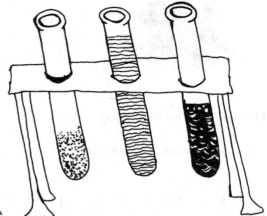

1. Perform the experiment that your teacher has provided for you to do. Follow the procedure carefully.

2. Look through the science experimentation books that are provided at this center.

3. Look for the materials you need in the science kit.

4. If you can't find exactly what you need, try to locate them at home tonight, or ask your teacher for help.

5. Try out your experiment several times. Make sure it works.

6. Show your experiment to the class and explain the scientific principle that is involved.

MAZE CENTER

At this center you may . . .

1. Choose one of the maze activity sheets from the basket.

2. Use a Visa-Vis™ pen to work through your maze.

3. When completed, use the special spray bottle of solution to clean off your laminated activity sheet.

PUZZLE/GAME CENTER

At this center you may . . .

1. Assemble one of the jigsaw puzzles. (If there is a piece missing, please indicate that on the box so the next person knows about it.)

2. Play one of the board games. If you are unsure about a rule, read the directions.

3. Make sure all the pieces have been returned.

RESEARCH CENTER

At this center you may . . .

1. Look through the materials and books provided. Find something that interests you.

2. Do an activity sheet **or** choose a book to find out some interesting facts. *The Guinness Book of World Records* is always a good place to locate some unusual facts.

3. Write five new things you learned by looking through the books. Write them on the 5" × 7" index cards found at this center.

4. Write five questions from the facts that you will use to try to stump your classmates. You might become a research wizard!

5. At the end of the period, share the questions and/or facts with your classmates. See if they know the answers.

6. Place your completed index cards in the *Research Question Stump Box*. Other students can read your questions and try to locate your answers in the encyclopedia, almanac, atlas, or other reference book.

DEPARTMENT STORE CENTER

At this center you may . . .

1. Choose a catalog from the ones provided at this center.

2. Use the order form to select $75 worth of merchandise. Fill out the order.

3. Add up your total and be sure to figure out sales tax.

4. Create your own catalog using merchandise from the catalogs provided. Make your own order form.

5. Select a family member or friend. Create a poster showing what you would buy for that person. Write an explanation of why you chose that person, and why you choose the merchandise you did. Limit your spending to $25.

6. Create your own fashion show of childrens' and adults' clothing on paper. Include men's, women's, boys' and girls' clothing.

7. Create a new name for a department store and create a shopping bag to accompany the merchandise people will purchase.

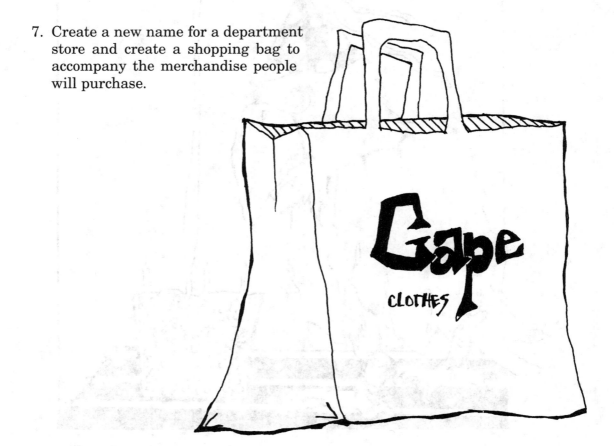

COMICS GALORE CENTER

At this center you may . . .

1. Glance through the laminated comic strips that you find in the box at this center.

2. Look for words that are specific to comic strips (zap, pow, zow, yikes, etc.).

3. Create your own comic character. It may be a hero or heroine. Use colored pencil, crayons, markers, or regular pencil for your drawings. Put him/her in a four- or five-frame comic strip.

4. Practice drawing cartoon characters from the art books that are provided.

5. Create a cartoon expressing your opinion or idea about something you believe in.

RESTAURANT ROUND-UP CENTER

At this center you may . . .

1. Choose a menu from the many that are available in the container provided.

2. Pretend you are going out for dinner and you are going to take along your best friend.

3. You have $25 to spend.

4. You are to purchase an appetizer, an entree, a dessert, and a beverage.

5. Try to get as close to the $25 limit as possible.

6. Select your food and write out an order form.

7. Add up the total. Don't forget to figure sales tax.

8. Add up the two figures.

9. Now multiply your food total (without the sales tax) and add a 15% tip.

10. Design your very own menu for a restaurant that you create. Name your restaurant, your logo, your uniforms for waiters and waitresses, and your menu.

THE CODING/DECODING CENTER

At this center you may . . .

1. Look through the different types of codes that have been used throughout history.

2. Practice some of the codes to see if you can gain some mastery of them. Use the books and activity sheets that are provided.

3. Write a new code of your own. Write a symbol for each of the letters of the alphabet, plus the numbers 1 through 10.

4. Create a message of your own. Try to make it at least 10 words long.

5. Have a partner decode your message.

6. Create a rebus story. Have a friend decode your story.

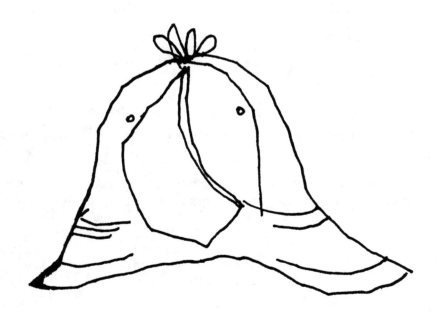

WORD SEARCH CENTER

At this center you may . . .

1. Use one of the word search sheets and find all the words from the word bank.

2. Create your own word search using words from the dictionary, spelling lists, or the thesaurus. Make a list of all the words you are using for your partner.

3. Have a partner locate the words you have selected on your word search. Have your partner use a yellow highlighter.

4. Put your name and your partner's name on your finished papers.

```
M E D D L I N G A N X I O U S L C L H K B
C O I N C I D E N C E S G L O O M Y O K B
I E S U P E R M A R K E T V X Y O P R J O
R M A N F L I C K E R I N G D R N K R U U
C A P H Z E I P A R T I T I O N S J O D N
U R P A C C L U M S Y E L E V A T O R G C
I T E L S T O M A C H A C H E R E D S M I
T I A L G R A V E Y A R D S R L R I G E N
S A R O E I M U S T Y C O L L A P S I N G
R N E W A C B P T R I L L I O N S G N T U
P F D E R I A B R I D G E D A D R R G L P
L I D D P A S S A G E W A Y D L M A E I R
U L A D H N C O N C E I V E E O U C R T O
C T B R O D E L I C A T E H D R E E L O P
K H B E N A N T E N N A S U K D X A Y I P
E Y L A E M A C I A T E D P E E P H O L E
D V E R S I O N O I T P R I N C I P L E D
Y Z D Y C V C R E A T I O N R A I L I N G
M U S C L E S W E I R D P E C U L I A R T
```

TECHNOLOGY CENTER

At this center you may . . .

1. Play a computer game.

2. Use the GeoSafari.

3. Listen to a soundstrip.

4. Listen to and watch a video.

THE MINI-MARKET CENTER

At this center you may . . .

1. Look through the newspaper food sections that are available on the table.

2. Plan one day of meals for your very own family. That means you need to have three (3) meals.

3. Think of having well-balanced meals with good nutrition, but don't forget to throw in some snacks and dessert.

4. You have $25 to spend.

5. Look for the pictures in the newspaper to show a visual, plus the price of the items you are buying.

6. Cut the item out of the ads and also show its price.

7. Use the construction paper provided at this center. Divide it into four equal sections—one marked *breakfast*, one marked *lunch*, and one marked *dinner*. The last one can be marked *snacks*.

8. Glue your pictures and prices onto a piece of construction paper.

9. Using your calculator, figure out how much your items will cost. Fill out the order form.

10. Be neat and make sure your name is on the paper.

11. When completed, put your paper in your PDR Folder.

WHY TEACH THEMATICALLY?

As teachers, we seem to be in competition with the fast-moving world of television, high-action video and computer games, and the excitement and stimulation of the world outside of the classroom. Holding the attention of our students for any long period of time in the traditional manner isn't working. We must rise to the challenge and create a rich environment that actively involves our students, so that they do engage themselves educationally. Allowing children to make choices about their education and the way they learn, and giving them a variety of experiences that tap their natural curiosity, will hopefully revive and redirect their natural high energy level. Through thematic teaching, students take a more responsible posture in active learning opportunities, and extend their enthusiasm outside of school and into their homes and community. By creating child-centered, meaningful environments for all students, the competition of the outside world can be minimized, but also harnessed and utilized.

Within the upper-grade classroom, students stay more focused on what they are learning if they can see that it is connected and relevant to their own lives. The goal of the teacher should be to motivate students by "hooking" them into what they are learning, and making them feel an important part of the curriculum. One way of doing this is through the thematic approach. Whether it is on an individual classroom basis, grade-level basis, or school-wide, when teaching and learning is done through integrated themes, students and teachers alike begin to see connections to the past, present and future, and gain new knowledge of how the disciplines interrelate.

When the curriculum is taught as an integrated theme, students have a variety of methods to experience learning and access knowledge. Through the use of their individual learning modalities and their multiple intelligences, students learn collaboratively, as well as independently. The teacher uses a balance of direct teaching strategies, as well as giving students the responsibility of learning on their own through hands-on curriculum-based centers, or by giving students a choice in activities that otherwise would be mandatory for all students. The word *balance* is emphasized. Teachers cannot totally eliminate direct teaching, but they must continue to search for more current strategies that take the emphasis off them, and put responsibility on active participation by their students.

A thematic program that engages students in their learning, lets them learn through hands-on activities, and gives them opportunities to understand and apply what they have learned is essential to a successful educational experience. The assessment element must also be added to make the program complete.

The use of thematic teaching is important because it focuses teachers on the concepts that are to be developed within their activities and class lessons. It also can make a somewhat isolated profession come more alive because it gets teachers to work together in keeping the students motivated. Seeing an entire school all involved in one theme, but with a variety of connections, makes for real excitement on the part of parents, teachers and students, alike. A sense of community develops as students work to see the broad understanding of the theme. People who never saw connections before within the theme become more creative and interested in how everything interrelates.

IS THERE A DIFFERENCE BETWEEN A TOPIC AND A THEME?

Differentiation between a topic and a theme needs to be made clear. A theme normally is looked upon as a broad area that integrates the subject areas and makes meaningful connections between them, allowing students to participate in activities that involve them in reading, writing, speaking, listening and, of course, thinking. Broad themes that can be used for long periods of time, and have a wide variety of directions that a teacher or school could pursue, might include: Connections, Patterns, Structures, Heritage, Treasures, Marvels, Frontiers, Survival, etc.

Looking at the theme of survival, one teacher and his/her students may choose quite a different direction to take compared with the teacher down the hall. One person may develop the concept of survival in everyday life skills for math; in other words, making sure that students see that they have to understand math to be able to figure sales tax, be consumers, eat at restaurants, use the TV Guide, buy a car or a house, etc. Whereas, another teacher might approach the theme by developing concepts around the environment and ecology focused on weather, climate, plants, etc. Whichever direction the class takes, students need to have clear understanding of the theme's importance and how it relates to them. This assures the teacher that students will deem it important to study it in depth.

A team of teachers may want to combine the concepts of survival into a totally integrated, long-term unit that can span a semester. This could cover aspects of survival physically, emotionally, intellectually, and socially. It could conceivably involve math, science, social studies, health, physical fitness, the fine arts, and more.

Many teachers use theme in the narrower sense of the word and center units around topics such as bears, bugs, monsters, apples, elephants, whales, etc. Regie Routman, in her book *Invitations*, distinguishes between themes and topics. She indicates that topics such as those mentioned above provide activities that are creative and interesting, but often they lack substance and are not based on major concepts. The development of important concepts and skills that make meaningful connections to the curriculum and to the children's lives can expand a topic into an educational thematic unit. A topic can be designed to give the same depth of skill and concept development as a theme, but it does require extra effort.

SHOULD A THEME BE DEVELOPED BY AN INDIVIDUAL, TEAM, OR SCHOOLWIDE?

In some schools, the thematic approach is schoolwide, as is the case of Howard Gardner's Key School in Indianapolis. Each semester the Key School teachers introduce a schoolwide theme and try to weave it throughout the entire school curriculum. Each teacher is responsible for implementing the theme in his/her own way, deciding which topics or concepts he/she would like to develop. Collaboratively, the teachers and students research existing curriculum materials and create those materials that aren't available. Changes and growth are made as teachers plan and assess the unit's value and progress. Brainstorming sessions are held with all teachers and staff, and three themes are chosen for the year. Students are given choices and led through a project related to that theme. Throughout the theme, students are planning and assessing their work. Parental and community involvement are utilized.

At the end of the semester, individual classes and students are brought together on a schoolwide basis, and the students present their projects.

Peer-, teacher-, and self-evaluation are built solidly into the theme projects.

Since everyone is at a different stage of thematic development, a schoolwide theme may be overwhelming to a staff. Therefore, teachers may want to begin in smaller steps by planning individually, in grade levels, or in other configurations of teams.

For an individual teacher interested in creating a theme alone, the task may seem monumental. Highly creative teachers may be able to see the way a theme may be laid out and may see connections easily. The task seems to be much easier when the team approach is used. Bouncing ideas off each other motivates the creation of new ideas. Teachers who work in small teams also have the advantage of lessening the load of theme creation, but can, in the end, share the ideas, possibly creating two separate thematic teaching units that can be used in several classrooms. By dividing up the work, more units are created and more students can reap the benefits of the thematic approach. Some modifications of the units may be necessary as the unit is implemented in other classrooms.

Engaging the older students into theme development as a class makes good sense because then the students feel they are part of the planning process, and their thoughts are important and valued. As the curriculum becomes child-centered, relevant and meaningful, students begin to develop responsible attitudes toward their education and connect them to the pursuit of lifelong learning.

How do you get started developing a thematic teaching unit?

1. Look carefully at the content areas and objectives of the curriculum you are going to teach and select a theme that takes into consideration the needs and interests of your students.

2. Look for literature that is related to the theme.

3. Determine the curriculum goals, objectives, and understandings you want to develop.

4. Through brainstorming with your class, other teachers, and parents, develop activities, experiences, and learning that support and foster skills and concepts that relate to the theme.

5. Find out what the children already know and what they would like to find out.

6. Organize ideas into content areas taking into consideration how children learn and relating them to the seven intelligences where possible.

7. Gather materials and resources to support your major concepts and understandings. Inform your parents and the community of your theme and request their assistance in supporting and expanding the theme.

8. Set up centers or assign activities that give choices to the students which foster investigation, hands-on experiences, exploration, and critical thinking. These elements should be implemented through a variety of grouping strategies, independent, as well as cooperative learning, and teacher-directed class lessons.

9. Evaluate student growth and success through the process of teacher-, peer- and self-evaluation.

THEMATIC UNIT: "MYSTERY AROUND US"

WHY THIS THEME?

The world is filled with mystery. Discovering these mysteries helps us to better understand ourselves, our lives, and what it truly means to be human. The art of investigating the clues that permeate our world opens up the world to us and gives us a clearer meaning of life itself. As we grow and develop, we discover that many things that appeared to be obscure at one point of time in our life can become clearer, and no longer present the mysterious view we saw before. Sometimes clarification of the world around us comes because we gain scientific explanation, or gain new knowledge in math that we are developmentally ready to understand.

In our everyday lives, we each become our own detectives, scientists, or mathematicians who unlock the unsolved mysteries that we have not understood. As we read a good detective story, we become involved with the development of clues that unlock the case or crime. In the real world, we must continually do the same kind of investigative work to solve the meaning of words, unlock the secrets of spelling, decipher the symbols in reading, find the hidden pattern or decode the secrets of numbers, or try to find the answers to unexplained or unclear events. In all areas of our educational pursuit, we explore and investigate clues to gain clearer understanding of our world.

HOW DOES IT FIT INTO THE CURRICULUM?

The theme of mystery within the classroom lends itself to all areas of the curriculum and gives room for each student to discover—through reading, writing, listening and speaking—the understanding that mystery abounds in our world. Within the parameters of their developmental level, students will explore the world of mystery and how it relates to the world around them. The theme of mystery encompasses the areas of math, science, language, geography, history, music, and art. Through activities and projects, each child will begin to develop keener observation, as well as deductive reasoning and critical-thinking skills.

Within this study, students will begin to understand that many things that appear to be mysterious can be understood when the clues are looked at carefully. This knowledge can assist in helping to find a solution to make events and situations clearer.

WHERE DO WE START?

Core Literature To get things started, students read several mystery stories. For fifth and sixth graders, three books that appear to hold their interest are *The Egypt Game*, *The Westing Game*, and *Scared Stiff*. The importance of having more than one work to study during the thematic unit is so that students can compare, contrast, and analyze the literature to gain insight into the basic elements and writing styles of the authors. Through oral and written language, students may expand their mystery knowledge and relate it to things outside the classroom.

Resource Books and Materials Having readily available resource books to motivate students to go beyond the literature is absolutely necessary. Almanacs, encyclopedias, reference materials about unsolved mysteries, people, etc., should be placed around the classroom. The public library is a good source of these materials, and as you make parents aware of the theme, students will just start bringing in more materials than you can even imagine. Videos, sound strips, pictures of famous detectives, and posters may also act as motivation for students to get involved.

Bulletin Board and Room Environment　At least one large bulletin board with a heading such as *Mystery Abounds, All the World Is a Mystery*, or *Mysteries Around Us* also acts as a focus and a motivator for students. This board should develop over the course of the unit and it should be student-centered. Student work showing understanding of key concepts can be displayed as a continual form of assessment. The game Clue®, mystery puzzles and words, and activity centers may be available for the students as they progress through the unit.

Community Involvement　Parents and other community resource people can be utilized in the pursuit of the theme. Ask for their assistance in giving greater direction and richness to the unit. They may help you become more aware of resources like guest speakers, field trips, and additional materials. Through parent communication such as a newsletter, let others know what you are doing. Experts on fingerprinting, court reporters, detectives, FBI agents, and attorneys, etc., will give more depth and interest to the unit. Exhaust your resources. Let your principal and other teachers also know about your quest.

At-Home Activities　Ask the students to expand their knowledge of mystery by looking through the TV program guides to see what fits into the thematic unit. Programs like "Unsolved Mysteries", and specials about the Loch Ness Monster, the Bermuda Triangle, mysteries in outer space, and mysteries of the deep abound, and parents and students may be willing to videotape them for you to show to the entire class. Television guides should be scanned for commercial as well as public television viewing ideas.

Parents can also get involved in helping their children to complete the *Who Am I? What Am I?* project. (See the end of this section.) By assisting them in learning how to move from the general to specific, they will see how a set of mystery clues in literature can unfold.

Encourage each child to watch a television detective story such as "Perry Mason", "Ellery Queen", "Murder She Wrote", "Mc Cloud", etc., or watch a mystery video or movie that will give a broader understanding of mystery. (See the parent letter and Mystery Movie Review form at the end of this section.)

Whole Class Lessons—Directed by the teacher

1. Watch the video *Whodunit: The Art of the Detective Story* or another similar film that shows how mystery stories are written.
2. Compare and contrast core literature books and make connections between authors' styles of writing, characters, setting, and other story elements.
3. Give guidelines on how to research using reference books, and modeling how to write a good research paper.
4. Discuss coding and decoding, fingerprinting, and evidence collection in murder cases.
5. Review how to use an almanac.
6. Review math concepts that students need for the math center.
7. Read to the class from *Two-Minute Mysteries, Sherlock Holmes, Mysteries of the Mind and the Senses*, or other short stories that will capture the students' interest.

HOW LONG SHOULD A THEMATIC UNIT TAKE TO COMPLETE?

The theme of mystery could take a class anywhere from a few weeks to several months. With the reading of three books, and the time for analyzing, synthesizing and evaluating this reading material, the unit will probably last for six to eight weeks. If children are totally immersed in the theme through reading, writing, speaking, listening, thinking, observing, and exploring, then the experience is worthwhile and keeping focused will be easy for a long period of time.

Centers supplement the curriculum. Since there are eleven mandatory centers and two optional centers, teachers may choose to provide center time as it fits into their individual program. Whether daily, every other day, or twice a week, students like to know when they can expect mystery centers to be set up. Many students like the consistency of knowing what is going to happen and when it will take place.

If students complete visiting all of the centers in two weeks, additional completion time must be provided either in class or at home. Most students cannot finish all that is required in the class periods. An additional week of short work sessions can be allocated for students to put finishing touches on their activities. The centers are again set up and students may revisit any center to complete the activity.

WHAT ABOUT EVALUATION?

It is recommended that throughout the unit, the teacher and students continually assess their progress. During center time, the teacher should be available and ready to assist. The teacher should become the observer who watches for active participation by each child and to see that the tasks are being done with understanding and quality. Students should write daily about what they accomplished (see *Mystery Center Daily Review and Recording Sheet* at the end of this section) and should be given opportunities to discuss with their classmates the progress they have made on their stories and other theme projects. Sharing each day on accomplishments that have been achieved at the centers gives good modeling for the students who have not already visited that center.

The teacher may keep records of his/her observations as he/she checks the students and their progress. These may be used for reference in parent conferences. The teacher should be available to check the understanding of information and to answer and clarify questions the students may have.

The use of a video camera adds another element of assessment as children progress through the unit. The mystery theme bulletin board holds a child-centered display of student work that shows the evolution of the theme. Research reports, mystery stories, reader's theater, drawings, etc., should be evaluated by the students themselves, their peers, and the teacher.

Parents are also asked to evaluate their child's mystery story. (See *Parent Evaluation Mystery Story Writing* at the end of this section.) Having the parents evaluate their child's story unites the home, school and child, and builds effective communication. **Note:** Students evaluate themselves on this assignment, as well as the teacher and parent. (See *Self-Evaluation* and *Teacher-Evaluation of Mystery Story Writing* at the end of this section.)

As a culminating activity, students should evaluate their theme development, and what they have learned. (See *Self-Evaluation of the Mystery Thematic Unit* at the end of this section.) Inviting parents into the classroom to see the results of the students' learning is also a good idea.

How Can Technology Be Used in This Unit?

During the course of the unit, exposure and use of technology should be encouraged. Having computers available for students to use for writing their research papers and mystery stories, the use of the video camera to record their presentations, taking snapshots as the activities unfold, the television, VCR, tape, filmstrips, CD and tape player all become a significant part of the unit and the implementation of it.

When Are Curriculum Centers Set Up?

After the students become motivated in the theme, and the teacher has given a foundation and general understanding of the importance of mystery in their lives, centers may be set up. Since this type of center is curriculum-based, students will rotate into all of the centers by visiting one per day. Approximately 40 minutes should be given for student completion of each center activity. Since some centers take longer to finish than others, it may be necessary for students to work on a previous day's activity at another time. If they complete all the work at a center before the end of the activity period, they may choose to work on the previous day's activity. The research, creative writing, and drawing centers seem to take a lot more time than is provided in class and may need to be assigned as homework. There are two optional centers (music and reader's theater) that may be used as students complete their work.

What Does a Mystery Center Look Like?

Each of the mystery centers is constructed with two pieces of 12" × 18" chipboard that are taped together. The display board is covered with a designed, black-and-white self-stick vinyl. The directions, along with other pictures and illustrations that make the board appealing to the students, are glued onto the board. Before attaching them to the board permanently, these items are framed with colored construction paper and laminated for durability. Reference books, student activity pages in labeled construction paper folders, and other materials needed at the center are placed in a basket or tub, and are set out in front of the display board.

How Should Students Be Chosen for Center Groupings?

Since the students will be at centers for a minimum of eleven days, it is important that the teacher helps to form workable teams. Cooperation is essential in making center time flow smoothly. Heterogeneous groups should be formed so that teams can assist each other in the center process. Students who are in need of more assistance on the tasks can be given cooperative help from their peers. Promoting the idea of cooperation should be a year-long journey. It is always a good idea to remind students that there is more than one teacher in a classroom.

MYSTERY CENTER ACTIVITIES

Note to the teachers: All of the activity pages and forms referred to for use in these station centers are found at the end of this section.

Station 1: Drawing Center

- At this center you will look at a number of pictures of **famous detectives** in the world (Sherlock Holmes, Ace Ventura, Brenda Starr, Nancy Drew, The Hardy Boys, Scooby Doo, Ellery Queen, Perry Mason, Columbo, McCloud, Jessica Fletcher, etc.).

- You are to use your imagination and create your own detective. You may make him or her realistic or animated. Use the available books to gather your ideas, but use your own creativity.

- If you finish, put your detective into a two-, three- or four-framed comic strip. Use the paper provided. You may want to sketch a rough draft and then perfect your character with markers or colored pencils.

- You may also want to make a *Wanted Poster* for your criminal. The sheet is provided in the folder.

- Keep this activity in your Mystery Folder.

Station 2: Vocabulary Center

- At this center you will find a class-generated list of words that relate to the theme of mystery.

- Use the words provided, and have your team members brainstorm with you to generate other words you can use. Try to think of at least ten of your own words.

- Be sure you make an answer key for this vocabulary project.

- Have another classmate highlight the words or write in the words.

- Place the finished wordsearch or crossword puzzle in your Mystery Folder.

Note: See Mystery Word Bank at the end of this section. Students should also be provided with graph paper at this center.

Station 3: Research Center

- At this center you will find an almanac, encyclopedias, library books, and other reference books that will assist you in finding out about people, places, and things that are connected to the theme of mystery.

- Use the available resources and write a research paper of approximately one to two pages telling about the information you have discovered.

- You may look for more information outside of class. Make sure you use several sources of information and remember not to copy directly from the books; put the information into your own words.

- To get you started, there is a notetaking sheet that will assist you in gathering your notes in some kind of order.

- Also use the *Information about Your Report* sheets to assist you in recording the titles of resources you use.

- You may use the computer center for in-class work. All final reports must be typed.

- Choose from these topics or find another place, creature, phenomenon, or person involved with mystery that you are interested in, and ask the teacher if it is okay to write your report on it.

    The Bermuda Triangle
    Easter Island
    Stonehenge
    The Great Wall of China
    The Black Hole
    The Lines of Nazca
    The Lost Continent of Atlantis
    The Pyramids
    The Abominable Snowman
    The Loch Ness Monster
    UFOs
    ESP
    Houdini
    David Copperfield
    Agatha Christie
    Sherlock Holmes

- You may want to include a picture, map, or illustration of your own or choose one from the book *Places of Mystery* found at this center.

Station 4: Code and Decoding Center

- In our everyday lives, we need to look at symbols and figure out their meaning. Young children look at letters and words, and decode the symbols to learn how to read. We all learned to unlock the math symbols to add, subtract, multiply, and divide.

- Your job is to look over the samples of **codes** we use in our world, or that have been used in the past. Decipher one of the codes.

- Create your own code by developing a symbol for each letter of the alphabet.

- Write out your code on an index card.

- Write a message in code of **at least three complete sentences (about 20 words)**.

- Have a member of your group decode your message.

- Place your work in your Mystery Folder.

Station 5: Mapping Center

Note to the teacher: Before the students visit this center, they must be informed about the shoe boxes. See the Mystery Shoebox assignment at the end of this section.

- At this center, you will **create a treasure map** that someone in your group must be able to follow. Be very specific. Include turns, steps, directions, corners, exact number of feet to travel, landmarks, etc. Use words and pictures to help your partner locate the real treasure. Don't forget any details. Make your map colorful and readable. Make an X on your map where your "treasure" will be found.

- You will also need to **write out** in words the steps and directions your partner must follow. This is a backup in case your map is not clear. When you go on your "treasure hunt," your partner will be assured of finding your box.

- At a specific time that your teacher chooses, you will hide your "treasure box," and your partner will attempt to read your map and follow your directions.

- When you locate the box, you will attempt to read the clues and find out who your mystery person truly is.

- Place your finished work in your Mystery Folder.

Note to the teacher: See Evaluation of Mystery Shoebox and Treasure Map Activity at the end of this section.

Station 6: Science Center

- At this center you will be working with two investigations. First, you will be looking at different **mystery powders** you can find in your own kitchen or bathroom. By touching, smelling, tasting, and observing the powders, you must investigate and try to discover what they are.

- Everything is edible. A *Mystery Powders Observation Sheet* is provided for you to write down notes and observations.

- Second, you will read the materials about how scientists are able to identify fingerprints, and be able to recognize the special characteristics of fingerprinting.

- After that, you and a partner are to **fingerprint** each other using the *Finger Printing Form* that is provided. Your partner will help you to ink your fingers, one at a time, and will gently press your prints onto the fingerprinting sheet. This is done with a rolling motion.
- Then fill out the entire sheet with the information that is asked for.
- Place your work in your Mystery Folder.

Note to the teacher: Some of the powders that can be used for this center are: powdered sugar, granulated sugar, salt, baking soda, cream of tartar, Nutra Sweet®, Wondra® Flour, baking soda tooth powder, nondairy creamer, garlic salt, garlic powder, cornstarch, pancake mix, powdered milk, regular flour, and baking powder. Store the powders in ziplock baggies and label each as Mystery Powder #1, etc. Each baggie should have a spoon to scoop out a little bit of the powder onto a piece of wax paper or foil.

Station 7: Geography Center

- At this center you will find a world map. Using your almanac and other reference materials, find out where the **mystery places and creatures** are located and mark and label them on the map. These mysterious places fall into the categories of the prehistoric past, ancient civilizations, natural wonders, and our modern world.

> Easter Island
> The Great Pyramid
> The Bermuda Triangle
> The Loch Ness Monster
> The Abominable Snowman
> The Lines of Nazca
> Stonehenge
> Machu Picchu
> Northern Lights
> Ring of Brogar
> The Great Wall of China
> The Emperor's Army
> The Plaster Figures of Pompeii
> The Lost Continent of Atlantis
> The Grand Canyon
> Yellowstone National Park

- If you can think of another area you would like to locate on your map, add it.
- Place your completed map in your Mystery Folder.

Note to teacher: You will need to provide a copy of a world map outline for students to use for this activity.

Station 8: Creative Writing Center

- At this station, you will be planning out your own **mystery story**. Since you have read several mystery stories already, have watched a mystery unfold on the television, and have discussed the elements of a mystery story in class, you should be ready to do some serious planning.

- Use the *Mystery Story Planning Sheet* that you find in the folder. Use your time wisely. Remember that a great story takes good planning.

- The detective you created at Station 1, Drawing Center, should be included with this story.

- When you are ready with your finished draft, place your *Mystery Story Planning Sheet*, your story, and your pictures from the Drawing Center inside a story folder. Your folder should include a title, your name, and the date. Keep all your work together.

- When you have finalized your mystery story, you will fill out the *Self-Evaluation Sheet*.

- Place everything inside your Mystery Folder.

Station 9: Game Center

- At this center you will have the opportunity to investigate and play the game of Clue®.

- Your teacher has gone over the rules of the game with the entire class.

- If you have forgotten any of the rules, read the highlighted directions inside the box.

- Use your mystery reasoning skills to help you find the real murderer, where it took place, and with which weapon.

- Place your "guess sheet" inside your Mystery Folder.

Station 10: Math Center

- At this center you will find a number of **math puzzles, mazes, tricks, math codes, secrets,** and **math mysteries** that will take some time to figure out why and how they work.

- You may use your calculator, dice, cards, spinners, graph paper and paper and pencil to assist you in exploring the mysterious and wonderful world of math.

- You may choose which activities you would like to investigate, but be ready to write down what you did and what you found out.

- Keep all your records in your Mystery Folder.

Station 11: Listening Center

- At this center you will be able to **choose one** soundstrip, filmstrip, or video you would like to listen to and find out more about. Sherlock Holmes, The Bermuda Triangle, The Loch Ness Monster, and Edgar Allen Poe are some topics that will be available to you.

- When you are finished listening to the soundstrip, filmstrip, or video you should be able to make a list of some facts you learned. If you are having difficulty remembering what you listened to, talk about these things with your partners as you are making your list.

Station 12: Music/Movement Center (optional)

- Listen to the theme from *The Pink Panther*.
- See if you can think of words that could go along with the theme.
- Try to think of some easy steps you could teach to younger children that would go along with the rhythm.
- Play the song on the keyboard.
- You will also find some music themes from television shows of the past and present. You might have heard some of the older program themes because the reruns of these programs can still be seen on television. See how many of these you can identify: *Alfred Hitchcock Presents*; *Magnum P.I.*; *Hawaii Five-O*; *The Rockford Files*; *Murder, She Wrote*; *Matlock*; *Perry Mason*; *Mission Impossible*.

Station 13: Reader's Theater Center (optional)

- At this center you will find four mystery reader's theater scripts.
- With a partner or partners, take a part and read it orally using your dramatic skill.
- Take a short part and read it with your partners to the class.

BIBLIOGRAPHY AND RECOMMENDED RESOURCES

Barker, Linda. *Origami*. New York: Smithmark Publishing Inc., 1993.

California State Department of Education. *It's Elementary* (elementary grades task force report). 1992.

Churchill, E. Richard. *Paper Airplanes*. New York: Sterling Publishing Co., 1991.

Cole, Joanna, and Calmenson, Stephanie. *Crazy Eights and Other Card Games*. New York: A Beech Tree Paperback Book, 1994.

Elkind, D. "Developmentally Appropriate Practice: Philosophical and Practical Implications," *Phi Delta Kappan*, 71(2), 1989, 50–57.

Erlenbusch, Sue Jones. *Tales of Mystery, Suspense, and the Supernatural*. West Nyack, NY: The Center for Applied Research in Education, 1994.

Forester, Anne D., and Reinhard, Margaret. *On the Move*. Winnipeg, Canada: Peguis Publishers, 1991.

Hohmann, Charles, and Buckleitner, Warren. *Learning Environment*. Ypsilanti, MI: High/Scope Press, 1992.

Huckle, Helen. *The Secret Code Book*. New York: Dial Book, 1995.

Kostelnik, Marjorie. "Myths Associated with Developmentally Appropriate Programs," *Young Children*, 47(4), May 1992, 17–26.

Kramer, Emmanuel M. *Places of Mystery*. Philadelphia: Running Press, 1994.

O'Neill, Katherine. *Amazing Mysteries of the World*. Washington, D.C.: National Geographic, 1983.

Routman, Regie. *Invitations*. Portsmouth, NH: Heinemann Educational Books, Inc., 1991.

WHO AM I? WHAT AM I?

A project in mystery and intrigue

1. Due Date _____ Name _____

2. Choose a famous person, place, or thing—someone or something that everyone knows about.

3. Find interesting information about your subject by using the research center. Books like *The Guinness Book of World Records* and the almanac may be very helpful.

4. Write 6 to 8 clues about your subject that someone could use to try to "track" him, her or it down.

5. Make your clues very **general** at first. Gradually get more **specific**.

6. At the very end, show a picture of the object or the object itself.

7. Write your clues on a 5" × 8" index card.

8. Practice your clues at home with your family. See if they can help you to make your clues harder to solve in the beginning and easier to solve near the end—just like in a mystery novel.

9. Bring your item or a picture of your item to school in a brown paper bag.

10. Present your clues to your class.

(date)

Dear Parents,

    This letter is written to let you know that your son/daughter is about to be immersed into the wonderful world of mystery! The next month and a half will be full of mysterious people, places, and things. I am hoping you will continue this study by watching for interesting information about mysterious things in the newspaper, on the television, and of course through books and the library. I have already "cleaned out" the public library, so that our students will have a multitude of books to use as resources.

    Each of the children will be involved in thirteen mystery centers during the next few weeks. The centers involve math, reading, researching, writing, vocabulary, music, art, science, and geography. We will be locating mysterious places of the world, learning to research materials and write a research paper, and write a mystery story.

    By tomorrow, your child should have completed his/her first mystery library book, and created a flowchart to show understanding of the book. During this month, your child will be reading another mystery library book, and will show how these two mystery books of the month compare and contrast using a graphic organizer.

    In class your child has begun to read a mystery literature book called _____ _____ .

HOW CAN YOU GET INVOLVED?

1. Watch a television detective story or see a good detective movie with your child. This will assist the child in seeing how clues evolve throughout the movie, and will assist him/her in writing his/her own detective story. Help your child to understand what are the characteristics of a good detective. (Murder, She Wrote; Matlock; Perry Mason; Columbo; Sherlock Holmes; Nancy Drew Mysteries; etc., might give you a few places to start.)

2. Help your child to write good clues for his/her mystery shoebox project, which will be the "treasure" a partner will be looking for. Also help your child to write general to specific clues about himself/herself for the *Who or What Am I Project*.

3. Help your child to write complete, clear instructions for the treasure map the students will draw in class. Each student must lead a partner to his/her personalized shoebox through instructive words, and again through pictures on a map.

4. Help your child to carefully burn the edges of his/her treasure map.

5. Assist your child in making a good choice on which research topic to get involved in. Any mysterious person, place, or thing that is appropriate would be acceptable. The paper will be approximately three pages in length and should have two or three references. There are plenty of materials in class.

6. Take out a map and let your child show you where places such as the Bermuda Triangle, The Great Wall of China, Stonehenge, Easter Island, and the lines of Nasca are located.

7. Look into the many mysteries of the world including mysteries of the mind, mysteries of the universe, mysteries of the ancient world, mysteries of the deep, mysteries of the animal world, etc.

Please note that your child will be having time in class to work on each center activity. Some students will need more time at home to complete some of these activities. Each center day will take approximately 30 to 40 minutes. If your child doesn't have a start on an activity, you may want to ask him/her why. There will be a due date for each of the center activities. They will be announced to the children as we get further into the unit.

If you have any special talent or interest, or know someone who is an expert in any field of work that would unlock the understanding of mystery in the lives of our children, please let me know.

Thank you.

_____
(teacher)

MYSTERY MOVIE REVIEW

Student's Name _____

Now that you are involved in the theme of mystery, you are going to learn more about the art of the detective story. Here's how you will do it . . .

1. Select a television or theater mystery movie. By watching this program or movie, you will begin to see how clues evolve to unfold the plot and the crime. You will also begin to see the characteristics of a good detective. Some programs or movies you might want to watch are: *Murder, She Wrote*; *Matlock*; *Perry Mason Mysteries*; *Columbo*; *Sherlock Holmes*; *Magnum, P. I.*; *Nancy Drew Mysteries*; *The Rockford Files*; *Ace Ventura, Pet Detective*; etc. Don't forget that you can also rent a movie, or go to the movie theater to see a more recent mystery film.

2. Critique the film by doing the following activities on a separate sheet of paper.

    a. Name of program or movie: _____

    b. Location where I saw the program or movie: _____

    c. Attach a newspaper article showing the movie advertisement or the television guide entry. (*optional*)

    d. Write a ¹/₂- to 1-page summary of the movie.

    e. List the main character and describe him/her physically and tell several things about his/her personality.

    f. What was the crime involved and how was it solved?

    g. Tell how the detective or main character discovered the truth about the crime.

    h. List three of the clues that led to the solving of the crime.

    i. Tell why you liked or disliked the program or movie. How would you rate this program or movie? 1 (poor) — 5 (fantastic)

    j. If you could change the ending of the program or movie, how would you make it better?

    k. Why is this program or movie considered a mystery?

WANTED

Right Thumb

Left Thumb

AGE:_____ BORN: _____ EYE COLOR: _____

HEIGHT: _____ WEIGHT: _____ HAIR COLOR:_____

OCCUPATION:_____

SCARS/MARKS: _____

ALIASES: _____

OTHER
INFORMATION:_____

_____

CAUTION

MYSTERY WORD BANK

Here are some words to get you started thinking about mystery in your world. While you are reading and talking with your friends and family members, see **how many other words you can find**.

accident
alibi
bloodhounds
bribe
burglar
caution
crime
criminal
crooks
danger
deceptions
decode
description
details
detective
disguises
disappearance
DNA
evidence
eyewitness
expert witness
FBI (Federal Bureau
   of Investigation)
fingerprint
flashlight
footprint
forgery
framed
fraud
guilty
hair and thread
   analysis

handwriting
   analysis
highjacked
hostage
identification
identify
identity
information
innocent
intruder
investigator
kidnappers
magnifying glass
motive
mugging
murder
mysterious
mystery
police
ransom
rescue
retrace
reward
robbery
scientific evidence
secrecy
secretive
security
shoplift
solution
suspect
suspense

suspenseful
suspicious
thief
undercover
victim
weapons

_____

_____

_____

_____

_____

_____

_____

_____

_____

INFORMATION ABOUT YOUR REPORT

Student's Name _____

1. To write this report, you will need to use *three* references or sources. You should have at least **one encyclopedia** and **one book**. You might also have a magazine or pamphlet.

2. As you start to take notes, jot down the important information about the book or encyclopedia that you are using.

3. Make a list of the information in the spaces below.

BOOK

Title of book _____

Author _____

Publishing company _____

Where published _____

Date published _____

Pages used _____

ENCYCLOPEDIA

Title of article _____

Name of encyclopedia _____

Volume number _____

Year of publication _____

Pages used _____

PERIODICAL/MAGAZINE/PAMPHLET

Title of article _____

Author _____

Title of magazine _____

Volume number _____

Month and year of publication _____

Pages used _____

....

    If you have other books, encyclopedias, or pamphlets, list them below in the same manner as shown on these two pages.

_____

_____

_____

_____

_____

_____

_____

_____

_____

_____

_____

_____

_____

_____

THE MYSTERY SHOEBOX

Student's Name _____

Before your visit to the Mapping Center, you will need to create your very own, personalized Mystery Box. In this box you will gather together approximately 8 to 10 clues about your true identity in the form of evidence.
Here's your specific mission:

1. Locate a shoebox from home. If you don't have one, borrow one from your neighbor, relative, classmate, or teacher.

2. Think of 8 to 10 items or exhibits that tell something about you. This is *evidence*. Here are a few examples of what your items might be: a very young baby picture of yourself, a magazine picture of your favorite sports star, an ad from your favorite restaurant, a small toy you enjoy playing with, a list of your family's first names, your parent's license plate number, your telephone number, a copy of your favorite recipe, a pair of earrings you like, etc. These items should be personalized. Try not to give yourself away to your partner too easily.

3. Place all your items neatly into the shoebox. You may want to place each one in an envelope marked *Clue #1*, and so on. **Make sure your name is not on any items**.

4. Place your shoebox into a brown paper bag with your name on the outside. This is so no one can see your shoebox before the Treasure Hunting Day. Hand it to your teacher before the assigned day of the "hunt."

5. You will be given a special time of the day to place your box in the correct location as seen by an X on your treasure map.

6. Your map and directions will be given secretly to another classmate, who will attempt to locate your mystery box by following your written directions and your map.

7. When, and if, your partner locates your mystery box by following your map, he or she will then try to figure out whose box it is. Let's hope your clues aren't too easy!

8. Your partner will then evaluate how well you organized your map and clues by filling out the *Evaluation of Mystery Shoebox and Treasure Map Activity* sheet.

EVALUATION OF MYSTERY SHOEBOX
AND TREASURE MAP ACTIVITY

Detective's Name _____

List the items of evidence you found: _____

_____

_____

Whose Mystery Box do you think you have found? _____

_____

Why do you think it belongs to him/her? _____

_____

What was the most important clue that gave you the idea that you knew whose box it was? How did it help you? _____

_____

How good were the clues that were given? Were they too easy, too hard? Did the person take enough time to give you a true picture of him-/herself? (Use a scoring system of 1 to 10 with 10 being the best and 1 being the least.) Explain your answer.

_____

_____

How well drawn was the treasure map? Were the directions exact and clear? Were the measurements correct? Were the symbols and words easy to follow? Was it too easy? Was it too difficult? Did the person seem to put effort into the map? Explain. (Evaluate with scoring system of 1 to 10.

_____

_____

_____

MYSTERY POWDER
OBSERVATION SHEET

Your Name _____

At this center you are to observe and explore the mystery powders in the containers. Explore through the use of all your senses. The powders can usually be found in your kitchen or bathroom. They are edible. Record your results. Write a brief, but detailed, explanation of each powder. Use descriptive words—use the thesaurus if you have difficulty. Remember a good detective has to keep explicit notes.

Mystery Powder 1: _____

_____

Mystery Powder 2: _____

_____

Mystery Powder 3: _____

_____

Mystery Powder 4: _____

_____

Mystery Powder 5: _____

_____

Mystery Powder 6: _____

_____

Mystery Powder 7: _____

_____

Mystery Powder 8: _____

_____

Mystery Powder 9: _____

_____

Mystery Powder 10: _____

_____

Mystery Powder 11: _____

_____

Mystery Powder 12: _____

_____

Mystery Powder 13: _____

_____

FINGERPRINTING FORM

Last name_____ First name _____ Middle name _____

Place of birth _____ Date of birth_____

Address of person being fingerprinted _____

Occupation _____

Height _____ Weight _____

Hair color_____ Eye color _____

Female / Male (circle one)   Race _____ Citizenship _____

Body marks, scars _____

Other names used (aliases) _____

_____

Signature of person being fingerprinted _____

School where fingerprints are being taken _____

1. Right Thumb	2. Right Index	3. Right Middle	4. Right Ring	5. Right Little
6. Left Thumb	7. Left Index	8. Left Middle	9. Left Ring	10. Left Little

Left four fingers taken simultaneously	Right four fingers taken simultaneously

Signature of official taking fingerprints_____ Date_____

MYSTERY STORY PLANNING SHEET

Your Name _____

1. Describe the setting of your story. _____
_____
_____
_____

2. Name your main characters and tell something about each. _____
   a. The detective _____
_____
_____
_____

   b. The criminal _____
_____
_____
_____

   c. The victim _____
_____
_____
_____

   d. Other main characters _____
_____
_____
_____

3. Motive (the reason for the crime): _____
_____
_____
_____

4. How is the crime committed?_____

_____

_____

_____

5. Is there a weapon used? _____

_____

_____

_____

6. What are some of the clues that led you to the solution of the crime? _____

_____

_____

_____

7. Explain how the mystery is solved. How does the story end? _____

_____

_____

_____

8. Remember, this is just a plan sheet. Your story should be neatly written in ink or typed.

9. You might want to look over the mystery flow chart that you used earlier in this unit. This will guide you into how a mystery unfolds.

10. Include a cover on the outside of your story.

11. Draw a picture of your main character and include it with your story.

12. Include this sheet at the back of your story.

13. Read your finished story to an adult.

14. Play the game Clue® if possible sometime in the next week.

15. Have fun!

16. You may work with a partner to get some ideas, but the story itself must be written by you.

17. Due Date: _____

SELF-EVALUATION MYSTERY STORY WRITING

Student's Signature

_____

Title of Work

_____

Date Completed

_____

One thing I really like about this piece of work is . . .

_____

_____

_____

I think this story would be even better if . . .

_____

_____

_____

Evaluate yourself on the following areas with a +, √, or −

Mystery elements: _____

Introduction/Closing: _____

Neatness: _____

Character development: _____

Use of time/planning: _____

PARENT EVALUATION MYSTERY STORY WRITING

Student's Name _____

Parent's Signature

_____

Date _____

Title of Work _____

One thing I really liked about what you wrote is . . .

_____

_____

_____

_____

One suggestion I would like to make is . . .

_____

_____

_____

_____

Did you observe your child breaking up this story writing into small, manageable segments of time, or did he/she procrastinate?

_____

TEACHER EVALUATION
MYSTERY STORY WRITING

Student's Name _____

Date _____

Teacher's Signature

_____

I think the special strengths of this piece are . . .

_____

_____

_____

_____

I would like to see . . .

_____

_____

_____

_____

AREAS OF EVALUATION:

Mystery elements: _____

Introduction/Closing: _____

Character development: _____

Neatness: _____

Use of time in class: _____

Overall grade: _____

Other comments:_____

_____

_____

_____

MYSTERY CENTERS
DAILY REVIEW AND RECORDING SHEET

Name _____

  Each day you will be visiting a new mystery center. At this time, you will be using your skills to perform certain tasks. Since the centers have already been planned for you, you will do the assigned activities, and then review and evaluate your progress. Briefly write about what you actually accomplished or learned, and tell what techniques or skills you used, who you worked with, and how you worked. Also jot down any questions or difficulties you need answered or problems that you might have met up with.

  Each day after rotating to centers, you will have five minutes of reflective, evaluation time to fill out this sheet. Keep it in your Mystery Folder for your teacher to see and evaluate.

DRAWING CENTER _____
_____
_____
_____

VOCABULARY CENTER _____
_____
_____
_____

RESEARCH CENTER _____
_____
_____
_____

CODE AND DECODING CENTER _____
_____
_____
_____

MAPPING CENTER _____
_____
_____
_____

SCIENCE CENTER _____
_____
_____
_____

GEOGRAPHY CENTER _____
_____
_____
_____

CREATIVE WRITING _____
_____
_____
_____

GAME CENTER _____
_____
_____
_____

LISTENING CENTER _____
_____
_____
_____

MATH CENTER _____
_____
_____
_____

MUSIC/MOVEMENT CENTER _____
_____
_____
_____

READER'S THEATER _____
_____
_____
_____
_____

Name _____

MYSTERY FLOW CHART

Make a flow chart for the mystery book you read in conjunction with this unit. Use geometric shapes such as triangles, squares, and circles. Write the necessary information. Use one color of construction paper for the background and another color for the parts.

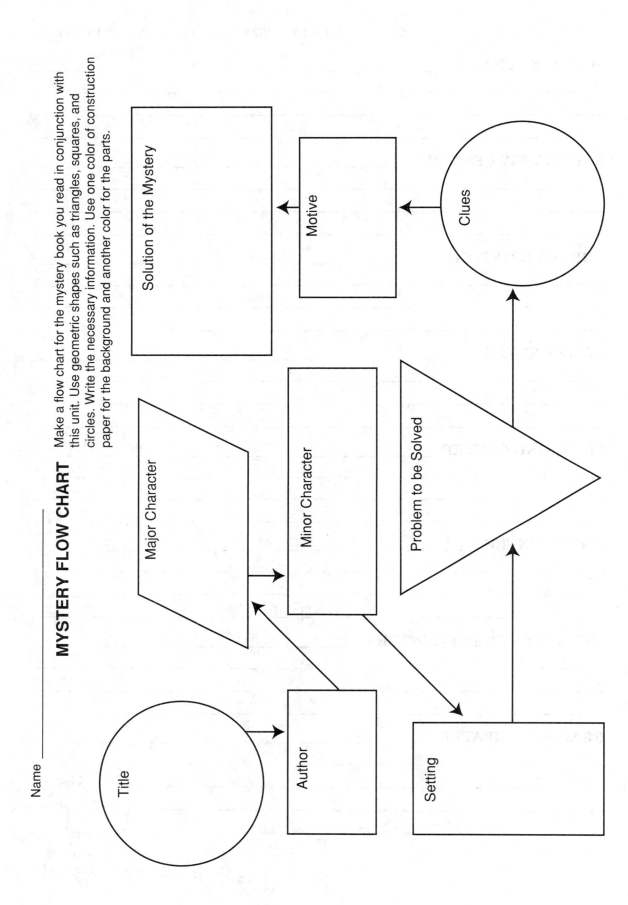

Title

Author

Major Character

Minor Character

Problem to be Solved

Setting

Solution of the Mystery

Motive

Clues

MYSTERY NOTETAKING SHEET

Student's Name _____

On this sheet of paper you will begin to record information that will be included in your mystery report. While you are reading from the many books provided, jot down some important facts you want to remember. In the column on the left, write the author's last name and the page number on which you found the fact. If you need more space, staple this sheet to any other pieces of notebook paper where you take notes. You'll use these notes to help you write your mystery research paper.

Author's Last Name	Page Where Found	Notes

SELF-EVALUATION OF
THE MYSTERY THEMATIC UNIT

Student's Name _____

1. Make a list of skills you think you improved on by doing this unit.

   _____

2. Tell five facts that you learned by research and studying mystery in our world.

   _____

3. Tell how you think mystery effects you in your everyday life and what part it will play as you grow older. _____

   _____

   _____

4. Tell how your family got involved in the theme of mystery. _____

   _____

   _____

5. What things do you think could be added to improve this unit? _____

   _____

   _____

6. Tell what things you enjoyed most during your mystery study and briefly explain why. Also indicate what you liked least and explain your reasons. Use the back of this sheet for your answers.

7. How do you rate yourself in completion and quality of work while doing this unit? (1 to 10 with a 10 being the best) Explain to your teacher why you deserve the grade you gave yourself.

   _____

   _____

   _____

   _____

MYSTERY FOLDER CONTENTS:
WHAT ITEMS SHOULD YOUR FOLDER CONTAIN?

Name _____

Check off each item you have completed in your Mystery Folder.

_____Mystery Movie Review

_____Word Search (a partner should have done it)

_____Additional mystery words for word search

_____Listening Post Summary

_____Mystery Powder Observation Sheet

_____Fingerprinting Form

_____Coded Message

_____Decoded Message

_____Mystery Story Planning Sheet

_____Mystery Story

_____Mystery Story Parent Evaluation

_____Mystery Story Self-Evaluation

_____Detective from Drawing Center

_____Wanted Poster

_____Comic strip

_____Notetaking Sheet

_____Research Paper

_____List of references used for your research project

_____World Map from Geography Center (must be colored)

_____Treasure Map

_____Set of written instructions for treasure hunt

_____Evaluation of the Mystery Shoebox and Treasure Map Activity

_____Daily Review and Recording Sheet

_____Self-Evaluation of the Mystery Thematic Unit

_____Other

INCREASING HOME/SCHOOL COMMUNICATION AND PARENT INVOLVEMENT

It is well recognized that the key element for a successful school is shared responsibility or "partnership in education," involving teamwork of school personnel, parents, students, and the community. The research is clear that children do better in school when parents are involved and play a positive role in their children's education. One of the strengths of our elementary school is the very active, involved, and supportive parent community we are fortunate to have. Parents are an integral part of our school program. Their tireless efforts, commitment, and willingness to help and support in a myriad of ways has enabled us to provide a quality program for the children. As our school is a magnet and the majority of our students are bussed from neighborhoods around the city, we have a large non-resident population. Finding ways to reach and encourage our non-resident parents to become more actively involved with the school has always been a challenge.

STRATEGIES FOR INCREASING PARENT PARTICIPATION IN SCHOOL ACTIVITIES AND FUNCTIONS

- Provide interesting and motivational activities for the whole family to participate in.
- To attract parents to school functions, provide child care for younger siblings, transportation for parents who need it, refreshments, and door prizes as appropriate.
- Student performances and recognition activities are powerful incentives to bringing parents to the school.
- Involve the students by having them make invitations; reward classes with the greatest parent response to school activities.
- Provide translation in different languages as needed.

- Information and notices regarding upcoming school functions should be sent out well in advance on school calendars and in newsletters.

- Bombard parents with advertisements. Colorful notices should be sent out, with follow-up notification, posters around the school, use of school marquees, etc.

- Remind parents who have signed up to participate in activities via personal phone calls.

- Many teachers give bonus points to students whose parent(s) come to certain events, such as Open House.

- Many schools issue a "no homework pass" redeemable for one homework assignment; or have a "no homework night" given to students who are participating in family workshops or school functions with their parent/guardian.

- There are many types of workshops that are hands-on, interactive, and very well received. In our district, *Family Math* and *Family Reading* workshops are quite popular.

- One school has a Pajama Night. Parents bring their children to school in their pajamas. The children go into different classrooms where a variety of adults read to the children for half an hour. Then everyone comes back to the auditorium for milk and cookies before going home.

- Our elementary had a Welcome Back to School Sock-Hop—sponsored by the PTA, with music, dancing, refreshments—which was held the first week of school. This brought a large turnout of families to meet informally, be introduced to staff, and have a lot of fun.

- Early in the school year many schools have a Back to School night, during which time teachers typically give a short presentation about their expectations, curriculum, etc., and open the lines of home/school communication. Some schools have a staggered schedule with, for example, primary grades meeting with teachers the first half-hour; and upper grades, the second half hour to accommodate families with more children at different grade levels. Some schools spread Back to School nights over two or three different evenings (i.e., kindergarten, 1-2, 3-5) in order to accommodate the needs of parents. At our Back to School nights teachers try to recruit as many parent volunteers as possible, letting parents know they are always welcome in the classroom, and that their help is needed in many ways (both in and out of the classroom).

- Volunteer Appreciation celebrations of various kinds (teas, banquets, luncheons) providing recognition and thanks to parents, community members, etc., who volunteered in any capacity during the school year are strongly recommended.

- School programs often attract more parents/families when they are coupled with ice cream socials, barbeques, etc.

- Many schools have special multicultural fairs and programs to celebrate diversity. Our school has a multicultural fair in which all classrooms select a different country. Those countries are studied in the class for their literature, culture, and geography. In preparation for the multicultural fair, the students learn a dance or song from their country to perform. The various national flags and currency of that country are made. With the help of our parents each class, on the day of the fair, has tables set up for each of the different countries represented. Items are displayed from the country and foods are prepared for students to sample. After all of the class performances, students walk around to the different tables and are able to use their currency (everyone receives the same amount) to "purchase" the foods of their choice. We also have multicultural game days in which students are taught to play a variety of games from several different countries.

- There are countless school events that serve to motivate and recognize students, attract parents/families to school, and increase involvement, such as: science fairs, art fairs, musical festivals, chorus programs, school/class plays, and performances of various kinds.

- Many schools have exhibitions of different kinds. One middle school has an Eighth-Grade Exhibition every year, during which students individually share with a community member what they enjoyed learning that year, what was important and meaningful to them, and allowing the community members to view the students' portfolios of favorite work samples for the year.

- It is recommended to send home parent surveys (translated as needed) to determine the opinions, concerns, interests, and needs of parents.

- One middle school has a "Shadow Your Student" half-day. Parents follow their children from class to class on a shortened schedule, and then all students/parents have a barbeque lunch together.

- Invite parents to be guest readers, speakers, share about jobs/professions, different interests, hobbies, skills, cultures, etc.

- One administrator shared how parents/guardians/grandparents are much more comfortable coming to the school when they feel the staff's warmth and friendliness that is unsolicited.

MORE SCHOOL OUTREACH EFFORTS

- Many schools have parenting classes on topics such as Helping Your Child with Homework/Study Skills, positive discipline, and so forth.

- One vice principal shared how important it is to make the school the hub of the community again and, in so doing, to allow and encourage access of the facility for the community. The school maintains close contact with the homeowners' association that helps school/community interaction and partnership.

- Another elementary school with a very diverse population has many classes at the facility provided through the community college district, such as English as a Second Language (ESL) free of charge for interested parents. Child care for parents attending classes is provided. This school has strong community outreach. It is a high crime neighborhood that has a number of social agencies in the area. Therefore, in conjunction with these agencies, they are able to provide after-school tutoring, parent institutes/classes, gang-prevention programs, and provision of social services.

- Often home visits are required to reach and elicit support of parents. Districts that are fortunate to have the resources to do so have home-school liaison personnel whose job is to facilitate home/school interaction.

- Some districts make a signficant outreach effort to the parents of their limited English speaking students. Through bilingual facilitators, bilingual school personnel, and translation of materials in represented languages, they work to help involve parents in their children's education. Some provide workshops to parents—giving concrete suggestions and materials in how to help their children succeed at school. Some schools have resources and materials for parents to check-out and use at home with their children.

- Ask parents for help, letting them know their assistance is needed and welcomed in countless ways. Provide a list of activities and supports that would be helpful so parents can see there are jobs to be done in and out of the classroom that would be very helpful to the teacher and students.

- Welcome parent volunteers in the classroom, and let parents know they are always permitted to visit their children's classes.

- Communicate information about the school in local newspapers, school marquees, newsletters, etc.

- Communicate information about your class in a monthly newsletter for parents. (See the end of this section for two sample classroom monthly newsletters.)

- In scheduling conferences with parents, provide scheduling options (e.g., evenings or Saturdays).

- Some schools make videotapes of school events to be checked out by parents who may not be able to attend, but wish to see some of the school's activities/events.

- Some schools establish parent hotlines.

- Other schools have established a Homework hotline. Teachers use their voice mail to record homework assignments so students/parents can check or double-check the assignments.

- See the parent letter at the end of this section for several recommended ways parents can actively communicate with their child and build the home/school connection.

INCREASING COMMUNICATION AND PARTNERSHIP WITH PARENTS OF STUDENTS WITH SPECIAL NEEDS

For any student experiencing difficulty academically and/or behaviorally, a critical intervention is to increase the communication between home and school and establish *teamwork* on the child's behalf. Students who have learning disabilities, ADHD, and other special needs will require far more frequent monitoring, reporting, and communication than will be necessary for the average student in the class. Parents need to be willing to share information with teachers, ask how they can help, and try to support the classroom teacher in any way possible. Teachers need to be open and receptive to implementing the interventions and supports to help meet the students' individual needs. They need to be sensitive to the input of parents and willing to make accommodations as appropriate.

- Many students who exhibit behavioral challenges in the classroom will need behavior contracts, charts, and various management plans devised to help them improve these skills. Often these plans and systems require close parental involvement to help reinforce the mutual expectation (home and school) of appropriate school behaviors. (See Section 4, *Behavior Management and Positive Discipline*.)

- Students who have difficulty with study skills and do not follow through on homework assignments will need closer parental monitoring. In order for the parents to be able to help, they need assignments recorded on a consistent basis, and make sure the necessary books/supplies are brought home. This is one of the biggest frustrations of parents who have children with ADD; these children need help recording homework assignments and monitoring for needed materials before they leave school. (See the two sample monitoring forms at the end of this section and additional monitoring forms in Section 4, *Behavior Management and Positive Discipline*.)

- There is no substitute for parent-teacher conferencing on students. Teachers need to meet with parents/guardians and have the time to talk, show work samples, answer parents' questions, and listen to them share about their children and any concerns, etc., in order to be most effective in reaching/teaching their children. For students experiencing difficulty in school, *it is critical* to meet and plan interventions together. It often takes persistence and a great deal of effort to arrange these meetings, which are often involving support staff as well as parents and teachers. Sometimes it requires significant flexibility on the part of school personnel to accommodate parents' needs to be able to schedule meetings. However, in order to help our students, it is important to try doing whatever we can, even when it causes a lot of inconvenience.

One of the most outstanding and valuable programs in our school district is the **Parent Facilitator** program of San Diego City Schools. Special education parent facilitators are parents who have children with special needs. They are employed by our school district to provide information and support to other parents who have children with exceptional needs regarding programs and services available to them and their children. Parent facilitators understand special education program options and procedures from personal exerience, and they know parents' rights and responsibilities. They provide parent education and consultation on a variety of topics, including California law regarding special education, individualized education program procedures, child growth and development, and community resources.

Not only are the supports and services of parent facilitators extremely helpful and beneficial for parents of children with special needs, but their assistance and intervention is very valuable to schools as well. (We wish to thank Linda Eckert, our most wonderful and dedicated parent facilitator who has served our school and our parents for many years.) For more information about this unique and highly effective program, write to: Special Education Parent Facilitator Program, San Diego City Schools, Dana Center, 1775 Chatsworth Boulevard, San Diego, CA 92107. Phone: (619) 225-3623.

WHAT TYPES OF HOME/SCHOOL COMMUNICATION MIGHT I USE?

- Send home weekly, bi-weekly, or monthly newsletters to parents informing them of what is taking place in class, projects students should be working on at home, ways parents can be helping and supporting, and so forth.

- Team teachers often write a joint newsletter to send to the parents of students in their classes.

- Most schools have newsletters or bulletins that are sent home on a regular basis to inform parents of what is happening schoolwide. Check if your school does.

- Schools with linguistically diverse populations have all notices automatically translated into represented languages.

- Send home weekly communication forms in order to inform parents of students' behavior and work performance during the week. Typically, parents are asked to sign the form and return it to school.

- Secondary schools often send home progress reports mid-quarter, or notify parents when students are receiving unsatisfactory grades prior to report cards being issued. Many secondary school teachers use point systems to determine grades. They often keep students' points computerized and know at any time what each student's standing is in the class. Parents can simply request progress reports from teachers if they have concerns about how their child is performing or keeping up with the class.

(Note: For additional ways of involving parents in the classroom, see Section 2, Learning Developmentally. Reproducible and sample communication forms are found at the end of Section 4.)

BIBLIOGRAPHY AND RECOMMENDED RESOURCES

California Association of Resource Specialists (CARS) has a newsletter that contains a Parent Page along with a great deal of valuable information regarding helping children with learning difficulties. Write to: CARS, P.O. Box 7469, Citrus Heights, CA 95621-7469.

Hollis, Barbara. *Form Letters and Assessment Comments for Your Whole Language Classroom* (1992).Teacher Created Materials, Inc., P.O. Box 1040, Huntington Beach, CA 92647.

Parent Journal, Parents' Educational Resource Center, a quarterly publication for parents of chidren with learning differences. A program of the Charles & Helen Schwab Foundation/PERC, 1730 S. Amphlett Blvd., Suite 130, San Mateo, CA 94402.

Radencich, Marguerite, and Schumm, Jeane Shay. *How to Help Your Child with Homework* (for parents of children ages 6-13). Minneapolis: Free Spirit Publishing Co.,1988.

Steding, Laurie. *Teachers' Messages and Notes Home.* Mahwah, NJ: Troll Associates, Inc., 1994.

ROOM 12 MONTHLY NEWSLETTER
OCTOBER 4

Dear Parents,

We have made it through the first full month of school and everything seems to be going fairly smoothly. We are getting into the regular routine of Room 12. Almost everyone has fallen into the routine very successfully. It always takes a few weeks for students to get used to their new environment and expectations, and for teachers to size up the class and its members. I can see the wheels turning in some of the students' heads, checking me out to see if I will notice they are eating in class or have forgotten their homework. I keep saying, "Do you think I just fell off a turnip truck?" Some of you must have used that expression because a few of the students know what I mean.

I really appreciated seeing so many of you at school for Curriculum Night. It is always a wonderful experience to meet the family of the children I spend my day with. Let's keep in contact. If there is a concern, or you need further information about something we do in class, please let me know. Communication between school and home is an important part of my educational philosophy.

Book of the Month: Mystery/Horror
                        Project: Written report/pop-up book

Cereal Box Project: Last week students were actively involved in discovering everything they could about cereal. The investigation involved becoming a cereal scientist, a *cerealologist*, and researching the boxes they see on the grocery shelves. Nutritional information such as fat, cholesterol, protein, etc., were talked about and pondered. Nurse Sandy will be discussing other points of nutrition next week. The purpose of this assignment is to make students more conscious of what they are eating. Students will be using their background information from last week, and coming up with their very own cereal. They will be responsible for creating the name of the cereal, the company that produces it, and the box it will come in. Students will also discuss the propaganda/advertising techniques that companies use to sell their products.

Students may work on this project alone or in pairs. If the partnership idea is used, time together will be necessary at home, since very little time will be spent in school for the creation. Boxes may be spray painted, covered in foil or wrapping paper, or covered in butcher paper at school. When I have done the project in the past, there are always some fantastically creative ideas produced. The box must have the key elements that are asked for on the sheets we have used in class. Ask your child to see his/her sketch sheet. We have done a lot of discussion about the packaging of a product and why adults and children alike like different cereals. I have tried to get into the "psychology of buying."

All cereal boxes are due this Friday. Commercials will be produced according to a 30-second time schedule, and will be taped on the video camera for your child's first graded oral language experience. Selling techniques discussed in class such as join the bandwagon, testimonial, repetition, emotional words, etc., should be used.

Science: During the month of October students will be completing the study of unusual weather conditions, and beginning to delve into the different biomes of the world. We have already begun the study of the biomes in Canada since we are currently reading *Hatchet*, the story of a boy who is forced to survive in the wilderness of Canada after his plane crashes and leaves him alone. Students will learn outlining techniques and test-taking strategies.

At the end of the month, I would like students to investigate the subject of pumpkins. Students will be able to tell if pumpkins float, if the lines on the outside are indicators of anything on the inside, if the size has anything to do with the number of seeds, what significance the stem has, and numerous other questions. The investigation will take two complete afternoons. I like students to work in groups of two or three. The scientific process will be explained and reinforced during these days.

In order for this to be successful, I would appreciate it if you could donate a small pumpkin to the class. We need at least ten to fifteen for the best results. Also, we need a few parent helpers to assist. This is a lab situation, and I would like to have several parents to supervise, especially in the cutting of the pumpkins. Mark your calendars for October 28 and 29 after 12:30, and let me know if you can come.

Math: We always have to do some review of concepts at the beginning of the school year. We have reviewed place value and multiplication. Sixth graders, as a group, had some difficulty with the unfamiliar concept of exponents. We will continue to use this pre-algebra idea in extended form throughout the year.

Our next concept will be to cover decimals. For both fifth and sixth grades this is a difficult concept, and many students traditionally have been unsuccessful at grasping the idea. Several new concepts in this area cause difficulty.

Other Needs: I am looking for other things to assist in reading and in math within the classroom. If you have any of the following items and don't know what to do with them, please send them in: old calendars with pictures; comic strips from the Sunday newspaper (in color); catalogs from department stores (Sears, Penney's, etc.); menus from restaurants. All of these items are very important to assist children about the environment in which they live. I use the catalogs and menus for extended math, and the calendars and comic strips in language arts extension. I appreciate your help.

Geography: Students will be learning about the area of Canada, while we are reading *Hatchet*. This week they should be using their almanac to research the important information about the country. Next week they should be using an encyclopedia or other reference book to find out more information about the country. This week they should be able to memorize the provinces of Canada.

Television Survey: Students this week will be filling out five television evaluations of programs they watch during the week. They should be watching for content, and for the propaganda techniques that are used in the commercials. I also want them to be aware of how much time is used in a half-hour slot for commercials, and how much actual programming play time there is. I think they will be very surprised. They should have a stopwatch or watch with a second hand so they can record the number of minutes of both program and commercial times. After watching one program, they are to write a brief summary of what the program was about and evaluate it. If they watch the news, they may write five facts about what they learned. A summary sheet is in your child's notebook (I hope). If you do not have a television or do not allow your child to watch television, please let me know and I'll give an alternate assignment.

Thanks for your support!

Julie Heimburge

- -

(Please detach and return to Room 12)

I have read the October Newsletter.

Student's Name _____

Parent's Signature _____

Comments:

_____

_____

_____

Dear Parents,

As part of our magnet theme *Interpersonal Communication,* your students are involved in the study of families. Through the creation of our own in-class families and through the literature we have been reading, students have discussed the ways families are alike and how they differ. The students have made a personal coat of arms, developed a "family bond" with their kindergarten buddies, and discussed some of their own individual characteristics. In math we have worked on "families of facts." Through the various areas of the curriculum, we have—and will continue to have throughout the year—discussions, writing, and reading about the importance of developing communication within our own families.

As the students reach the adolescent years, peer communication seems to become a very important part of a child's life. It is essential that within our own families we keep the lines of communication flowing smoothly, and not let the "outside" influences take the place of family. Throughout the year we will ask that your family take an active part in your child's education. It is our hope that the school, the child, and the home all communicate with each other on a regular basis to provide a clear and open path for the successful interchange of information, feelings, and concerns of all three parties.

The following activities will be helpful in assuring your child of a successful year through the theme of interpersonal communication, combining the home-family and the school-family into an interconnecting unit. Please make a choice of how you will approach interpersonal communication with your child within your family, and make a check mark where you think you can be of the most help. Of course, we know that not everyone can be a participant in every activity, but we hope you will make an asserted effort to choose several.

_____1.   Attend Curriculum Night, Open House, and other school events.

_____2.   Volunteer a minimum of one hour of your time per semester in your child's classroom

_____3.   Share a special talent, skill, or your career with your child's class.

_____4.   Watch a television program with your child. Talk about the program and how you related to it. Have your child retell the storyline to you. Did he/she comprehend the main ideas?

_____5.   Read a story to or *with* your child at least once a week. Ask him/her some key questions to see if he/she understands the main points. Have your child retell the story as he/she remembers it. Write a summary of the chapter or pages together. You might want the whole family to get involved.

_____6.   Write a brief essay about your child. It may be a special memory, event, or experience that touched you in a special way. This paragraph can be read aloud to the class or placed on the bulletin board for the students to read. Include a picture, if possible.

_____7. Have a conference with your child's teacher. Include your child in part of the conference.

_____8. Eat dinner together as a family with no interruptions allowed. Talk to your child about school, and what are his/her feelings, concerns, likes, dislikes, fears, etc.

_____9. Go to a movie, play, or recreational event with your child. Have your child talk with you about what he/she liked and disliked about the event, and how it could be improved. Have your child write a summary of the time you spent together, and make a choice of what he/she would choose to do on another outing.

_____10. Plan a family picnic. Have your child assist you in the preparations and details. Have him/her organize the food and activities, and write a summary of the day.

_____11. Have your child spend several hours at work with you, if possible. At the end of the day, have him/her write up a summary of this time.

_____12. Have a "No Television Day." As a family, plan what you will do to fill the time when the television would normally be on. After the "experiment" is over, have your child write a paragraph focusing on the positive and negative points of the day.

_____13. Have your child interview the oldest member of your extended family. Help him/her think up some interesting questions before giving the interview. Then discuss the interview and write a paragraph with the most important things that were learned. You may also make a tape (video or audio) of the interview, copy the tape, and send a copy to another younger member of the family.

_____14. Have your child write a letter to a family member who hasn't seen him/her for a while **OR** send a 2- to 3-minute voice tape to them discussing all the changes that have occurred since he/she last saw them.

_____15. Make a family video showcasing all members of your immediate family. Makes sure all family members describe themselves thoroughly and tell about their hobbies, talents, strengths, favorites, etc. This may be done in interview or in newscast form. Have your child share the video with his/her class.

_____16. Start a personal scrapbook of your life together as a family. Include pictures, ticket stubs, brochures of events you attended together, etc. Bring the scrapbook to share with the class sometime during the year.

_____17. Cook together as a family where everyone has a certain responsibility in the kitchen. Have your child write a paragraph describing the event and what each person did. Also include a section on how the food tasted, and how this could work out better the next time.

_____18. Start a family cookbook. Write at least five favorite "secret" family recipes everybody loves and everybody wants to know about. Keep the recipe book updated. Share the book with the class.

_____19. Listen to three generations of music as a family. Have each generation select a favorite selection from their era. It may be on the radio, tape, or CD. Listen to each selection and discuss the music. Compare and contrast the changes in the music of each generation. Write a paragraph explaining your discussion and what you discovered as a family.

_____20. Share a *family* hobby with your child's class. Include your child in the presentation.

_____21. Participate in "Bring Your Grandparent to School Day" (date to be announced).

_____22. Make up your own family communication activity. Have your child write the idea and share it with the class.

Thank you.

_____
Teacher

(Please return to your child's classroom teacher)

We have chosen the following activities to assist our child in the understanding of interpersonal communication focusing on our family.

_____
(Please list the numbers of the items you feel that you can participate in.)

Child's Name _____   Parent's Name _____

INFORMATION NOTE

Name: _____ Date/Week of: _____ Phone: _____

Periods	Teacher's Initials	Class Performance (circle one)	Assigned Homework	Upcoming Tests?	Missing Work?
		G Great A Average U Unsatisfactory			
		G Great A Average U Unsatisfactory			
		G Great A Average U Unsatisfactory			
		G Great A Average U Unsatisfactory			
		G Great A Average U Unsatisfactory			
		G Great A Average U Unsatisfactory			
		G Great A Average U Unsatisfactory			

Comments:

_____

_____

_____

_____

_____

Counselor's Signature: _____

Parent's Signature: _____

_____
Date

Dear _____ ,

    I am sending you this letter to let you know that _____ has not been completing his/her homework assignment. It is my hope that you and I can work as a team to assist him/her in being more successful in these assignments. During this last reporting period, your child has handed in _____ of the required assignments. Class assignments not completed at the morning check-in time may be handed in for late credit. Options for homework not turned in on time include staying in at morning or noon recess, or Friday detention. I would prefer not to deny these activity times from the students, so I would appreciate your assistance.

    In order to build a feeling of success in your child, we need to monitor his/her behavior on a regular basis. I am sending this report indicating what assignments are missing. I will send a similar _Assignments Missing Form_ each Friday until we begin to see a change in the behavior. Please note that in my class, homework is not busy work. Instead, it is part of the classroom work that, if not completed, makes the child unprepared for the following day's in-class work. Most of the time, the at-home work takes about 20 to 30 minutes to complete.

Thank you.

_____
Teacher

- -

ASSIGNMENTS MISSING FORM

Your child is missing the following assignments:

Monday	Tuesday	Wednesday	Thursday	Friday

_____   _____
Parent Signature   Date

BEHAVIOR MANAGEMENT AND POSITIVE DISCIPLINE

Wouldn't it be a wonderful dream if we could walk into each of our classrooms at the beginning of the year and know that what we faced as teachers were students eager and motivated to do their best work, comply with our rules and procedures, treat one another with respect, and look up to us with high regard? Behavioral management is a vital issue for teachers, especially when classrooms have more and more students who exhibit very challenging and disruptive behaviors. Section 4 contains advice and recommendations based on a number of sources including recognized experts in the field, literature on this topic, and practical experience of well-respected educators in public schools. School administrators, district counselors, and classroom teachers from several schools in San Diego County were interviewed about positive practices and behavioral interventions they use within their schools and/or classrooms. The authors are grateful for their time and willingness to share with us what they find effective.

When it comes to behavioral management, the less a teacher needs to rely on extrinsic incentives and motivators, the better. There will be fewer discipline problems and behaviors requiring correction and intervention if students' basic needs are being met within the classroom.

WHAT DO STUDENTS NEED?

- a structured, positive classroom that is welcoming and inclusive
- a teacher who is a good role model; someone who is firm, fair, and clearly in charge
- to feel safe and comfortable in the classroom environment (knowing that they will be treated with dignity and respect; and not deliberately criticized, embarrassed, or humiliated in front of their peers)
- to feel confident that their teacher cares about their needs and can be trusted

- a chance to voice their feelings, worries, concerns, and ideas
- to feel they have choices and are involved in some decision-making
- instruction and materials that motivate, engage their interest, and keep them involved—therefore, minimizing both boredom and frustration (from which many inappropriate behaviors stem)

WHAT SHOULD TEACHERS DO?

- establish reasonable rules, procedures, and guidelines
- explain rationale for rules and procedures
- have clear, fair, logical consequences for misbehavior and enforce with consistency
- make rules external (post them; use photos or pictures to depict rules and procedures)
- use modeling, practice, and frequent review
- provide structure and routine
- follow through in a timely manner
- establish clear, fair consequences
- allow students to participate in determining consequences and rewards as appropriate
- establish warm, firm, positive relationships with students
- maintain positive and high expectations
- model respectful language, tone of voice, body language
- focus classroom management on problem *prevention*
- smile, laugh, and communicate that you enjoy teaching and being with students
- be positive and reinforcing
- try very hard not to respond to students out of anger
- communicate to students through daily interactions that you care about them and aren't going to give up on them
- document inappropriate behavior and log actions/interventions
- contact parents at first sign of problems
- make parent contacts by phone and/or conference so that lines of communication are always open
- develop action plans with parents
- invite parents to come to school and visit the classroom
- buddy up with other teachers for support and collaboration
- watch for warning signs of potential problems (*anticipate*) and *intervene* early
- be flexible and willing to accommodate individual needs of children

WHAT SHOULD SCHOOLS DO?

- make greater use of student study teams in the referral/suspension process to develop student plans for improvement, including academic, behavioral, and other goals
- utilize mentoring/coaching among teachers

- provide more training to staff regarding classroom management; ADD/ADHD awareness and effective teaching strategies for ADHD students and other children with special needs, learning styles, cultural/ethnic diversity and sensitivity; motivational techniques/strategies for engaging students and reducing opportunities for misbehavior
- devise a schoolwide discipline plan that is well thought out and consistently implemented
- encourage teamwork so that students, parents, and staff are all accountable for student behavior
- be certain that policies and rules are communicated clearly to all students, parents, and staff
- initiate counseling and intervention when behavior problems first occur, involving parents immediately
- provide adequate supervision during recess, lunch, and passing periods
- provide counseling and guidance sessions of various kinds (growth groups, conflict-resolution training, social skills) and topics (peer pressure, name calling)
- utilize peer mediation to settle conflicts
- consider change of classroom or schedule for certain situations
- carefully consider classroom placement for certain students
- target certain students in need of extra positive attention and guidance by having support staff and all auxiliary staff "adopt" certain students; this might mean the librarian, P.E. teacher, VP, custodian must take an interest in the particular student, offering assistance as needed, asking how he/she is doing, checking up on him/her, and so forth
- make the environment and physical campus more child/student oriented, reflecting student interests, ownership, and pride (e.g., student-made murals, art work and projects displayed for all students to see)
- maintain the expectation from *all* on campus (students, full staff, parents) that we respect one another in words, actions, and body language

PREVENTION OF STUDENT MISBEHAVIOR AND MILD INTERVENTIONS

In most classrooms students' behaviors can be managed through basic structuring of the environment with rules, consequences, and consistent enforcement. With a management system that focuses on *prevention* of problems, and through mild interventions when problem behaviors do occur, generally students' misbehaviors can be brought under control. The following are general principles and strategies for preventing behavioral problems, and interventions to employ within the classroom.

Establish 4 to 5 rules positively stated, posted, and referred to frequently. Here are five examples.

1. Do your best work.
2. Cooperate with others.
3. Treat everyone with respect.
4. Stay on task at your seat.

1. Bring all needed materials to class.
2. Be in seat and ready to work when bell rings (pencils sharpened, paper/pencil out, warmups started).
3. Obtain permission before speaking or leaving your seat.
4. Respect and be polite to all people.

---

1. Come prepared to work.
2. Follow directions and stay on task.
3. Keep hands, feet, and objects to yourselves.
4. Be kind and courteous to others.

---

1. Follow directions.
2. Pay attention.
3. Work silently during quiet time.
4. Do your best work.

---

1. Be on time.
2. Be verbally and physically considerate.
3. Use time wisely.
4. Bring necessary materials.
5. Put forth your best effort.

The following are examples of schoolwide expectations from two different middle schools:

School A:
1. Be here * Be on time * Be prepared (bring books, paper, pens, notebook, planner, and PE clothes).
2. Show respect (for adults, for students, for property, for yourself).
3. Behave safely (no fighting, no threats, no profanity).
4. Dress appropriately (no hats inside, follow school guidelines).

> **School B:**
> **RESPECT FOR LEARNING:**
> I will be punctual and prepared for classes, listen carefully,
> ask pertinent questions, and give my best effort to each task.
> **RESPECT FOR PEOPLE:**
> I will behave and cooperate in ways that help myself and
> others feel safe, respected, and cared about.
> **RESPECT FOR PROPERTY:**
> I will take pride in the care of my school. I will care for
> my own belongings and respect the property of others.

At our elementary school, the rules/expectations are:

> **At Benchley-Weinberger every student R.E.A.D.S. well!**
> R = RESPECTS the rights and property of others
> E = is EQUIPPED for learning
> A = ACCEPTS responsibility for their actions
> D = DRESSES appropriately for school
> S = practices SAFETY for self and others

The following is a junior high school discipline/accountability plan that is signed by students and parents. (See the end of Section 10, *Team Efforts*, for a similar home-school compact used in the San Diego City Schools.)

> **Students Are Responsible For:**
> 1. Coming to school daily to learn.
> 2. Following the directions of all adults on campus.
> 3. Respecting and caring for school property and property of others.
> 4. Demonstrating good citizenship and behavior.
> 5. Being on time and being prepared to work until dismissed by the teacher.
> 6. Maintaining and bringing a 3-ring notebook daily, which is to include: assignment sheets filled out daily, pens, pencils, erasers, paper, subject dividers.
> 7. Writing all classroom activities and homework assignments on weekly calendar.
> 8. Showing courtesy and respect for everyone.

Staff Is Responsible For:

1. Respecting the dignity and individuality of each student.
2. Reflecting enthusiasm for learning.
3. Offering a program that provides for individual differences.
4. Guiding students in making appropriate choices.
5. Communicating with students and parents in a regular and positive manner.
6. Posting student rules and consequences in the classroom. **Note:** Rules must be discussed with students on an ongoing basis, and enforced in a consistent, fair and equitable manner. Teachers will communicate their expectations for students to parents, so that we develop a shared partnership in assisting our students with appropriate behaviors.
7. Creating a positive learning environment.

Parents Are Responsible For:

1. Reinforcing your child's desire to learn.
2. Guiding your child to develop acceptable behavior that includes self-control and accountability for his/her actions.
3. Knowing, understanding, and supporting the rules your child is expected to follow.
4. Cooperating with school officials in reinforcing appropriate discipline consequences.
5. Communicating with the school regularly.
6. Being sure your child is in school regularly and on time.
7. Notifying the school when your child is absent.
8. Ensuring that your child is clean, in good health, and properly nourished.
9. Providing a quiet time and place to study.

POSITIVE BEHAVIORAL STRATEGIES

Structural Variables

- Clarify expectations (teaching, modeling, guided practice, communication of those expectations to students and their parents).
- Ask individual students to state the appropriate rule when an infraction occurs.
- Review behavioral expectations prior to the activity.
- Give attention to students who are engaged in appropriate behavior.
- Praise and give positive, specific, descriptive feedback to students meeting expectations. "I like the way Michael is standing in line quietly with his hands to himself. Nice job, Michael." "I see that Jodie has her book open to the right page, and her paper and pencil are out. Jodie is ready to work."

- Try increasing the immediacy of rewards and consequences.
- Use preventive tactics (anticipating problems and avoiding through careful planning).
- Provide frequent activity breaks and opportunities to move around.
- Delay instruction until it is quiet and students' attention is focused.
- Position self at door and greet students individually as they enter the room.
- Immediately direct students as they enter the room to routine warmup activities (journal entries, interpreting brief quotation on board, writing sentences using vocabulary words, math drill of facts, etc.).
- Prepare for and help students through transitions, change of routines, and unstructured situations.
- Utilize proximity control; circulate among students or stand next to desk of student who is misbehaving or prone to do so.
- Increase ratio of positive to negative comments to students to at least 3:1.
- Try ignoring minor inappropriate behavior, particularly if student's misbehavior is not purposeful or intentional.
- Train other students to ignore.

Environmental Variables

- Change student seating (closer to center of instruction, closer to teacher, away from friends, away from distractors).
- Remove distracting items/objects (toys or objects they are playing/fidgeting with) from students.
- Increase distance between desks and provide more space if possible.
- Try using music for transitions and for calming/relaxing students.
- Scan room frequently and stay alert to what students are engaged in at all times.
- Arrange environment for easy access to all parts of the room and visibility of all students; seat disruptive students closer to you.
- Examine environmental variables for students' individual needs.

Affective Variables and Personalized Efforts

- Provide teacher assistance to individual students on a personal 1:1 level.
- Acknowledge and validate what students are thinking and feeling.
- Try to be as empathetic and understanding as possible.
- Talk with former teacher(s) regarding strategies and interventions they may have found effective, and check cumulative record for information that may be significant in trying to help certain students.
- Make eye contact and use prearranged teacher signals and cueing. This can be a specific trigger word or nonverbal signals/gestures that the teacher sets up privately with individual students and uses as a way of warning or redirecting the student (without having to nag or call negative attention to that student in front of peers).

- In some cases fidgety children who seem to need having something in their hands actually do better focusing when given something that they can squeeze or hold. Some children with ADHD **need** to keep their hands busy to stay alert. In this case it might be helpful trying a special arrangement with this child to be given a small piece of clay at his/her desk or be given a key ring with some small object attached that can be clipped somewhere out of sight for the student to hold as needed. The student can be told that as long as this doesn't become a distractor to the other students, he/she may have this privilege.

- Provide a cooling-off period for students who are becoming agitated or angry.

- Discuss situations individually with students in a calm, quiet voice.

- Try to remove the student from an audience of peers when discussing misbehaviors with him/her.

- Maintain positive expectations for students' success.

- Use humor to de-escalate problem situations and to provide student support.

- Avoid lecturing, nagging, and criticism.

- Try lowering your voice, rather than raising it.

Instructional Variables

- Have clear choices and options of activities for students who complete work early to avoid problems that arise out of boredom.

- Make sure independent work is developmentally appropriate and within student's capability of doing successfully.

- Be careful not to assign seatwork or independent tasks that a student is not capable of doing—a prime invitation to acting out from frustration!

- Make sure lessons and activities are engaging and motivating, and students understand the relevancy.

- Utilize effective questioning techniques.

Most teachers at all grade levels use some kind of step system or discipline hierarchy of consequences for general management. In many schools this is a consistent system used throughout the school as part of the site discipline plan. Although the specific steps and consequences vary, the general sequence is that for the first offense or infraction of rule, the student receives a minor consequence (e.g., 5 minutes away from group); the next offense results in a stronger consequence (10 minutes away from group; then a longer period away along with a phone call home; then perhaps time away in a neighboring classroom or counseling center with work to do, or problem behavior sheet to be filled out, standards to be written, etc.; then, as a next step, being sent to the office to see the principal or vice principal).

Here is an example from *elementary classroom A*:

1. Verbal warning
2. Second warning
3. Time out (5 to 10 minutes at time-out desk in classroom)
4. Time away in partner classroom (also has a time-out desk)
5. In-school suspension

Note: In elementary classroom A, these steps are used with all of their fourth-grade classes (and most of the school). There are four fourth-grade classes that work collaboratively in planning for their students. Teachers have buddied up so that in each partnership they team teach (one teaches both classes language arts/social studies; and one teaches the two classes math/science). They are also the time-away class for the buddy teacher. In all of their classes the fourth-grade teachers utilize a token economy system, with paper "bucks" that are passed out to students with high frequency throughout the day for positive behaviors. The teachers usually keep large amounts of these bucks (tokens) in their pocket and walk around the room distributing to students for appropriate behavior. Students are then able to use their tokens/bucks to purchase items in a weekly classroom store. Students need to use 10 tokens to leave class for the bathroom, which has greatly reduced students' requests to leave the classroom. Students are also fined tokens for late or missing homework assignments.

The following is an example of a *middle school discipline plan*:
Consequences apply when a student does not meet expectations.

First offense: Conference with student.

Second offense—Level 1 (teacher action and choice of consequences including):
• time out in class • detention with teacher after school • detention in shared time place or class • behavior journal • trash pick up • conflict busters referral • peer helpers referral • lower citizenship grade • letter writing to parent by student (teacher edits) • phone call to parent by student (teacher edits)

Third offense: Teacher calls parent and explains steps taken for first and second offenses. Explains next steps if continues. In addition, a behavior contract is set up with student.

Fourth offense—Level 2 (teacher action and choice of consequences assigned by teacher including): • mediation in class • consult with support teacher • time out in buddy's class • parent conference • written plan using Glasser or other model • detention on Thursday • teacher can suspend from class for day of offense and following day

Problem continues—Level 3 (consequences): • counseling group referral • detention room referral

Problem continues—Level 4 (consequences): • behavior contract in Student Services • consultation team referral • Saturday School assigned by administrator • In-school suspension assigned by administrator

Problem unresolved after all levels attempted: Referral to administrator for advanced intervention/action.

BEHAVIOR MONITORING AND COMMUNICATION SYSTEMS

Color-Coded Cards

Many elementary school teachers use a colored card system along with the increasing levels of consequences. This is a graphic system for monitoring behavior and there are many variations of this system. It usually involves a pocket chart with an individual pocket or envelope for each student. Every student's name or number is on an individual pocket. Each day the students all start the day with a certain color (e.g., pink: "I'm in the pink"). After a warning, when there is an infraction of the rules, the student's card is changed to the next color along with consequence #1. This procedure continues throughout the day. In some classes there is a notebook kept in a designated part of the room. When a student needs to change his/her color, it is the student's responsibility to record in the notebook the time and date of the infraction, and what the student did that was against the rules.

Some teachers reward students daily who didn't have their card changed during the day, or for those who by the end of the week didn't have their colored card changed more than a certain number of times. For students with more challenging behaviors, teachers often work out a system with parents to send home a message of the student's final color or the number of times the card was changed that day. Sometimes this is tied to a home/school reinforcement program.

Numbered Cards

Some teachers utilize a system of briefly conferencing individually with specific students about their overall behavior for the day. Then the teacher assigns a number to be sent home at the end of the day to indicate to parents how well the student followed rules and expectations. Often this system is tied to a home/school reinforcement system. Students receive a predetermined level of rewards at home for good behavior days, when the student receives a 1 or 2 card. They receive a predetermined consequence when the number card sent home is 4 or 5. For example:

---

1. Very well behaved. Great day!
2. Good day
3. Fair day (so-so)
4. We had some trouble today.
5. We had a very difficult day.

Behavioral Improvement Forms

Many schools use a system of having students fill out some kind of form describing the problem or situation he/she is in trouble for, and identifying a more appropriate strategy or way to deal with the problem or situation if it were to occur again. Depending on the age/level of the student, these problem identification and behavior improvement forms vary. Some teachers, counselors, and administrators use forms that simply have the child write what happened, with whom the situation happened, and one alternative strategy they could try next time if the situation were to occur again. Younger children, or those who have difficulty writing, could draw rather than write about the situation or more appropriate strategy for dealing with it. It was pointed out by counselors and teachers that just this act of having the students identify the problem from their perspective is very helpful.

The form always serves as a springboard for discussion when the student is then seen by the teacher, counselor, or administrator. Younger students can be asked, "Now tell me about your picture." As one counselor shared, "We're trying to teach students that if their behavior isn't good, they didn't make a fatal mistake. Having a chance to share and talk with somebody not directly involved about what happened that got them into trouble and what they can do differently is cleansing. It gives the child a fresh start. It allows an impartial person to listen, not respond out of anger or negativity, and credits the child with some dignity." (See the end of this section for sample forms students need to fill out.)

Class Meetings and Problem Solving

This is a system used to discuss and problem-solve issues happening in and out of the classroom. Using a problem board or clipboard, students write problems that occurred. As one counselor described this system, "This gives the child a place to temporarily dump the problem." At the end of the day the teacher does a priority check. He/she asks, "Jeremy, has your problem been resolved during the day?"

On the recording form the student needs to write his/her name, the person with whom he/she is in conflict, and briefly explain what happened. The situation is shared with the class, and the class decides on a consequence upon consensus.

Some teachers conduct regularly scheduled classroom meetings for a designated amount of time (e.g., 15 minutes twice/week or 1/2 hour meeting weekly). Students record problems they have been experiencing with other students on a special recording sheet on a clipboard. The rules in some classes are that the student needs to try at least one strategy for solving the problem before he/she is allowed to enter it on the board, and only at designated times of the day. During these class meetings, if the problem still exists, the person accused of being involved has the chance to respond. Once again, if a rule has been broken by either party, the consequences are nominated by the class and voted on. In addition, the class shares suggestions for avoiding or dealing with such situations in the future. The teacher always screens the problems recorded and handles those situations inappropriate for this format in other ways.

> *Note: See Section 9, Programs for Building Positive Relationships, Social Skills, and Conflict-Resolution Skills, for problem-solving/conflict-resolution techniques and programs that are being used schoolwide.*

It is well known and substantiated by countless studies in the literature that positive reinforcement—catching students doing what they should be doing and providing positive feedback and reinforcement for those appropriate behaviors—is the most effective approach in the classroom. The following lists some positive reinforcers and consequences that are being used successfully with students. It contains a mix of reinforcers for both the elementary, middle and secondary level.

Positive Incentives:
- verbally praise specific behaviors
- positive notes and calls to parents
- certificates/photos taken of excellent and improved citizenship
- special assemblies, awards, and recognition for good or greatly improved behavior (families invited)
- awards and certificates
- class money or points redeemable at auctions/lotteries or class store

- leaving early for lunch or recess
- first in line
- a minute or two earlier dismissal from class for passing periods
- special activity day, field trip, party, movie at end of the month
- honor roll system to reward students who improved their grades or performance during a grading term
- lunchtime activities and dances
- earning time in class or period to catch up on work while listening to students' choice of music
- lunch intramurals (students earn participation in various sports during lunch)
- extended lunchtime
- free tickets awarded to school sporting events, school plays, dances, concerts, etc.
- drawings/raffles for donated prizes by local merchants
- postcards (students receive postcards for positive achievement in class)
- party or dance at end of semester for all students who stayed off detention list
- privileges (job monitors, taking care of class pet, taking attendance, passing out papers, sharpening pencils, operating AV equipment)
- tutor a younger child
- extra physical education, music, art, computer time
- play a game with friend(s)
- tangible reward (food—preferably healthier snacks such as pretzels, crackers, popcorn, breakfast cereal, low-fat cookies—or stickers)
- earning treasure chest items (small toys, trinkets, pencils, erasers, etc.)
- choose class game or book to be read
- class or school store credit
- work posted, picture taken
- breakfast or lunch with teacher, VP, principal, other staff member
- ice cream party or pizza party (for class or group of students arriving at certain goal)
- awarded a "no homework pass" for the evening or good for one assignment
- more convenient parking space
- release time to go to gym/shoot baskets, go to library, listen to radio with earphones, use computer
- free time (individual or class earned) for games, talking with neighbors, listening to music, drawing, doing activity of choice
- sit by friend/choice of seating for the day or week
- work at art center
- take off one bad grade from daily assignments recorded
- take one problem off a test
- "caught being good" coupons to be used for school or classroom raffles
- pizza parties, ice cream parties, breakfasts/lunches for great improvement in behavior

One elementary school has an I Can Manage Myself (I.C.M.M.) Club. Students become I.C.M.M. members when they have four consecutive days of completed assignments and no time-outs. They remain in the club until they miss turning in a homework assignment or need to be disciplined by going to time-out. They may re-enter the club as soon as they again have-four consecutive days with the same criteria. These students school-wide earn several privileges. For example, the principal may ask a teacher to send his/her I.C.M.M. members to help collate papers in the office, set up chairs in the auditorium for a special program, or perform other special jobs and privileges. The classroom teacher will award privileges to I.C.M.M. members as well, which includes being able to go to lunch a few minutes earlier.

In addition to positive reinforcement for appropriate behavior, teachers will need to enforce consequences for misbehavior. It must be kept in mind that our goal in providing any negative consequences to students is not to punish for the sake of punishing, but to *teach* students the need and expectation to behave appropriately and follow rules—to ensure that the classroom is a place where all students can learn. The following lists some guidelines, strategies, and consequences used effectively for reducing misbehavior in elementary and secondary schools.

Negative Consequences in Response to Problem Behaviors

Note: All consequences should be given without lecturing and delivered unemotionally, in a "matter of fact" manner.

- change of color card with corresponding consequence
- change of number card to go home
- last person to line up or be dismissed
- loss of recess or part of recess or free time
- owing time, e.g., one or two minutes of time for each incident (of interrupting class) to be paid back prior to going out to recess, at lunch, or at end of day (this consequence should be delivered calmly as "since the student took class/teacher time away from instruction, student owes you that time")
- time out from class participation, but within the room at a designated area

Note: Students need to know exactly which behaviors will result in time-out. Many teachers have a specific time-out activity (such as writing standards) for the designated amount of time.

- work center or detention
- filling out a think-about-it sheet
- student writes a letter home
- teacher calls or conferences with parents
- student calls parent from the school to discuss behavior (**Note:** Teachers who have telephones in their rooms and are able to have a student call parent at the time the problem occurs find this to be a highly effective consequence)
- student documents own behavior (e.g., in class book, recording sheet)
- student writes an apology letter
- student writes standards

- student writes a paragraph or two about situation and better strategies for dealing with such a situation if it should occur again
- playground restriction from certain games or areas
- walking or standing with playground supervisor
- time away in neighboring class (student should be sent with work that can be done independently for a limited amount of time depending on age of student)
- time-out in counseling center
- loss of points earned
- being "fined" or losing tokens/tickets, etc., which are redeemable for rewards when using a token economy
- restriction from privileges
- behavior contract
- daily report card

ALTERNATIVES TO SUSPENSION/EXPULSION

For students whose behaviors are more significant—having reached the point where administrative involvement takes place—the administrator should consider a variety of alternatives to formal suspension. As one principal explained, "The only thing that suspension does that is positive is to document the severity of the problem, and get the attention of parents when it happens. Formal suspensions always involve reentry conferences with parents, as well, to work out a plan for the student." The following are some alternative interventions that could be assigned by the administrator:

- Time-outs/time away in another classroom, counseling center, office
- Loss of activities (such as a field trip)
- Saturday school (offered at some schools)
- In-school suspension: This has the advantage over formal suspension in that it still keeps the student in school and supervised. If our goal is to help students be successful and learn appropriate behavior, in-school suspension can be an effective consequence and deterrant. To be effective, though, it is critical that the day be absolutely dull and nonreinforcing for the student. It also requires that there be a physical place (counseling center, office) where the student can stay and work with direct or indirect adult supervision. The student needs to be given work to do independently during the day. One school shared that it has teachers place extra copies of papers they have run off in a box/tray in the work room for their grade/range of student independent reading levels. Different packets of these materials are prepared for students to do independently for in-school suspension or extended time-outs.
- Parent shadowing of the student for the day or part of the day is a popular and often highly effective alternative to suspension. Teachers of older students (particularly in middle school or junior high) who have had a parent shadow them find this strategy an excellent deterrant to future misbehavior. It is helpful to meet with the parents as a team or part of a team while the parent is at school and formulate a behavioral plan at that time.

- Shortened/modified days: This is sometimes used particularly for younger students who are unable to maintain a full-day in school without significant behavioral issues. It is a temporary intervention that may be employed for students experiencing a lot of difficulty.

- Modified schedule: This is an intervention that is used most often at the middle school or high school level when classes are changed for students who function better at certain times of day. One school shared that in order to help a severely ADHD student succeed, he was scheduled two P.E. periods—one in the morning and one in the afternoon, which was a very effective intervention for this student.

- School/community service: One middle school principal shared that if students at her school are caught littering or defacing school property, she assigns them to be on the campus clean-up patrol. They need to help pick up trash around campus, and do certain reasonable jobs assigned by the custodian during noninstructional time. Another middle school principal has a "gum patrol" to which students caught breaking the NO CHEWING GUM rule are assigned. The principal assigns any student referred for chewing gum to Thursday afternoon gum patrol duty. She monitors their participation in scraping off gum around campus. Other kinds of school service assigned by the administrator may include: shelving books in the library, helping in the cafeteria to clean up after lunch, working in the computer lab to dust off computers and clean keyboards, etc.

One very touching story was shared by a junior high school administrator when asked about any creative alternatives to suspension that he may have used at his school. This vice principal was getting so tired of constantly dealing with the negative behaviors of one very challenging student, that for an alternative to suspension he decided to try assigning "Randy" school service. This particular school service turned out to have made a significant difference in the life of this student. The administrator told the eighth grader, "You are always taking the time and energy of everyone on this campus, and it's now time for you to start learning how to give." He brought Randy to the teacher of a special education class for severely handicapped students on the campus and told the teacher that Randy would be there to help him for a couple of weeks. During lunch time and Randy's elective class (woodworking), he was assigned to help the students in many different ways.

It was truly amazing what a difference Randy's involvement helping these children made for him and the students in the classroom. The teacher shared how Randy was kind and sensitive to the needs of the students, and able to bring so much laughter into the classroom that hadn't been there before. Randy continued to volunteer his time working with these students, and turned around in his behavior and attitude. As a result, he was abundantly rewarded by the school for his positive change in behavior and citizenship, now receiving numerous privileges and rewards rather than punishments and negative attention.

This same junior high school also has another creative community service alternative to suspension. The school has earlier start and dismissal times than its neighboring elementary school. The junior high dismisses at 2:10 p.m.; the elementary school, at 3:20 p.m. The junior high school buses students in from other parts of the city, but has late buses assigned by the district three times/week for after-school activities. As an alternative to suspension, some students are assigned the community service job of tutoring at the elementary school from 2:10 until 3:15 on the late bus days. Many students gain from the tutoring opportunity, and continue to volunteer some of their time doing so.

Note: In all of the consequences assigned, parents are, of course, communicated with. Conversations with parents should be taking place from the beginning of the problem to the last step; and that sometimes means making home visits or staying for late afternoon conferences. It was stressed by one administrator that when parents are contacted regarding discipline issues by teachers, counselors and administrators, school personnel must approach the topic from the position of, "Let's work together on this matter." Care must be taken to never be accusatory, but to approach discipline issues from a team/partnership perspective.

SCHOOL COUNSELING ASSISTANCE

School counseling centers that are proactive in providing support to students and staff, and offer various types of services and training to students are vitally important in inclusive schools. In our district's schools it is the counselor who coordinates and facilitates the Student Study Team process. The counselor and guidance aide work with students throughout the day with problem solving, conflict resolution, listening to children and providing support, teaching lessons on self-esteem, social skills, self-control, etc. The counseling center is used as needed for time-outs, and providing 'growth groups' for targeted groups of children experiencing similar needs. Numerous meetings with parents are arranged, and home visits made by the counselor. The district counselor often runs a series of parenting classes on a variety of topics and issues. Agency referrals via school team are made through the counselor (or school nurse). In addition to other supports, it is the counselor who assists classroom teachers in setting up behavioral contracts, charting and monitoring systems, and helping with other strategies and techniques for improving behavior. (See sample Counseling Center Behavior Plan at end of this section.)

PROBLEMS THAT ARISE OUTSIDE OF THE CLASSROOM

In many cases the most significant behavioral issues occur outside of the classroom—on the playground, in the lunch area, in the bathroom, between classes, and so forth. The following are recommended practices that schools have found to be effective in reducing the number of discipline problems that take place during these times.

On the Elementary School Playground

- Increase the amount of supervision to allow for adequate monitoring of students.
- Add more structure by teaching and enforcing specific rules as to how supplies and equipment are to be used appropriately, checked out and returned, signals for lining up to return to class, etc.
- Use a-one bell signal that means for everyone to FREEZE, then a second signal or bell for students to line up to return to class (preferably walking).
- Provide several choices of activities that children can participate in during recess, allowing all students who wish to engage in activities the opportunity to play. It is helpful if certain areas of the playground are designated for particular games. Many discipline problems can arise out of frustration—having to wait without being able to actively participate (which is especially true for children with ADHD).

- Make sure there is a variety of games, ideally ones that can run themselves with minimal adult supervision. In addition, there should be sufficient supplies/equipment to accommodate children who wish to use hoola hoops, individual jump ropes, etc.

- If certain students/groups of students who play together at recess are frequently in conflict, assign an adult to target that group of students, adding more structure and direct supervision to those children.

- Have an option (if possible) available to those students who are uncomfortable on the playground, perhaps having open time in the library or counseling center where quieter games (board games) are available to play, books to read, etc.

- Many schools have *student conflict managers* who have been trained by the counselor to handle problems of younger students (not their own peers) that occur on the playground. They give the younger students a choice: "Do you want me to help you with the problem or get a grown-up?" After approximately six weeks of training through sessions with the school counselor, these conflict managers shadow a senior conflict manager for a week or so. Then the senior conflict manager supervises the new trainee. At a final meeting with the counselor, they are asked if they think they are ready to begin the responsibility. Conflict managers on the playground have been very effective in helping with student-problem resolution. (See Section 9, *Programs for Building Positive Relationships, Social Skills, and Conflict-Resolution Skills*, for more information on conflict managers.)

- In some schools the aides supervising on the playground are given a clipboard to carry with forms attached to fill out, documenting behavioral problems that arise. When a problem occurs, it is first discussed with the child. If the behavior continues, students are often sent out of the activity to a supervised area (bench, wall) near the playground. The aide fills out the form, which designates the behavior, and drops it into the teacher's mailbox. The classroom teacher decides on the action, which includes the following options: (1) no action needed; (2) school service; (3) assign student to write a letter to parent; (4) parent call; (5) refer to principal.

Note: Some elementary schools have found that by having the students play first during the lunch break and eat later, they are calmer when returning to class after lunch. However, one of the problems that schools with this system found is that some children are slow eaters or—due to the cafeteria line—are late getting served and don't finish eating before it is time to go back to class.

Reducing Out-of-Classroom Behavioral Problems in Middle Schools

- One middle school principal shared how the school significantly reduced behavioral problems during the lunch period by splitting the lunch, with all sixth graders eating at the same time as half of the eighth graders. At the second lunch period, all of the seventh graders eat with the other half of the eighth-grade class. By splitting the eighth graders ("divide and conquer") and providing a lot more equipment to use during lunch, they found it to be very beneficial.

- This same principal found a creative way to reduce behavioral issues and improve cleanliness in the school bathrooms by making separate sixth-, seventh-, and eighth-grade bathrooms, and running school contests to see which grade could keep its bathroom the cleanest. The winning class received special awards or privileges.

- Increase teacher supervision during passing periods.
- Station teachers at the door to greet students as they enter class.
- Encourage parent participation so parents are a visible presence on campus.
- See Section 9, *Programs for Building Positive Relationships, Social Skills, and Conflict-Resolution Skills,* for the **Conflict Busters Program** and other outstanding conflict-resolution programs used with great success in middle schools and junior high schools.

STUDENTS WITH CHRONIC DISRUPTIVE BEHAVIORS

In most classes there are a few students who are more challenging in trying to manage and who require more behavioral interventions than the other students in the class. With these students it is easy to lose our patience, become frustrated, and feel inadequate in our skills. First of all, it is important to look at each of these students as individuals and try to see past the behaviors to the whole child. A number of the students who are disruptive in the classroom and may become oppositional are very often children with ADHD (diagnosed or undiagnosed). If this is the case, remember that their disruptive behaviors are based on a neurobiological disorder, and are typically not deliberate.

Bring students who pose chronic behavioral issues in class to your Student Study Team. Refer these children not just for disciplinary purposes, but also for a multidisciplinary look at the student and examination of his/her school history. In doing so, you may be instrumental in helping to identify some students with ADHD, learning disabilities, or other special needs who slipped through the system without ever having been identified or understood. There are more and more children who are now being diagnosed in middle school and high school with ADD, and are receiving treatments and interventions that are making a significant difference in their lives. Other children who are defiant and oppositional are likely in need of other supports, and outside referrals that also require a team approach (teacher, counselor, social worker, nurse, parents, administrator) to provide the student appropriate intervention and help. The following strategies are necessary for this population of students:

- Watch for what triggers the child over the edge to begin a plan of early intervention. Change what you, as the teacher, are able to change. Sometimes a change of seating, buffering from certain peers, or adding some structure before and during transitions makes a big difference.
- Spot early warning signs of potential problems and divert from the situation; intervene early to avoid escalation.
- It is critical to establish close communication with these parents and a clear understanding that you, as teacher, are trying to help their child. It may require extraordinary effort to meet with some of the parents—including making home visits, going to the parents' workplace, or staying at school until late in the day to accommodate parents' work schedules. However, if a positive relationship can be established, it will be well worth the time and effort.
- Do whatever it takes to try establishing rapport and trust with these students. Consider it a challenge that you are going to meet and do whatever possible to reach

these children, who may be very used to teachers who write them off and only try to get them out of their classes.

- Increase amount of positive feedback (private cueing and signals, notes to student, praise of specific appropriate behaviors, and positive reinforcers).

- No matter how much you are provoked to responding out of anger, try to remain calm, and avoid being put in those situations where you end up reacting or engaging in a power struggle. This will require thinking about and planning in advance how you will deal with certain situations.

- Utilize individual behavior plans with students having chronic behavioral problems and when the general classroom management system is not sufficiently working for that student.

- A contract may be needed that is a written agreement among student, teacher, support staff, and parents. It is negotiated, understood, agreed to, and signed by all parties. As a team you decide on a target behavior that the student needs to improve. With what behavior do you want to replace the inappropriate behavior? Establish what will be an achievable goal and determine what will be the reward the student can receive, and criteria for receiving that award if the goal is met. A contract should be for a limited amount of time and then be reviewed. Decide on the time frame that the contract will be in effect; and plan for a review date.

SAMPLE BEHAVIOR PLANS AND MONITORING SYSTEMS

One of the most common methods for monitoring and reinforcing students are charts that the child keeps, and on which the teacher records if or to what degree the student met the target behavior during certain intervals. In the elementary school, those intervals are usually every half hour to hour period, or monitored three times a day (before recess, after recess, and after lunch). At the middle school level, the chart or card is generally recorded on by the teacher every period. We find it necessary to have many of our ADHD students on charts to monitor a *target behavior or two* (e.g., staying in seat, raising hand, on-task, keeping hands and feet to self) and *either work to completion or reasonable amount accomplished*.

The reinforcer and frequency of reinforcement is determined depending on the needs of the child. Some students need to have a daily reinforcer if they meet the goal, which is awarded at the end of the day at school. Some are reinforced on Wednesdays and Fridays if daily is too frequently and weekly is too long a time span. Most students work toward a weekly privilege at school (e.g., extra computer time, choosing from a school treasure box) if they have accumulated enough points, teacher initials, or smiley faces. The most effective plans are those that can be coordinated between home and school and in which the parents are full partners in the system. If the reinforcer is given at home, it is very important that parents follow through as agreed upon, and that the reinforcer is absolutely contingent upon the student having met the goal of the chart or contract, and cannot and will not be granted to the child in any other way. If the parents agree, for example, to taking the child to an arcade, a movie, out for pizza, renting a video of the child's choice, allowing the child to stay up later, or inviting a friend to sleep over on the weekend; it needs to be clearly and exclusively a reward for meeting the goal of the home/school contract, and *not* granted if the child *failed* to meet the goal.

We have some of our very impulsive students on a system that involves taping a card to the student's desk with one or two behaviors listed on the card. For example:

1. I remember to raise my hand and wait to be called on.
2. I ask permission before I get out of my seat.

The teacher and student agree to a reinforcer that the student is motivated to work towards receiving, and the number of points that it will take to earn the reward.

The teacher makes a great effort not to call on or acknowledge this student who cannot seem to help blurting out answers or talking before being called on. When the teacher notices the student remembering to raise his/her hand, the teacher makes every effort to call on that student. In addition, the teacher will walk over and place circles with his/her initials (written in ink) on the card as a positive reinforcement. These are the points that the student is earning. By writing them in ink with the teacher's initials, it makes it difficult for the student to try cheating and drawing his/her own points on the card. While walking around the room among the students, the teacher will give points on the child's card quietly praising him/her for remaining in his/her seat and remembering to raise his/her hand.

There is also a *response cost* tied to this system. When the student blurts out without waiting to be called on, or is out of seat inappropriately, the teacher may cross one or two points (initialed circles) from the card. It is important to try to catch this student behaving appropriately and positively reinforcing at a higher frequency so that he/she doesn't get too discouraged as points are removed from the card. If this happens, the student will perceive the goal as unattainable and will lose interest and motivation.

Note: We highly recommend the Tough Kid Tool Box (Jenson, Rhode, and Reavis) as an outstanding resource for every school site committed to meeting the individual needs of its students. It includes numerous charts, forms, and other reproducible graphic tools for: monitoring and tracking student behavior and performance, communicating between home and school, and motivating students to improve behavior and work production. Some of our students (e.g., those with ADHD) are in need of more intensive behavioral intervention and monitoring by teachers and parents than the average student. That book contains a vast array of ready-to-use tools for both elementary-, middle-, and secondary-level students in need of such intervention. The Daily Tracking Form and Monitoring Behavior Form at the end of this section are from that valuable resource.

In 1995 the movie *Dangerous Minds* was released. This movie is about the challenges a new teacher, portrayed by Michelle Pfeiffer, faces when she accepts a teaching position in an inner-city high school with students who are considered incorrigible and unteachable. The movie moves us to analyze what this one teacher does to eventually reach her students and change their behavior and attitude. The movie begins with her facing a class of completely noncompliant, disrespectful students who hate school and don't want to be there. These students have managed to drive out every teacher within a few weeks or months, and are rather confident they will be able to do the same to this new teacher as well.

During the course of the movie, the new teacher—through determination, perseverance, extreme dedication, and an attitude of "I'll do whatever it takes"—learns through trial and error to be a powerful teacher. She ends up being the kind of teacher we all hope to be—one who makes a significant difference in the lives of needy students. What specifically did this teacher do to change the chaotic, crisis situation she walked into?

- She first figured out that she needed to somehow get her students' attention, so she used concrete examples and demonstrations. (Since she was an expert in martial arts, she initially used karate as a means of getting their attention.)

- She started using tangible positive reinforcers immediately (rewarding students engaged appropriately).

- She told her students that currently each has an 'A' and all they need to do is to keep it. **Note:** None of her students ever thought they would have an opportunity to earn an 'A.'

- She began stressing, discussing, and bombarding her students with the words "It's your choice."

- She realized the curriculum materials were not engaging her students because they were not relevant to their lives, so she changed—presenting lessons and examples her students could relate to and have feelings about: "I wish to die. I choose to die."

- She offered a high incentive to her class. If they all completed a particular assignment (one that was motivating and within their reach and ability to accomplish successfully), the teacher promised to take them to an amusement park. She kept her promise.

The teacher was successful in slowly gaining her students' trust—probably the most critical factor in making a difference. Building and maintaining their trust was the foundation upon which everything else was built. She accomplished this by showing her humanness, and by trying to "walk in the shoes" of her students. She proved her commitment to her students over and over again by being their strongest advocate not only with parents, but with administration.

This teacher did what it takes to make contact with some parents. She made a persistent effort and was willing to go to the home. In one moving scene, she makes an unexpected home visit in order to tell the parents that she is proud of their son (and that they should be, too) and that she enjoys having their son in her class. The teacher shows interest in and respect for the family—and demonstrates how willing she is to go this extra mile. This personal effort enables her to reach this student, gain his trust, and make the connection that is critical for his success.

The teacher recognized that the curriculum that had been used with her students was not motivating or effective. She knew she had to use activities and materials that would tap their interests, and connect to their real lives. For those students whose basic needs are often those of survival; for school to be important to them, it has to be personal—a place of hope and affirmation, a beacon to light the way for them. This teacher made the learning experiences meaningful. In her English class she used lyrics/poetry to which her students could relate. She utilized effective questioning techniques—ones that were open-ended, allowed individuals to discuss their interpretations, and asked questions such as, "Who agrees? Who sees it differently?"

We educators are in the profession because we hope for those magical moments when we can reach a child, and inspire him/her to be the best he/she is capable of being. The movie's teacher possessed those particular traits that enabled her to be successful in reaching and teaching her challenging students: She communicated in every action that she had high expectations for her students, that she cared about them and believed in them. This teacher put all of her energies into building positive relationships with her students. She tried to be nonjudgmental in her interactions with her students, and to avoid reacting out of anger and frustration. Instead, she used proactive strategies. She recognized what wasn't working, and went about trying to change what wasn't working. Rather than blaming her students, she worked on changing what she was able to change—her own behavior and ways of handling situations. The teacher treated her students with dignity, allowed her students and herself to laugh and have fun; and was a motivator, an encourager, and inspiration.

BIBLIOGRAPHY AND RECOMMENDED RESOURCES

Canter, Lee. *Positive Reinforcement Activities (Grades 7-12)*. Santa Monica, CA: Lee Cantor & Associates, 1987.

Canter, Lee, and Canter, Marlene. *Succeeding with Difficult Students*. Santa Monica, CA: Lee Cantor & Associates, 1993.

Garber, Stephen, Garber, Marianne, and Spizman, Robyn. *Good Behavior—Over 1,200 Sensible Solutions to Your Child's Problems from Birth to Age 12*. New York: St. Martin's Paperbacks, 1987.

Goldstein, Sam. *Understanding and Managing Children's Classroom Behavior*. New York: John Wiley & Sons, Inc., 1995.

Jenson, William R., Rhode, Ginger, Reavis, H. Kenton. *The Tough Kid Book (Practical Classroom Management Strategies)*. Longmont, CO: Sopris West, 1995.

Jenson, William R., Rhode, Ginger, Reavis, H. Kenton. *The Tough Kid Tool Box*. Longmont, CO: Sopris West, 1995.

McCarney, Stephen, Wunderlich, Kathy, and Bauer, Angela Marie. *The Pre-Referral Intervention Manual—The Most Common Learning and Behavior Problems Encountered in the Educational Environment*. Columbia, MO: Hawthorne Educational Services, Inc. 1993.

Perlstein, Ruth, and Thrall, Gloria. *Ready-to-Use Conflict Resolution Activities for Secondary Students*. West Nyack, NY: The Center for Applied Research in Education, 1996.

Sloane, Howard N. *The Good Kid Book—How to Solve the 16 Most Common Behavioral Problems*. Champaign, IL: Research Press, 1988.

Sprick, Randall S. *Discipline in the Secondary Classroom: A Problem-by-Problem Survival Guide*. West Nyack, NY: The Center for Applied Research in Education, 1985.

MONITORING BEHAVIOR FORM

Student's Name: _____ Date: _____

Teacher's Name: _____ Class: _____

Periods	Performance Rating	Teacher's Comments
	1 2 3 4	
	1 2 3 4	
	1 2 3 4	
	1 2 3 4	
	1 2 3 4	
	1 2 3 4	
	1 2 3 4	
	1 2 3 4	

Rating Scale — Circle a Number

1 = Needs Improvement   **2** = Barely OK   **3** = Average   **4** = Great

If the teacher agrees with the student rating, put a line across the circled rating. ⊘

If the teacher does not agree with the student rating, put an "X" across the circled rating. ⊗

Behavior(s) Being Rated: _____

_____

_____

_____

_____

_____

DAILY TRACKING FORM

Student Name _____ Date _____

Period	On Time?		Behavior					Prepared?		Assignment(s) Completed?		Homework Assigned?		Teacher's Signature/Initials
	Yes	No	Excellent				Poor	Yes	No	Yes	No	Yes	No	
1	☐	☐	5 ☐	4 ☐	3 ☐	2 ☐	1 ☐	☐	☐	☐	☐	☐	☐	
2	☐	☐	5 ☐	4 ☐	3 ☐	2 ☐	1 ☐	☐	☐	☐	☐	☐	☐	
3	☐	☐	5 ☐	4 ☐	3 ☐	2 ☐	1 ☐	☐	☐	☐	☐	☐	☐	
4	☐	☐	5 ☐	4 ☐	3 ☐	2 ☐	1 ☐	☐	☐	☐	☐	☐	☐	
5	☐	☐	5 ☐	3 ☐	3 ☐	2 ☐	1 ☐	☐	☐	☐	☐	☐	☐	
6	☐	☐	5 ☐	4 ☐	3 ☐	2 ☐	1 ☐	☐	☐	☐	☐	☐	☐	
7	☐	☐	5 ☐	4 ☐	3 ☐	2 ☐	1 ☐	☐	☐	☐	☐	☐	☐	

Homework List (Continued on Back): _____

_____

_____

_____

_____

Tracking Form Reviewed by:

_____

(Signature)

ELEMENTARY SCHOOL   BEHAVIOR PLAN
Counseling Center

Name: _____ Date: _____

Teacher/Room: _____ Grade/Track: _____

To be monitored by: _____

Behaviors that student needs to work on:

_____

_____

What does the student need to achieve to receive reward? (Outcome)

_____

What will be the reward? _____

_____ Weekly _____ Daily   Given by _____ Time _____

Time-out: minimum time for time-out: _____

Contract desired: _____ bubble sheet _____ hourly sheet _____ daily sheet

_____ multi-behavior / daily sheet

IMPORTANT: PARENT CONTACT

_____ I have contacted the parent/guardian regarding my concern and they have agreed to support this contract and follow through at home with consequences and rewards.

_____ I am unable to reach parent/guardian, HELP!

BEHAVIORAL IMPROVEMENT FORM

Student's Name _____   Date _____

1. What is the situation you were involved in? What rule(s) were broken?

_____
_____
_____
_____

2. How do you feel about what just happened?

_____
_____
_____
_____

3. If a similar situation were to happen again, what would you do differently?

_____
_____
_____
_____

_____   _____
Student's Signature   Reviewed by (Staff Member)

WEEKLY PROGRESS REPORT

Child's Name: _____

For the Week of: _____

Please review this progress report and any attached work with your child. After reviewing, please sign this form and have your child return the entire report to school on Monday morning.

Behavior

☐ Very Good
☐ Satisfactory
☐ Unacceptable

Work Habits

☐ Independent
☐ Distracted
☐ Need Guidance
☐ Unacceptable

Work to finish at home? ☐ **YES (attached)**   ☐ **NO**

Comments from school: _____

_____

_____

_____

_____

DAILY RECORD	Monday	Tuesday	Wednesday	Thursday	Friday
HOMEWORK					
WORK HABITS					
BEHAVIOR					

Parent/Guardian Signature: _____

Comments from home: _____

_____

_____

_____

_____

GETTING STUDENTS ORGANIZED FOR SUCCESS: HOME AND SCHOOL STRATEGIES

Many students in our classes are lacking in their organization and study skills. For some children (especially those with ADHD), disorganization is a hallmark characteristic of the disorder. There is a lot that both parents and teachers can do to help organize our children, which will allow them a far greater chance for success throughout their lifetime.

PROVIDE STRUCTURE

For children who have weakness with internal organizational skills, the adults in their lives need to provide more external structures to help them improve these skills. Teachers and parents can provide this assistance and structure by:

- helping to organize the student's work space and materials
- teaching time management/awareness
- making sure the student knows how to tell time and read a nondigital clock
- making sure the student can read calendars and schedules
- calling attention to due dates
- assisting with prioritization of activities and workload
- breaking down longer assignments into smaller, manageable increments
- helping to plan for short-term assignments
- expecting assignments to be written down consistently, teaching how to do so, and monitoring that it is done
- teaching and utilizing "things to do" lists (writing down and then crossing out accomplished tasks)

147

- teaching standards for how to organize written products to be reader-friendly (e.g., awareness and use of spacing, margins, headings)
- helping with preparing and following schedules
- providing time and assistance as needed for cleaning out/sorting the students' messy desk, backpack, and notebook
- providing necessary supplies to help the student get organized

RECOMMENDED SCHOOL PROGRAMS-SYSTEMS

The most outstanding program we are aware of for training students in the skills and strategies necessary for school success is *Skills for School Success*, developed and written by Dr. Anita Archer and Mary Gleason. We have been using this program schoolwide in our elementary school for the past few years. Each lesson in the program easily integrates into the classroom curriculum and provides teacher-guided instruction of numerous organization and study skills, including the following:

- *School Behaviors and Organization Skills:* Using appropriate before- and during-class behaviors; organizing and using notebooks; writing entries on an assignment calendar; using a calendar to plan homework; how to organize assignments on paper; organizing desks and other materials
- *Learning Strategies:* For completing assignments with directions; memorizing/studying information; answering chapter questions; proofreading written assignments; previewing chapter content; active reading; taking notes on written material and taking notes on lectures
- *Test-Taking Strategies:* Studying for and taking multiple-choice, true-false, short-answer, content-area and skill-based tests
- *Textbook Reference Skills:* Using table of contents, glossary, index, etc.
- *Graphics:* Reading and interpreting various types of graphs and tables
- *Reference Books:* Alphabetizing; locating words and entries in dictionaries and encyclopedias

A main component of Archer and Gleason's *Skills for School Success* program, and one which we have found to make a profound difference in the overall study skills and organizational habits of our students, is the consistent use of certain materials. Beginning in third grade, each student is required to use a 3-ring notebook (binder) with subject dividers, and a zippered pencil-pouch. Students are encouraged to have supplies such as pencils, highlighters, pens, and extra notebook paper with them at all times in their binders. Notebooks have pockets at the front and back that are labeled: "Take Home/Leave Home" and "Take Home/Return to School." (**Note:** This program is a schoolwide program and even students from kindergarten through the primary grades also have a folder with labeled pockets they use daily.)

All students are also required to carry a backpack or bookbag; and notebooks are carried to and from school in their bags daily. With this requirement being consistent schoolwide, over the past few years our students have developed the habit, and parents become trained in asking to see students' notebooks in the evening. Parents are also made aware of the need to check the pockets of notebooks for important home/school communication.

It is a very helpful practice if teachers provide all handouts, notices, and papers to students that are already 3-hole punched. By doing so, and directing students to place them in the proper section of their notebooks, it cuts down considerably on papers that are crumpled up and shoved into backpacks, desks, and books.

Another key component of this program is the monthly assignment calendar that all students keep towards the front of their notebooks. The monthly calendar, which when opened in notebooks is 2-pages in width, is where students are directed to record all assignments (on the due date for that assignment, test, project). Through teacher modeling and guided instruction, students learn how to record assignments properly. This is an *essential* teacher responsibility—one that will help countless numbers of students who have difficulty following through with homework, and who need assistance in building organization and study skills. **Note:** Student planner books that are organized Mondays–Fridays with lots of space for recording "things to do" under each day are preferable for many students. Many of these student planner notebooks are 3-hole punched and can be inserted inside binders. Their weekly format with Mondays–Fridays having the most space, and weekends less, are easier for many students to utilize.

Remember that all assignments, due dates, page numbers, and so forth need to be presented to students both verbally and visually. It is important to keep assignments posted on the board for students to copy. It is very helpful to students when teachers try to take a few moments (at the end of the subject period or school day) to *lead* students in the recording of assignments on their calendars. Teachers must communicate and maintain the clear expectation that all assignments are to be recorded on their calendars; and they must monitor that this is occurring. Students with special needs often need additional assistance either directly from the teacher, or from peer partners/study buddies. Teachers can routinely ask table partners or groups seated together to check each other that everything is accurately recorded.

Archer and Gleason also developed *The Advanced Skills for School Success* program for the secondary level which continues to build on the elementary skills. This program, designed for grades 7-12, includes four modules: Module 1 (school behaviors and organization skills), Module 2 (completing daily assignments), Module 3 (effective reading of textbooks), and Module 4 (learning from verbal presentations and participating in discussions).

Another excellent resource written to and for middle school students is *School Power* by Jenny Shay Schumm and Marguerite Radencich. It provides practical guidance and strategies on a variety of topics to help students of this age range be successful in school, and includes the following chapters:

- Get Your Act Together
- Listen and Take Notes
- Speak Up
- Become a Better Reader
- Write Right
- Study Smarter
- Tools for School Success

Teachers will be vastly rewarded for their extra efforts in training and assisting students with these critical organization and study skills. They will find great improvement in students' study habits, accountability for homework, and work turned in on time. Parents will also be very grateful for the teachers' efforts to help their children and improve the home/school partnership.

WHAT ELSE CAN TEACHERS DO TO HELP STUDENTS GET ORGANIZED?

- Attach a "things to do" list on student desks, and help students get in the practice of crossing off items as they are completed.

- Prepare important notices and handouts on colored paper, preferably color-coded for certain categories: for example: weekly/monthly newsletters all in blue, spelling lists in pink, etc.

- Provide schedules and checklists.

- Break down long-term assignments into shorter, manageable increments with teacher feedback to students along the way.

- Allow time for cleaning out desks, notebooks, and lockers. Have periodic desk and notebook checks. Positively reinforce for organization of work space and materials (e.g. prizes, certificates, privileges such as "no homework tonight passes"). **Note:** See the *Notebook Check* form at the end of this section.

- For some students it is necessary to periodically have another person (adult or student) *help them* sort through their desks, backpacks, and notebooks. They may need to dump everything into a shopping bag and bring to another area or room while working on this organization project. Then student and helper together can recycle unnecessary papers, put paper hole reinforcers on torn papers as needed, 3-hole punch other miscellaneous papers and refill appropriately in notebooks, throw out trash and non-working pens, sharpen pencils, and so on.

- Provide certain places (trays, shelves, color-coded file folders) in the room where students know consistently to place completed or incomplete work, and turn in assignments.

- Assign study buddies to help each other. These partners can be responsible for checking each other to make sure assignments are recorded on calendars; and, when absent, to have the buddy collect all handouts, notices, and assignments. Buddies exchange phone numbers to call each other when the other is absent and communicate about what was missed that day in class.

- Encourage students to use and, if necessary, provide them with self-stick notepads for marking pages in books and jotting down key words and notes.

WHAT CAN PARENTS DO TO HELP THEIR CHILDREN GET ORGANIZED?

- Provide your child with a backpack/bookbag, notebook/binder according to the teacher's specifications.

- Provide all necessary supplies for school and homework. (See the Homework Survival Kit supply list.)

- Together with your child choose a place in the home that has adequate lighting, is comfortable for working, and is as free from distractions as possible.

- Set a schedule for homework. Some children like to come home and immediately get part or all of their homework done and out of the way. Others need a break before tackling any homework. Together with your child plan a schedule or time for homework that can be adhered to as consistently as possible.

- Post a master calendar or wall chart for important events and activities. Remember to refer to it often.

- Help transfer important extracurricular activities/scheduling onto your child's personal calendar/planner.

- If possible, be available when your child is doing homework to help as needed; but don't get in the habit of having your child rely on you. *Don't do the work for your child.*

- Ask daily for any home/school communication.

- Ask to see how the child is recording assignments. Praise all efforts at being organized.

- Expect your child to have all assignments recorded. If your child is one who tends to have difficulty keeping up with assignments, turning work in on time, or following through with projects and daily homework, see the teacher! Let the teacher know this is an area of weakness for your child, and that you want to be in a position to help. Request the teacher's help in making sure all assignments are recorded daily. Then be sure to follow through by reviewing the recorded assignments with your child.

- Reinforce with your child the need to not leave school until he/she checks his/her assignment sheet/calendar. Make sure the child has any necessary books and materials needed to do the homework.

- Be sure to ask for progress notes that keep you appraised as to how your child is doing. If you haven't received any communication or feedback for a while, call the teacher or write a note.

- Provide the structure and environment that will be conducive for home study.

- Get your child a watch to wear and a clock that is accurate in his/her room.

- Consider "no phone call" times in the evening.

- Support your child from being distracted by the TV by turning it off.

- Help the child divide the workload and assignments into manageable chunks. Ask to see what he/she has accomplished after a certain amount of time, or to show you when a particular assignment is done.

- Consider using a timer if your child has difficulty staying on task. Sometimes a "beat the clock system" is effective in motivating children to complete a task before the timer goes off. Ask to see the completed task, and reward if it was done with relative accuracy and neatness. Even more effective is having the child self-monitor, requiring that he/she take a few minutes more to check over the work and self-correct as needed.

- Communicate your expectations that homework is a priority. In today's busy society, many families are over-extended with the number of extracurricular activities they are involved in. If there is very little time in an evening to devote to schoolwork, perhaps you need to re-examine your commitments and activities and give up something.

- Encourage your child and emphasize *effort* as the most important criteria.

- Praise for being on-task, getting to work, and taking responsibility. Give extra praise for accomplishment and progress.

- If homework assignments are taking an inordinate amount of time and your child is struggling, make an appointment with the teacher. Special modifications may need to be arranged (e.g., shorter assignments, child dictates and you transcribe for him/her). See Section 8, *Interventions and Adaptations for Accommodating Special Needs*.

- Together with your child, carefully examine his/her work space. Make sure there is available a large working surface (desktop) free from clutter. If your child has a computer, don't place it on the desk, which cuts down considerably on the working surface area. Instead, place the computer on a separate desk or table.

- Have your child clear out desk drawers and shelves of work, projects, and papers from previous school years. Together, decide on what you would like to keep and make a portfolio of that work to be stored out of the way.

- Provide your child with a corkboard and pins to hang up important papers.

- Dry-erase boards and markers are helpful to hang in the kitchen and your child's room for important notes and messages.

- Provide a file with color-coded folders in which your child can keep things stored categorically.

- Besides a family master calendar, provides your child with a desk calendar that serves as an overview of important dates, activities, and events.

- Encourage and help your child get in the habit of putting all books, notebooks, signed notes, and other necessary materials inside the backpack before bedtime. Place in the same spot every night.

- Use self-stick notes to place on mirrors, doors, and other visible places for reminders.

- Supply your child with a portable homework survival kit. A smaller version for the car is also helpful. (See the letter to parents at the end of this section for recommended school supplies for the beginning of the school year.)

HOMEWORK SURVIVAL KIT

Parents can help their child considerably in cutting down on wasted time spent searching the house for necessary homework supplies and materials. Not only is it a frustrating waste of precious minutes, but it also causes a major break in productivity—pulling children unnecessarily off-task. Providing all necessary supplies in one place, where the child is working, will eliminate the need to get up and look for a sharpened pencil, paper, eraser, and so forth.

This *homework survival kit* can be stored in anything portable, preferably a lightweight container with a lid. Some children work at their desks; others, on kitchen or dining room tables; still others prefer to spread out on their beds or the floor. With this system, it doesn't matter the location of where children choose to study. The necessary supplies can accompany them anywhere!

- notebook paper
- unlined paper

- ruler
- calculator

- sharpened pencils
- erasers
- glue stick
- scissors
- transparent tape
- masking tape
- white correction fluid
- ballpoint pens (black and blue)
- colored pencils/pens/markers
- hole puncher
- pencil sharpener

- 3-hole puncher
- compass
- dictionary
- thesaurus
- protractor
- crayons
- stapler/staples
- paper clips
- staple remover
- self-stick notepads
- index cards

Many adults have established the habit of carrying a book, newspaper or magazine, and notebook/pen in the car for those times they need to wait for appointments, have to sit in the car waiting for someone, etc. It is a good idea to have our children do the same. They can keep a book or magazine, and a much smaller version of the homework kit in the car. This would enable them to accomplish some productive school work during those times they are on errands with parents, in transit, and so forth.

BIBLIOGRAPHY AND RECOMMENDED RESOURCES

Archer, Anita, and Gleason, Mary. *Skills for School Success* (grades 3-6). Curriculum Associates, Inc., 5 Esquire Road, N. Billerica, MA 01862-2589. Phone: 1-800-225-0248.

Archer, Anita, and Gleason, Mary. *Advanced Skills for School Success* (grades 7-12). Curriculum Associates, Inc.

Parker, Harvey. *ADAPT Student Planbook.* Available through ADD WareHouse Catalog, 300 Northwest 70th Ave., Suite 102, Plantation, FL 33317. Phone: 1-800-233-9273.

Rief, Sandra. *How to Reach and Teach ADD/ADHD Children.* West Nyack, NY: The Center for Applied Research in Education, 1993.

Rooney, Karen. *Independent Strategies for Efficient Study.* Available through ADD WareHouse.

Schumm, Jeanne Shay, and Radencich, Marguerite. *School Power—Strategies for Succeeding in School.* Minneapolis: Free Spirit Publishing, 1992.

Spizman, Robyn, and Garber, Marianne. *Helping Kids Get Organized.* Carthage, IL: Good Apple, 1995.

_____ (Date)

Dear Parents,

Every year we, as upper-grade teachers, are asked what materials the students should obtain for the opening of school in September. With the drastic cut in district funding, we are asking students to bring some of their own materials, all of which will be beneficial to them in making their school year run more smoothly and efficiently.

We have compiled a list of school items that are used most often by upper graders during the school day. The ones with the stars are essential to all students. The other items are strongly suggested.

* 3-ring binder
* notebook dividers
* 3-hole notebook paper
* extra pencils
* blue or black ballpoint pens
* thin, black, felt-tipped marker
* scissors
* calculator
  glue stick
  ruler
  colored pencils
  crayons
  thin, colored markers
  compass
  protractor

We understand that not all students will be able to bring all of the materials, but we hope this will assist you in helping your child to be better prepared for school. We find that when students have their own items, they appreciate them and are more apt to take better care of them. Coming prepared for school on the first day will help your child feel organized and ready for a successful school year.

Thank you.

_____

Teacher(s)

NOTEBOOK CHECK

Student's Name _____   Date _____

Evaluator's Name _____

_____ **YOUR NOTEBOOK ORGANIZATION IS OUTSTANDING. THANK YOU FOR BEING RESPONSIBLE IN KEEPING YOUR NOTEBOOK ORDERLY.**

_____ **YOUR NOTEBOOK IS IN SATISFACTORY ORDER.**

_____ **YOUR NOTEBOOK IS NOT IN SATISFACTORY ORDER. PLEASE ORGANIZE IT TONIGHT. YOU MAY HAVE IT RECHECKED AGAIN TOMORROW.**

_____
Parent Signature

NOTE TO THE TEACHER

In the upper grades and middle schools, students need to organize their materials responsibly. At our school, all upper graders are required to have a three-ring binder.

This form is issued at the end of each week for the first four weeks of school. As the year progresses, most students are weaned from it, while others must continue with its use.

Since it is a time-consuming task for the teacher, it is suggested that a parent volunteer or aide looks over the notebooks regularly. Occasionally our principal or vice principal drops by for a notebook check. Notebook standards and teacher expectations should be established early in the year.

PROGRAMS AND STRATEGIES FOR FOSTERING STUDENTS' SELF-ESTEEM

Throughout this book our focus is on providing the classroom and school environment with activities, strategies, supports, and interventions that will enable all students to develop their self-esteem. In order to be successful, all children need to experience and internalize positive feelings about themselves as capable, competent learners and valued, respected, cared-for individuals.

> "The teacher gives not of his wisdom,
> But rather of his faith and lovingness."
> *The Prophet*, Kahlil Gibran

ENVIRONMENTS THAT PROMOTE POSITIVE SELF-ESTEEM

A classroom or schoolwide *climate* is the atmosphere felt on a daily basis and permeates the entire environment. Schools, such as ours, that are noted for their positive climates are often described as humanistic, warm, welcoming, and accepting. Over the years countless visitors to our school have commented that they feel a difference as soon as they walk onto our campus. Adults and students appear happy and treat each other respectfully. It is a comfortable, inviting environment to be in. The following are some of the necessary ingredients for a positive school climate:

- an atmosphere of trust
- support and encouragement from teachers, administrators, staff, and other student peers
- respect and appreciation for diversity (ethnicity, cultural, learning styles, etc.)

157

- clear, high expectations for students and staff
- community and parental support
- variety of teaching strategies and delivery systems to address the range of learning styles in the classroom
- clear academic and behavioral goals
- motivating, relevant, and challenging learning tasks and integrated curriculum
- lots of engaging, fun activities for students
- regular and frequent monitoring of student work
- kind, accepting, fair, nonjudgmental teachers who have an awareness of the developmental range and various needs of students in the classroom
- a sense of belonging/community
- an emphasis on cooperation, communication, and bringing out/recognizing the strengths of everyone
- student work displayed around campus
- positive recognition of students and staff members
- incentives and rewards
- administrative expectation/modeling of positivism, kindness and respect; and enforcement of that expectation schoolwide

The administrator is the *key* person to set the emotional climate and tone of the school. A positive, innovative, upbeat, administrator with strong leadership skills and commitment to teamwork can turn around an entire school. In addition, there are some schools with a few teachers who may actually be harming students with their negative attitudes, inflexibility, humiliation, or criticism of students. Administrators must not allow teachers to treat children in such ways, and must use their authority and all of their efforts in dealing appropriately with such teachers.

CLASSROOM STRATEGIES AND PROGRAMS TO PROMOTE SELF-ESTEEM

- Provide an atmosphere of acceptance when ideas are being generated. Don't reject ideas in brainstorming sessions.
- Encourage students to express feelings.
- Use questioning techniques and sharing methods that allow all students to have the opportunity to be heard and share with equity. (See Section 11, *Effective Questioning Techniques for the Classroom.*
- Welcome students as they enter the room with a smile and by greeting them personally.
- Write students personal, positive notes to place on their desks, attach to their work that you return to them, or mail home (postcards).
- Write specific messages as often as possible on student work.
- Send special messages and notes to students recognizing their efforts and behaviors you are pleased with.

- If you know which students will be in your classroom before the beginning of the school year, make personal phone calls to introduce yourself, or mail notes during the summer telling the students you are looking forward to having them in your class.

- Teach students how and then make the time to have them write positive notes, thank-you letters, get well cards, etc., to other students, staff members, substitute teachers, guest speakers, and parents. Some elementary teachers who use centers in their room have a special center/area with supplies for making cards and banners when there is time during the day.

- Find the humor in situations, and try to bring fun and laughter into the classroom as much as possible.

- Incorporate literature into the curriculum that helps students express and understand feelings and emotions, that ties in thematically with a variety of topics such as caring and determination, belonging and acceptance, rejection and taunting, handicaps, etc.

- Call one parent each night to report positive things about his/her child's efforts.

- For every phone call home that is to discuss negative behaviors, make a few positive phone calls home to share good news with parents.

- Teach students how to make positive statements, compliments, and recognize/use esteem-building language. Enforce in the classroom that "in here we only say positive things about ourselves and others and that no put-downs or negative comments to or about others are acceptable." Some elementary teachers call positive statements/compliments "sparkles," "builder-upper words," "fuzzies." They make a hand signal that indicates positive statements heard, and whenever the teacher or other students hear someone saying something positive to another student, they make the hand signal indicating they heard a "builder-upper statement." A list can be kept or chart made to record self-esteem language heard. Some middle school teachers refer to their classroom as "home court"; they teach students that home court means it is a supportive environment, filled with fans who are encouraging and cheering each other on. When any negativity is heard, the cue to be more positive is to simply state, "Remember we're in home court."

- Teach students how to accept compliments appropriately.

- Discuss negative comments and how those words make us feel. Name those negative comments (put-downs, zingers) and use a cue word/signal to remind students not to use esteem-hurting language.

- Schedule brief 5- to 10-minute conferences with each student as frequently as possible throughout each grading period.

- Some teachers have a breakfast each week or every other week (providing the juice, muffin/toast) with different small groups of students from the classroom. Other teachers schedule a picnic lunch with a different group of students each time on a regular basis (often providing the dessert or beverage). This special time with the teacher is less formal, and allows students to talk about topics other than schoolwork in a very pleasant way. It allows you to connect with students and build a positive relationship.

- Take photos of students engaged in a variety of activities and/or videotape frequently. Display photos and show the video to students and parents.

- Teach about and talk about learning styles and multiple intelligences, and address these at every opportunity. (See Section 1, *Reaching All Students Through Their Multiple Intelligences and Learning Styles.*)

- Many teachers have students applaud their peers' accomplishments, positive behavior, and so forth.

- Help students recognize their strengths and competencies. Keep a record or profile of what students do well.

- Designate students as "class experts" on certain topics or with specific skills that they shine in or have a special interest in.

- Provide many activities and opportunities for students to showcase their strengths; teach other students what they know how to do well; perform, share about their hobbies, interests, and so forth.

- Create a class book on OUR STRENGTHS with each student having his/her page. Each student can provide pictures, and/or write about his/her strengths and what he/she does well, positive character traits, etc.

- Many teachers have a bulletin board devoted to a different student each week. This "Student of the Week," "Student Standout," or "Student in the Spotlight" is generally asked the week or weekend before it is his/her turn to bring in pictures and any objects they would like to display about themselves. They often need to write a short biography; and parents are asked to write at least a paragraph sharing positive things about their child. Some teachers pass out strips of paper to each student in the class, and they need to write something positive about the student in the spotlight (e.g., character traits/attributes, what they think that student does well, what they like or appreciate about that person, etc.). The student in the spotlight can pass out additional strips of paper to family members, other staff members, and friends to add to his/her collection. At the end of the week, these positive comments can be mounted on a poster to take home. (See the sample "Student Standout" instructions at the end of this section.)

- Buddy up a child with low self-esteem with a younger child as a cross-age tutor to that younger child. Cross-age tutoring and upper-/lower-grade buddy systems are a wonderful way to boost self-esteem of all children.

- Model how to use positive self-talk, especially to illustrate how to think positively and not give up when frustrated.

- Point out students' errors in a way that is not demeaning and respects their efforts. On written work, take care not to mark up students' papers (especially with red ink!). It is often helpful and respectful to indicate errors in the margins, or on self-stick notes when possible. When teaching students to peer edit, train students and model how to always share positive comments first—what they liked about the work (even if it is only a choice of one certain vocabulary word)—before making any recommendations for improvement.

- Many classrooms have their own class pet and their own patch/area of school garden to care for, which helps students to feel good about themselves and more connected to their class and school.

SCHOOLWIDE PROGRAMS AND STRATEGIES

There are many ways that schools recognize students, provide rewards and positive reinforcement, and work to build students' self-esteem. The following are examples of various schoolwide efforts and strategies for increasing students' self-esteem that were shared by school personnel and other resources:

- Staff members "adopt" a student identified as having need of extra support and attention. All staff are asked to check up regularly on their student, spend time talking with them, and provide extra supports and reinforcement as they wish.

- Many schools utilize a "Caught Doing Something Good" or "Gotcha" program. All staff members are given tickets to pass out to students they catch in the act of doing something kind for someone else, being helpful, or performing a targeted social skill being practiced (e.g., courtesy, good manners). Tickets are either accumulated by students for purchases from a school store, or are placed in a central raffle box for a weekly drawing, with those 4 to 5 students whose names were drawn receiving recognition and a prize of some type. (See Section 9, *Programs for Building Positive Relationships, Social Skills, and Conflict-Resolution Skills.*)

- At one elementary school each teacher keeps his/her own box for students to place their "Caught Being Good" tickets as they receive them. Every Thursday the classroom teachers select three names from their boxes. Those students whose names were drawn are all sent to the library during the last twenty minutes of the day for a make-your-own ice cream sundae reward. In some secondary schools, if a certain number are acquired, the "Gotcha" tickets are redeemable for a free yearbook or other substantial award.

- Most schools have recognition assemblies throughout the year, with parents invited, pictures taken of the students to be displayed and/or published in newsletters, and refreshments served. Students have the opportunity to be recognized at these assemblies for any number of reasons that are positive and show student growth or service (such as reading with your partner the best you can, best helper in the classroom, being an ambassador to a new student, showing the most progress in returning homework). Students can be rewarded and recognized for improvement, effort, cooperation, spirit, attendance, positive attitude, friendliness, and so forth.

- At our elementary school we have an early morning assembly once a month outside on the blacktop. Each classroom or team of classrooms is in charge of a brief performance or leading the school in song, etc. Then after some announcements, we recognize all of our "students in the spotlight" for that month from each classroom. Those students all go up front while they are cheered by the school and receive a special pencil from the principal. In this way *all students* in the school are recognized at one of the school assemblies, in addition to other assemblies where students are recognized for school service, good attendance records, achievement, and so forth.

- School clubs are widely used to provide opportunities for students to become involved in the school community and expand social interactions. In so doing, they grow in their positive feelings about themselves. There are numerous clubs to address a wide range of interests and activities. Some clubs/organizations are formed to specifically target individual students in need of involvement and reward those who are making efforts to improve themselves.

- One vice principal at a middle school shared how they formed a "Hiking Club" and a "Builders' Club" at their school. The Hiking Club is geared for those students who have had problems that involved a lot of management or intervention from school staff, but who have managed to "turn around" in their behaviors, achievement, and/or attitude. Students are selected by any staff member to be in the Hiking Club. Twice a month, this group of students—along with the few staff members involved with this club—hike the trails of a regional park in the area. Then, they stop for a cold soda and students are driven home. The Builders' Club is also a "prestigious" club of students who are recommended for acceptance by staff members who notice the student making a positive effort to improve citizenship. Some of the activities they do in the Builders' Club is paint the benches, decorate/paint the trash cans, plant trees, help construct things, and work in conjunction with the local Kiwanis Club to collect toys for the toy drive.

- One middle school principal shared, "The best self-esteem builder is for the students to discover that they are *great*, not because someone tells them, but by achieving success. At their school teachers give grades of A, B, C or 'Do Over'. There are no D's and F's. If a student hasn't passed a test or received a passing grade on an assignment, he/she is assigned a study buddy/peer tutor and/or other teacher support and assistance to provide the help necessary for the student to be able to raise his/her grade to a 'C'." She shared that they have vastly fewer students experiencing failure.

- To set a positive tone first thing in the morning, many staffs are encouraged to greet students as soon as they set foot on school grounds. At elementary schools, the reward for staff members is a lot of hugs from arriving students (a wonderful way to start our day, as well!).

- School counseling centers provide many services designed to build students' self-esteem, such as: growth groups, new student orientation, teaching conflict resolution and social skills, coordination of agency services, providing interventions for attendance problems, etc. (See Section 9, *Programs for Building Positive Relationships, Social Skills, and Conflict-Resolution Skills*.)

- When necessary, refer students to support staff or to the Student Study Team for assistance in helping students with a variety of needs. When children having any number of problems receive the appropriate intervention to meet their needs, they are enabled to achieve success and grow in self-confidence and self-esteem. Many children need help addressing physical, social, health and medical issues, speech/language, as well as learning difficulties.

- One middle school principal shared that she established a "Principal's Forum." Students sign up to meet with her to discuss things they would like to see happen at the school, or any problems and possible solutions. This is a way she keeps in touch with students' needs/concerns; and it promotes student self-esteem—knowing their issues are being listened to by the principal.

- There are numerous rewards and incentives used as positive reinforcements for students by individual teachers and schoolwide. (See Section 4, *Behavior Management and Positive Discipline*, for a comprehensive list of positive reinforcers effective in elementary, middle, and secondary schools.)

- Principals do a variety of things to give positive attention and recognition to students, such as: welcoming students/personal greetings as they arrive at school, or having teachers send students to the principal's office for achievements and improved behavior. (Principals call home with the "good news".) Elementary school students are often given little treats (pencils) by the principal on their birthdays. Awards/certificates are given, and pictures are taken of students who have met certain goals and deserve recognition. Students are showcased on designated office/school bulletin boards, in school newsletters, and so forth. Administrators who make a strong effort to get to know students are approachable and supportive, and are committed to an inclusive, positive school environment, do a lot to foster student self-esteem.

- Schools have many kinds of clubs, support groups, and programs that are very helpful in providing more opportunities for students to grow in self-confidence and self-esteem. Tutorial programs under a school-community partnership provide students with role models as well as academic help. Mentoring programs and clubs/interest groups are very effective and necessary for students. Many schools with diverse student populations have clubs/organizations to meet the needs of different cultural/ethnic groups such as Southeast Asian, African-American male, Latina female, etc.

One of our district's elementary schools with 1,300 students (1,000 of whom are Limited English Proficient, with 97% below the poverty level) has numerous programs for students designed to enhance self-esteem and meet the needs of their diverse population. Working together with several agencies in the area through school/community partnership, the school is able to provide after-school tutoring, gang-prevention programs, and on-site counseling from various agencies, in addition to school guidance/counseling. The school also has social work interns on campus who help provide extra support and intervention.

COMMUNITY SERVICE

Many schools provide opportunities for their students to *reach out* into the community. Through the act of providing a needed service and making personal connections with others, students acquire a good feeling about themselves; thus, enhancing their self-esteem. Depending on the location, some schools are able to partner with convalescent and nursing homes. The children visit the residents, play games with them, make cards and pictures, write poems and stories to send them, sing and perform on holidays, and so forth.

One middle school administrator shared how the students work schoolwide on a project to help the homeless in the city. They collect clothing, toiletries, and blankets; make quilts, bag food, etc., for delivery. Our elementary school has an annual project that we have been able to do with the help and commitment of our wonderful P.T.A. parents. Each class designs and makes its own special quilt, which is later donated to children in need within the community.

It is very important to instill in our children a sense of obligation and responsibility for helping others, and involve them in community service projects whenever possible. Hopefully, this is occurring outside of school, as well, with their families and churches/synagogues. Any opportunity we provide to involve our children in service projects will be of value to the community and society. The additional benefit is that most people gain in self-esteem, feeling very positively about themselves when they experience the act of giving to others.

BIBLIOGRAPHY AND RECOMMENDED RESOURCES

Borda, Michele. *Esteem Builders* (K-8 Self-Esteem Curriculum for Improving Student Achievement, Behavior and School Climate). Rolling Hills Estates, CA: Jalmar Press, 1989. Phone: 213-547-1240.

Borda, Michele, and Borda, Craig. *Self-Esteem: A Classroom Affair, Volume 2.* San Francisco: Harper & Row Publishers, 1982.

Brooks, Robert. *The Self-Esteem Teacher.* 4201 Woodland Rd., Circle Pines, MN: American Guidance Service, 1991. (Part of the Seeds of Self-Esteem Program, Treehaus Communications)

Gibbs, Jeanne. *Tribes—A New Way of Learning Together.* (1994). Center Source Publications, 305 Tesconi Circle, Santa Rosa, CA 95401.

Teolis, Beth. *Ready-to-Use Self-Esteem & Conflict-Solving Activities for Grades 4-8.* West Nyack, NY: The Center for Applied Research in Education, 1996.

Vurnakes, Claudia. *201 Strategies for Teacher Advisors—A Source Book for Affective Learning (middle and upper grades).* Frank Schaffer Publications, Inc., 23740 Hawthorne Blvd., Torrance, CA 90505.

STUDENT STANDOUT
FOR THE WEEK OF _____

Student's Name _____

CONGRATULATIONS! You have the distinct honor of being room _____ 's Student Standout for next week. Please review the following items carefully and come in next Monday prepared to share them with your classmates.

1. Bring pictures of yourself at different stages of your life. These will be placed on the student standout board for the entire week. All pictures will be returned to you next Monday.

2. Have your mother, father, grandparent, aunt, uncle, sister, or brother write a brief paragraph about you (something funny that they recall, a favorite memory, or just some nice thoughts about you). See, even your parents get homework in this class!

3. Bring in an article of clothing or something that is special to you (t-shirt, hat, uniform, stuffed animal, etc.) to help your classmates learn something new about you.

4. Have a friend make a list of the things he/she likes about you. Include it on your board.

5. Share your hobby with us during your special week. Bring your collection, special talent, etc., and share it with the class.

6. If you play an instrument, play something for the class.

7. Bring in your favorite game. You will have a special game time allocated to you. (It can be a computer game!)

REACHING ALL STUDENTS WITH SPECIAL NEEDS

To be an effective teacher it is imperative to have awareness, sensitivity, and understanding of the academic, behavioral, and social/emotional difficulties some of our students have. We need to be able to teach and adapt our instruction for all levels of ability (gifted and special education students). We need to create a learning environment that will be motivating and comfortable for the full range of diversity among our students. In today's classrooms all teachers have students with ADD/ADHD (attention deficit hyperactivity disorder) and with learning disabilities (LD). In many of our classrooms there are students who are gifted, and those who are Limited English proficient (LEP). Numerous children are growing up in home environments and living situations that place them "at risk." More and more children are moving up in the grades who had been prenatally exposed to one or more drugs; and we may have students who have a variety of other disabilities or medical conditions.

Teachers need ongoing training in the teaching strategies, structure, environmental modifications, curriculum adaptations, and support that will allow *all* children—those with and without special needs—to achieve. First and foremost, we need to see our students *as children*. They are all unique, special individuals; but they are all just kids—with *far* more similarities than differences. Some may present more challenging behaviors, and teachers may need to dig deeper into their bag of tricks in order to reach them and help them learn. However, *all* of our students *can* learn. They all want to be successful in school and gain competencies and skills. They all want to have fun, make friends, be accepted, and feel part of the "community."

In this section, you will be presented with characteristics, background information regarding specific needs, and recommended resources for assuring the success of these particular populations of students:

- Children with learning disabilities
- Children with ADD/ADHD
- Children who were prenatally exposed to drugs
- Children who are Limited English Proficient
- Children who are gifted and talented

It is interesting to note the similarity in educational needs of these children. They all require many of the same sets of teaching strategies and techniques. The literature and research on effectively teaching all of the above diverse populations of children keeps leading to the same conclusions: These children all need hands-on, active learning that is stimulating, relevant, developmentally appropriate, and taps their learning strengths. They need to be provided with choices, structure, and clarity of expectations within an accepting and nurturing environment. This is great news to teachers! When we work to increase our teaching skills and repertoire of instructional strategies for today's classroom, we are indeed working to meet the needs of *all* our students.

CHILDREN WITH LEARNING DISABILITIES

Learning disabilities can cause difficulty with language, memory, listening, conceptualization, speaking, reading, writing, spelling, math, and motor skills—in various combinations and degrees. *Learning disabilities* (LD) is a term used to describe a neurological handicap that interferes with someone's ability to store, process, or produce information. It affects approximately 10 percent of the population. Each individual is unique in the combination of strengths and weaknesses, and degree of impairment. Learning disabilities can be quite mild and subtle, and may go undetected; or they may be quite severe—greatly affecting one's ability to learn many academic, communication, functional, and social skills. Specific learning disabilities affect individuals in ways similar to a telephone switchboard that has some problems in the circuitry of the system, causing difficulties with incoming and/or outgoing messages.

The types of learning disabilities may affect any combination of: the reception or input of information into the brain (visual and/or auditory perception), the integration of that information in the brain (processing, sequencing, organization), the retrieval from storage (auditory and/or visual memory), and the output or expression of that information (communicating motorically or through oral/ written language).

Learning disabilities create a gap between a person's true capacity and his/her day-to-day productivity and performance. In years past children with learning disabilities were frequently mislabeled as having limited capacity to learn (or as being lazy) and were typically segregated or cast out of the system. In fact, the criteria for classification as learning disabled requires that the child has *at least* average intelligence, yet is underachieving to his/her measured potential in one or more academic areas (e.g., reading, math, written language); and this significant discrepancy between his/her measured ability and performance is *not* due to mental retardation, emotional disturbance, environmental deprivation, or sensory impairment.

Fortunately, over the past 20 to 25 years there has been much more education and awareness regarding specific learning disabilities. It is far more recognized now that these children are certainly not lazy or unmotivated. Many are gifted with exceptional aptitude in some of their multiple intelligences (e.g., spatial, musical, bodily-kinesthetic). We know much more about how to teach through these children's strengths—through the channels that will help them to learn more effectively. We must allow children with learning differences to try bypassing or compensating for their weak areas by utilizing the appropriate tools and strategies. It is important to remember that these children do have many strengths along with their weaknesses. They *can* learn. If we, as teachers, haven't found the best avenues through which to reach them, it is our responsibility to keep on trying until we do.

Common Characteristics of Children with Learning Disabilities

Symptomology Checklist
SYMPTOMOLOGY CHECKLIST—LEARNING DISABILITIES
(Check behaviors seen. Mark: S = sometimes; O = often)

Visual Perceptual Deficits
____ reversals: *b* for *d*, *p* for *q*

____ inversions: *u* for *n*, *w* for *m*

____ yawns while reading

____ complains eyes hurt, itch/rubs eyes

____ complains print blurs while reading

____ turns head or paper at odd angles

____ closes one eye while working

____ cannot copy accurately

____ loses place frequently

____ rereads lines/skips lines

____ does not recognize an object/word if only part of it is shown

____ reading improves with larger print/fewer items on page/uses a marker to exclude portion of page

____ sequencing errors: *was/saw*, *on/no*

____ does not see main theme in a picture, picks up some minute detail

____ slow to pick up on likenesses-differences in words; changes in environment

____ erases excessively

____ distortions in depth perception

Visual Perceptual/Visual Motor Deficits
____ letters collide with each other/no space between words

____ letters not on line

____ forms letters in strange way

____ mirror writing (holding paper up to mirror and you see it as it should look)

___ cannot color within lines

___ illegible handwriting

___ holds pencil too tightly; often breaks pencil point/crayons

___ cannot cut

___ cannot paste

___ messy papers

Auditory Perceptual Deficits

___ auditory processing: cannot understand conversation or learning delivered at the normal rate/may comprehend if information is repeated very slowly

___ auditory discrimination: does not hear differences in sounds: short *i, e*; sounds *b, p, d, t, c, g, j, n, m*; does not hear final consonants accurately

___ cannot tell direction sound is coming from

___ does not recognize common sounds for what they are

___ cannot filter out extraneous noise; cannot distinguish teacher's voice from others—hears wrong answers, steadfastly maintains "teacher said it" (Some children get very tense in noisy classroom)

___ does not follow directions

___ does not benefit from oral instruction

Spatial Relationships and Body Awareness Deficits

___ gets lost even in familiar surroundings such as school, neighborhood

___ directionality problems, does not always read or write left to write

___ no space between words

___ cannot keep columns straight in math

___ bumps into things; clumsy, accident prone

___ does not understand concepts such as *over, under, around, through, first, last, front, back, up, down*

Conceptual Deficits

___ cannot read social situations, does not understand body language

___ cannot see relationship between similar concepts

___ cannot compare how things are alike/different; classification activities are difficult

___ does not understand time relationships—*yesterday, today, tomorrow, after/before, 15 minutes versus 2 hours, "hurry"*

___ does not associate an act with its logical consequence. "If I talk, I get detention" (being punished for no reason. Unfair.)

___ little imagination

___ no sense of humor; cannot recognize a joke/pun

___ tends to be expressionless

____ slow responses

____ not able to create, to "think," to create poetry, original stories

____ cannot make closure; cannot read less than clear ditto; cannot finish a sentence such as "I like it when. . . ."; difficulty filling in blanks

____ excessively gullible

____ cannot do inferential thinking: What might happen next? Why did this happen?

____ great difficulty in writing

____ bizarre answers/or correct answers found in bizarre ways

____ cannot think in an orderly, logical way

____ does not understand emotions, concepts such as *beauty*, *bravery*

____ classroom comments are often "off track" or reasons in bizarre ways

____ difficulty grasping number concepts: *more/less*; >/<; can't estimate

____ mispronounces common words

Memory Deficits

____ cannot remember what was just seen (was shown)

____ cannot remember what was just heard

____ cannot remember sequence of 4 numbers given auditorally

____ cannot copy math problems accurately

____ cannot remember spelling for common/frequently encountered words

____ remembers things from long ago but not recent events

____ poor sight vocabulary—few words known to automatic level

____ slow to memorize rhymes/poem (makes many errors)

____ appears to know something one day but doesn't know it the next

____ limited expressive language; does not remember names for objects—"that thing"

____ limited receptive language

____ makes same error again and again; does not seem to benefit from experience

____ writing poor—cannot remember to capitalize, punctuate, skip a line, indent, and so on

Motor Output Deficits

____ perseveration—gives same response again and again

____ distortions in gross motor functions—cannot skip, hop, hit ball, and so on

____ difficulty cutting, pasting, coloring, writing, (can point to correct way to form a letter but cannot produce it on paper)

____ can point to correct spelling but cannot copy it accurately

____ can dictate story or paragraph but cannot write it

____ does not communicate orally to a degree appropriate for age

____ mouth noises

____ tics

Behavioral Components

Attention Deficit Disorder

___ good days—bad days

___ cannot sit still

___ cannot stand still

___ impulsive; does not consider consequence before acting

___ low frustration tolerance: short fuse

___ cannot finish assignments in allotted time

___ visually distractible; looks up to all visual stimuli

___ auditorally distractible; responds by looking up to noise

___ fidgety: drumming fingers, tapping toes, rolling pencil, fooling with objects; makes mouth noises; incessant talking

___ short attention span

___ spaces off—confused—does not sit up/head on desk/"tired"

___ negativistic/oppositional behavior

___ little work produced; daydreams

___ reads something correctly, but mind is elsewhere as evidenced in poor comprehension

___ overreacts to stimuli (cannot mind own business)

___ does not follow rules; often claims didn't hear them

___ may be cruel, mean to others; makes fun of them

___ mood swings

___ disorganizes; loses books, papers, lunch box, coat

Failure Syndrome

___ describes self as "dumb"

___ does not take reprimands well

___ tends to avoid group activity

___ avoids activity; does little; claims illness

___ daydreams/withdrawal

___ class clown—acting out behavior

___ immature behavior; babyish, seems younger, dependent

Serious Emotional Overlay

___ explosive, unpredictable, dangerous behavior, lashing out

___ preoccupation with death, destruction

___ no work produced, coupled with lack of enthusiasm for anything

___ tells bizarre stories and purports they really happened

___ shallow feeling for others

___ cannot distinguish reality from fantasy

___ withdraws; alone; little communication

___ feels "picked on"; uses projection, denial; never assumes responsibility for actions

___ fearful, anxious, insecure, tense

Used with permission from Joan Harwell, *Complete Learning Disabilities Handbook* (West Nyack, NY: The Center for Applied Research in Education, 1989).

National Organizations

National Center for Learning Disabilities
99 Park Avenue
New York, NY 10016
212-687-7211

Council for Learning Disabilities
P.O. Box 40303
Overland Park, KS 66204
913-492-8755

Council for Exceptional Children
1920 Association Drive
Reston, VA 22091-1589
1-800-232-7323

Learning Disabilities Association of America, Inc. (LDA)
4156 Library Road
Pittsburgh, PA 15234
412-341-1515

Orton Dyslexia Society
Chester Bldg., Suite 382
8600 La Salle Road
Baltimore, MD 21204

CHILDREN WITH ADHD

Attention Deficit Hyperactivity Disorder (ADHD) is believed by most experts in the field to be a neurobiological disorder characterized by developmentally abnormal degrees of inattention, impulsivity, and hyperactivity. ADHD often interferes with a child's ability to function with success academically, behaviorally and/or socially, and affects approximately 3 to 5 percent of the population. There are different subtypes of the disorder, which are all classified under the general term ADHD, and are defined under the new DSM-IV criteria. **Note:** The most current term or acronym for attention deficit hyperactivity disorder is AD/HD. However, the authors will be referring to ADD or ADHD throughout the text instead of AD/HD.

ADHD is often described by the medical/scientific community as a "neurological inefficiency" in the area of the brain that controls impulses, aids in screening sensory input, and focuses attention. According to the researchers, they have found that there is *less* activity (e.g., lower electrical activity, less blood flow) taking place in that portion of the brain. ADHD is viewed by many as a biological disorder of which there is a chemical imbalance or deficiency in certain chemicals called neurotransmitters in the area of the brain responsible for attention and activity, and the ability to inhibit or control behaviors. The causes of ADHD are not known, but it is most frequently attributed to heredity (genetic factors) as it commonly is found to run in families. Various prenatal factors, lead poisoning, and complications or trauma at birth have also been identified as possible causes of ADHD.

According to Dr. Russell Barkley, one of the leading experts in the field, it is a neurological disorder characterized by problems with *disinhibition* (controlling emotions, delaying responses, and ability to wait) and *sustaining attention, effort, and persistence.* Within the last few years scientific studies have shown that ADHD may perhaps not be primarily a disorder of paying attention, but one of self-regulation, of poor inhibition of behavior. Dr. Barkley states in his book *Taking Charge of ADHD* (1995) that "ultimately ADHD may be renamed to reflect this new view, perhaps as *behavioral inhibition disorder.*" ADHD causes highly inconsistent performance and output. It is not that children with ADHD lack the skill or ability, or know what to do; instead, they have difficulty demonstrating or acting on it with any consistency. When it comes to performance, it is very frustrating and perplexing to parents and teachers, because one day or minute the child is able to do the work, and the next he/she is not.

One of the most insightful and outstanding books on attention deficit disorder is written by two doctors whose practice is to treat children and adults with ADD. The authors of *Driven to Distraction*, Dr. Ned Hallowell and Dr. John Ratey, have ADD themselves and speak from personal experience and insight. Some of their descriptions of living with ADD are as follows: "You don't mean to do the things you do do, and you don't do the things you mean to do. People with ADHD live in distraction and chaos all the time—bombarded by stimuli from every direction and unable to screen it out." They also describe ADD similar to being nearsighted. "You don't focus very well . . . you have to strain to see clearly . . . and memories are porous." According to the doctors, medication used in the treatment of ADHD "helps take the static out of the broadcast. It works like a pair of eyeglasses, helping the individual to focus."

The clinical definition of ADHD is provided by the Diagnostic and Statistical Manual (DSM) of the American Psychiatric Association, and has been revised several times over the past 15 years. The most recent clinical definition of ADHD is in the new DSM-IV manual (4th edition, 1994). It contains 18 symptoms of ADHD which are listed in two separate categories:

Nine symptoms of **INATTENTION***:* fails to give close attention to details or making careless errors in schoolwork or other activities; has difficulty sustaining attention in tasks or play activities; often appears not to listen; does not follow through with instructions or fails to finish tasks (not due to resistance or a lack of understanding); has difficulty with organization; avoids tasks that require sustained mental effort such as schoolwork; loses things necessary for tasks or activities; is easily distracted by extraneous stimuli; is forgetful in daily activities.

Nine symptoms of **HYPERACTIVITY-IMPULSIVITY:** fidgets with hands or feet, or squirms in seat; is unable to sit during periods of time when remaining seated is expected; runs about or climbs excessively in inappropriate situations (with adolescents or adults this is usually manifested as restlessness); has difficulty playing quietly; is on the go constantly as if "driven by a motor"; talks excessively; blurts out answers to questions; interrupts others; has difficulty waiting in line or waiting turn in games.

DSM-IV sets an inclusion criterion (**six or more of the nine symptoms in a category must exist and have persisted for a length of time and degree that it is maladaptive and inconsistent with a child's developmental level**). The symptomatic problems must have persisted for at least six months in both of the categories. The onset of the hyperactivity-impulsivity symptoms must be no later than seven years of age, and present in at least two or more situations. **Three types of ADHD are possible: Inattentive (ADHD-I), Hyperactive-Impulsive (ADHD-HI), or Combined (ADHD-C).**

There are no objective tests (i.e., blood tests) to identify children with ADHD. In addition to meeting the DSM-IV diagnostic criteria for ADHD, a diagnosis is based on the following: special clinical interviews with parents and children; questionnaires and rating scales to be filled out by parents, teachers, and others working closely with the child; detailed health and developmental histories; and a thorough physical examination to rule out other medical problems. A comprehensive evaluation also includes a collection of work samples, observations of the child in a variety of settings, and often psycho-educational evaluations/assessments.

This information is interpreted by *clinicians* who must determine the pervasiveness of the symptoms (in different settings) over a period of time; and must also rule out a host of other possible causes. These could include: factors in home/personal life causing great stress or anxiety; depression; medical or psychological problems; learning problems; language disorders; auditory processing disabilities; substance abuse; etc., that produce similar symptoms and behaviors.

It is imperative that educators take great caution in their role of identifying students who may or may not have ADHD. Teachers must *not* be "diagnosing" ADHD or sending parents off to the doctor telling them that their child has ADD. The role of educators is to share objective observations and concerns about their students with parents. They need to consult with appropriate school personnel (school nurse, counselor, and other support staff) regarding those concerns and how to provide educational interventions and support to the child. Along with instructional, behavioral, and environmental modifications to assist the student, the teacher should be documenting these interventions and their effectiveness. The teacher should be communicating with parents about steps he/she is taking to help the student, and be establishing and building teamwork with parents.

The most effective way to facilitate referrals for evaluation of students who display the characteristics of ADHD is through the Student Study Team process. A multidisciplinary *team* approach to intervention, provision of information to parents, and a coordinated effort to meet the child's needs is recommended. The staff members most appropriate for making medical referrals are school nurses, *not* classroom teachers. (See Section 10, *Team Efforts.*)

Typical Characteristics and Behaviors of ADD/ADHD

At the elementary school level we see children with ADHD as highly impulsive (blurting out in class, acting on impulse, not being able to wait or delay gratification). They lack self-control and regulatory behavior, have a high activity level, trouble sitting, and are constantly touching or playing with nearby objects. They are distractible, and have trouble getting started on tasks, staying on task and completing assignments. These children have great difficulty sustaining attention and effort without prompting, incentives, and refocusing. They bore easily, usually are very disorganized, and have great difficulty with written work/output.

It is important to note that not all children with ADHD have these hyperactivity/impulsivity characteristics. There is that category of children who have the predominantly inattentive type of ADHD. These children usually have fewer disciplinary problems in school, as their behavior is not disruptive. However, they often have difficulty with achieving to their potential due to the other problems of output/performance deficiencies, distractibility, and inability to sustain attention and complete tasks. Many have accompanying learning disabilities as well.

Most individuals with ADHD continue to have symptoms persist through adolescence and adulthood. The behaviors caused by the disorder may change or manifest themselves differently as the child matures. Adolescents with ADHD show the following characteristics: erratic academic performance, underachievement, forgetfulness, inconsistency, bore easily and seek diversion, attraction to high stimulation/high-risk behavior, disorganization, impulsivity, problems with moodiness, often depressed, poor self-image, restlessness, fidgetiness, and difficulty getting started on tasks and following through.

Once again, we must remember to *focus on the positive*, and recognize all of the desirable traits that are also associated with having ADHD. Some of these traits include the following:

- resiliency
- ingenuity
- creativity
- spontaneity
- boundless energy
- sensitivity to the needs of others
- accepting and forgiving
- risk taking
- intuitive
- inquisitive
- imaginative
- inventive
- innovative
- resourceful
- empathetic

- good-hearted
- gregarious
- observant
- full of ideas and spunk

WHAT DO CHILDREN WITH ADHD AND/OR LEARNING DISABILITIES NEED?

- Clarity of expectations
- Structuring of work environment, tasks, and materials
- Assistance through transitions
- External assistance in helping to get and maintain attention
- Cueing, prompting, and reminders
- Active learning
- High-response opportunities
- Help with organization and study skills
- Multisensory instruction
- Learning-style accommodations
- Written output modifications
- Escape valve outlets
- Predictability of schedules and routines
- Extra time to process information and output/perform tasks
- Extra space
- Creative, engaging curriculum
- Help with coping skills and feelings of frustration
- Adaptations and modifications of the curriculum and environment
- Modeling and teacher-guided instruction
- Meaningful learning experiences that help them to make connections and see relevancy
- Choices
- Teaching strategies that build on their strengths and help bypass their weaknesses
- Teachers in their lives who are positive and flexible . . . who are encouragers and motivators, and are able to see past the behaviors to the *whole child*; they need teachers who have a sense of humor and make learning experiences both *novel and fun*

Note: How to Reach & Teach ADD/ADHD Children by Sandra Rief provides in-depth strategies/interventions and guidance on helping children with learning and attention difficulties.

See the end of this section for additional recommended resources regarding attention deficit hyperactivity disorder.

Federally Sponsored ADD Training and Dissemination Projects

Continuing Education Program on ADD, The Council for Exceptional Children, 1920 Association Drive, Reston, VA 22091; Phone: 703-620-3660.

Enhance Knowledge & Skills of Personnel to Meet the Needs of Students with ADD, University of Miami, School of Education, P.O. Box 248065, Coral Gables, FL 33124-2040; Phone: 305-284-3003.

Regional Consulting Center to Assist School Personnel Working with Adolescents with ADD, Lehigh University, Dept. of Counseling, School Psychology and Special Education, 111 Research Drive, Bethlehem, PA 18015; Phone: 215-758-3258.

Chesapeake Institute, ADD Resource Bank, 2030 M Street, N.W., Suite 810, Washington, D.C. 20036; Phone: 202-785-9360.

ADD Special Project, University of Alabama, Box 870231, Tuscaloosa, AL 35487; Phone: 205-348-7340.

Specialist Level Training Program to Serve Children & Youth with ADD, University of Kentucky, College of Education, Dept. of Education and Psychology, Lexington, KY 40506-0349; Phone: 606-257-1381

ADDNET—A Network of Live Broadcasts Concerning ADD, University of Georgia, 570 Aderhold Hall, Athens, GA 30602; Phone: 800-296-4770.

Preservice & Inservice Training Program for General and Special Educators, Parents, and Children with ADD, University of North Carolina at Chapel Hill, CDL, CB#7255, BSRL, Chapel Hill, NC 27599; Phone: 919-966-1020.

Development, Evaluation and Distribution of an ADD Inservice Program, Arkansas Children's Hospital, Pediatrics Dept., 800 Marshall, Little Rock, AR 72202; Phone: 501-320-1021.

Novelty Interventions for Youth with ADD, Purdue University, LAEB #5144, West LaFayette, IN 47907; Phone: 317-494-7332.

PROJECT ADEPT: Attention Deficit Education for Professionals & Teachers, University of Arizona, College of Education, Tucson, AR 85721; Phone: 602-621-3248.

SEA/IHE Collaborative Inservice, Preservice and Mini-Team Personnel Preparation Project for Service Students with ADD, Kansas State Board of Education, 120 SE 10th Avenue, Topeka, KS 66612; Phone: 913-296-3867.

ADD Special Project to Develop an Inservice Training Curriculum, University of Massachusetts at Boston, 100 Morrissey Boulevard, Boston, MA 02125-3393; Phone: 617-287-7250

JAADD ADD Project for Inservice Educator Training and Parent/Child Training, Jewish Association for ADD, 1416 Avenue M, Suite 202, Brooklyn, NY 11223; Phone: 718-376-3079

CHILDREN PRENATALLY EXPOSED TO DRUGS WHO ARE AT RISK

Over the past few years teachers (particularly in preschool and primary grades) have been feeling the impact of children in their classrooms who had been prenatally exposed to drugs. Now this first wave of children are moving up in the grades. There is very little known as to long-term effects of prenatal drug exposure. There are also many myths, particularly as to who is affected. The problem of drug-exposed babies crosses all socioeconomic and ethnic barriers. It impacts both rural and urban areas and school districts throughout the country.

According to a study by the National Association for Perinatal Addiction Research and Education in Chicago (Chasnoff, Landress, and Barrett, 1990), there was no significant difference between the percentage of middle- and upper-income women using drugs during pregnancy and low-income and minority women. Dr. Ira Chasnoff testified before a hearing of the Select Committee on Children, Youth, and Families of the House of Representatives (1986) about the importance of considerations other than prenatal exposure to drugs that effect the outcomes for school-age children. "It is not simply a matter of drug use. The issues are very complex, and the quality of parenting that each child receives from his parents is more a factor in the long-term outcome of these infants than their actual exposure to drugs." Dr. Chasnoff et al. (1992) further explained that "the long-term effects which will be found within the general population of drug-exposed children will not be explained by drug exposure alone. Before we can predict the developmental outcomes for these high risk children we need further research into the additive and interactive effects of the multiple risk factors to which they are exposed, including in many cases the global effects of poverty, multigenerational substance abuse, and the impact of growing up in a drug-seeking environment."

John Flynne, author of *Cocaine* (1991), states that "there are an estimated 5-6 million regular users of cocaine in the United States." Data compiled in 1988 indicate that one-half million children from 12-17 years of age had used cocaine during the past year. In young adults from 18-25 years of age, 3.5 million had used cocaine in the past year.

Congressman Charles B. Rangel testified to the House Select Committee on Children, Youth and Families in 1989 that 10 percent of pregnant women have tried cocaine at least once during their pregnancies. Rangel went on to say, "The National Institute of Drug Abuse estimates that there are 6.5 million people using drugs in a way that seriously impairs their health and ability to function. Yet nationwide, at any one time, there are only 240,000 drug abusers in treatment." (Referenced from: *Born Hooked Poisoned in the Womb*, compiled by Gary E. McCeun. Hudson, Wisconsin: Gary E. McCuen Publications, Inc.)

NAPARE (National Association for Perinatal Addiction Research and Education) conducted a nationwide survey of 36 hospitals (Ruhmkorff, 1989) finding 11 percent of the women in the hospitals had used illicit drugs, and that 10-20 percent of the deliveries tested positive to cocaine. Some physicians believe that as many as two-thirds of the children born with cocaine in their systems go undetected because hospitals do not routinely screen all newborns nor do many of them have screening protocols to follow (Conner, 1990).

According to Dr. Marie Kanne Poulson in a 1990 report she prepared for the California State Department of Education, "Educational Needs of Children at Risk Due to Factors Related to Substance Exposure," children prenatally exposed to drugs can be described as *low threshold* (showing uneven maturation of their neurological system in being able to control or modulate their own behavior in response to social or physical environments), hypersensitive, *and hyper-reactive* to sensory and emotional situations. "Their disorganized oftentimes out of bounds behavior, seen by many as destructive and intentional, stems from an overload of sensory or emotional input to the CNS (central nervous system)."

Dr. Poulson shares that the influence of drugs on the central nervous system creates a wider range of variability in the child's capacity for:

- organization of his/her play and daily living activities
- precision and direction of movement
- learning continuity and learning strategies
- sense of self and interactive behaviors

In the organization of play and daily living activities, one might see a child who is more distracted and less focused, has little self-initiation, and has little organized follow-through of play learning and self-help activities. In the area of precision/direction of movement, the child prenatally exposed to drugs may have difficulty with spatial relations and motor coordination. As for learning continuity this child may experience sporadic mastery; a concept, skill, or strategy he/she learned one day may have to be relearned another. The behavioral risk factors the prenatally exposed child might exhibit are: (1) shows behavioral extremes, (2) is easily overstimulated, (3) has a low tolerance for changes, (4) constantly tests the limits, (5) has difficulty in reading social cues, and (6) has difficulty with peer relationships (Poulson, 1990).

Currently, the scientific research has not yet proven any causal relationship between prenatal drug exposure and ADHD. The similarities in many of the characteristics, however, are striking. It is not surprising since with prenatal drug exposure the child's central nervous system is often affected, and he/she may have sustained neurological damage. However, just because some of the symptoms are the same, it does not mean that these children have ADHD. Nor does it mean that children who have ADHD and those who were prenatally exposed to drugs respond to the same treatments. It falls in the hands of the medical/scientific community to pursue the research and answers as to how we can best help these children, as far as any possible medical intervention is concerned.

Research as to effective practices in working with prenatally exposed children stresses the importance of: developmentally appropriate curriculum, structure and consistency, routines and rituals, flexible room environments, student readiness, and transition time plans. The following are some recommended strategies found effective for teaching children prenatally exposed to drugs. This partial list was extracted from one compiled by teachers in the Prenatally Exposed to Drugs (PED) Program at Salvin School. The Los Angeles Unified School District's Salvin School is one of the first pilot programs in the nation designed specifically for this population of children.

- Provide support and emotional reassurance.
- Establish classroom routines with minimum number of transitions.
- Consider the developmental level of the child.
- Use physical, concrete, and verbal cues to direct and redirect the child in tasks or activities.
- Recognize and consistently praise the child's attempts and accomplishments.

- Prepare for and guide through transitions.
- Provide the child a schedule of play and rest activities to help develop regular patterns.
- Respond to specific needs of the child with predictability and regularity.
- Elicit eye contact and/or touch the child before giving verbal commands.
- Talk the child through to the consequences of his/her actions.
- Provide the child with explicitly consistent limits of behavior.
- Use close proximity and gestures.
- Create a stable environment where the child feels safe to express feelings, wants, and needs.
- Use hands-on activities.
- Verbalize expected behaviors.
- Set consistent limits on inappropriate behavior, but allow for expression of feelings.
- Provide a variety of tactile and small-motor activities.

Salvin School has found that there is no typical profile for a drug-exposed child, but that impairments fall along a continuum from minimal symptomology to severe impairment in all areas of development (Cole, 1989.)

Once again, what research and experimentation are finding as to successful teaching practices and strategies for this population of children is very similar to what we know to be effective in meeting the needs of our other children (with ADHD or LD). This is good news to teachers who want to *reach and teach every child in their classrooms.* As educators it is our responsibility to do all we can to help our students be successful. Fortunately, we have it within our power to make a significant difference in the lives of our students. In spite of the difficulties they may be entering our classes with, the at-risk situations in which they may live, we *can* help considerably in overcoming those obstacles. We need to be careful not to automatically make assumptions as to the causes of some of our students' behaviors. We certainly have no right or qualifications to make judgments or attempt to diagnose! What we need to do as teachers is try as hard as possible to establish rapport and partnership with the family, and to provide the best education, interventions and support that we can.

Note: The authors are grateful to Carol Pearson Donahue who provided all of the research for this section in her doctoral dissertation (June, 1994) for the University of La Verne, California entitled: A Case Study: Strategies, Skills and Techniques Educators Will Need in Teaching Children Prenatally Exposed to Drugs as They Approach Kindergarten and Formal Education.

See the bibliography and recommended resources at the end of this section for more information.

STUDENTS WHO ARE LIMITED ENGLISH PROFICIENT

Our schools are filled with many children for whom English is not their primary language, and are limited in their English proficiency (LEP). Teachers need to have basic awareness of how a second language is acquired, and general recommended practices for instructing children who have not yet acquired the ability to understand or produce English.

One of the most accepted approaches to teaching second language acquisition (English to non-English proficient students) is the *natural approach* described by Tracy Terrel (1977, 1981). According to Terrel, there are four stages of second language acquisition: The *pre-production*, *early production*, *speech emergence*, and *intermediate fluency* stages.

The first stage of *pre-production* is a silent period for the learner that may last up to several months. During this time, the student is dependent upon modeling, visual aids and context clues to obtain and convey meaning. Lessons should focus on listening comprehension and building the student's receptive vocabulary. During the *early production stage* students begin to speak using one or two words or short phrases. Activities in class should be designed to motivate students to produce vocabulary they already understand. The *speech emergence stage* is when students start to speak in longer phrases and complete sentences. Lessons and activities are designed to develop higher levels of language use, and expand their receptive vocabulary. During this stage the student is able to respond to literal questions that have been made comprehensible. *Intermediate fluency* is the stage students reach when they are able to engage in conversation and produce full sentences. At this stage they should be challenged to produce responses requiring critical thinking skills and complex sentence structures.

Another leading expert on language acquisition is Dr. Stephen Krashen, who developed several important hypotheses on the acquisition of language. According to one of his hypotheses, everyone learning a language goes through a silent period. This is the period before speech is produced in either the first or second language, when the child must listen and develop an understanding of the language before beginning to speak (1980). According to Krashen's *natural order* hypothesis, grammatical structures are acquired in a predictable sequence, with certain elements usually acquired before others. He also poses his *affective filter hypothesis* and concludes that several affective variables are important in second language acquisition. These include low anxiety in the learning situation, high motivation, and self confidence.

Krashen also is responsible for the *comprehensible input hypothesis*, which states that growth in language occurs when the learner receives comprehensible input, or input which is just beyond what the learner already understands. According to the input hypothesis, it is the teacher's responsibility to provide speech modified to the point that a listener can understand the message and get the message across using visual or contextual clues, by dealing with familiar topics, using body language, etc. The input needs to be interesting and motivating and embedded in context so that the LEP student can move easily through the different natural stages of language acquisition.

Effective Strategies for Teaching LEP Students

- Use visuals/graphic representations with high frequency.
- Use a great deal of body language and gestures.
- Keep relevant maps, posters, and students' productions around the classroom.
- Don't teach vocabulary in isolation; use several examples and move from example to definition, and back to more carefully prepared examples.
- Build on students' prior experience.
- Increase wait time (at least 5 seconds) for student to respond to any question.

- Provide numerous opportunities to work in partners and triads, mixing the LEP student with a fluent English speaker. It is very helpful to work in triads or cooperative learning groups with bilingual, LEP, and one or two fluent English speakers as a team.
- Assign a student buddy to help whenever additional assistance is needed to understand directions.
- Create a comfortable environment that encourages risk-taking.
- Teach and model learning strategies.
- Provide more opportunities for classroom interaction.
- Slow down speech and repeat as needed.
- Paraphrase.
- Use fewer idioms and pronouns.
- Modify language to be more comprehensible for the proficiency level of the student.
- Use fewer multisyllabic words.
- Speak naturally, but slowly.
- Provide peer tutoring.
- Provide many opportunities for hands-on, active learning.
- Provide a great deal of background information to increase comprehensible input and comprehension.
- Preview and review material and lessons.
- Provide graphic organizers.
- Use dramatization and role play.
- Draw illustrations and pictures to define.
- Provide teacher modeling throughout all instruction.
- Provide students with many opportunities to respond to questions and verbalize without ridicule.
- Listen patiently and attentively to students.
- Try to assess the student's learning style, presenting information and using approaches that best reflect those learning preferences.
- Teach through relevant familiar topics.
- Focus on communication and comprehension.
- Teach key words/vocabulary in context.
- Utilize questioning techniques appropriate to the stage of language acquisition.
- Check frequently for understanding.
- Foster a low-anxiety environment in the classroom.
- Create an environment that gives the message to children that all linguistic and cultural backgrounds are recognized, appreciated, and valued.
- Use thematic/integrated teaching approaches.
- Focus on meaning and making connections in learning.
- Celebrate the students' efforts and successes.

- Make newly arrived students feel comfortable by providing fun activities and plenty of opportunity for listening.
- Facilitate LEP student involvement in games, sports, or activities. Through playing a game, one soon acquires the rules as well as the vocabulary in context.
- Provide a stimulating, supportive environment.
- Avoid correcting errors of pronunciation, structure, or vocabulary. Accept the student's effort or, if necessary, state the response correctly without comment.

One of the strengths of our nation is the diversity of our population. For example, California has the largest number of immigrant children within our schools; so our districts have been experimenting with strategies, techniques, and programs for meeting the needs of immigrant children more intensively than most districts in the country. These children bring with them a wealth of talent, global perspectives, and motivation to learn—great potential for educating us and enriching all of our lives. They also have many needs and face countless challenges as they enter our schools. As educators, we must do all we can to help them overcome the many obstacles, meet the challenge, and achieve success.

In an article entitled "The World Enrolls," written by Laurie Olsen and Marcia Tien-Hsiang Chen in *California Tomorrow* (Spring, 1988), the following statistics were provided: The number of immigrant students in California are up 250 percent in the last decade and they make up at least 5 percent of the student population in half of state school districts. Nearly all large districts are at least 15 percent limited English proficient; some districts are more than half immigrants.

Olsen and Tien-Hsiang Chen share, "School age immigrants from dozens of nations represent a potential filled and fast growing portion of California's future. Eager, almost desperate, for the two things public schools are designed to supply—socialization and knowledge—these young people relish the life and freedom of the U.S., yearn to fit in and learn, and study on average longer hours than their native-born peers. However, they also bring unique, sometimes daunting, needs. They generally don't speak English. Many have been psychologically traumatized—by war, the immigration journey, lack of documentation, and poverty. Many bring little formal education, and suffer from astounding culture shock here."

In the two-year study by *California Tomorrow* interviewing immigrant students as well as hundreds of teachers, parents, administrators, and community experts, Olsen and Tien-Hsiang Chen identified four broad areas prime for change. Though focused on immigrants, these "calls to action" seek to renovate how we educate *all* students:

Call to Action #1: *Cultural Orientation.* Immigrant children need a practical orientation to U.S. schools and what they do. Fear, intolerance, ethnocentrism, and prejudice prevail in the absence of information about each other. Schools should have classes that initiate communication between immigrants and others. Relations with immigrant parents and communities can be strengthened through orientations, native-language newsletters, advisory committees, etc.

Call to Action #2: *Counseling for Psychological Stress.* Many immigrant children have been through so much that schools' efforts to teach them English or subjects are wasted without counseling first. Whether from the schools themselves or community agencies, these students need bilingual counseling, peer discussion, and support groups—involving parents whenever possible. Teachers in districts heavily impacted by immigrant students need training in identifying and referring traumatized children.

Call to Action #3: *Teaching English.* Activities that teach immigrants English must become a central part of the schools. The state must recruit, train, and employ more bilingual teachers and aides. Excellent bilingual and ESL program models exist: the schools and districts that have them must spread the word; districts missing these resources must seek them out. In districts enrolling high percentages of immigrants, every teacher should be trained in English as a Second Language (ESL) techniques.

Call to Action #4: *Teaching Subjects While Teaching English.* Many of these children are not adequately assessed and are placed in situations where they become bored and angry over being held back academically. Others find themselves in classes way over their heads. For those with tremendous academic gaps to overcome, the sense of being so far behind can turn into hopelessness and discouragement.

The results of the two years of research by *California Tomorrow* is published in a 130-page report, "Crossing the Schoolhouse Border," which examines the needs of immigrant students, lists resources and model programs for serving them, and recommends action to policymakers, educators, communities and the media for educating and socializing newcomers. The report is available from: Ft. Mason Center, Bldg. B, San Francisco, CA 94123. See the end of this section for additional references and recommended resources.

CHILDREN WHO ARE GIFTED AND TALENTED

The category of "giftedness" is one that many people don't view as fitting under the umbrella of exceptionality or special needs. However, children who have very high intellectual functioning and/or academic skills are in need of instruction and educational opportunities that stretch their academic potential and meet their unique needs.

There may be quite a bit of variation from state to state and district to district in the criteria for serving gifted and talented populations of children. In California the program for teaching gifted and talented children is referred to as GATE. According to our district's GATE Curriculum Framework (published in 1991): "Current state legislation allows the district to select one or more of the following categories for identification of gifted and talented students:

- intellectual ability
- high achievement
- specific academic ability
- creative ability
- leadership ability
- visual and performing arts talent"

San Diego Unified School District identifies and offers programs to gifted and talented students in the following categories:

- *Intellectual ability:* Students who demonstrate exceptional intellectual development, whose general mental development is significantly accelerated beyond that of their chronological peers. (Mental ability is demonstrated by scores within the superior range on standardized tests of mental ability.)

- *High achievement:* Students who consistently produce advanced ideas and products and/or score exceptionally high on achievement tests. (These are students with superior achievement in reading, language or math as demonstrated by superior scores in two total areas over a timespan of two years.)
- *Specific academic ability:* Students who consistently function at highly advanced levels in particular academic/ability areas (secondary level only).

The Curriculum Framework continues, "The GATE program views gifted and talented students as those possessing the *potential for excellence* as reflected in superior ability levels that may include several dimensions such as abstract thinking, linguistic ability, creative processing, logical reasoning, persistence and concentration, visual reasoning, etc. The traditional perception of intelligence is seen as too narrow and is not adequate in the fair assessment of all students who possess such a capacity for excellence. Evidence of the student's eligibility for the Gifted and Talented program must be based upon multiple criteria, with documentation of these traits attained from a variety of sources."

Recommendations for Meeting the Needs of Gifted Children

- Revolve instructional practices around abstract, complex understandings.
- Focus discussions, presentations, and materials on concepts and generalizations that transfer within and across disciplines.
- Build abstractness and complexity into the curriculum.
- Allow for higher levels of thinking and processing.
- Use a high percentage of open-ended activities that stimulate further thinking and investigation.
- Use discovery approaches, allowing students to use their inductive reasoning processes to discover patterns, ideas, and underlying principles.
- Provide students the opportunity to express their reasoning and how they went about solving problems.
- Involve student products with real problems presented to real audiences.
- Allow for many choices in activities and projects.
- Use a variety of methods that maintain students' interests and accommodate different learning styles.
- Use a student-centered, personalized learning environment.
- Focus on independence and student initiative.
- Have an accepting, nonjudgmental environment.
- Provide challenging tasks, complex ideas, and sophisticated methods.
- Use various and flexible instructional methods and styles.
- Focus on the teacher as an instructional manager/facilitator.
- Use community resources and resource persons.
- Telescope the common core; teach conventional subject matter in less time, allowing for acceleration of conventional curriculum.
- Vary the pacing for learning by appropriation of longer or shorter time spans based on students' needs and abilities.

- Use programmatic augmentation, adding dimensionality (depth and scope) to the conventional curriculum.
- Use relevant, interdisciplinary, thematic teaching across the curriculum.
- Use a qualitatively differentiated program that modifies or adjusts the content, process, product, and learning environment in ways that build on and extend the special characteristics of gifted students.
- Expand basic skills.
- Use out-of-school augmentation, providing students opportunities to apprentice with outstanding producers and performers. Provide field trips, seminars, and other out-of-school educational opportunities.
- Create opportunities and options.
- Use project-oriented curriculums.
- Use novel approaches.
- Provide mentorship opportunities.
- Make available technology and information access.

Characteristics of Gifted Children

- Highly curious, questioning
- Often plays/clowns around, but tests well
- Discusses in detail/elaborates
- Shows strong feelings and opinions
- Constructs abstractions
- Prefers adults
- Prefers to work alone
- Draws inferences
- Initiates projects
- Is intense
- Manipulates information
- Creative/inventive
- Is a good guesser
- Thrives on complexity
- Is keenly observant
- Is highly self-critical

See the end of this section for recommended resources and references regarding children who are gifted. You might also contact the following association for additional information:

National Association for Gifted Children
1155 15th Street, NW, Suite 1002
Washington, D.C. 20005
202-785-4268

BIBLIOGRAPHY AND RESOURCES FOR HELPING
CHILDREN WITH LEARNING DISABILITIES

Bloom, Jill. *Help Me to Help My Child: A Sourcebook for Parents of Learning Disabled Children.* Boston: Little Brown, 1990.

Brooks, Robert. *The Self-Esteem Teacher.* Circle Pines, MN: American Guidance Services, Inc., 1991.

Cummings, Rhoda, and Fisher, Gary. *The School Survival Guide for Kids with Learning Differences.* (Free Spirit Catalog and Hawthorne Educational Services, Inc.), 1991.

Greene, Lawrence J. *Learning Disabilities and Your Child.* New York: Fawcett Columbine, 1987.

Harwell, Joan M. *Complete Learning Disabilities Handbook.* West Nyack, NY: The Center for Applied Research in Education, 1989.

Levine, Melvin. *All Kinds of Minds.* Cambridge: Educator Publishing Service, Inc., 1993.

Levine, Melvin. *Keeping a Head in School.* Cambridge: Educator Publishing Service, Inc., 1990.

Levine, Melvin. "Learning Disorders and the Flow of Expectations," *Their World Magazine,* a publication of the National Center for Learning Disabilities, 99 Park Avenue, New York, NY 10016.

McMurchie, Susan. *Understanding Learning Differences* (Available from Free Spirit catalog)

Pierangelo, Roger, and Jacoby, Robert. *Parents' Complete Special Education Guide.* West Nyack, NY: The Center for Applied Research in Education, 1996.

Shapiro, Edward. *Academic Skills Problems: Direct Assessment and Intervention,* 2nd Ed., New York: Guilford Press, 1996.

Shapiro, Edward. *Academic Skills Problems Workbook.* New York: Guilford Press, 1996.

Silver, Larry B. *The Misunderstood Child: A Guide for Parents of Children with Learning Disabilities.* Blue Ridge Summit, PA: TAB Books, 1992.

Smith, Sally L. "How to Spot Learning Disabilities in Children," *Bottom Line,* Vol. 8, No. 5, March 15, 1987.

Smith, Sally L. *Succeeding Against the Odds—How the Learning Disabled Can Realize Their Promise.* New York: G.P. Putnam's Sons, 1991.

Videotapes

Lavoie, Rick. *How Difficult Can This Be?* (F.A.T. [Frustration, Anxiety, Tension] City Learning Disability Workshop) Available through A.D.D. Warehouse or PBS Video, 1320 Braddock Place, Alexandria, VA 22314; Phone: 1-800-424-7963.

I'm Not Stupid. Videocassette, 51 minutes. Gannett Broadcasting Group. Available through: Learning Disabilities Association of America, 4156 Library Road, Pittsburgh, PA 15234; Phone: 412-341-1515.

Page Fright: Inside the World of the Learning Disabled. Videocassette, 28 minutes. Available through: Filmmakers Library, 124 East 40th Street, New York, NY 10016.

Rief, Sandra. *How Can I Help My Child Succeed in School?* (*Strategies and Guidance for Parents of Children with AD/HD and Learning Disabilities*). Available through Educational Resource Specialists, P.O. Box 19207, San Diego, CA, 92159; Phone 1-880-682-3528.

BIBLIOGRAPHY AND RESOURCES FOR
HELPING CHILDREN WITH ADHD

CH.A.D.D.
499 NW 70th Avenue, Suite 308
Plantation, FL 33317
305-587-3700

This is the national organization of Children and Adults with Attention Deficit Disorder). CH.A.D.D. has national, state and local chapters, conferences, conventions, etc., and produces two excellent publications (*Attention!* and *CHADDER Box*) with up-to-date information and articles and other resources.

There are also many other local support groups dedicated to providing information and support to families with ADD/ADHD. Ask your school nurse, local hospitals, physicians, and other parents of children with ADD regarding what supports are available in your community.

Recommended Books

Bain, Lisa J. *The Children's Hospital of Philadelphia: A Parent's Guide to Attention Deficit Disorders.* New York: Delta Books, 1991.

Barkley, Russell A. *Taking Charge of ADHD—The Complete, Authoritative Guide for Parents.* New York: Guilford Publications, Inc. 1995.

Coleman, Wendy. *Attention Deficit Disorders, Hyperactivity & Associated Disorders—A Handbook for Parents and Professionals.* Madison, WI: Calliope (2115 Chadbourne Avenue, 53705-3927), 1993.

Dendy, Chris A. Zeigler. *Teenagers with ADD—A Parents' Guide.* Bethesda, MD: Woodbine House, 1995.

DuPaul, George and Stoner, Gary. *ADHD in the Schools: Assessment and Intervention Strategies.* New York: Guilford Press, 1994.

Flick, Grad L. *Power Parenting for ADD/ADHD: A Parent's Guide for Managing Difficult Behaviors.* West Nyack, NY: The Center for Applied Research in Education, 1996.

Fowler, Mary C. *Maybe You Know My Kid: A Parent's Guide to Identifying, Understanding and Helping Your Child With Attention Deficit Disorder.* New York: Carol Publishing Group, 1990.

Goldstein, Sam and Goldstein, Michael. *Hyperactivity: Why Won't My Child Pay Attention?* New York: John Wiley & Sons, 1992.

Goldstein, Sam. *Understanding and Managing Children's Classroom Behavior.* New York: John Wiley & Sons, 1995.

Hallowell, Edward and Ratey, John. *Driven to Distraction.* New York: Pantheon Books, 1994.

Ingersoll, Barbara, and Goldstein, Sam. *Attention Deficit Disorder and Learning Disabilities (Realities, Myths and Controversial Treatments).* New York: Doubleday, 1993.

Johnson, Dorothy Davies. *I Can't Sit Still: Educating & Affirming Inattentive and Hyperactive Children*. Santa Cruz, CA: ETR Associates, 1992.

Jones, Claire. *Sourcebook for Children with Attention Deficit Disorder—A Management Guide for Early Childhood Professionals and Parents*. Tucson, AZ: Communication Skill Builders, 1991.

Moss, Robert A. *Why Johnny Can't Concentrate: Coping with Attention Deficit Problems*. New York: Bantam Books, 1990.

Parker, Harvey. *The ADD Hyperactivity Handbook for Schools*. Plantation, FL: Impact Publications, 1993.

Parker, Harvey. *The ADD Handbook for Parents, Teachers and Kids*. Plantation, FL: Impact Publications, 1988.

Rief, Sandra. *How to Reach and Teach ADD/ADHD Children*. West Nyack, NY: The Center for Applied Research in Education, 1993.

Shapiro, Edward, and Cole, Christine. Behavior *Change in the Classroom: Self-Management Interventions*. New York: Guilford Publications, Inc., 1994.

Wodrich, David L. *What Every Parent Wants to Know: Attention Deficit Hyperactivity Disorder*. Baltimore: Paul H. Brookes Publishing Co., 1994.

Videotapes

ADHD: *Inclusive Instruction & Collaborative Practices* (developed and presented by Sandra Rief) 38 min., 1995. National Professional Resources, Inc. Also available through Educational Resource Specialists, Phone: 1-800-682-3528; CEC catalog; and ADD Warehouse.

Inclusion of Children and Youth with Attention Deficit Disorder (Bruce Buehler, M.D. and Joseph Evans, Ph.D.) 40 min., National Professional Resources, Inc.

ADHD in Adolescence: The Next Step (Arthur Robin, Ph.D.) 90 min., Available through ADD Warehouse.

ADHD: What Do We Know? (Russell A. Barkley, Ph.D.) 35 min., Guilford Press Video.

ADHD: What Can We Do? (Russell A. Barkley) 35 min., Guilford Press Video.

ADHD in the Classroom: Strategies for Teachers (Russell A. Barkley) 40 min. (focus is on younger students) Guilford Press Video.

Answers to A.D.D.—The School Success Tool Kit (John F. Taylor). 102 min., Salem, OR: Sun Media 1992.

Why Won't My Child Pay Attention? (Sam Goldstein, Ph.D. and Michael Goldstein, M.D.) 76 min., Salt Lake City,: Neurology, Learning and Behavior Center, 1989.

Educating Inattentive Children (Sam Goldstein, Ph.D. and Michael Goldstein, M.D.) 120 min. Salt Lake City: Neurology, Learning and Behavior Center, 1990.

Education of Children with Attention Deficit Disorder. A kit for parents and educators including a video for parents (*Facing the Challenges of ADD*), a video for teachers (*One Child in Every Classroom*) and other written information from the Division of Innovation and Development, Office of Special Education Programs, Office of Special Education and Rehabilitation Services, U.S. Dept. of Education), 1995.

BIBLIOGRAPHY AND RESOURCES FOR HELPING AT-RISK CHILDREN PRENATALLY EXPOSED TO DRUGS

National Association for Perinatal Addiction Research and Education (NAPARE)
11 E. Hubbard Street, Suite 200
Chicago, Illinois 60611
312-329-2512

Salvin Elementary School
Prenatally Exposed to Drugs (PED)Program
Los Angeles Unified School District
1925 Budlong Avenue
Los Angeles CA 90007

Project DAISY (another nationally recognized program for PED children)
District of Columbia Public Schools
415 12th Street NW, Room 415
Washington, D.C. 20004

Hillsborough Educational Partnership Foundation of Tampa
Hillsborough County Schools
1202 East Palm Avenue
Tampa, FL 33605

Request a catalog from ONCADI Publications
National Clearinghouse for Alcohol and Drug Information (ONCADI)
Office for Substance Abuse Prevention (OSAP)
P.O. Box 2345
Rockville, MD 20847-2345
1-800-729-6686

Council of Exceptional Children (CEC) Resources Catalog
Dept. K4092
1920 Association Drive
Reston, VA 22091-1589
1-800-232-7323

National Professional Resources
25 South Regent Street
Port Chester, NY 10573
1-800-453-7461

Chasnoff, Ira J. Cited in Ninety-ninth Congress, 1986. *Placing Infants at Risk: Parental Addiction and Disease.* Hearing before the Select Committee on Children, Youth and Families, House of Representatives, Washington, D.C.: U.S. Government Printing Office.

Chasnoff, Ira J. "Use treatment, not punishment." In *Born Hooked Poisoned in the Womb*, compiled by Gary E. McCuen. Hudson, WI: Gary E. McCuen Publications, Inc., 1989.

Chasnoff, Ira J., M.D., Landress, Harvey J., A.C.S.W., and Barrett, Mark E., Ph.D. "The Prevalence of Illicit Drug or Alcohol Use During Pregnancy and Discrepancies In Mandatory Reporting in Pinellas County, Florida." *The New England Journal of Medicine*, 322 (April 1990): 1202-1206.

Chasnoff, Ira J., M.D., Griffith, Dan R., Ph.D., Freier, Catherine, Ph.D., and Murry, James, Ph.D. "Cocaine/Polydrug Use in Pregnancy: Two-Year Follow-Up." *Pediatrics*, 89 (February 1992): 284-289.

Cole, Carol K. *Young Children at Risk Due to Prenatal Substance Exposure*. Los Angeles: LA Unified School District, 1989.

Conner, Kim. *California's Drug-Exposed Babies: Undiscovered, Unreported, Underserved*. Sacramento, CA: Joint Publications, 1990.

Davis, Diane. *Reaching Out to Children with FAS/FAE*. West Nyack, NY: The Center for Applied Research in Education, 1994.

Donahue, Carol Pearson. *A Case Study: Strategies, Skills and Techniques Educators Will Need in Teaching Children Prenatally Exposed to Drugs as They Approach Kindergarten and Formal Education*, doctoral dissertation for the University of LaVerne, CA., 1994.

Flynne, John. *Cocaine*. New York: Carol Publishing Group, 1991.

National Association of State Directors of Special Education. *Children Exposed in Utero to Illegal Drugs: Education's Newest Crisis*. Liaison Bulletin. January 19, 1992.

Odom-Winn, Danni, and Dunagan, Dianne E. *Prenatally Exposed Kids in School*. Baldwin, NY: Educational Activities, Inc., 1991.

Poulson, Marie Kanne. *Perinatal Substance Abuse, What's Best for the Children. A report by the Child Development Program Advisory Committee*. Sacramento: State of California Child Development Program Advisory Committee, 1992.

Poulson, Marie Kanne, Ph.D.. *Educational Needs of Children at Risk Due to Factors Related to Substance Exposure*. Prepared for the California State Department of Education, 1990.

Rangel, Charles B. "A Comprehensive National Anti-Drug Strategy Is Needed." In *Born Hooked Poisoned in the Womb*, compiled by Gary E. McCuen. Hudson, WI: Gary E. McCuen Publications, Inc., 1989.

Ruhmkorff, Ann K. "Drug Addicted Babies: A National Perspective." In *Born Hooked Poisoned in the Womb*, compiled by Gary E. McCuen. Hudson, WI: Gary E. McCuen Publications, Inc., 1989.

Villareal, Sylvia Fernandez, McKinney, Lora-Ellen, and Quackenbush, Marcia. *Handle with Care: Helping Children Prenatally Exposed to Drugs and Alcohol*. Santa Cruz, CA: ETR Associates, 1992.

BIBLIOGRAPHY AND RESOURCES FOR HELPING LEP CHILDREN

Crawford, Alan N., Ph.D. "Research Update—Second Language Acquisition." *The California Reader*, September/October, 1982. V-2A to V-12D.

Duvall, Lynn. *Respecting Our Differences—A Guide to Getting Along in a Changing World,* 1994. Available through Free Spirit catalog, for ages 13 and up.

Garcia, Shernaz B. *Addressing Cultural & Linguistic Diversity in Special Education—Issues and Trends,* 1994. Available through Council for Exceptional Children catalog.

Krashen. D.D. *Bilingual Education and Second Language Acquisition Theory. Schooling and Language Minority Students: A Theoretical Framework.* Sacramento: Office of Bilingual Bicultural Education; California State Department of Education, 1981.

Olsen, Laurie, and Tien-Hsiang Chen, Marcia. "The World Enrolls." *California Tomorrow.* Spring, 1988. 8-20.

Terrel, T.D. "A Natural Approach to Second Language Acquisition and Learning." *Modern Language Journal,* 1977. Vol. 61. 325-337.

Terrel, T.D. *The Natural Approach in Bilingual Education. Schooling and Language Minority Students: A Theoretical Framework.* Sacramento: Office of Bilingual Bicultural Education, California State Department of Education, 1981.

BIBLIOGRAPHY AND RESOURCES FOR HELPING GIFTED CHILDREN

Clark, Barbara. *Growing Up Gifted: Developing the Potential of Children at Home and at School.* Columbus: Merrill Publishing Co., 1992.

Gallagher, James J., and Gallagher, Shelagh. *Teaching the Gifted Child.* Boston: Allyn & Bacon, Inc., 1994.

Kamiy, Artie, and Reiman, Alan. *Curriculum Activities for Gifted and Motivated Elementary Students.* West Nyack, NY: Parker Publishing Company, 1987.

Maker, C. June, and Nielson, Aleen B. *Teaching Models in Education of the Gifted.* Austin, TX: Pro-Ed, 1995.

Renzulli, Joseph S. *Schools for Talent Development: A Practical Plan for Total School Improvement,* 1994. Available through CEC catalog.

San Diego City Schools GATE CURRICULUM FRAMEWORK. July, 1991. Available from: San Diego City Schools, Schools Services Division, Exceptional Programs Department, Dana Administrative Center, Room 247, 1775 Chatsworth Boulevard, San Diego, CA 92107.

Schmitz, Connie C., and Galbraith, Judy. *Managing the Social and Emotional Needs of the Gifted: A Teacher's Survival Guide.* Available through Free Spirit catalog. Minneapolis, MN: Free Spirit Publishing, 1985.

Van Tassel-Baska, Joyce. *Planning Effective Curriculum for Gifted Learners.* 1992. Available through CEC catalog.

Winebrenner, Susan. *Teaching Gifted Kids in the Regular Classroom: Strategies and Techniques Every Teacher Can Use to Meet the Academic Needs of the Gifted & Talented.* 1992. Available through CEC catalog and Free Spirit catalog.

RECOMMENDED CATALOGS OF VENDORS

ADD Warehouse
300 Northwest 70th Avenue, Suite 102
Plantation, FL 33317
1-800-233-9273
(Resources for parents, teachers, children and other professionals regarding ADHD)

Hawthorne Educational Services, Inc.
800 Gray Oak Drive
Columbia, MO 65201
1-800-542-1673
(Resources on pre-referral ADD, LD, speech/language, behavior, gifted, early childhood, etc.)

National Professional Resources, Inc.
Dept. C95
25 South Regent Street
Port Chester, NY 10573
1-800-453-7461
(Resources on ADHD, LD, special education inclusion, school discipline and violence prevention, collaboration and teaming, school reform and management, children and youth at risk, multicultural, etc.)

Free Spirit Publishing
400 First Avenue North, Suite 616
Minneapolis, MN 55401-1730
1-800-735-7323
(Resources on parenting and teaching, self-help for kids, creative learning, learning differences, gifted and talented)

Council for Exceptional Children Resources, CEC Publications,
1920 Association Dr., Dept. K4092
Reston, VA 22091-1589
1-800-232-7323
(Resources on teaching practices, inclusive schools, collaboration, school reform, transition, life and work skills, gifted, ADD, behavioral disorders, cultural diversity, at risk, etc.)

The Master Teaching Planning Catalog
Leadership Lane
P.O. Box 1207
Manhattan, KS 66502-0038
1-800-669-9633
(Resources on ADHD, inclusion, at risk, discipline, etc.)

OTHER NATIONAL ORGANIZATIONS/ASSOCIATIONS FOR HELPING CHILDREN WITH SPECIAL NEEDS

Council for Exceptional Children
1920 Association Drive
Reston, VA 22091-1589

National Information Center for Children & Youth with Disabilities
P.O. Box 1492
Washington, D.C. 20013-1492
1-800-999-5599

American Speech-Language-Hearing Association
10801 Rockville Pike
Rockville, MD 20852

Tourette Syndrome Association
4240 Bell Boulevard.
Bayside, NY 11361-2874
718-224-2999

American Occupational Therapy Association
1383 Piccard Drive
Rockville, MD 20852

American Psychological Association
1200 17th Street, N.W.
Washington, D.C. 20036

INTERVENTIONS AND ADAPTATIONS FOR ACCOMMODATING SPECIAL NEEDS

This section is designed to provide suggested interventions and adaptations you may wish to use in your attempt to provide inclusive education for all students. They may be helpful as pre-referral strategies; or considered when writing IEPs or 504 Intervention Plans. Many of these interventions are critical for the success of students, particularly those with learning disabilities and/or ADHD. We need to look at accommodations for students that allow them to bypass as best as possible their areas of disability. Inclusive classroom teachers are open and willing to examine which factors need to be adjusted or modified (instructional, environmental, organization, behavior management, assessment, etc.) in order for each student to achieve success.

FOR STUDENTS HAVING DIFFICULTY WITH ATTENTION & DISTRACTIBILITY

- Make use of non-verbal signals (e.g., flashing lights, ringing a bell) to cue students prior to transitions, or to stop all activity and focus on teacher.
- Increase teacher proximity to student (standing near or seated close by).
- Provide preferential seating: up front; within cueing distance of the teacher; away from doors, windows, and high-traffic areas of the room.
- Seat distractible students surrounded by well-focused students, and with good role model(s) facing them.
- Increase physical prompting of student (e.g., hand on shoulder).
- Increase visual prompting/cueing of student (eye contact, private hand-signals).

- Increase auditory cues and signals to student (private signal words to serve as reminders).
- Vary tone of voice when presenting to students (avoid monotone).
- Present at a snappy, lively pace.
- Keep 'brevity' in mind (instruction, explanations, etc.).
- Provide study carrels or partitions to reduce visual distractions during seatwork or test-taking as appropriate. (*Note:* These "privacy boards" or "office areas" should not be used if they are viewed by the students in the class as punitive measures, or in singling out certain students only).
- Provide earphones for students to reduce auditory distractions as appropriate, preferably not the kind that have cords as part of a listening post. Have four or five sets of earphones available and encourage experimentation among all students.
- Provide more physical work space
- Have student clear desk of distractors (allowing only essential items to the task on the desk)

Some children, such as those with ADHD, have the need to touch objects for stimulation to keep alert and focused. Experiment after making private arrangements with the student. It may be necessary to remove all of these toys/objects or it may be helpful to allow the use if controlled. For example:

- Allow some children with the need to have something in their hands to try holding a small piece of clay, play dough, or squishy ball—as long as it stays within their hand and is not a distractor to others. Allow some children to attach something to a belt loop that they can touch, such as a keychain with a small object attached.
- Use a timer to complete certain tasks and then reward student for completion or on-task behavior during that time segment.
- Assign seatwork tasks that are at the appropriate level, and can be done independently.
- "Block" pages of work assigned as seatwork so that it doesn't overwhelm or cause a student to give up or completely avoid the task. Blocking pages means to cover up part of the page or folding it in segments so that lesser amounts are visible at one time. This is very helpful if someone can monitor/give feedback after the shorter blocks of work are completed. Breaking the assignment into these smaller chunks helps keep students more motivated and on-task, as well as reducing frustration.
- Actually cut assignments or work pages in half, giving only one half at a time.
- Reward students for a certain number of completed items that are done with accuracy.
- Provide the student with written examples for reference.
- Color highlight directions and important words on the assignment.
- Provide guided practice before having a student work independently on the task.
- Provide a study guide or some graphic tool for students to use accompanying verbal presentation. *Note:* It is helpful for maintaining attention to be jotting down a few words or filling in missing words in a guided format.
- Make sure necessary supplies are available.
- Allow students to ask buddies for clarification on seatwork.

- Utilize a contract for on-task behavior with positive incentives and perhaps response costs.

- Significantly increase opportunities for active student involvement in the lesson, and utilize questioning techniques that engage all students (See Section 11 *Effective Questioning Techniques in the Classroom*)

FOR STUDENTS NEEDING INTERVENTION TO BYPASS MEMORY DIFFICULTIES

- Teach and practice how to categorize and chunk information.
- Teach a variety of *mnemonic (memory) devices* and strategies:

  —**How to make associations** (visually, conceptually, or auditorily to help memorize). For example, given a group of words or terms, teach how to place in categories. Look for ways the items go together, sound alike, look alike, etc., to help remember.

  —**How to pair** unfamiliar, new terminology with similar sounding, familiar words. There is a technique called *Key Word* mnemonics that is very helpful in remembering new vocabulary. For example, *eclectic*, which means "selecting from various sources" sounds similar to "electric." There is electricity in many sources. So, for some people, making an association between eclectic and electric may help them remember. To make the association even stronger, one can visualize someone who stuck a finger in an electrical socket and has hair sticking out in all directions, or many different places.

  —How to draw and **visualize ridiculous pictures** that create a vivid image. This technique greatly aids recall of rote information

  —**Use of acronyms** (D.E.A.R. = "Drop everything and read").

- Teach how to make up silly sentences with the beginning letter of each word in the sentence standing for information to be memorized in sequence. For example, to learn the planets in sequential order from the sun (Mercury, Venus, Earth, Mars, Jupiter, Saturn, Uranus, Neptune, Pluto), encourage students to invent a silly sentence they can remember (and hopefully visualize) such as "Mary's very elegant monster just swallowed up nine porcupines."

- Use this technique for remembering spelling patterns/rules such as: "Generally double letters f, s, l, z when they follow a short vowel." (ie. cuff, stiff, pass, mess, toss, fuss, will, bell, dull, fizz, jazz. Four silly little zebras represents letters f,s,l,z. By recalling that phrase, it can aid the recall of those spelling patterns.

- Teach and practice visualizing with huge size, lots of color and motion.

- Teach and model how to practice memorizing by repeating the information orally several times

- Teach how to memorize small chunks of information by reading, covering the information up and saying verbally, checking self, writing down key words, etc.

- Have students repeat instructions given by teacher back to the teacher before beginning the task.

- Have students paraphrase instructions or information to be learned.
- Color highlight important information and concepts to be learned.
- After directions are given, have student tell his/her partner what he/she is to do.
- Increase the amount of practice and review in a variety of formats.
- Require that students write down all assignments, preferably on an assignment calendar that is kept in the same place consistently.
- Teach, model, and expect all assignments to be recorded, and monitor that students have done so. This often requires monitoring by way of teacher initialing assignment calendar, or student partners check each other and initial each other's assignment calendar.
- Utilize checklists and things-to-do lists.
- Allow use of tools and aids, such as multiplication charts and tables, spell-check devices (e.g. Franklin Speller).
- Encourage use of electronic organizers

FOR STUDENTS NEEDING ADAPTATIONS IN TESTING/ASSESSMENT

Note: The following is an extensive list of possible adaptations to be considered when trying to provide a fair assessment of students' learning. Included are some recommendations that teachers should keep in mind when preparing exams for all students. Some of the other interventions should be considered as special accommodations for students with moderate to severe reading, writing, or attention difficulties, who are unable to demonstrate their comprehension or mastery of the content material under normal testing conditions and criteria.

- Provide students with all handouts/test copies that are easy to read (typed, clear language, at least double-spaced, clean copies, ample margins).
- Avoid handwritten tests.
- Eliminate unnecessary words and confusing language on the test.
- State directions in clear terms and simple sentences.
- Underline or color highlight directions or key words in the directions.
- Provide opportunities for short-answer assessment (multiple choice, matching).
- On vocabulary tests give the definition and have student supply the word, rather than providing the word and student needing to write out the definition.
- Provide word bank to select from for fill-in-the-blank tests.
- Allow extended time for completing the test.
- Take exam in the classroom, then in a small group or with special education teacher and average the two grades.
- Provide students an example when possible of different types of test questions they will be responsible for on the exam.
- Provide more workspace on the tests (particularly for math tests).

- Allow students to use graph paper or other paper to solve math problems and attach to test, rather than require that computation must be done on the limited work space directly on the test.

- Enlarge the print.

- Divide a test in parts, administering on different days rather than rushing students to complete lengthy tests in one class period.

- Allow student to retake the test orally after given in written form to add points to his/her score if he/she is able to demonstrate greater knowledge/mastery than shown on written tests (especially for essay questions).

- Administer frequent short quizzes throughout the teaching unit and review the next day; thus providing feedback to students on their understanding of the material. These short quizzes do not need to be graded for a score, but to help students in their learning and confidence prior to the exam.

- Substitute an oral for a written test as appropriate.

- Assign take-home tests on occasion.

- Allow taped tests if needed, and permit student to tape-record answers to essay questions rather than write them.

- Read test items orally to student(s).

- Don't penalize for spelling, grammar, etc., on tests that are measuring mastery of content in other areas.

- Give credit for what is done correctly.

- Read aloud the directions for the different parts of the test before students begin the exam.

- Before providing final grade on test, point out test items that you spot are incorrect, and allow student to try self-correcting careless errors before scoring.

- Give reduced spelling lists for students who struggle with spelling; for example, 15 words rather than 20 or 25. When dictating the words on the test, dictate those 15 words in any order first; then continue with the other words for the rest of the class. Those students on modified lists have the option of trying the additional words for bonus points. (See Section 12 *Motivating Techniques for Teaching Spelling and Vocabulary*)

- Score tests for number correct/total number assigned per student (which can be shortened assignments or tests for individual students).

- Eliminate need for students with writing difficulties to copy test questions from the board or book before answering.

- Teach students the strategies and skills for taking a variety of tests (true/false, multiple choice, fill in the blank, essay, fill in the bubble, etc.).

- Practice all types of testing formats.

- Collaborate with special educators to rewrite the tests for special needs students (shorter sentences, simplified vocabulary, easier to read format).

- Test what has been taught.

- Avoid questions that are worded in a way to deliberately trick the student.

- Write multiple-choice questions with choices listed vertically rather than horizontally (as it is easier to read).
- Utilize portfolio assessment (progress evaluated on individual performance and improvement as opposed to comparing to other students).
- Reduce weight of test grade.
- Color the processing signs on math tests for students who don't focus well on details and make careless errors due to inattention. For example, highlight yellow = addition problem, green = subtraction, blue = multiplication.
- Utilize privacy boards at desks during test-taking time, and/or find other means of reducing distractions when students are tested.
- Allow use of a calculator on math tests that are assessing problem-solving skills, not computation.

MODIFICATIONS OF PRESENTATION FOR STUDENTS WITH DIFFICULTY FOLLOWING DIRECTIONS AND PROCESSING AUDITORY INFORMATION

- Vary your verbal style (volume, tone, pitch) to avoid monotone presentation.
- Keep your presentation lively and active.
- Supplement verbal presentation with visuals, graphics, and demonstrations.
- Use a great deal of hand signals and motions, gesturing and non-verbal communication.
- Use fewer words and more visual examples.
- Increase amount of modeling and guided practice.
- Allow extra time for processing information.
- Increase amount of eye contact with students.
- Increase wait time to at least 5 seconds before asking students to respond to questions.
- Provide directions in written as well as verbal form.
- Speak slower and avoid giving directions or speaking when not directly facing the class.
- Paraphrase using similar language.
- Be aware of your use of complex sentence structure and sophisticated vocabulary, and which students may have difficulty comprehending.
- Monitor frequently for student understanding.
- Adjust lessons in response to student performance.
- Increase student response opportunities significantly. (See Section 11 *Effective Questioning Techniques in the Classroom*)
- Teach throughout the day with multisensory techniques.
- Utilize a great deal of color, movement, and graphics.
- Write major points or content outline on board.

- Offer many choices that involve creative expression.
- Provide outline or overview of the lesson.
- Relate information to students' experience and background information.
- Have students share what they already know about a topic before instructing on that topic.
- Limit the number of new concepts introduced at one time.
- Pause during oral presentations/lectures, and allow students a few minutes to work with partners to briefly discuss the content and share their understanding.
- Provide many opportunities to work with a partner, triad, and group of four to five students.
- Summarize key points, and let students know what is important for them to remember.
- Use game format for drills.
- Clearly state lesson purpose.
- Provide instruction that accommodates full range of learning styles in the classroom.

Note: See additional strategies recommended for students having difficulty with attention and distractibility.

FOR STUDENTS NEEDING ADAPTATIONS IN TEXTBOOKS AND HELP WITH CIRCUMVENTING READING DEFICIENCIES

See Section 14, *Strategies for Helping Students with Reading and Writing Difficulties.*

FOR STUDENTS NEEDING INTERVENTIONS TO BYPASS WRITTEN LANGUAGE DIFFICULTIES

See Section 15, *Strategies for Helping Students with Reading and Writing Difficulties* and Section 13, *Motivating Techniques for Teaching Spelling and Vocabulary.*

FOR STUDENTS NEEDING INTERVENTIONS FOR BEHAVIORAL DIFFICULTIES

See Section 5, *Behavior Management and Positive Discipline,* Section 7, *Reaching All of Your Students with Special Needs,* and Section 9, *Programs for Building Positive Relationships, Social Skills, and Conflict Resolution Skills.*

ACCOMMODATIONS FOR STUDENTS HAVING DIFFICULTY WITH ORGANIZATION AND PLANNING

See Section 5, *Getting Your Students Organized for Success.*

FOR STUDENTS NEEDING INTERVENTIONS AND ADAPTATIONS TO BYPASS MATH DIFFICULTIES

See Section 17, *Motivating Students to Be Successful Mathematicians.*

FOR STUDENTS NEEDING INTERVENTIONS DUE TO LANGUAGE DIFFICULTIES

See Section 13, *Motivating Techniques for Teaching Spelling and Vocabulary*, Section 16, *Making Oral Language Come Alive in the Classroom*, Section 8, *Reaching All of Your Students with Special Needs.*

FOR STUDENTS IN NEED OF INTENSIVE MONITORING AND HOME/SCHOOL COMMUNICATION REGARDING BEHAVIOR, CLASS PERFORMANCE/WORK PRODUCTION

See Section 4, *Behavior Management and Positive Discipline* and Section 4, *Increasing Home/School Communication and Parent Involvement*, which include monitoring/tracking forms appropriate for elementary and middle school level.

FOR STUDENTS NEEDING INTERVENTION IN SELF-AWARENESS AND SELF-ESTEEM

See Section 7, *Programs and Strategies for Fostering Students' Self-Esteem*; Section 2, *Reaching All Students Through Their Multiple Intelligences and Learning Styles*; and Section 3, *Learning Developmentally.*

UTILIZE THESE INTERVENTIONS AS PRE-REFERRAL STRATEGIES

Prior to referring a student for possible special education services, it is necessary to initiate modifications and accommodations as appropriate. The following steps are recommended:

- Establish parent contacts and communication.
- Try providing as much supplementary assistance as possible (e.g., cross-age tutor, peer tutor, parent/community volunteer, aide, computer aided).
- Review student's cumulative folder.
- Conference with former teacher(s).
- Confer with support staff and any appropriate school personnel. See the pre-referral communication form at the end of this section.
- Initiate a home/school contract for one or two targeted behaviors. (See Section 5, *Behavior Management and Positive Discipline*.)
- Make any environmental modifications that seem appropriate, such as change of seating.

- Select a few interventions to try implementing, discuss with parents your plans to try providing the modifications/interventions over the next few weeks, and then assess effectiveness prior to making a referral. Keep good documentation/records during this period. Share informally with appropriate member(s) of the support team your concerns regarding the student and steps you are taking at this level. This informal communication with support personnel is helpful prior to referral.

Pre-referral communication form

When teachers meet with our student study team members at the informal level to share concerns about students, we use the Informal Student Needs Review form (found at the end of this section) which is filled out together at the time of the informal meeting. (See Section 10, *Team Efforts* for more information.) If there is no written format used for communication at the pre-referral level, it is still important to at least bring concerns to the awareness of appropriate support staff member(s). The special education teacher, counselor, nurse, speech/language therapist, etc. should be alerted about students in need; and are, therefore, able to advise and support the classroom teacher. When there is a student with more significant problems, the team can prioritize that student, perhaps make some observations, and schedule a more immediate student study team consultation on that student.

Checklists of interventions

The checklist at the end of this section (Have You Tried These Interventions and Modifications?) is a simple format for having teachers examine a variety of modifications and accommodations. It allows teachers to think about which accommodations they are already providing in the classroom, and to select which ones they would like to try and focus on next. It is recommended that student study teams use this checklist or something similar when meeting with teachers and planning for interventions. It helps to select a few of the strategies on the checklist and color highlight them as the new interventions to be tried.

IEP Alternative Means and Modes

In our district there is an additional page that is part of the IEP and is filled out for the special education student entitled IEP Alternative Means and Modes and Differential Proficiency Verification Form. The checklist form includes some modifications/adaptations of assessment (e.g. oral tests, modified tests, taped tests, short-answer tests, extended time for completing tests); presentation and instruction (e.g. increased verbal response time, repeated review/drill, reduced paper/pencil tasks, shortened assignments, note-taking assistance, taping lectures, alternative materials). **Note:** Only special education students in Grades 9-12 may have modified proficiency standards in certain courses as determined by the IEP team.

Summary Letters

One of the ways that we try to ensure that all key players are aware of the intervention plan when we meet on children with more significant needs and issues, is to write a summary of the concerns shared and decisions/interventions agreed upon. Typing a summary letter is usually done for those students who have the involvement of other care providers (counselors, psychiatrists, medical doctors, etc.). Typically, one of the team members will write the summary, with copies for parents, members of the team, and any other professionals outside of school who are involved in the care of the child. The following is an example of one summary letter for a student with ADHD. In this case, as the student's parent does not speak English, it was translated into Spanish for the parent, and the mother signed a release of information form allowing us to send a copy to the child's physician.

SUMMARY OF SCHOOL OBSERVATIONS AND CONCERNS REGARDING: MANUEL L.

SCHOOL: _____ DATE:_____

WRITTEN BY: _____ POSITION: _____

PHONE NUMBER: _____

Manuel has been a student in my Resource Specialist Program for the past few years. He is a capable, intelligent boy, with a great deal of talent in art (particularly drawing). Manuel has identified learning disabilities in auditory and visual sequential memory, with above-average cognitive functioning on measured assessments. Manuel has always been extremely impulsive and highly distractible since he entered our school three years ago. It is a challenge to focus his attention even in small group settings or working 1:1. Of all the students with ADHD with whom I have worked over the past several years, I would consider Manuel's degree of impulsivity - particularly his difficulty inhibiting vocal responses—to be among the most severe. He has a constant need to talk, which has been problematic in that he blurts out answers, interrupts constantly, and can't wait to tell or talk about things that come to mind (which are often totally unrelated to the task at hand). Other students become very impatient and exasperated with his interruptions, and it has been my observation that he receives a lot of negative feedback from his peers. Work production has been minimal over the years because of the above behaviors.

Since Manuel has been taking a second dose of medication at school, I have observed a significant improvement during the time I work with him (12:30-1:15 three days/week). There has definitely been less impulsive behavior, and he is much better able to inhibit the constant chatter. Manuel does ask numerous questions, requesting clarification. He has always done so. His confusion, not understanding, and need to have things repeated frequently is compounded because of the inconsistent attention (due to ADHD), learning disability in short-term memory, and difficulty comprehending in terms of language. **Note:** *Manuel continues to receive ESL services as he is still limited English proficient.*

Manuel's classroom teacher has also noted improvement in behavior during the afternoons since he has been receiving his medication at 11:45. Mornings continue to be inconsistent—some days he has great difficulty controlling impulsive behavior and staying on-task; other days, he does better. His teacher's main concerns at this time are: • difficulty listening and following directions • very disorganized (loses things frequently) • many incomplete and missing assignments • difficulty taking turns and functioning without social problems in groups

As we discussed at our meeting (including classroom teacher, special education teacher, mother and interpreter), the following interventions are currently in place and/or will be provided for Manuel's success:

- *A great deal of 1:1 verbal and nonverbal signaling and cueing*
- *Focusing 1:1 (beginning the task with Manuel and asking him to show or tell what he needs to do next).*
- *Frequent opportunities to work with a partner on his work, and for clarification*
- *Up-front, preferential seating directly in front of teacher*
- *Teacher using daily assignment calendar for recording all homework assignments. Before Manuel leaves for the bus he must show calendar to teacher for her initials to indicate that*

assignments are all recorded accurately on the calendar. Mother is to ask to see calendar every day after school which should be initialed by teacher. If it is, then he earns extra TV time that evening; if not, he loses some TV privileges.

- *Use of monitoring chart for on-task behavior. Manuel will earn reward in-school (he chose time with a friend to play on computer or time to use special art supplies) if he meets goal for the week.*

- *Once/week Resource teacher or aide will help Manuel organize materials, and check for progress on long-range assignments (reports, projects).*

- *Manuel will be encouraged to use our Drop-In Center (which is a service we provide students through our resource program). Our room is open the last hour of the school day for students needing help with classroom assignments, getting started on homework, and other assistance. It is manned by special ed teachers, aides, and high school student volunteers. Students can come for all or part of the period. Manuel knows that whenever he feels the need for extra help (e.g., is confused, overwhelmed, needs help pulling projects together, gathering resources, getting caught up, and so on) to ask his teacher, and she will send him to Drop-In or help him in class.*

- *Continued special education services through Resource Specialist Program of direct-instruction in reading/writing , in-class support and collaborative assistance.* **Note:** *See assessment reports and current IEP.*

- *We will evaluate effectiveness of interventions within the next few weeks.*

BIBLIOGRAPHY AND RECOMMENDED RESOURCES

Bos, Candace S., and Vaughn, Sharon. *Strategies for Teaching Students with Learning and Behavior Problems, Third Edition*: Needham Heights, MA: Allyn & Bacon, 1994.

Custer, S., McKean, K., Meyers, C., Murphy, D., Olesen, S., and Smoak, S. *SMARTS: A Study Skills Resource Guide* (Studying, Memorizing, Active Listening, Reviewing, Test Taking & Survival). Longmont, CO: Sopris West, Inc., 1990.

McCarney, Stephen, and Wunderlich, Kathy Cummins. *The Pre-Referral Intervention Manual.* Columbia, MO: Hawthorne Educational Services, Inc., 1993.

Murphy, Deborah, Celia, Meyers, Olesen, Sylvia, Custer, Susan, and McKean, Kathy. *Exceptions—A Handbook of Inclusion Activities for Teachers of Students at Grades 6-12 with Mild Disabilities.* Longmont, CO: Sopris West, 1995.

Parker, Harvey. *ADAPT: Attention Deficit Accommodation Plan for Teaching.* Plantation, FL: Impact Publications, Inc., 1994.

Rief, Sandra. *How to Reach and Teach ADD/ADHD Children.* West Nyack, NY: Center for Applied Research in Education, 1993.

Wood, Judy W. *Adapting Instruction for Mainstreamed and At-Risk Students.* New York: MacMillan Publishing Co., 1992.

INFORMAL STUDENT NEEDS REVIEW
AND RECOMMENDATION PROCESS

Student Name: _____ Teacher: _____

Grade: _____ School: _____ Date: _____

Please circle your concern(s):

Academics   Behavior   Health/Environment   Other

Describe your concerns: _____

_____

_____

_____

What concerns do the parents have? _____

_____

_____

_____

Did last year's teacher have these concerns?   yes   no

If so, what did he/she do to intervene? _____

_____

_____

_____

Consultation from: _____ Counselor _____ Resource Teacher _____ Nurse

_____ Speech/Language Therapist _____ Psychologist _____ Adaptive PE

_____ Administrator _____ Other

Dates: _____ Plan developed _____ Plan reviewed _____ Follow-up

Explanation: _____

_____

_____

HAVE YOU TRIED THESE INTERVENTIONS
AND MODIFICATIONS?*

ENVIRONMENT

____Seating up front, close to teacher

____Giving student extra work space

____Seating away from distractions (e.g., the door, learning centers, noisy heaters/air conditioning units, high traffic areas)

____Limiting visual distractions and clutter

____Monitoring noise level

____Reducing noise level during tasks requiring concentration (tests, reading)

____Designing the room to accommodate different learning styles

____Seating among well-focused students

____Use of study carrels or privacy boards during seatwork and test-taking

____Models and visual displays for student reference

____Appropriate-sized furniture

ORGANIZATION

____Assignments written on board as well as presented orally (and left recorded on board)

____Assignment calendar used daily—with teacher monitoring and expectation of usage

____Teacher, aide, or student buddy to assist with recording of assignments

____End-of-day clarification of assignments/reminder to students by teacher

____End-of-day check by teacher/aide for expected books and materials to take home

____Providing students with handouts that are already 3-hole punched

____Student requirement to have notebook, dividers, plastic pouch with teacher checks

____Provide assistance organizing materials (e.g., papers in proper place in notebook)

____Color-coding books, notebooks, materials

____"Thing to Do" list taped to desk

____Breaking down long assignments into smaller chunks/increments—with teacher checking student and providing feedback with each increment

____Limiting the amount of materials/clutter on the student's desk

* Revised from How to Reach and Teach ADD/ADHD Children by Sandra Rief

INCREASED COMMUNICATION AND TEAMWORK

_____Daily or weekly home/school communication to be signed by parents (e.g., monitoring forms or charts indicating behavior and work completion)

_____Increased phone contact with parents (remembering to share positive observations as well as concerns)

_____More frequent conferences/planning meetings with parents (trying to build a partnership on behalf of student)

_____Communicating concerns with support staff members at the informal level

_____Involving your site consultation/student study team (referral to team)

_____Buddy up with another teacher for discipline, team-teaching, joint activities

_____Let student know you are interested in helping him/her; dialogue with student(s) about their needs, encourage open communication

CLASSROOM MANAGEMENT

_____Increasing the amount of structure and monitoring of behaviors

_____Clearly defined expectations and consequences (reviewed frequently)

_____Utilizing teacher "proximity control" (standing near disruptive student, eye-contact)

_____Delaying instruction until it is quiet and teacher has engaged everyone's attention

_____Providing significantly more positive reinforcement (e.g., praise, notes/calls home)

_____Praise _specific_ behaviors (what student is "doing right")

_____Use of a contract or charting/reinforcement system for specific behaviors (on-task, staying seated, raising hand/not calling out, work completion)

_____Private, personal cueing and signals with student

_____Providing for frequent breaks and opportunities to move

_____Extra assistance and structure during transitional times of day

_____Allowing student to participate in selection of rewards/consequences

_____Using short reinforcing periods with teacher evaluation of effectiveness

INSTRUCTION AND EVALUATION

_____Allowing extra time for processing information (speak slower, give more "wait time")

_____Increasing the amount of modeling, demonstration, and guided practice

_____Many opportunities to work cooperatively with a partner or small group

____Many opportunities to verbalize in class and respond in a "safe" climate without fear of ridicule

____Regular feedback and progress check re: homework, class assignments, etc.

____Teaching throughout the day with *multisensory techniques* (using clear verbal presentation, many visuals, hands-on activities and movement)

____More student participation in projects involving creative expression

____Allowing and encouraging the use of computer, typewriter, word processor

____Modified, shortened assignments

____Accommodating written output difficulties by:

    ____allowing extended time to complete written assignment

    ____allowing oral responses

    ____permitting student to dictate responses/someone else transcribes

    ____reducing written requirements/permitting alternative means of sharing

    ____allowing parent to initial or sign-off homework after student has spent specified amount of time on assignment

____Extra one-to-one assistance (from teacher, aide, parent volunteer, cross-age tutor, student/peer buddy)

____Have student repeat directions/instructions prior to starting assignment

____Allow extra time for taking/completing tests

____Alter type of examination (true/false, short-answer, multiple choice, essay, demonstration, oral presentation, creative project)

____Allow student to have tests read to him/her if needed

____Provide student with color-coded, highlighted text

____Provide student with outline or overview of lesson

____Provide student with audio cassette of text

____Use a variety of questioning techniques/allowing for more response opportunities

____Allow student to use learning aids (e.g., Franklin Speller, calculators, reading markers)

____Provide handouts that are clean, easy to read

____Have students read assignments in pairs

PROGRAMS FOR BUILDING POSITIVE RELATIONSHIPS, SOCIAL SKILLS, AND CONFLICT-RESOLUTION SKILLS

Most of us who read or listen to the daily news reports are numbed and sickened by the intolerance, prejudice, and ever-increasing violence that is so threatening to the very core of our nation and world. Children *must* learn to get along with their neighbors in order to survive and coexist. The reality for many of our children is that in their homes, neighborhoods, and communities they are surrounded by hostility and violence. It may be rare for them to hear people speak to each other in civil, respectful language. Many may not know that there are peaceful ways to solve conflicts. Manners and social skills may never have been modeled or expected of them.

What are some ways to help teach our children how to build positive relationships, treat each other with understanding and respect, and resolve conflicts peacefully? This section describes some programs being used with success in San Diego City Schools that address some of these most critical skills our children need to learn: tolerance and acceptance of others, resolving differences and conflict through mediation and compromise rather than violence, and building social skills and positive relationships.

THE CONFLICT MANAGER PROGRAM

The Conflict Manager Program used by many of our district's elementary schools since 1983 was written by Michael Calamar, a district counselor in San Diego City Schools. He had adapted the Conflict Manager Program that had been developed in California's Bay Area Schools prior to this time. According to Calamar, "The program seeks to teach students that conflict is a natural part of life and an opportunity to learn, but can also be dangerous. Since conflict is here to stay, our young people must learn the skills they will need to manage a lifetime of conflict peacefully. This program is developmental, preventive, and proactive. It is not a quick fix. The skills taught must be practiced over and over again for many years before we can expect students to be comfortable with them, and before they are their automatic responses to conflict. Conflict management skills are as 'basic' as academic skills and as necessary for our students' success and survival."

The purpose of the Conflict Manager Program is to train elementary students in conflict resolution so they can assist fellow students to peacefully resolve conflicts during recess. The role of the conflict managers is to serve as helpers—assisting other students to solve playground problems. They are not replacements for yard duty, nor are they acting as police or judges. They are one part of a comprehensive plan to improve the playground atmosphere. Conflict managers only work with students who agree to accept their help. When students are having a problem on the playground, they have the choice of working with either a conflict manager or an adult. The conflict managers are monitored by adults outside and can provide help immediately, if needed. It is recommended that each playground has 3 to 4 conflict managers, who usually are given bright orange vests to wear.

Students are selected for the program by nominations of teachers, students, principal, district counselors, etc. Not only should model citizens be given the opportunity to assume this responsibility; it should also involve a diverse selection of children. The district counselor sets up a schedule with teachers for training the conflict managers chosen. Training consists of 8 to 10 sessions that last between 40 to 45 minutes. Groups generally consist of 6 to 8 students who serve one day a week for one quarter or semester. As new conflict managers are trained to replace them, the veterans help provide assistance and support on their first day or two of duty.

The counselor is responsible for training each new group of students, introducing the conflict managers to the student body, conducting regular meetings to review the process and provide a forum for sharing concerns/questions, as well as recognizing their contributions at the end of each term of duty.

For more information, including a 17-minute video and guide by Michael Calamar, contact: Race/Human Relations and Guidance Dept., Dr. Eloiza Cisneros, Asst. Superintendent, and Dr. Francine Williams, Instructional Team Leader, School Services Division—Area IV, San Diego City Schools, Dana Center, 1775 Chatsworth Blvd., San Diego, CA 92107. Or call RHR and Guidance Department, San Diego City Schools at (619) 225-3850.

SOCIAL SKILLS TRAINING/REINFORCEMENT IN ELEMENTARY SCHOOL

Some elementary schools provide social skills training through a variety of lessons and units taught by classroom teachers to the whole class, or in sessions facilitated and presented by the counselor either in classrooms or in small-group sessions outside of the classroom.

One elementary school shared how it has a schoolwide social skills program that involves selecting one topic/behavior each month (e.g., respect, courtesy, listening skills, friendship). Every teacher spends time at the beginning of the month discussing the topic/skill of the month with his/her students. All adults on campus wear a badge of the month that has the targeted topic/word(s) printed on the badge. In addition, all staff members are given ten "I Got Caught" slips of paper. These are distributed throughout the month to students exhibiting the targeted positive behavior (being respectful, being courteous, being a good friend, being helpful, etc.).

Note: Teachers are not allowed to give out tickets to their own students, which increases the awareness to be looking to reinforce for positive behaviors of *all* children around campus.

Students who receive the "I Got Caught" tickets are to write their names on the tickets and place them inside a huge jar in the school media center. Every Friday the secretary pulls out four tickets from the jar; and those students have their names published in the teacher's bulletin, the parent bulletin, and are able to select a reward from the principal's treasure box.

MIDDLE SCHOOL CONFLICT MEDIATION

Conflict Busters

Students are trained to be conflict mediators at the middle school level, as well. One middle school (Farb) in our district has a program called Conflict Busters, which was started in 1988 by Coach Steve Kaplan. It was an outgrowth of a leadership group that was set up at the school by our district's Race/Human Relations Department. Teachers and counselors identified a number of positive and negative leaders in the school, who were selected to be trained as student mediators. Much of the training came from the Student Mediation Handbook developed and used by a local agency called SAY San Diego (Social Advocates for Youth), which works together with many of our schools. The conflict busters are trained by school counselor Mary Jo Housman and Coach Kaplan in the mediation process which involves the following stages:

1. *Introduction*—Welcoming the disputants, mediators introduce themselves and explain their role, briefly explaining the process and the ground rules (no interrupting, name calling or put-downs; and confidentiality of mediation session except in certain situations that require adult intervention).

2. *Uninterrupted time*—To give disputants an opportunity to express their issues and how they feel about them.

3. *Exchange*—To help each person understand how the other experiences the conflict. Mediators ask each disputant to tell about his/her feelings and how he/she views the problems. Each disputant has to listen carefully and restate what the other one said.

4. *Building the agreement*—Mediators help the disputants share responsibility for the problem, talk about how to solve the problem, and begin to reach a mutually acceptable agreement.

5. *Writing the agreement*—Mediators write the agreement on an agreement form that is signed by disputants.

6. *Closing statement*—To formally close the mediation session.

After they receive the training, the conflict busters handle most of the problems in peer relationships (name calling, spreading of rumors, threats) that occur among students at the school. During 5th period, the schoolwide 30-minute block of time of sustained silent reading (SSR), the conflict busters (of which there are about 30 trained) go every day to the rooms designated for this purpose. Students who have had conflict throughout the day get a pass and are sent for conflict resolution to see the conflict busters during this period. They may be referred by their teachers, aides, other adults, or request a pass themselves. When they are not in direct mediation, the conflict busters are involved in different training activities with the instructors/supervisors on topics such as active listening, rephrasing, and so forth.

The area used for this purpose at the school is a loft with separate rooms that have windows. The supervisors are able to check in to see how things are going. There are two conflict busters involved in the mediation process, seated between the students in conflict. They do not solve the problems or tell the conflicting parties what they should do. Their role is to serve as a vehicle for the students involved to solve their own problems. Conflict busters are trained to ask questions such as, "How did that make you feel?" and to have students share, "It really hurt me when you . . . ," and so forth. They help guide the process for reaching an agreement on resolution, and putting the agreement in writing for the conflicting parties' signatures. According to Coach Kaplan, this process has had a very significant positive impact on the school, resulting in much less need for disciplinary action and more accepting of responsibility by students.

Peer Counselors

This same school trains *peer counselors* twice a week throughout the year to provide assistance and support to students for a variety of reasons. Peer counselors may be assigned to new students for orientation and until they get to know some other people at the school. It may be the recommendation of the Student Study Team to connect certain students with a peer counselor. For example, students who are having difficulty in any of their classes or having social problems (e.g., being teased by other students) may be assigned a peer counselor for help and support.

A peer counselor is someone to talk to, someone who may help with intervening when students are having problems in a class. They are to refer the student to school *staff* on issues that are of a personal nature and for help with any problems that are more significant. If a student is having trouble in a class, the peer counselor arranges a time to talk with the student, and then together they arrange a meeting with the counselor and teacher. They ask what the problem is and what they should work on. Then the peer counselor assists in whatever way he/she can to help the student meet the teacher's expectations. A follow-up meeting is then arranged with the teacher that they attend together.

THE MIDDLE SCHOOL ADVISORY PROGRAM

Common among middle schools across the country is the *advisory program*, which should take place during a structured time under the leadership and guidance of an advisor teacher. An effective advisory program helps young adolescents feel good about themselves and the contributions they can make to their school, community, and society. It is intended to provide consistent, caring, and continuous adult guidance at school through the organization of a supportive and stable peer group. An outstanding book highly recommended for all middle school personnel is *The Definitive Middle School Guide* by Forte and Schurr. (See the resources at the end of this section.)

According to the authors of that guide, an advisory program provides a structured time during which special activities are designed and implemented to help adolescents find ways to fulfill their identified needs. It is a vehicle for helping students through the "turbulence and hurdles of early adolescence." An advisory program also helps to bridge the gap between elementary and high school by providing every student with an advisor who has a special concern for the student as an individual and encourages independence and personal growth needed for high school success.

Forte and Schurr list important characteristics of a quality advisory program and effective advisors:

- Advisory periods meet a minimum of three times/week for 20 to 30 minutes a day, daily if possible, and generally for the first part of the school day.

- Groups are manageable in size (no more than 20 to 22 students); and planned activities are varied and student-centered.

- Advisory sessions have a common core curriculum with flexibility in its implementation—involving a number of hands-on/interactive activities, and open-ended questioning and discussion sessions that are intended to stimulate thinking and listening to different perspectives.

- An advisory program has its own name, logo, and identity.

- An advisory teacher is highly informed about the unique needs and characteristics of his/her advisees, supports the advisory concept, and works to increase his/her knowledge and understanding of it.

- The advisor should be the main advocate for his/her advisees, and the single most important adult in the school for his/her advisory students. The advisor is kept informed of all activities regarding his/her advisees and should act on the information accordingly.

- The advisor needs to work to develop a feeling of trust and caring in the advisory group, which is an evolving process. It is essential that privacy and confidentiality are respected and maintained in all circumstances except those that reveal the student or another is in real danger. The personal growth skills an advisor needs to be willing to work on developing are being: a good listener, tolerant, open-minded, and nonjudgmental.

- An effective advisor is able to open up and share personally with students as/when appropriate, and infuse humor and fun into the sessions.

MIDDLE SCHOOL P.E. SOCIAL SKILLS PROGRAMS

Many children are deficient in their social skills. For whatever reasons that high numbers of our students lack social skill competency, it is clear that they need these skills to be *taught*, *modeled*, and *practiced*. In order to do so, schools are attempting to teach and reinforce social skills training in creative ways, such as through middle school physical education programs.

In some of San Diego's middle schools, students are taught specific target social skills in three-week units (e.g., encouragement, giving/accepting compliments, manners, sportsmanship, responsibility). The skills are discussed in terms of what it would "sound like" and "look like" to display those particular skills, as well as the rationale for using the skill. For example, *encouragement* might look like: thumbs up, a pat on the back, a smile, a high five. It might sound like: "nice try," "you can do it." Then, through a number of entertaining and motivating cooperative games and activities, the skills are practiced and reinforced. Students receive positive reinforcement in a variety of ways for exhibiting those skills. Students are also responsible for processing and evaluating how well they and their group performed regarding use of the specific social skill.

THE HIGH SCHOOL PEER COUNSELING PROGRAM

Typically, peer counseling programs take place at the high school level. Peer counselors are teens who receive educational training related to drug abuse and skills training for helping to positively influence others who are having problems. There are many peer counseling programs across the country. One model used in some San Diego schools is from *The Peer Counseling Training Course*. (See the recommended resources at the end of this section.)

Students who become peer counselors are often trained during a separate elective class at the high school, which teaches students skills such as: active listening, effective message sending, self awareness, values clarification, decision making, and starting and ending a helping relationship.

Initially, an effective way of recruiting prospective peer counselors is to contact teachers of elective classes in social studies and health-related areas to arrange informal talks with their students. Recommendations may also be requested from guidance counselors and other school personnel. As the program develops, peer counselors will often be the best recruiters. According to Phillips, author of *The Peer Counseling Training Course* manual, there are certain qualities necessary for becoming successful peer counselors. Students need to be responsible. Peer counselors do not need to be top or above average students, but they do need to take the class seriously and be able to keep confidentiality. Peer counselors should consist of a cross section of students from the campus. All academic levels should be represented, as well as diverse social, racial, and cultural backgrounds. Peer counselors need to be sensitive to the needs of others and demonstrate a strong desire to learn to help other people. They must be open to expanding their own self awareness, which will involve their willingness to take risks in training groups of other students.

THE WORLD OF DIFFERENCE PROGRAM

A World of Difference is an outstanding program developed by the Anti-Defamation League to combat prejudice and discrimination in the classroom. This multicultural awareness program, designed to teach tolerance and reduce racial, ethnic, and religious friction in the classroom, is based on the concept that our differences are cause for celebration—and that our nation's diversity is our greatest strength.

ADL's *A World of Difference* program is a powerful means of training teachers to combat bigotry and encourages understanding and respect among racial, religious, and ethnic groups in the classroom. The program helps teachers of all grade levels to:

- address diversity in their classrooms
- examine their own and others' biases
- expand their own cultural awareness, as well as that of their students

The overall goal of the program is to assist educators in creating multicultural, non-biased learning environments in which all children can succeed. Interactive workshops provide participants with materials and strategies designed to:

- confront their own biases as well as those of their students
- encourage the use of effective techniques for promoting attitudinal change
- integrate human relations materials into the curriculum
- increase opportunities for students to achieve success and experience a sense of accomplishment
- utilize cooperative learning and conflict-resolution
- demonstrate how diversity can enrich the classroom

Note: The above description of A World of Difference is taken from ADL's published brochure. For more information about this powerful, very valuable program, contact: Anti-Defamation League—A World of Difference Institute, Anti-Defamation League, 823 United Nations Plaza, New York, New York 10017; Phone: (212) 490-2525.

BIBLIOGRAPHY AND RECOMMENDED RESOURCES

Cohen, Richard. *Students Resolving Conflict—Peer Mediation in Schools* (Grades 6-12). Glenview, IL: Good Year Books, Scott Foresman, 1995.

Cowan, David, Palomares, Susanna, and Schilling, Dianne. *Teaching the Skills of Conflict Resolution* (Activities and Strategies for Counselors and Teachers). Spring Valley, CA: Innerchoice Publishing, 1992.

Forte, Imogene, and Schurr, Sandra. *Advisory Middle Grades Advisee/Advisor Program.* Nashville, TN: Incentive Publications, 1991.

Forte, Imogene, and Schurr, Sandra. *The Definitive Middle School Guide.* Nashville, TN: Incentive Publications, 1993.

Metcalf, Linda. *Counseling Toward Solutions.* West Nyack, NY: The Center for Applied Research in Education, 1995.

Phillips, Maggie. *The Peer Counseling Training Course* (revised and expanded by Joan Sturkie). San Jose, CA: Resource Publications, Inc., 1991.

Schrumpf, Fred, Crawford, Donna and Usadel, H. Chu. *Peer Mediation—Conflict Resolution in Schools.* Champaign, Illinois: Research Press Co., 1990.

Telesis Peer Counseling Program, Telesis II of California, Inc., 3180 University Avenue, Suite 640, San Diego, CA 92104.

TEAM EFFORTS

Many people spend a lifetime searching for the perfect partner. The energy put into this quest is monumental. Whether the search is for personal reasons (like finding a spouse, a best friend, or a roommate) or for more professional reasons (such as finding a business partner) life experiences tell us that "clicking" with another person or persons in a good partnership is rare indeed.

In the teaching profession, the idea of teaming or partnerships makes good sense for everyone involved. When we take the full gamut of an elementary school teacher's day, we begin to realize that we cannot do "it" all. An elementary teacher is expected to teach all academic subjects well, plan special activities and programs, while attempting to meet all the special emotional, physical, social, and intellectual needs of each child. This is all to be done with very little aide time, and with little or no prep period built into the program. Many schools have learned to juggle their schedules and use special personnel to cover classes so that teachers can be given grade-level planning time.

It has been said that teaching is a lonely profession. Elementary teachers are in their classrooms for about six and a half hours per day with little time to communicate and exchange ideas and frustrations with other adults. As elementary teachers, we find that our room becomes our "home" where we spend the entire day working and planning for the day and the rest of the week, correcting papers, putting up bulletin boards, filling out paper work, plus a myriad of other tasks. Monitoring and assisting students who need extra help often shorten our breaks and lunch periods, again lessening our time to chat with fellow teachers.

For many teachers, team teaching has become a way to meet the challenge of the self-contained classroom and the isolation that often accompanies it. There are many issues to consider when setting up teaming situations within any school.

ISSUES TO CONSIDER WHEN TEAMING

In order for a team to function successfully from the start, all members must embrace the philosophy that:

- Teaming will make their teaching more effective.
- Teaming will improve the individual growth and development of the students.
- Teaming will better meet the needs of both teachers and students.

It is important that when beginning to form workable teaching teams, there is a search for balance. Teachers should seek out other team members who have complementing teaching styles and temperaments. An over abundance of any one individual teaching style or personality causes an imbalance in the team that affects the students' ability to grow and develop in a successful way. Team members should possess traits that enhance the team effort such as:

- flexibility
- good communication skills
- professionalism
- desire to work well with others; a team player
- humor
- respect for other's similarities and differences

In addition to these personal traits, a team must have some basic components that allow members to work together as team players, such as:

- A supportive and open sharing environment where ideas and teaching styles are respected and appreciated
- Members who have the ability to listen carefully to each other's needs and wants, and who can offer constructive criticism and praise
- Teachers who have interests, talents, and personalities that complement each other
- Common goals for students and teachers
- A common vision for students
- Reasonable standards and expectations of students and team members

It should be remembered that teaming development, whether in the elementary or middle school, is ongoing. Each day, week, and month is new and becomes an adventure. The kinks in the program can be worked out over the course of time, as the teachers together see any need for changes. New ideas can be implemented, modified or revised, when necessary.

A FIFTH/SIXTH GRADE TEAM

At our school, all upper grade teachers are involved in teaming situations. The fifth/sixth grade team has grown into a very effective partnership, starting with two teachers the first year, and increasing to three teachers in subsequent years.

How does the fifth/sixth grade team work?

- Each teacher is responsible for his/her own language arts program within the home-room setting.

- All teachers contribute ideas to core literature thematic teaching units to show continuity to the students within the team.

- Each teacher chooses a teaching area of the curriculum that either he/she feels is a strength, or one in which he/she wants to extend or foster more interest in for personal growth.

- For four days of the week, children rotate into these three curriculum areas of math, science/art history, and social studies. These periods are 55 minutes long. The children are exposed to three different teaching styles by three unique teachers.

- Students do not rotate on the fifth day. This day is saved to work closely with the homeroom children in language arts, centers, computer, and library studies.

- Planning sessions are held weekly in a more formal manner, and more informally, as needed. No common prep period is available for team planning, so all meetings are held during lunch or after school.

- Parent conference sessions were held separately by the homeroom teacher for the first report period, except where either the parents or team teachers desire a combined conference. Additional conferences are held throughout the year by the team or the individual teacher as deemed necessary. Parents are always encouraged to ask for a conference whenever a need arises. In the case of students who are experiencing difficulties with academics, homework, and/or discipline, often the child's presence is requested at the conference.

- A discipline program is implemented and supported by each teacher within the team to be used in their classrooms.

- Those students who have difficulty with behavior or who don't complete their work are given detention on Friday afternoon in one of the team member's rooms, while the other students have a "choice" physical education period or free-time activity supervised by the other two teachers.

- Collaboration with the resource teachers was set up to assist students in need of extra help. The resource teachers taught special lessons within each classroom sometime during the week, and resource aide time was assigned to each team teacher.

- A "drop-in" period was set up every afternoon in the resource room to assist any students who needed help on assignments generated by the team. Students did not need to be identified as "resource" to use the "drop-in center".

- Each fifth/sixth grade class was "buddied" with a kindergarten classroom. Special activities and celebrations are shared with buddies each week. Upper-grade students are given a buddy to partner with during the year.

- Thematic teaching units, including mystery, mythology, space, and survival, are created collaboratively for team use.

WHAT ARE THE ADVANTAGES TO THIS TEAM APPROACH FOR THE TEACHERS?

- The camaraderie keeps teachers from being so isolated in their own classrooms.

- Brainstorming sessions help to define and improve teaching. As ideas are bounced off each other, new ideas are created to challenge and motivate the students.

- Evaluation of projects and activities by three people helps to improve the program. Having three teachers scrutinize a project design or activity helps to iron out problems that might arise during implementation.

- Teamwork allows each person to use his/her unique skills, and to provide a renewed abundance of their energy to teaching. As one person volunteers to work on one aspect of the program, the others find their own tasks to make everybody's life a little less stressful. Just like a family, when everyone pitches in, we have more time to focus on our part of the job. Division of the workload makes our teaching lives more simplified.

- The creation of thematic units by three teachers that could be used for 100 students also saved time and effort. Instead of one literature unit, each teacher had three to use with their own class.

- A teacher and student who have difficulty relating to each other, or whose personalities just don't "click" on a particular day, know that after an hour, they can have a break from each other. The period of separation gives both student and teacher "breathing time" to regroup and deal with each other later in the day, or on the next day.

- Conferencing with parents seems more manageable. As teachers, we could present a whole child's evaluation from three perspectives, not just one. Parents can see we are a team working to assist their child in becoming more successful in their academic, social, emotional, and physical needs. The teachers and parents are pulled together to create a better monitoring program designed to unite the home and school for the benefit of the student.

- Communicating regularly with each other about the students gives all three teachers greater awareness about the whole child. Expectations are set high, and students know what is expected. This brings consistency to the program.

- Working collaboratively with our two resource teachers, the students' needs are met more effectively. The ratio of teacher to student is lowered, enabling students to obtain more direct teacher assistance and monitoring.

- The resource teachers and aides, in concert with the classroom team teachers, form a collective team that thoroughly addresses the needs of our special education students. As we enter into conferences with parents of students with special needs, we now have a full team of five teachers who can identify specific academic, as well as emotional, strengths and weaknesses of the students. Many students will never again have this full experience of true collaboration.

WHAT ARE POSITIVE ASPECTS ABOUT TEAMING FROM THE PERSPECTIVE OF THE STUDENTS?

- There are fewer discipline problems. As the students rotate, they seem to feel a sense of self-control and responsibility. They like the more grownup feeling—being treated like they were more mature.

- The opportunity to be mobile during the morning segment helps some of our behaviorally challenged students to get a stretch break every hour. This helps them to stay more focused when instruction is given.

- They have a chance to deal with three different personalities of teacher, each with his/her own teaching style. This seems to be helpful in creating the feeling of a middle school environment within the elementary school. Our goal is to implement an innovative, challenging, and high-quality program that will keep our sixth graders motivated and on target. The students respect our similarities and differences. They also learn that we not only know them in one subject area, but also know them in the way they dealt with their other subjects.

- They feel a very gradual transition into what their remaining adolescent years of schooling will be like.

- There is a diminished sense of competition among students in all three classrooms. Sixth graders tend to become very territorial and loyal to their own environment. In the teaming situation, the three classrooms unite and work as a team or as a family. Although each classroom does have its own personality, all the students come together and feel a sense of school spirit and cohesiveness. The students like the feel of being one, big, happy family.

- The students view that they have three teachers to relate to, and many times bring their individual concerns not to their homeroom teacher, but to one of the other team members. In a world where adolescents diminish their communication with adults and talk more often with their own peers, this building of trust within the team gives students a feeling that they have three classroom teachers who care.

How does being involved in a team change a teacher?

- It generates a new understanding of their own teaching personality and a deeper knowledge of their own teaching style.
- It brings forth a renewed sense of enthusiasm.
- It provides a healthier, more balanced environment for everyone involved.
- It inspires teachers to stay abreast of current ideas in their field.
- It gives teachers an opportunity to extend their interpersonal skills.

As cooperative learning has rocketed to the top of teaching strategies to use with students, we must see the benefits that cooperative teaching practices can offer each of us within our profession.

STUDENT STUDY TEAMS

Many schools utilize a process for identifying students in need of intervention of various kinds known as the Student Study Team (SST) process. In our district we refer to this multidisciplinary team, which meets regularly (once/week), as a consultation team. It is a function of general education, not special education; and our team leader and facilitator is the district counselor at each site. Students are referred to the team generally by classroom teachers, but any parent or staff member may refer a child to the team.

In our elementary school the team consists of the counselor, school psychologist, nurse, special ed staff, principal and classroom teacher(s). We meet on Friday afternoons when all team members arrange their schedules to be on site, and we usually are able to discuss/plan for three different students every SST meeting. Thanks to the support of our principal, we are able to provide for coverage of teachers' classrooms in order to release the teacher from class to attend the meeting. We believe that one of the strengths of our school is the effectiveness of our student study team, the high level of mutual respect for each other's expertise and professionalism, and the commitment of all members to meeting the needs of our students.

Students are referred to the team for behavioral, social, academic, emotional concerns, medical, and attendance issues. Effective, proactive student study teams encourage this identification process at their school, and want students brought to their attention who are exhibiting problems of any kind. It is highly recommended that if teachers are considering a referral to special education, they utilize the Student Study Team process first, sharing their concerns and the strategies/interventions they have taken to meet the child's needs. However, it is not a requirement that special education referrals must follow this procedure.

In our district we *do* ask teachers to channel through SST the students whom they feel may have ADD/ADHD, and are in need of additional intervention. San Diego Unified Schools has the PARD Project (Project for Attention Related Disorders), which is a systemwide approach used in our schools for identifying and providing intervention to students who present the characteristics and symptoms of ADHD. District health services personnel have had several meetings with the major medical providers in our city. It was agreed upon that before children are referred by the school for a medical evaluation due to problems related to attention, impulsivity and hyperactivity, they need to first utilize the SST process—and provide documentation of school interventions that have been tried to help the child. Our elementary school has always followed this practice—asking teachers to bring to the team students who exhibit the behaviors associated with ADHD, so that we can assist in helping with providing appropriate intervention.

It is a requirement that teachers share concerns with parents *prior* to referring them to the Student Study Team. In addition, we want to make sure that teachers are trying a number of different strategies before the child is brought through the SST process. We ask that classroom teachers share any concerns they may have about students at the *informal* level with any of the team members as they feel appropriate. For example, for health/medical concerns, possible ADD/ADHD, emotional issues, etc., the teacher should first meet with the school nurse. For behavioral, social, or attendance issues and concerns, the counselor or the school psychologist should be seen. Teachers should meet with the resource teacher for concerns about learning difficulties and academic problems, or the speech/language therapist or adapted P.E. teacher as those specific needs and concerns arise.

It is much more efficient if teachers first meet informally to share their concerns with the appropriate support staff. They receive help at this level with recommendations of interventions to try. Sometimes observations are made by team members. Teachers can receive help with planning and implementing behavioral interventions (behavioral charts, contracts, monitoring systems, reinforcements). Academic assistance may be offered at the informal level in a number of ways.

A follow-up within a few weeks enables the teacher/support team member to see if there is improvement or if the student should be referred to the SST for further intervention/planning. In this manner, when the student is discussed in SST (with parents invited as important team members), we are not wasting time with preliminary steps, but are now at a point where we are ready for the next step—whatever that may be, as determined by the team.

Our team reserves a few minutes at the end of our meetings to briefly share which students were brought to our attention at the informal level. Many times these same students have issues/concerns that are known to other members of the team, and it is recommended on the spot that a particular student should definitely be scheduled for a Student Study Team meeting.

When SST meetings are scheduled, parents are invited to attend. Parents are an integral part of the team, and their input and involvement in the team process is very important and valuable. It should never be a surprise to parents to be notified about the SST meeting, because the classroom teacher should be in close contact with the parents, keeping them informed of interventions they have been implementing prior to this time. The teacher should let parents know when they are moving to the next step—referring to SST for additional assistance in trying to help their child. If parents are unable to come to the meeting, they are contacted after the meeting, sharing with parents the intervention plan that was decided upon.

Student study teams may recommend and form an action plan that involves any number of possible interventions which may include:

- observing the student in various settings
- revising, revamping, helping to create behavioral plans (e.g., contracts, charts, reinforcement systems)
- identifying and recommending specific strategies (instructional, environmental, behavioral) for the classroom, home, other school settings
- providing small group, one-to-one assistance from available resources
- recommendation to assess the student—providing a psycho-educational evaluation at the school site to determine eligibility for special education services (I.E.P. process)
- referral to outside agencies/care providers (medical referrals, counseling, social services); in this case, parents need to sign a release of information form enabling the school to share information. If such referrals are made, the parents give permission for the school to gather data and provide documentation of specific concerns, performance, and behavior of their child.

See end of Section 8, *Interventions and Adaptations for Accommodating Special Needs* for an Informal Student Needs Review and Interventions/Modifications Checklist recommended for use at SST meetings.

SPECIAL EDUCATION COLLABORATIVE MODELS

Across the country many special education personnel are using collaborative models to meet the needs of their students. There are countless models that are being experimented with in schools everywhere. We provide a resource program at our school which incorporates a great deal of collaboration. All of our special education students are served in an inclusive classroom for the majority of the day; services for our students with special needs are provided through a number of different avenues. In our resource program about half of the delivery of services to our students takes place within the classroom, and the other half is provided through pull-out services and direct instruction. We have not discarded the pull-out model for delivery of services which many districts and schools have done. As with most aspects of education, we find that balance is needed in programming and delivery models in order to meet the needs of students most effectively.

At our school the special education teachers directly team teach in some of the classrooms—working jointly with some of the classroom teachers in teaching reading (e.g., part of the reading rotation in class with groups of students), teaching skill groups to part of a class or the whole class for a limited amount of time (e.g., 4–6 weeks, once/twice a week), teaching special "guest" lessons, and co-teaching with certain teachers for a particular subject throughout the year. We use most of our aide time to the program for providing direct service, support and monitoring of our students within their classrooms—enabling them to keep up with and be successful in their daily work. We also have pull-out services—scheduling some groups of students for direct instruction on I.E.P. goals (reading, writing, math) in the resource room (generally 30–45 minute sessions 3–4 days/week).

We disagree with the philosophy that special education students are best served only within the classroom setting. The location is not the key factor, rather it is the type and quality of instruction that takes place. It is our experience that elementary-level children are typically eager and happy to come to the resource room for small group instruction. In many cases children need to physically leave the large classroom for part of the day to regroup. Often, distractible students are far more focused and attentive in a resource room setting for part of their instruction.

Scheduling is always a challenge (sometimes a nightmare) for teachers who are committed to teaming and collaborating together. Special education personnel often have very large caseloads, with students scattered throughout all classrooms, not clustered in a limited number of classrooms. It takes a great deal of effort to try accommodating the needs of each of the individual classroom teachers when scheduling and still be able to effectively serve our special education students.

A very critical aspect for the success of special education students within an inclusive classroom setting is close communication between classroom teachers and the special education teachers. The special educator needs to be aware of the instruction (e.g., literature being read, dates of exams, projects and other assignments taking place in different classrooms), so appropriate supports can be provided for students as needed. In our resource program, part of what we do in our collaborative model is help the classroom teachers to restructure and design some of the materials and tests; make some audiocassettes of books being read in the upper grades; and basically help our students to better access the curriculum successfully.

Special educators serve as a resource and support to the classroom teacher as well as to the students. When classroom teachers feel supported, they are far more willing to go the extra mile in meeting the special needs of their students. As resource specialist teachers, we often provide materials that are used to supplement instruction in the classroom. Sometimes we provide study sessions prior to exams; help students (not just special education students) find materials/resources they need for projects; monitor students' organization and study skills; participate in conferences with parents along with the classroom teachers, and so forth.

At our school we have been able to provide another wonderful service over the past few years. We call it our *drop-in center*, scheduled during the last 45 minutes of the school day in the Resource Room. Students from our local high school, taking a community service project elective course, have been working to help us run the 'drop-in center'. One year our principal was able to provide additional aide time (nonspecial ed) to support this service. We allow and encourage any students in need of extra help in their classroom work to drop in to the *center* during this time. This includes clarification and support on completing classroom assignments and projects (e.g., research reports), getting started on homework, using the computer, and getting help with typing up papers, etc.

Not only are those students who are in our special education program welcome, but we often recommend that students with ADD/ADHD, who are not in special education but could use the support, make use of the Drop-In service. Other students who wish to be there for help on specific assignments are also aware that the center is open for this purpose, and may send students when they wish. We ask our students who struggle with keeping up in the classroom to ask their teachers to be able to come and see us when they feel they need the extra help. It is always a surprise to see who shows up each time! The drop-in center is very popular and is never perceived as a negative place to be. We want students—particularly those in the upper grades—to learn that it is a good strategy to make use of available tutorial help; we want them to make use of any such services in the middle school that will help them to be successful. The drop-in center is a positive, comfortable environment to be in and students are particularly motivated and happy to work with our high school helpers who are excellent role models and supports for our children.

SPECIAL ED/GENERAL ED COLLABORATION: CO-TEACHING AND HAVING A GREAT TIME!

Over the years we (both authors) have had the pleasure of co-teaching and working collaboratively together. Julie has always had clusters of students in her classes with learning disabilities and certified into our resource program. It often makes sense to serve her special education students directly in her classroom. Currently Julie is teaching math to all three classes in her team. Hands-on math has always been one of Sandra's strengths and interests; so we scheduled this school year for Sandra to co-teach math with Julie during the first period of the day—when Julie has the straight fifth-grade class from the team in her room. This particular class has six students with IEPs and goals in math, in addition to some other students with special needs.

We teach math through a lot of hands-on and problem-solving activities. Having two teachers working together to plan, model, and monitor students' participation and performance is very helpful. In addition, when teaching computation and processes that are confusing to students, we sometimes split the class randomly in two parts—bringing half to the resource room, the other half to remain in the classroom. In this way, we can both be teaching a smaller group, using our overhead projectors, and monitoring more closely whoever may be having difficulty. Sometimes we have review sessions in smaller groups as well. We take turns working with the students in need of extra reinforcement of skills. In this way the class does not perceive Sandra (the special education teacher) as always working with those students in need of help.

Some students need a variety of modifications of their work in order to be successful. (See Section 8, *Interventions and Adaptations for Accommodating Special Needs* and Section 16, *Motivating Students to be Successful Mathematicians*). Being right there in the classroom makes it easier to help provide on-the-spot interventions/modifications; and know how well students are keeping up with the classroom work on a daily basis. As soon as they start to slip, it is easier to intervene in school and to elicit parent help, as well.

TEAMWORK WITH PARENTS

As has been discussed throughout this book, parents are an integral and vitally important part of the team. Without their assistance, involvement and support, we as school personnel are very limited in how effectively we are able to reach and teach our students. (See Section 3, *Increasing Home/School Communication and Parent Involvement*; Section 2, *Learning Developmentally*; and Section 5, *Getting Students Organized for Success: Home/School Strategies*)

Many schools are requiring that all parties (parents, teachers, students, and administrators) work collaboratively to achieve our educational goals for students—sharing responsibility in the learning process. Home/School Compacts (such as the sample at the end of this section) must be agreed upon and signed by parents, school staff, and students at the beginning of the school year.

At our school we are very committed to working with parents of students with special needs, providing support and education in a variety of ways. We established a lending library in our resource room of books, audio, and videocassettes on several topics of interest for parents of children with learning, behavioral, and attention difficulties. Our school nurse runs a very well-respected support group for parents of children with ADD/ADHD that has been extremely helpful to many families in our community over the years. We also take full advantage of an outstanding service to parents of children with special needs offered by our district's Parent Facilitator Program. (See Section 3, *Increasing Home/School Communication and Parent Involvement* for more information on the Parent Facilitator Program.)

SITE GOVERNANCE TEAMS

Many schools are committed to shared decision-making among the various constituents of the school community: certificated staff, classified staff, parents, and administrators. Elections are held to select representatives who are responsible for making recommendations and decisions on a variety of agenda items brought to Site Governance Teams, such as those regarding: curriculum, programs, budget, discipline policies, staffing, assessment, community/parent involvement, and so forth. Schools that have active and empowered governance teams find that, in most cases, staff and community feel they have a voice in the important decisions affecting their school, and that it is a positive process.

We want to thank our team buddies—our teaching partners and student study team members. They inspire us, keep us motivated, are our supports, and make our jobs so much more exciting and rewarding. Thank you to Sue Sachs, Jim Solo, Kathy Aufsesser, Sandy Wright, Leah Edzant, Barbara Cleland, Bill Irwin, Steve Hill, Brenda Ferich.

SAMPLE HOME–SCHOOL COMPACT

Each student should be helped to reach his/her highest potential for intellectual and social growth. To achieve this, the home and school must work together by recognizing and agreeing upon the responsibilities of each party in the learning process.

As a student, I will be responsible for:

**1. Reading, or being read to, at least twenty minutes per day, four or more days per week.

2. Showing respect and cooperating with all adults at the school.

3. Coming to class on time, prepared to work.

4. Completing all assignments to the best of my ability.

5. Respecting the rights of others to learn without disruption.

6. Showing respect for people and property by not using profanity, stealing, or vandalizing.

7. Practicing the rules in the school's discipline code.

8. Spending time at home completing homework, reading, and studying.

Date _____ Student Signature _____

As a teacher, I will be responsible for:

*1. Communicating frequently to parents/guardians ways they can support student learning at home.

*2. Providing for two-way communication between classroom and home in order for parents/guardians to have reasonable access for discussing matters relating to their son/daughter.

*3. Scheduling parent/guardian/teacher/student conferences and/or workshops to accommodate parents'/guardians' schedules.

*4. Providing opportunities for parents/guardians to volunteer, observe, and participate in classroom activities.

5. Providing instruction in a way that will motivate and encourage my students.

6. Providing a safe and positive atmosphere for learning.

7. Explaining and modeling assignments so that my students have a clear understanding.

8. Communicating to parents/guardians the importance of reading daily with their son/daughter.

9. Discussing with parents/guardians the meaning of this compact as it relates to student achievement.

10. Supplying clear evaluation of student progress to students and parents/guardians.

11. Notifying parents/guardians of any concerns or problems in a timely manner.

Date_____ Teacher Signature _____

As a parent/guardian, I will be responsible for:

*1. Monitoring attendance, amount of television viewing, and providing positive use of out-of-school time.

*2. Providing a regular time, place, and supervision for homework completion.

*3. Attending at least one parent/guardian/teacher/student conference to discuss my son's/daughter's school progress.

*4. Volunteering, participating, or observing in my son's/daughter's classroom.

*5. Participating in decisions and/or workshops related to the education of my son/daughter.

**6a. Reading to my son/daughter daily for twenty minutes, four or more days a week. (Elementary), or

**6b. Ensuring my son/daughter reads daily for twenty minutes, four or more days a week. (Secondary)

7. Communicating the importance of education to my son/daughter.

8. Providing a caring environment, including adequate food and rest.

9. Helping my son/daughter to meet his/her responsibilities.

10. Notifying teachers of any concerns or problems that may affect school performance.

Date _____ Parent/Guardian Signature _____

As the principal/administrator, I will be responsible for:

*1. Ensuring that our school provides high-quality curriculum and instruction in a safe and supportive learning environment that enables all students to meet or exceed student performance standards.

*2. Providing for two-way communication between home and school, in order for parents/guardians to have reasonable access for discussing matters relating to their son/daughter.

3. Reinforcing the partnership between parent/guardian, student and staff by recognizing outstanding practices of individuals and/or groups.

4. Creating a welcoming environment for students, families, and community members.

5. Communicating to students and families the school's mission, goals, parent involvement policy, and ways to support student achievement.

6. Communicating to parents/guardians the importance of reading daily with their son/daughter.

7. Providing a process for ongoing planning, reviewing, and improving school activities and programs.

8. Soliciting feedback from students, families, and staff about school programs, policies, and activities; responding in a timely manner to such feedback.

9. Acting as the instructional leader by supporting teachers in their classrooms.

10. Providing appropriate training and workshops for teachers and parent/guardians.

Date _____ Principal Signature _____

Adapted from the California State PTA Parent Education Manual, *Parents Empowering Parents (Section 1, Exhibit H)*, to include school-parent compact requirements as stated in Title 1 of Improving America's Schools Act, Section 1118 (d), and district requirements

---

San Diego City Schools • Parent Involvement and Support/Consolidated Programs Services •
Helping Schools→Help Parents→Help Students

*Title I Requirements
**District Requirements

— *Section 11* —

EFFECTIVE QUESTIONING TECHNIQUES FOR THE CLASSROOM

One of the most important processes that takes place in a learning environment is that of asking and responding to questions. Many teachers inadvertently use questioning techniques that are highly exclusive of numerous children in the classroom. It is important to update our skills and increase our repertoire of effective questioning strategies that are inclusive of all our students.

In traditional classrooms, teachers will ask a question and then call on an individual student to respond, while the rest of the class is expected to sit quietly and listen to the interchange. In some classes it is possible for days, weeks, and perhaps even months to go by with some students never sharing their thoughts or ideas verbally in class. Research has shown that it is very common for classroom teachers to do the following, as well:

- First call on a student by name, then ask that student a question (automatically cueing the rest of the class that they won't need to answer that question).

- Ask a question and expect an immediate response without waiting for the student to process the question or have any think-time before responding.

- Call on the same 6 to 7 students habitually, often those whom the teacher can count on to respond with the answers the teacher wants to hear.

- Ignore many students, even when they raise their hand to respond.

- Call on low-achieving students with far less frequency than high-achievers.

- Call on males with higher frequency than females.

- Ask numerous questions that have a single answer that is either right or wrong, with a low percentage of open-ended types of questions being asked.

- Ask a low percentage of questions that require higher level, critical-thinking skills.

Typically, teachers are unaware of their own pattern of questioning and are surprised, even appalled, when they monitor themselves as to who is/is not being called on, and with what frequency. Students are very quick to pick up on the teacher's style and to assess the probability of their being called on; and, consequently, their need to participate and respond in that classroom. The following are *effective* questioning strategies and techniques for today's classrooms. They encourage high response opportunities for students, student accountability, critical/divergent thinking, and active participation—with everyone having a voice that is heard and respected. These are all strategies that are *inclusive* of every student in the class.

SOCRATIC SEMINAR

It is very worthwhile to have teams of teachers trained in the method of Socratic Seminar, which is a sophisticated method of leading dialogues in the classroom that focus on understanding issues from various viewpoints, not eliciting "right" answers or "covering" a topic. The Socratic method of teaching is based on Socrates' theory that it is more important to enable students to think for themselves than merely to fill their heads with the "right" answer. Students learn to think more critically, read more closely, and discuss ideas with clarity and confidence. The ability to ask the question that stimulates thoughtful and meaningful discussion is often more important than the answer.

Typically, for a seminar, the teacher selects a short reading (poem, article) that lends itself to ideas and issues worth discussing. It is the role of the teacher or seminar leader to formulate questions that have no single answer, can be answered best by reference to the text, and requires the student to apply the text and ideas to him-/herself. Seminars are generally conducted with everyone seated in a circle. Students are trained to not raise their hand during the seminar, but to take turns and join into the dialogue. Everyone in the seminar must be familiar with the material being discussed. Often the teacher reads the passage aloud to the class before asking students to study it for a given length of time on their own.

There are guidelines, skills, and behaviors that are explicitly taught to students before engaging in seminars, such as the following:

- Listen respectfully.
- Stay on the subject.
- Come prepared to the seminar ready to participate.
- Refer to the text and defend ideas from the text.
- It is all right to pass.
- Ask for clarification when confused about something.
- How to respond with statements such as, "I agree with _____ but I want to add _____." "I disagree with _____ because _____."

What the Teacher Needs to Do During the Seminar

- At the beginning of the seminar ask an opening question and then give students a certain amount of time to discuss in pairs or triads before beginning the group seminar.
- Allow at least 5 to 7 seconds for replies to questions, then follow with a clarifying question.

- Rephrase a question if not understood.
- Ask for clarification—for the student to be more specific, to rephrase, or elaborate.
- Request that reasons be given for answers.
- Allow and encourage discussion of differences; draw out reasons and implications.
- Ask interpretive questions, divergent questions, and questions that are open-ended with many possible answers.
- Keep refocusing back to the text.
- Ask students to paraphrase other students' responses and then respond or react to what the other student shared. (For example, "Janet, what did you understand Michael to say just now? Can you say that in your own words? Do you agree with that? What evidence do you find in the text to support that?")
- Keep a record of who has spoken.
- Encourage students to speak up.
- Return to students who pass.
- Have closure by having students summarize a few points made during the discussion.
- Accept students' responses without labeling them right or wrong.
- Pause and allow time after a student answers a question, giving all students the time to consider the given response. Then ask other students for their opinions about the response.

Examples of Socratic Questioning

1. In what ways are _____ and _____ alike (or different)?
2. What would you do (or say) if you were _____?
3. Can you think of an example to illustrate the point?
4. What if ____ happened (or were true) instead of _____?
5. In recent times, what well-known people are (were) like _____?
6. What would you do (or say) if you were _____?
7. How would _____ view this? (Why?)

> *Note: Additional recommended questions for the Socratic Seminar are found below under guided readeding.*

RECIPROCAL TEACHING

Reciprocal teaching is a comprehension-oriented process that can be used throughout the curriculum for all grade levels, and for high- and low-achieving students. Reciprocal teaching involves children in the cooperative process of: prediction, question generating, clarification or defining of unfamiliar terms or phrases, and summarizing. Students are taught each of the above strategies. After students have learned the strategies modeled by the teacher and practiced as a group, they take over the "teacher role" in their cooperative groups. It is an excellent vehicle for teaching comprehension and for training students in the art of questioning.

Reciprocal Teaching Strategies

- *Predicting* what the passage, article, story will be about by looking at the title, pictures, or any other clues. Predictions are confirmed or adjusted as we read.
- *Question generating:* Students are asked to construct teacher-like questions that begin with "What do you think . . . " "Why does . . . ", "How are . . . " etc.
- *Clarification:* Ask if there are any words used that they would like clarified or defined, or that a younger child might need clarified.
- *Summarizing*

Students are responsible for answering and recording their responses on paper to the following:

1. Predict what the story/article/passage will be about in one sentence.
2. Write three "teacher-like" or "test" questions about the story/article/passage. Write the answer and page number where the answer is found.
3. Write a one-sentence summary of the passage or pages that were assigned for today.
4. Write 3 to 5 words from today's assignment that your group or younger children would need to have clarified. After each word write the page number where the word can be found. Look up the definition. Write the meaning of the word as it is used in the story/article/passage.
5. If you did not read the whole story today, predict what you think will happen next.

GUIDED READING

One of the most important processes that takes place in any language arts classroom is *guided reading*. The teacher guides students to construct meaning from the text through appropriate questioning.

Effective Questions During Guided Reading Instruction

- What do you think _____ means?
- What do you see in the picture?
- What do you think _____ is thinking?
- What do you think will happen next?
- Have you ever felt like _____ did when he/she _____?
- Tell me something you thought was funny, sad, . . . in the story.
- Which character in the story would you choose as your friend? Why?
- What do you know by looking at this picture? Tell something about the culture from this picture.
- How does _____ relate to _____(other areas of study)?
- What message do you think the author is trying to get across?
- What clues tell you that _____ was probably poor?

- What season is it? How do you know?
- What other books have you read about a similar topic? Does the cover give you any clues? What about the table of contents or chapter headings?
- What is the tone of this passage?
- What does this part of the story remind you of? What is the same? What is different?
- How would you feel if you were _____?
- What caused _____ to _____?
- How do you think _____ and _____ were alike (or different)?
- How was _____ different at the end of the book? What do you believe caused this change?
- As you read, think how the text confirms, adds to, or changes what you already know about _____.
- Where is _____ probably going to go next?
- What effect did _____ have on _____?
- According to the passage, what caused _____?
- Which character do you feel you know the best? Why? Read the text again to see what else you can find out about that character.
- What do you think was the significance of _____?
- As you reread, think about the techniques the author uses to . . . (create mood, portray characters, etc.).
- Have you ever been in this situation?

Examples of Divergent Questioning

- List as many _____ as you can think of.
- How would this look to a _____?
- What would happen if there were no _____?
- What would happen if _____ were true?
- How would _____ view this?
- Suppose _____ happened. What would be the consequences?
- If you were a _____, what would you (see, feel, smell, taste)?

QUESTIONING TECHNIQUES TO INCREASE STUDENT RESPONSE OPPORTUNITIES

In all classrooms, teachers have students who are inattentive and easily distracted. There are children who, for whatever reason, are reluctant to participate and are passively rather than actively involved in the lesson. One of the most effective ways of ensuring that all students are actively engaged in the lesson is through specific questioning techniques that require a high rate of student response. The following are some methods to significantly increase student participation and response.

Eliciting Unison Responses

Teachers trained in direct instruction techniques are familiar with this method. What is required is to teach students that there will be many times when you will be asking questions that *everyone* will be answering at the same time. Students are trained (by modeling and practice) to respond to a teacher signal by *calling out the answer in unison*. This method is used when there is only one correct answer and that answer is short. Students are first focused by the teacher to be looking directly at him/her. The teacher then asks a question (that has a short, single answer) and pauses for a few seconds while students are to be thinking. Then, the teacher gives a verbal signal (such as, "Everyone . . . ") followed immediately with a visual signal (such as, gesture with arms/hands) that has been taught to students. At that signal, students call out the answer in unison.

This method is very useful when giving two choices. Example: "Is the number 68 even or odd?" . . . (pause/wait time) . . . "Everyone . . . " (followed by signal). At the signal, everyone calls out "even." It can be used throughout instruction to keep students alert and participating. Rather than asking one student for an answer, this method makes all students be accountable for thinking and participating. A follow-up question could then be directed to individual students to explain *why*. "How do you know that 68 is even?" . . . "Susan?"

This same direct instruction method is also used by focusing students on a visual stimulus (e.g., words written on the board, math facts on the overhead projector, etc.). For quick review or drill of addition, subtraction, multiplication, division facts, or for reading/decoding a list of words, this method of questioning is valuable. The teacher points to a stimulus, pausing for students to think, then gives a verbal signal (e.g., "What word? . . .) followed by a tap by a pointer next to the stimulus. Students call out the word in unison, greatly increasing their rate of response. When incorrect answers are called out, the teacher can immediately correct as a group and continue to practice as a group, without singling anyone out.

Another way of eliciting unison responses is to ask the class a question, pause for "think time," and ask them to write their answer on an individual chalkboard or dry-erase board. Then, after a teacher signal ("Boards up"), students hold up their boards for the teacher to see and quickly assess which students understand and who needs extra help. Students of all ages enjoy writing on the boards. For dry-erase boards, a tissue serves as an eraser. For chalkboard use, it is very helpful to store a piece of chalk inside a baby bootie, which serves as the eraser.

Group questions can be asked with students needing to respond with a thumbs up/thumbs down response. This can be used for indicating "yes/no," "I agree/I disagree," or for any "either/or" response the teacher wants. For example, a teacher might want to have students practice determining if sentences are statements or questions. A statement can be indicated by thumbs up; a question with thumbs down. Students can put their heads on desks (perhaps with eyes closed). The teacher can verbally make up sentences that are either statements or questions and determine which students understand the concept by their thumbs up/down responses. Other finger signals can be used with the teacher writing 4 or 5 response choices on the chalkboard. The teacher then asks students to determine which choice they think the answer to a question is by holding up the corresponding number of fingers. For example, "Which part of speech are the following words . . . " (1 = noun, 2 = verb, 3 = adjective, 4 = adverb).

Partner Response

Probably the best method for increasing student response opportunities is to pair students with partners. All throughout the school day teachers can ask partners to turn to each other and "tell your partner," "share with your partner," "brainstorm with your partner" any number of questions or topics. Of course, partners would need to be seated next to each other. If partners are numbered "1's and 2's, or A's and B's," then the teacher can direct even more specifically to make sure that within the partnership one person isn't the dominant speaker. For example, "A's, tell your partner what you think will happen next in the story." "B's tell your partner why you think Brandon ran out of the house in such a hurry." Large-group discussion can follow partner talk and sharing in all content areas.

It is important for the teacher to vary student partnerships. Partners may be rearranged by assigning students to work with the person next to them, diagonal from them, behind them, or across the table from each other. It is most beneficial to allow for easy access without a lot of movement other than turning their chair around or scooting in closer to each other.

CALLING ON STUDENTS EQUITABLY AND RANDOMLY

One technique many teachers use to ensure they are giving all students in class an equal opportunity to respond is to write each student's name on either a deck of cards or on tongue depressors (ice cream sticks). The cards or sticks are used to draw from when calling on students to answer questions. Once a name is drawn, the name card (or tongue depressor) is put in a different stack (or container). However, when using this technique it is important that students not "tune out" and stop paying attention once they have their turn. In order to prevent this from happening, it is good practice to draw a name from the "already called on" stack of cards (or can of sticks) every certain number of questions asked.

OTHER QUESTIONING STRATEGIES

- Play *Jeopardy* types of games with students where the answer is provided, and students need to determine the question.
- Review vocabulary words studied in class by playing *I'm thinking of . . .* The teacher states, "I'm thinking of a word that means curious." The child responds with, "What is 'inquisitive'?"
- Write terms on the board that are being studied in the content area. Students have to write a question that would have as an answer each of the terms.
- *Firing Squad:* Three to four students come to the front of the classroom with prepared questions pertaining to a subject being studied in class. In quick succession, students "fire" questions to their classmates. If the classmate cannot answer it, he/she says, "Pass," and a new student is chosen.
- Display a bulletin board of "I wonder . . . " or "I always wondered why . . . " Examples: "I wonder why an older person's hair turns gray." "I wonder why there are waves in an ocean." "I wonder why the moon looks different colors on different nights." "I wonder how the memory of a computer works."

These types of questions can be generated individually, in partners, or teams. This question board should be added to throughout the school year, and could prompt writing assignments, research, and other possible projects.

BIBLIOGRAPHY AND RECOMMENDED RESOURCES

Cushman, Kathleen. "Conversation in Classrooms: Who Are Seminars For?" *The Harvard Education Letter*, March/April, 1992.

Gray, Dennis. "Putting Minds to Work—How to Use the Seminar Approach in the Classroom." *American Educator*, Fall, 1989; pp. 16-23.

Hansen, Dr. Bobbi. *Effective Questioning Strategies: Helping All Students Feel SMART*, College of Education, California State University, San Marcos.

Mooney, Margaret. "Guided Reading Beyond the Primary Grades." *Teaching K-8*, September, 1995.

Schaffer, Jane C. "Improving Discussion Questions: Is Anyone Out There Listening?" *English Journal*, April, 1989, pp. 40-42.

Walker, Rena M. *Accelerating Literacy Handbook*. San Diego, CA: Walker Enterprises, 1995.

Wolf, Dennis Paler. "The Art of Questioning," *Academic Connections*, Winter, 1987.

MOTIVATING TECHNIQUES FOR TEACHING SPELLING AND VOCABULARY

TEACHING SPELLING SKILLS

In any classroom there is a tremendous range in students' ability to spell. We know that some children seem to be natural spellers and this skill comes very easily to them. They are the ones who spell most words correctly in their daily writing, get 100% on spelling tests with little effort, and are the winners of spelling bees and other competitive activities. These students may be very adept at visualizing and recalling the correct letter sequences and configurations of words they see in print. They often have a strong internal phonetic base, and can sound words out sequentially with ease. Generally they have the visual recognition skills to identify a word that is misspelled (doesn't look right to them) and, therefore, are able to edit their own work and self-correct.

We also know there are several children in the classroom who struggle with spelling, and get very frustrated in their attempts to do so. As teachers and as parents, our goal should be to help each child feel successful in his/her ability to spell. Not all children will become proficient spellers, but our responsibility is to make sure each child has some degree of success and develops a variety of strategies to build this important communication skill.

Whole language philosophy has certainly put spelling instruction through a great deal of transition during the past few years. It is believed that when children see the word in context, in the literature they are reading and discussing, they not only internalize the word's meaning, but are also more motivated to spell that word correctly. Spelling is a *functional* skill, necessary for expressing ourselves and accurately communicating in writing. As adults, we know the value of being able to present ourselves well on paper. It is important for students to be putting their effort into learning how to spell and recall the words they will be most likely to use in their writing. It is also necessary to teach students the patterns of our language so they will be able to generalize and make a strategic attempt to encode (spell) words they wish to use as they are writing.

Students acquire spelling skills in a variety of ways. We must provide our students with direct instruction in basic phonics skills (letter-sound associations and phonemes), word patterns (families of words that have the same cluster of letters), and word structures (syllabication, prefixes, suffixes). We must also increase student motivation to spell correctly by making the classroom spelling program one that is meaningful to them. It isn't a productive use of our students' time to select a number of words to memorize each week that in all likelihood they will never use in written communication, or remember how to spell a month later.

There are many words we can incorporate into spelling lists that are practical yet very challenging. A good source of words can be from any number of lists available of "spelling demons" (commonly misspelled words) in the English language. In addition, students should have regular opportunity to practice spelling *high frequency* words. Just one thousand words account for nearly 90 percent of the words adults find necessary for their everyday writing. High frequency words lists are also readily available. It is astounding how many upper-grade students incorrectly spell such *high frequency* words as: *said, they, could,* and *there.*

Since many schools no longer use a consistent spelling program, we strongly recommend that teachers make sure their students have practice learning the basic patterns of the English language by reading and writing words, such as the following:

- *Phonetically regular words*—including *short vowel* words (best, plant, rich, check, trust), *long vowel* words with different patterns of final 'e' (plate, dime, cute, whole), and *vowel digraphs* (chain, dream, sweet, groan), and so forth. Note: Approximately four-fifths of all words can be sounded out phonetically.

- *Multisyllable words with prefixes and suffixes* (unhappy, unable; recondition, reassign; slowly, wisely; imagination, discussion, attractive).

- *Word family/rhyming patterns* (thank, blank, crank; thick, trick, stick, quick; right, night, delight, bright; bold, cold, scold).

- *Focusing on patterns such as beginning blends/clusters* (drive, dropped, drink, dry; squeeze, square, squint; thrive, through, thrifty, throat)

- *High frequency words and commonly misspelled words*

  We also recommend some practice with dictation of sentences. Have students write two or three sentences from dictation, with immediate feedback and self-correction in spelling, capitalization, and punctuation.

By the upper elementary grades and secondary school, many students will need a minimal amount of teacher instruction in spelling skills. Yet others may require a great deal of structured, guided instruction to be successful. The following are proven to be successful classroom-tested methods and strategies for teaching spelling to students of all levels of spelling competency. Spelling instruction and opportunities to practice in ways that are effective for *all* children—regardless of their skill level or learning style—require *flexibility* and *choice* built into the program.

Ways to Formulate Weekly Spelling Lists

Many teachers create their own weekly spelling lists rather than use district spelling lists or commercial products. One example is to select 5 words weekly from the literature being read in class, 5 words from the content areas in science/social studies that students are currently studying, 5 phonetically-regular words following a sound association or phoneme (e.g., *ar* words such as: chart, sharpen, remark, hardly), and 3 to 4 difficult bonus words from the literature students are reading. Once again, words teachers select from the literature or content material for spelling lists should be the more *functional* words, and not the obscure vocabulary words that will have very minimal carry-over in students' writing (unless they are used as "bonus" words).

Weekly words can be introduced as a whole class with the teacher writing on the overhead or chalkboard, dividing the words into syllables, and determining if all students know the meaning of the words. Students who have difficulty with spelling are allowed the modification of a shorter list of words to learn for the week.

In some of the fifth/sixth grade classes at our school, students receive a teacher-selected list of words from the piece of literature they are currently reading in class. The list consists of 20 words, of which students are to select anywhere from 10 to all of the words to study that week. The choice of how many is based on the child's developmental level. Students who are high achievers in this area almost always select all 20 words, whereas those who are less proficient may take less words. The goal is to master learning the words selected, and students strive to achieve a high percentage correct on the final test.

Do some high-achieving spelling students take the easy way out by choosing fewer words than they are capable of doing? The answer is *not usually*. Do the children who struggle with spelling choose too many words to learn for the week? Often this does happen because children who are challenged by spelling don't want to admit they are having difficulty. They often want to take all twenty words (especially at the beginning of the school year), and consequently do poorly on the final tests. It is, therefore, the teacher's responsibility to talk with those students and make a plan for success. The teacher can encourage them to start with fewer words and build up throughout the year. Sometimes it is essential that the teacher actually assist the child in choosing his/her words. Remember, one of our goals is for our students to develop the self-awareness to make responsible choices for themselves. Upper-grade students should be able to select their own words for their developmental ability level. Teacher assistance should only be given when the child is not making appropriate choices, whether at the lower or upper level of the ability range. Through teacher modeling and individual teacher assistance, it has been our experience that most all students arrive at the point where they do make very appropriate choices when given this opportunity, and achieve success using this system.

WHAT ARE THE STEPS FOR THIS APPROACH?

- The teacher selects 20 words from the chapters the class is reading for that week, and prepares a copy of the list for each student. Next to the words are the page numbers where the students can and will locate the words in the text. Throughout the week's lessons, students are given scanning opportunities and activities that help them locate the words on those particular pages. Holes are punched into the paper so that the child may easily insert the page into his/her notebook. (See the samples at the end of this section.)

- Each child has a permanent list of spelling activities that are used weekly. These activities are kept for the entire year in the child's binder. They are run off on a colored piece of duplicating paper so the child can easily locate it in his/her notebook during the week.

- The teacher selects one or two activities he/she believes will build spelling skills that are being stressed for that week. These become teacher-directed activities that are mandatory for each child. This way the teacher has some control over assessing the students' needs for future lessons.

- Students themselves then choose 5 to 8 activities they think will help them learn the selected words for the week. Ultimately, the teacher is trying to have students choose a variety of activities throughout the week and throughout the year. Through student choice of activities, many students will approach spelling creatively, which will help them to remember the spelling of words throughout their lifetime and not only for the Friday test.

- The Spelling Activity List is always incomplete. Students have so many other ideas that are great additions. Always keep activities open so that the list can grow.

- On Thursday, all spelling activities are due. Selected students share with their classmates some of the creative activities they have done.

- Students orally quiz each other on Thursday to help prepare them for the test.

- On Friday all students take the final test. Spelling partners are chosen in a variety of ways (the person across from you, next to you, diagonal from you, the person with the same number of words you are taking) so that students do not always have the same partner.

- Partners are instructed to use each word in a sentence as they give the test. After the test is given, Partner A checks Partner B's test. As they check each other's test, any word that is incorrectly spelled is rewritten by the checker next to the incorrect spelling.

- Rechecking is done by the teacher or spelling expert.

- Any word missed on Friday is retaken orally by the child on Monday morning and grades are recorded by the student on his/her own progress chart. (See the *Spelling Test Recording Sheet* at the end of this section.)

- It is strongly recommended to children who have not successfully passed the test to decrease the number of words taken for the next week.

- As the year progresses, students are occasionally asked to select their own words from the literature selection. Certain ground rules are added, such as "no use of proper nouns." (See the sample *Student-Initiated Spelling* at the end of this section.)

Spelling Activities

1. Choose a long word from your list. See how many shorter words you can make from it using the letters in the word. Think of at least 15 words.

2. Make a word search on graph paper using all of your words. Include an answer sheet.

3. Write a poem using at least five of your spelling words.

4. In your neatest handwriting, write out each of your words three times.

5. Make a set of flash cards. Study each of your words with a partner. Leave out the words you missed. Restudy them.

6. At home, say your spelling words on a tape recorder. Spell them correctly into the recorder. Listen to yourself. Bring the tape to school.

7. Write the words by syllables in different colored markers.

8. Make a paragraph of your own using at least half of your spelling words. Make sure the paragraph makes sense.

9. Write each of your words in sentences to show that you understand their meaning. Make the sentences interesting and entertaining!

10. Make a rebus using ten of your words. Use syllables and pictures to get your idea across clearly.

11. Locate all the nouns in your list. Circle them on your paper. Write a describing word to precede each noun.

12. Make a word picture with your spelling words. Lightly draw with pencil a basic shape. In thin black marker, write your words in small lettering around your basic outlined shape. Now erase your pencil marks and your words will form the shape!

13. Create a crossword puzzle with your words. Write a good definition for each word so that your partner can figure out your puzzle. Include an answer sheet. Make sure a classmate does your crossword puzzle before it is due. Put your name and your partner's name on the paper.

14. Draw a cartoon sequence and use at least ten of your spelling words to create the text or dialogue. You may also use the drawings from a newspaper cartoon and replace the printed text with your own.

15. Write ten of your words in Morse Code.

16. Make up your own code and have a partner decode your ten words.

17. Give each letter of the alphabet a value (a = 1, b = 2, c = 3, d = 4, etc.). Then find the value of ten of your words.

    Example: Spelling: 19 + 16 + 5 + 12 + 12 + 9 + 14 + 7 = _____

18. Write the lyrics to a new rock or rap song. Use at least six of your words from the spelling list.

19. Create six new titles for new books. Use at least eight of your spelling words. Remember to capitalize your titles and underline them.

20. Create a holiday or everyday greeting card, either humorous or serious, using at least ten of your spelling words.

21. Find an antonym for five of your words.

22. Write a letter to your teacher using proper letter form to explain the importance of spelling to you. Use at least eight of your spelling words in the letter.

23. Write an advertisement for a new product. Include five of your spelling words.

24. Find letters in magazines or newspapers. Glue each letter down on a paper forming ten of your spelling words with a variety of printed letters.

25. Draw a picture for five of your words.

26. On your computer, write each of your words in different fonts and sizes.

27. Have your parents study your words with you. Have them initial this paper to show you did it.

28. Make up eight word skeletons from your word list. Give them to a partner and have him/her figure out the words.

    Example: (_ _ s _ r _ _ e _ t) for the word 'instrument.' You may need to give a clue if your partner is stumped. Check that your partner has spelled the words correctly.

29. Find synonyms for eight of your words.

30. Choose eight of your words and make a frame around each of them. Write the word in pencil first. Then erase the word and you will have formed a frame. This shows you the shape (configuration) of the word.

31. Place the first ten words on your list in alphabetical order.

32. With a highlighter, show all of the plural words. Alphabetize them.

33. Make all of the singular words into plural words.

34. Skim the page(s) in your literature book where your spelling words are located. Select three spelling words, and copy the complete sentences in which you find each spelling word.

35. Make three word maps. Select words from your list. First make an oval shape. Place your words inside. Think of, look up, and use your thesaurus to find four other words that mean the same as your word.

36. Scramble the letters of ten of your spelling words. Have a partner unscramble them.

37. Write ten of your words using some kind of alphabet manipulatives (e.g., magnetic letters, alphabet cereal, letter tiles, etc.). Have your parent initial that you actually did the activity.

38. Write an advertisement on an index card using five of your spelling words.

39. Write five couplets, using at least five of your words.

    Example: One day while I was at my file
                I found a cardboard crocodile.

40. Write out ten of your words. Circle the silent letters and underline the vowels.

41. Write five prepositional phrases using five of your words that are nouns.

42. Write eight of your words in a language other than English.

43. Study with a partner. Write your words on a whiteboard. Have your partner write down how many words you got correct.

44. Have someone dictate to you ten of your words. Write your words using the copy, write, cover, check (CWCC) method.

45. Write your words using the 'rainbow technique' of tracing over each of the words at least 3 different times in different colored pencils, crayons, chalk or markers.

46. Select 2 words from your list that are hard to remember the spelling of. Make a sentence out of the letters of those words to help you remember them. Illustrate the sentences. Then teach your memory tricks for learning those words with a partner.

    Example: **muscle:** *Mighty Ursula Squashes Cute Little Elephants.*

47. Select 5 words and find as many little words within them as possible (words in sequence only)

    Examples: **incredulous:** in, red, us **lieutenant:** lie, ten, an, ant

48. Select 1 or 2 words from your list and find as many words as you can using any of the letters within that word (any order or combination of those letters). Compete against a partner or members of your family. See who can find the most words.

    Examples: **incredulous:** dries, rules, cinder **lieutenant:** lit, neat, lean

49. Make up an activity of your own. Be creative.

Teacher-Directed Spelling Techniques and Strategies

- Introduce words on the overhead projector. As a class, ask students to look at the configuration, little words within the word, and any mnemonic clues that would be helpful in remembering to spell the word. Write the word in syllables in different colored pens. Discuss its meaning and use in context.

- When modeling and guiding students in sounding out a word in print, cover part of the word while demonstrating how to sound out one syllable at a time. Point to the individual sounds as you model decoding the word. Then slide your hand or finger rapidly under the letters as you blend the sounds to quickly say the whole word.

- Assign a group of Spelling Experts (those students who are skilled spellers) to act as peer tutors. They may also assist during other writing periods when some students *have to* know how to spell a word correctly, and get frustrated using a dictionary or spell-checker at that time. Spelling experts can also be assigned the task of rechecking spelling tests before grades are recorded.

- Have readily available several resources for student access such as: dictionaries, electronic spell-checkers (e.g., Franklin Spellers), lists of commonly used words, etc.

- Students frequently ask adults how to spell a word while they are writing. Rather than automatically spelling the word for the student, encourage students to use self-help strategies (looking up a word, locating the word in the text or on word charts to copy; using an electronic spell-checker; sounding out the word the best they can and then circling that word to check the spelling later). It is also helpful to allow students to ask peers for spelling assistance. **Note:** Some children get so bogged down in the spelling that they won't write unless they know how to spell the words. With these children, although it is important to encourage self-help strategies, it is advisable to help them with the spelling of some of the troublesome words. Writing them on a separate piece of paper or index card to copy is helpful.

- Use commercial games that teach and reinforce spelling and vocabulary in entertaining ways. *Examples:* Scattergories®, Scrabble®, Boggle®, hangman, Sniglets®, Clever Endeavor®. When playing games in which correct spelling is not a requirement, extra bonus points can be awarded for words that *are* spelled correctly to add the incentive for spelling accuracy.

- Have students develop their own personal lists, word banks, word cards attached to a ring, notebooks, card files, etc., for spelling words they wish to keep and practice. This is particularly useful when these personal spelling words are selected from misspelled words from the student's own written products.

- Teach students to look for patterns in words. Teach word families.

- Provide additional phonetic training to students who are deficient in this skill and are poor spellers. Many upper-grade students have never had teacher-directed phonics instruction and are totally unaware of letter/sound associations in our language. They may be able to decode and read adequately, identifying words from sight and context; but if they can't recall what a word looks like in print, they may have no strategies for spelling. **Note:** See the resources at the end of this section. Programs such as *Simply Phonics* (Rief), *Project Read—Phonology* (Greene and Enfield), *Developing Independent Readers* (Waring), and *Spelling Smart* (Stowe) are highly recommended.

- When reading student's written work, the teacher can make a check mark in the left margin on the line of a misspelled word. The student should try to find his/her own misspelled word(s) and self-correct whenever possible.

- Teach students to write rough drafts using every other line. When they are writing, they can circle, put a question mark, or write "sp" above any words they think are probably spelled wrong. This helps them to self-monitor. Then they can apply strategies for checking the spelling of those words.

- Give class points or table points for recognition of spelling words in a library book.

Other Multisensory Strategies for Enhancing Spelling Motivation

- Dip a clean paintbrush in water and write words on a tabletop or chalkboard.

- Pair movement with practicing spelling words (clap to each letter, bounce ball, yo-yo). Get creative!

- Tap out the sounds or syllables in words.

- Sing spelling words to common tunes/melodies.

- Write the word in the air while sounding it out.

- Using two fingers, write words in a flat tray or box filled with either sand or salt.

- Write words in glue or liquid starch on pieces of cardboard. Then sprinkle any powdery material, glitter, yarn, beans, macaroni, sequins, etc., to create textured 3-D spelling words. Substances such as sand, salt, and glitter are good to use for students who benefit from tracing the words with their fingers. **Note:** The act of tracing with your fingers on a texture helps make a sensory imprint on the brain that increases memory and retention.

- Pair students and have them write words on each other's backs with their fingers.

- While sitting on the carpet, have students practice writing the words directly on the carpet with two fingers using large muscle movements.

- Practice writing words on individual chalkboards or dry-erase boards with colored chalk and colored dry-erase pens (or use magic slates).

- Fingerpaint words on tabletops using shaving cream, pudding, whipped cream, or frosting, etc.

There are positive and negative aspects to any spelling program. As the teacher sees a need for change, the spelling program can be altered. Too many times teachers stay with a program that gets old for the students. Maintaining consistency is important, but having a change for a week or two might be that "shot in the arm" that students (and teachers) need to regroup, take a breather, and rejuvenate themselves.

- Give students a break with no spelling words for the week.
- Have students create their own lists from different sources.
- Have parents and students make up a list of family words.
- Make a spelling list of only 5 or 6 syllable words.
- Center spelling words around a holiday.
- Have students work cooperatively, making up spelling words and activities for their classmates.

Remember: *Variety adds a new dimension. By giving up some control of the spelling program to the students, the teacher is able to make observations on how the students truly work, and the manner in which they make responsible choices.*

TEACHING VOCABULARY SKILLS

The teaching of vocabulary should be infused throughout the entire curriculum, providing students with numerous opportunities to learn and use new words. Teachers need to seek "teachable moments" to motivate students to learn vocabulary relevant and meaningful to them. Most effective in doing so is through classroom discussion of current events, items of interest happening in the news that students are hearing about. What a perfect opportunity, for example, during high-profile trials to teach words such as: defendant, prosecutor, indictment, conviction, attorney, evidence, bail, and so forth.

It has been our experience that many students in our classrooms are unfamiliar with words that we assume they know. It is important to be checking for understanding when we are instructing and/or reading with our students. Over the years we have been amazed at words and terms students (native English speakers) didn't know the meaning of.

Recommended Teaching Strategies

- Model using words in various situations when teaching/introducing vocabulary.
- Define words for students and paraphrase.
- Have students locate vocabulary in context within the text/literature.
- Have students generate vocabulary lists individually, with partners, or in small groups that are categorical (action words, describing words, feeling words, connecting words). Then combine small group lists to formulate class lists/charts to be posted and added to throughout the year.

For example, students are frequently asked to give character *descriptions*. A chart can be generated to include words such as: inquisitive, stubborn, dedicated, ambitious, persevering, distant, obnoxious, mischievous, greedy, selfish, bitter, vivacious, adventurous, independent, resourceful, generous, sensitive, conscientious, loyal, sincere . A chart of *connecting* words might include: however, consequently, therefore, nevertheless.

Students have a particularly difficult time identifying and labeling *feelings* and often are stumped when asked questions such as, "How do you think the character felt?" *Feeling* word lists might include words such as: suspicious, elated, optimistic, concerned, confused, perplexed, discouraged, frustrated, overjoyed. This is a perfect opportunity to teach and practice use of the thesaurus.

- Model and teach sentence expansion. Start with a basic, simple sentence written on the board or overhead. Have students answer questions to add to the sentence for expansion, such as: How? When? Where? For whom? Why?

    Example: The girl worked. (How?) The girl worked frantically (Why?) in order to complete her assignment on time. **Note:** One of the components of *Project Read* (Greene and Enfield), entitled *Framing Your Thoughts*, very effectively teaches students the skill of expanding "bare bones" sentences through very concrete, hands-on techniques. (See the recommended resources at end of this section.)

- Use the newspaper for vocabulary sources and discussion.

- Teach techniques of visualization and association for learning vocabulary words. Use Scott Bornstein's methods for teaching students strategies of visualization, imagination, logic, and observation in making associations. He teaches how to make connections between the word and its definition. (See the recommended resources at the end of this section.)

- When teaching new vocabulary give examples and non-examples. Try this strategy: "This is a _____." "This is not a _____." "Is this a _____? How do you know?"

- Teach vocabulary essential for test-taking and following directions. Make sure all students understand the following words: synonym, antonym, opposite, summarize, illustrate, contrast, compare, connect, sequence, match, opposite, describe, underline, list, never, always, all, none, generally, usually, true, false, frequently, cross out.

- Use semantic mapping and webbing for vocabulary development. Place a topic word in the center and have students generate words or phrases related to that topic word. Write those words and phrases stemming away from the center word.

- Give students a list of commonly used words. In partners or small groups have them identify words that are synonyms that a primary grade child might use, an upper grader or teenager might use, an adult might use. These words can be assigned a monetary value, and are referred to as penny words, nickel words, quarter words, dollar words.

- Have students use a certain number of vocabulary words within a paragraph they write.

- Have students make flash cards with their vocabulary words (words on one side/definitions on the other) and practice with a partner.

- Teach dictionary and thesaurus skills. Model and practice how to use these references frequently. Teachers need to stress the importance of vocabulary development and the need to increase our repertoire of words to help express ourselves and communicate our true viewpoints and opinions. It is recommended that every student have his/her own dictionary and thesaurus (or one per every two students to share). Provide many activities and opportunities to use a thesaurus for enriching the vocabulary in oral/written communication and substituting for overused words.

- Have students create their own crossword puzzles, word matches, and word searches using new vocabulary words. There are computer programs that help students to do so, such as *Word Works*. (See the resources at the end of this section.)

- Play concentration games matching vocabulary words with definitions.

- As students are dismissed, enter room, etc., have them say a new vocabulary word and tell what it means, or use it in a sentence. This might be the students' "ticket out of the door" at the end of the day.

- Have cooperative groups work as a team to write one of the vocabulary words, illustrate it, and use creatively on a transparency. They then share with the whole class. All students keep a notebook or section in their binder for new vocabulary and must copy the words and meanings.

- If there are 10 vocabulary words to learn during a week, assign 10 students in the room to write one of the words on a sentence strip with a felt-tip marker. This is their word for the week. Anytime the word is used throughout the week, they are to stand up and hold up the word. Each week select 10 different students.

- Have students keep a notebook, card file, or word bank of new vocabulary words. Include the word, its definition, and an example or two of the word being used in a sentence.

- Give individual, table, or class points for finding vocabulary words of the week in library books.

BIBLIOGRAPHY AND RECOMMENDED RESOURCES

Bornstein, Scott J. *Memory Techniques for Vocabulary Mastery.* (1988) Bornstein Memory Improvement Programs, 8040 Deering Avenue, Suite 7, Canoga Park, CA 91304.

Forte, Imogene, and Pangle, Mary Ann. *Selling Spelling to Kids.* Nashville: Incentives Publications, Inc., 1985.

Franklin Learning Resources has a number of electronic aids from the simple to sophisticated, that make it easier for many students to find the correct spelling of words and definitions than through the use of dictionaries. Contact: Franklin Learning Resources, 122 Burrs Road, Mount Holly, New Jersey 08060.

Greene, Victoria E., and Enfield, Mary Lee. *Project Read—Phonology.* Language Circle, P.O. Box 20631, Bloomington, MN 55420. Phone: 612-884-4880.

Rief, Sandra. *Simply Phonics: Quick and Easy.* (1993) EBSCO Curriculum Materials, Box 11542, Birmingham, AL 35202-1542. Phone: 1-800-633-8623.

Stowe, Cynthia. *Spelling Smart! A Ready-to-Use Activities Program for Students with Spelling Difficulties.* West Nyack, NY: The Center for Applied Research in Education, 1995.

Word Finder: The Phonic Key to the Dictionary. Available through Pilot Light, 2708 47th Street S., Gulfport, FL 33711.

Word Works. EBSCO Curriculum Materials, Box 11542, Birmingham, AL 35202-1542 Phone: 1-800-633-8623.

SAMPLE: TEACHER-DIRECTED SPELLING LESSON

Name _____

Spelling: Week of _____ from *Hatchet*, Chapters 4 and 5

Word List A	Word List B
incredible (p. 31)	dizziness (42)
temperature (31)	immediately (45)
aches (33)	occurred (46)
forehead (33)	frantic (47)
swollen (35)	tomatoes (48)
bruised (35)	chocolate (48)
attempt (35)	positive (49)
mosquitoes (36)	silence (51)
scenery (38)	commercials (52)
channel (41)	wolves (55)

SPELLING ACTIVITIES

1. Highlight each of your words. Write each of your words neatly in cursive writing or in printing. Use the following guidelines: If you take all 20 words, write each word 1 ×; 14-19 words, write them 2 ×'s; and 10-13 words, write them 3 ×'s.

2. Combine a word from List A with a word from List B into one sentence. Write three of these sentences. Underline your words.

3. Locate the word *swollen* on page 35. Copy the entire sentence. Watch for correct spelling and punctuation.

4. Think of four other words like *wolf* that form the plural by changing the "f" to "v" and adding "es." Use your language book for help if you cannot think of any others.

5. Alphabetize List B.

6. Write a synonym for *silence*. Use your thesaurus.

7. Make up a word search on graph paper using all the words.

9. Have a friend or family member ask you your words. Have them initial this paper. _____

10.   Any word you miss on Friday must be retaken orally on Monday.

SAMPLE: TEACHER/STUDENT SPELLING UNIT

Name _____

Spelling: Week of _____ from *Scared Stiff*

position (150)	familiar (171)
calliope (159)	loudspeaker (170)
souvenirs (159)	microphone (170)
carousel (159)	genuine (172)
artificial (160)	bruise (175)
invisible (162)	bookkeepers (179)
opposite (166)	valuable (186)
investigate (167)	restaurant (187)
hesitate (167)	merry-go-round (187)
tourist-trap (168)	greasy (187)

SPELLING ACTIVITIES:

1. Highlight each of the words you will be taking this week.

2. Write your words in cursive, printing, various computer fonts, or in calligraphy.

3. Write each of the hyphenated words from this list.

4. Write each of the compound words in this list. Think of five other compound words that you use in your everyday language.

5. Scan page 159 and locate the word *calliope*. Write the entire sentence, underlining the word. Then look it up in the dictionary. What are the two guide words at the top of the page? Draw a picture of a calliope and explain what it is in your own words.

6. Choose 5 other activities from your *Spelling Activities* page.

7. Study with a partner. Have him/her initial this paper.

SAMPLE: STUDENT-INITIATED SPELLING UNIT

Name _____

Spelling: Week of _____

This week you will be developing your own spelling words and activities. Here is what you will be expected to accomplish.

1. Choose 20 words from the following chapters in your reading book. _____

2. You may use any word, except proper nouns—no names of people, places, or things.

3. Look for words that you will use in your everyday speech and writing—not words that are foreign to you, or that you will probably never use again.

4. Choose 6 to 8 spelling activities from your *Spelling Activities* sheet.

5. Study your words.

6. Take your test on Friday with a partner.

7. Staple your spelling activities and your test together and place it in the appropriate box.

8. Make sure your name is on your work.

9. Answer these questions:

    a, Did you do quality work? _____

    b. Did you study?_____

HOOKING IN RELUCTANT READERS/WRITERS

WHOLE LANGUAGE VS. SKILLS-BASED

Every six to eight years language arts instruction seems to take a new direction depending on the swing of philosophical thought. For those of us who have been teaching for twenty years or more, we have experienced the full cycle of reading/writing instruction. During the past few years the school of thought embraced by most districts is that students learn to read best through whole language. This integrated approach combines reading, writing, speaking, and listening, enabling children to see connections and acquire meaning from good pieces of core literature. Whole-class instruction of a piece of literature is often used with this approach in the upper-grade classroom. Teachers modeling good reading habits by reading from the text to their students, cooperative group or paired reading, and opportunities for individual reading are elements of this reading method. Furthermore, reading is more global, more significant to students, and the activities that support the reading are more creative and enriching than was the case in the last wave of reading instruction.

Throughout our educational history, teaching reading was much more fundamental, very directed by the teacher, homogeneous reading groups, drill, high focus on phonics, and worksheets. This method certainly seemed to show high performance on the standardized tests, and most students learned to read. However, the process and the reading materials used seemed to stifle creativity, and many of the students were bored with the trite passages and word-controlled stories. The teacher's editions of basal series were very easy to follow, but left very little room to veer from the scripted lessons. New teachers could easily teach reading because the guide was comprehensive, and there was no question what needed to be taught—it was all there right before the teacher's eyes. It was easy to make out report cards because the child took tests to show exactly where they were on the developmental or grade expectancy scale.

Need for a balanced reading program

Any reading program that is going to be successful will incorporate the best of methods and approaches that have been proven to be effective in teaching students. Children need reading material that will captivate their interest, fuel their creative thought, motivate them to think critically, and allow them to make meaningful connections to their lives. The whole language approach provides for these needs of children most effectively. In addition, we know that many children need a more direct approach for being taught specific skills fundamental to becoming fluent, competent, independent readers and writers. They need a more structured, teacher-directed approach for being taught those necessary skills. What makes best sense is to find a balance in language arts instruction, utilizing a host of strategies and techniques to meet the needs of all learners. Since every child learns reading in his/her own individual way, taking the best of both approaches (whole language and skills-based) will hopefully hit the mark for each student.

THE CHALLENGE OF MOTIVATING THE UPPER-GRADERS

In the primary grades students have insatiable appetites for books, and are motivated to read them because of the bright colors, large text, and phenomenally illustrative pictures. But what is there to captivate the upper-grade students? The subject matter must be interesting and make connections to the students' lives so that they will continue to read as the books increase in the level of difficulty, with more and more pages and chapters.

In the last decade, there seems to have been a general downward slide in students' desire to read for enjoyment, and in the ability to comprehend what is being read. This is most likely because of the fast- paced world in which the students live, and because television, current movies and videos are a much more attractive lure to those students who are having difficulty in the reading process. Today, tapes and videos of books are readily available, so some students wonder why they need to read at all. Unless we show our students a need for reading, our reluctant readers will continue to show a lack of enjoyment or appreciation for the place of a good piece of literature in their lives. The transition from picture books to chapter books is very difficult for our more reluctant readers. When something is a challenge, or overwhelmingly difficult, a certain percentage of our students will give up and stop trying. In the upper grades, we must search for stories and other reading experiences that enthrall the lower-achieving students, giving them a chance to be successful by building their self-esteem without defeating their self-images.

One of our goals in teaching reading to upper-graders is to provide them with opportunities to comprehend, appreciate, and respond to a wide variety of pieces of literature. Through their reading, we hope they will begin to synthesize their understanding of customs and beliefs of different cultures, and will compare and contrast their own lives to the characters in the books. We want to provide them with opportunities to read other materials besides books, so that they possess the survival reading skills needed in the world of their everyday lives. We must provide experiences for the reading of practical content reading, as well as self-selected, pleasure reading.

WHAT CAN BE DONE FOR THE UNDER-MOTIVATED READER/WRITER?

In every classroom, no matter how hard the teacher tries, there are going to be some students who are reluctant readers/writers. These are the students who have difficulty keeping focused for even short periods of time on the reading task at hand. They are sometimes apathetic and often disengaged during the reading period. So what are we going to do to motivate these reluctant learners?

POETRY

Poetry seems to bring out the best in children of all ages. It can become a motivating avenue to teach many aspects of language. Poetry seems to breathe life and enthusiasm into the reluctant reader. It gets them involved and makes them feel successful in one aspect of reading. Children who come to us with limited English proficiency also seem to pick up and enjoy poetry because of its simplicity and shortness. Students who are high achievers seem to thrive on the humor, the memory of the verse, and the elements that make it so magical.

Every child seems to relate to the contemporary feel of Shel Silverstein's and Jack Prelutsky's lively, fun, child-centered poetry. Whether the poem is about not wanting to go to school, having too much homework, a father who snores too loudly, or a four-leaf clover that brings bad luck, children tend to become active participants in the reading, listening, speaking and writing of these poems. They smile, laugh, readily read, listen, and respond to this poetry because it relates to their interests, is short and nonintimidating, and is enjoyable. For the reluctant readers, there is no threatening factor of too many words crammed on a page. The lines are fast-moving and rhyming, and have subjects that kids think about and are involved in regularly in their daily lives. Students who seem unable to stay focused because of factors in their lives outside of school, because of attentional difficulties, or just because they have low motivation in their learning style, tend to be quickly swept away in poetry because they can instantly be successful readers.

Skills Taught Through Reading/Listening to Poetry

- rhyme
- phonics
- parts of speech (nouns, verbs, adjectives, prepositional phrases)
- listening
- cooperation
- poetry form
- figurative language
- imagery
- memory

Getting Children "Into" Poetry

Beginning the day with a lesson on poetry usually is a cheerful way to get the morning started. How can students not feel welcomed in a classroom where the day begins with something light, enjoyable, and stimulating?

For classroom use, overhead transparencies are made for many of the poems. The overhead printing is enlarged to more than its actual size. When dealing with a class size of 30 or more, teachers need to be cautious when using the overhead projector so that students are able to read the text easily without straining their eyes. Care should be given to making the words large enough for all students to read. In our classrooms, the upper-graders may move closer to the screen by moving their chairs nearer to the front of the room, or by sitting on the rug area, which is directly in front of the screen. We find that upper-grade students do not mind sitting on the rug if it is made available and used early in the year.

The use of overheads in these poetry lessons seems more beneficial than handing out individual copies of the poem because it gets students focusing collectively. Students are more likely to listen because they know that the poem will not be up on the overhead for very long, but that it can still be reviewed if necessary. Also, in these times of disappearing funds for education, a transparency is more economical than class sets of poetry papers.

"Michael Built a Bicycle"—A Lesson Plan

In order to teach the concept of imagery and to help ensure that children are transitioning from picture books to chapter books, Jack Prelutsky's poem "Michael Built a Bicycle" from *The New Kid on the Block* (New York: Greenwillow Books, 1984) provides the perfect avenue to start. In this poem, Michael builds a bicycle that is overly accessorized.

Michael Built A Bicycle*

Michael built a bicycle
unsuitable for speed,
it's crammed with more accessories
than anyone could need,
there's an AM-FM radio,
a deck to play cassettes,
a refrigerator-freezer,
and a pair of TV sets.

There are shelves for shirts and sweaters,
there are hangers for his jeans,
a drawer for socks and underwear,
a rack for magazines,
there's a fishtank and a birdcage
perched upon the handlebars,
a bookcase, and a telescope
to watch the moon and stars.

There's a telephone, a blender,
and a stove to cook his meals,
there's a sink to do the dishes
somehow fastened to the wheels,
there's a portable piano,
and a set of model trains,
an automatic bumbershoot
that opens when it rains.

There's a desk for typing letters
on his fabulous machine,
a stall for taking showers,
and a broom to keep things clean,
but you'll never see him ride it,
for it isn't quite complete,
Michael left no room for pedals,
and there isn't any seat.

The following is the plan for teaching basic imagery for this poem.

Day 1

1. The students are asked to listen carefully to the unusual items that Michael places on his bicycle.

2. The teacher reads the poem to the students while their eyes are shut. This is important so they block out the other stimuli in the classroom and therefore, concentrate on the poem itself.

3. The students have lined paper on their desks. At this time, they are asked to list as many items that they can think of that Michael has on his bicycle.

4. As they are making their list, the teacher again reads the poem.

5. The students are then shown an overhead transparency of a basic bicycle frame.

6. They are given a piece of plain white paper and asked to draw a simple bicycle frame similar, but not exactly like, the overhead on the screen.

7. They are asked to *quick-draw* a picture of what Michael's bicycle might look like, using the list of items they have just formulated. (A sixth grader's sample quick-draw is shown in the illustration.)

8. After three minutes, the teacher asks for volunteers to draw some items on the overhead (birdcage, blender, bumbershoot [umbrella], cassette deck) to motivate some of the students who are a little artistically hesitant to get started. Just seeing a few ideas might be the catalyst to "jump start" a child who doesn't believe he/she can draw.

9. After ten minutes, the students are asked to stop their work. The students share their papers with their table partners (tables consist of 4 students).

10. Volunteers are asked to share their pictures with the entire class at the rug area.

11. The students are then asked to explain how this exercise is like transitioning from picture books to chapter books. (*When we have pictures in a book, they show us how the illustrator wanted the reader to see the story. When we read chapter books with no illustrations, we must fill in or create the illustrations or scenes in our own minds. It is similar to seeing a movie and reading a book.*)

Day 2

12. A few overheads are made of the students' bicycle pictures to share with the entire class.

13. A discussion may ensue on why the pictures all look different. (We all have *different* artistic ability; we all perceive the words differently; we all heard different things while listening.)

14. The poem is presented to the whole class on the overhead projector. The students see how James Stevenson, the illustrator of Jack Prelutsky's book, *The New Kid on the Block* , visualized the poem.

15. The students read the poem from the overhead again silently.

16. The children are each assigned one line of the poem to read independently in front of the class. They are given about 30 seconds to say the line out loud to themselves (in a whisper) and, if they don't know a word or words, they need to ask their partner.

17. The poem is read in its entirety by individuals. Everyone participates, and because everyone has heard the poem at least three times when the teacher read it, the child should be able to successfully read his/her part.

18. The poem is handed out to each pair of students. They are to highlight the rhyming words; then read the whole poem alternating every two lines of poetry. (This allows the reluctant reader to be a successful participant without being frustrated by having to read in front of too many other children.)

19. Parts of speech are easily taught through poetry. Since this poem is rich in naming words, the teacher might want to take this opportunity to review the idea of common nouns. Students with limited English proficiency might be asked to recite the nouns in their own language, while locating the same words in English from the poem.

Recommended poems for classroom use by *Jack Prelutsky* are listed below :

"My Brother Built a Robot" (creative writing about robots and what a child might program a robot to do; construction of a robot)

"Last Night I Dreamed of Chickens" (prepositional phrases)

"I Should Have Stayed in Bed Today" (verbs)

"The Turkey Shot out of the Oven" (verbs)

"When Tillie Ate the Chili" (verbs)

"Belinda Blue" (conversation, dialogue)

"A Remarkable Adventure" (creative writing: *What are your best excuses why your homework isn't done?*)

"The Flimsy Fleek" (imagery, adjectives)

"Gussie's Greasy Spoon" (nouns)

"I Found a Four-Leaf Clover" (verbs, creative writing: *What would happen to you if you found a four-leaf clover?*)

"My Dog, He Is an Ugly Dog" (adjectives)

"Homework! Oh, Homework!" (memorization, writing: *How do you feel about doing homework?* Create one homework assignment that you would like a teacher to give you. Explain why this assignment would be considered educational.)

"Louder than a Clap of Thunder" (comparisons, creative writing: *What is loud?*)

"Suzanna Socked Me Sunday" (repetition, dramatization)

Note: These poems can be found in Something Big Has Been Here *(Greenwillow Books, 1990) and* The New Kid on the Block *(Greenwillow Books, 1984).*

"Messy Room"—A Lesson Plan

Another poem that will motivate even the most reluctant readers/writers in the classroom is "Messy Room" by Shel Silverstein from *A Light in the Attic* (New York: Harper and Row Publishers, Inc.,1981).

This is a poem that students relate to for many reasons, but basically because at this age, children do not keep their bedrooms particularly tidy. In fact, in many homes, the "messy" room is a source of contention between parents and their children.

The following lesson has been utilized successfully with upper grade students.

1. The teacher reads the poem to the students without the use of the visual. He/she prefaces the reading by saying, "Today I am going to read a poem by Shel Silverstein entitled "Messy Room." Each of you should listen carefully and think about what you can see in this room."

2. The teacher then asks the students individually to write on paper or on a whiteboard what things they remember were in this particular bedroom. About three minutes are given for this task. This is an excellent time for the teacher to observe which children are having difficulty with listening. The auditory children will find this task very easy, but the visual children will probably be challenged by the task.

3. The teacher then reads the poem again to the students and when he/she is finished asks the students to add to their list.

4. The poem is read a third time and the students are allowed to add to their lists. They are asked to count the number of items they remember and place that number at the top of their page and circle it.

5. The transparency is now placed on the overhead.

6. One by one individual students come to the overhead and use an overhead marker to highlight the items found in the room. As one child is finished, he/she hands-off the pen to a member of the other gender. This person now highlights a new idea and *hands-off* to another student. This gets a number of students actively involved, and encourages some of them to participate who normally would not raise their hands. The uniqueness of using the overhead pen does motivate some of the students to become involved.

7. A discussion is then held about auditory and visual learners. Asking a question, such as "How many of you had difficulty remembering the poem when I only read it once to you? Twice? Three times? How many of you would have liked to have seen the poem from the very beginning?" Making students aware of how they learn is essential in the upper grades. Students need to know their style of learning and how they can compensate if they are weak in one of their modalities.

8. Students are then asked to write a paragraph describing their own bedroom. Some ideas covered in that paragraph should be color, wallpaper, window coverings, size, shape, bedspread, stuffed animals, and other details. Ten minutes are given to this task. It is a quick-write. Students should write for the full ten minutes and the teacher should also write, modeling good writing to the students. At the end of this time, all students are asked to turn to their partner and read their quick-write.

9. Students should be aware of the fact that a quick-write is not a final product; it is just a beginning. More time is needed to think about and expand the ideas. All students are asked to put finishing touches on their paragraphs at home and are strongly encouraged to read their paragraphs to their parents.

10. The teacher might already have a more thorough paragraph written so that the students can hear what the teacher is expecting. Good teacher modeling is essential to good student writing.

11. The next day, students read their completed paragraphs to partners.

12. A discussion is held to compare bedroom neatness. The teacher may ask, *How does your bedroom compare with the child's in the poem? Do you think the person in the poem is a boy or a girl? Why? How many of you have messy bedrooms? How many of you have neat bedrooms? How many of you share a bedroom? How many of you get into arguments with your parents because of the messiness of your bedroom? How often do you have to clean your bedroom? How does it feel when you can't find something you need because your room is too messy? How does it feel when you get grounded or restricted because of your room?*

13. This questioning leads the students into discussing their own personal styles. The teacher can probably guess which students have messy bedrooms and which ones have neat rooms, just from what is seen within the classroom. A child's style is very noticeable. One job of the teacher is to make students aware of how they approach life. By doing so, they learn to appreciate and understand who they are.

14. The poem is now brought back onto the screen and selected students are asked to read the lines. Since the students have all heard the poem several times, everyone should have some degree of success in reading it orally. Choosing the best readers first does give the students a refresher course in listening to the poem. Since the purpose of presenting fun poetry in class that everyone can relate to is to get students involved, everyone should

have a chance to read some part of the poem orally. Use of partners is also helpful. Partner A reads the poem to Partner B. Active participation by each student is a must. Limited English proficient students are able to enjoy and have fun with the shortness and content of this poem.

15. Students independently are now asked to write all of the pairs of rhyming words they can find in the poem. These are then highlighted by selected students on the transparency.

16. Cooperatively in groups of three, students are now asked to find as many naming words (nouns) that they can locate in the poem. The teacher may say, "I am looking for some other words that are like room. Find me at least ten other naming words (nouns: persons, places or things). You may find all of them if you want. You have five minutes. Remember that you can always test a naming word by putting 'the' in front of it (the room, the underwear, the chair)." **Note:** Although teaching parts of speech is not part of the whole language approach, students must have command of them, especially when they are dealing with a foreign language. If we teach the basics of speech, students will have a better foundation when they do have opportunities to learn a foreign language.

17. The students are now told they will have one week to become more familiar with their own rooms. Their task is to measure their room and to draw a sketch of what it looks like on graph paper, being careful to be exact. (This can be coordinated with the teaching of area and perimeter.) Some help may be necessary from parents. Extra tape measures may be borrowed from the teacher for those students who do not have their own. Students may work together. **Note:** Some students do not have bedrooms. We have to be careful to respect their need for privacy. Possibly letting them work with another student, or having them create the perfect bedroom on their own, would make them feel more comfortable.

18. It is always helpful to have a guest speaker come in who is a builder, contractor, or architect. They can make children more aware of how to draw doors, windows, etc., to scale. It is surprising how children perceive the world. Many of them, when drawing their doors, make them stick out into the room, instead of seeing them from a bird's-eye view, or from looking down upon them. It is a good idea to have a model or sample of what you want. You will probably have to restate the idea several times that they are looking at their room from a position hovering above it.

A Poetry Corner or Center

In every classroom there should be a place where students may visit to look at and review poetry books. The poetry center always seems to be popular. Students continue to borrow books from this center to take back to their own desks or to use during a "choice" period. (See "Planning, Doing, Reflecting" in Section 2, *Learning Developmentally*.)

As poetry is read, the teacher may ask the students to:

• Record and evaluate the poems on a special poetry log sheet that is kept in their three-ring binders throughout the year. (See the *Poetry Log* sheet at the end of this section.) Short, concise record-keeping is an easy way for the reluctant reader to summarize and recall the poetry that he/she has read.

- Keep a file of poetry selections that students cut out of magazines, newspapers, or rewrite themselves.
- Draw or illustrate their favorite poetry.
- Memorize a favorite poem.
- Share a poem with a partner.
- Dramatize a poem for the entire class.
- Write poetry of their own.
- Tape their reading of a poem and listen back to their way of reading it.
- Read their favorite poetry to younger students at school (buddies) or at home.
- Make a poetry board. Using a large white piece of tagboard, students might recopy (in printing or on the computer) a poem they like, illustrate it, present it to the class, display it on the bulletin board.

When the classroom is richly supplied with a large variety of poetry books for the students to use and enjoy, and the teacher gives instruction in basic poetry, students readily use poetry to express themselves. One of the most beautiful poems written in our classrooms was done by a reluctant reader/writer. During the Planning-Doing-Reflecting segment of the day, where students select a center they want to spend time at, Matt chose the Poetry Center. He read a few poems during that half-hour segment, but then took out a piece of paper and began to write. His poem was about an aunt who had recently died. The poem was an outpouring of sorrow that he felt compelled to write in order to give finality to the death. Matt was able to share the poem with his classmates during the oral "reflecting time." If this center had not been available at that particular time, would that student ever have had the opportunity to create it on his own?

Having poetry in the classroom provides wonderful opportunities for all students to be involved in reading and writing. Students' success in short, poetry-reading experiences may open the door to larger reading successes in the future.

TONGUE TWISTERS

These silly phrases and hard-to-say rhymes provide fun language experiences for all students. Those who are reluctant readers and speakers can become very successful at reading, reciting, and creating their own twisters.

Some examples from *Tongue Twisters* by Charles Keller (New York: Simon & Schuster Books, 1989) are:

- Seven silly sheep slowly shuffled south.
- Eight apes ate eight apples.
- Sister Sarah shined her silver shoes for Sunday.
- Round and round the rough and ragged rock the ragged rascal ran.

Students may begin by reading the twisters from the board or from books. Beginning with one-, two-, or three-lined rhymes and then progressing to more difficult ones seems to be a logical order.

You might involve students in tongue twisters by:

- Starting a file box or collection.
- Placing one twister on the board each week and asking those who have mastered it to say it to the class.
- Having students work in partners to master the skill.
- Writing tongue twisters of their own. Since tongue twisters use the literary element of alliteration, students might start with one example of their own using their name, such as: Mary mentioned money matters to her mother; Sue's sister sat sadly seeing the sinking ship; Jasmine jabbered joyously as the gelatin jiggled.

COMICS

Children from all academic ranges can enjoy the use of comics in the classroom. The reluctant reader views a comic strip as manageable because of its shortness and because there are pictures to accompany the words, which give clarification to the meaning.

Teachers may provide comics to their students in a variety of ways:

- A large supply of comic strips from the Sunday newspaper may be laminated and used for instruction. Having parents assist in the collection of comics is helpful so that there is more than one copy of each. Colorful comics tend to be more stimulating than black and white for most students.
- Small-group instruction using the same comic may be used with the reluctant readers, or with LEP students who have difficulty understanding the more sophisticated strips.
- For whole-class instruction, a comic strip may be placed on the overhead projector, read, and discussed.
- Teachers should select the comic strips that are age appropriate for their students. Children can become frustrated with some of the more complicated story lines.
- A comic center may be set up for students to visit when their work is completed or during the Planning-Doing-Reflecting part of the day (see Section 2, *Learning Developmentally*). Laminated comic strips may be used to read, summarize, and keep a record. (See the *Comic Strip Recording Sheet* at the end of this section.) Students may create their own comic characters and comic strips.
- Children may want to dramatize the comic strips from the newspaper or the ones they have created themselves.
- Students may use a transparency to share their comic strips with the entire class, or the teacher may duplicate a student's comic strip on an overhead transparency.
- Individual comic strips such as Blondie, Dennis the Menace, or Peanuts can be collected over several months. Cooperative groups may work together to see how the characters change, or what their experiences are over a longer period of time. Reviewing comic strips in this way allows children to see that many characters do not change—that they keep their basic personalities over weeks, months, years, or even decades.
- Children should be provided opportunities to read the comics out loud with partners and to be able to discuss them within cooperative groups.

- Limited English proficient speakers or learning disabled students may have difficulty understanding the humor in the comic strips. Therefore, small-group instruction may assist these students in translation or explanation of the meaning. It is helpful to pair students who speak the same native language when discussing figurative language. A student who is bilingual may be able to explain the true meaning of an expression to another limited English proficient student who translates literally instead of figuratively. This partner may be able to explain the humor in the comic in his/her partner's native language.

There is a wonderful book called *Teaching with Calvin and Hobbes* by Mary Santella-Johnson and Linda Holmen that we highly recommend. The authors use very humorous *Calvin and Hobbes* comic strips to motivate upper-grade students while teaching a variety of skills: vocabulary, comprehension, figurative language, and problem solving.

CEREAL BOXES

What would life be without the cereal aisle at the grocery store? Have you ever watched little kids in their baskets reach out at the brightly colored boxes that seem to beckon them to come closer? Have you noticed how cereal commercials fascinate the young and old alike on Saturday mornings? Every morning across America there are thousands of children "reading" the back of those cereal boxes.

The question then is, why don't we as teachers use this motivating and easily accessible instructional tool in the classroom to "hook" students to the real world? At our school, we have done just that.

This cereal box activity extends across the curriculum. To supplement the classroom literature units, students (even those who are reluctant readers) will come alive, and see that reading can also come in little bites. A cereal box contains a lot of reading material, but also gives visual motivation and cues. When kids see that reading is a life skill that will extend their everyday knowledge, then reading becomes more meaningful.

Since this activity is only a supplement to the regular math, language arts, health, science and art curriculum, the number of minutes and number of days that the teacher can incorporate it into the instructional program is an individual concern. Fitting it into 20 to 30 minute blocks of time seems to fit well for some.

A Week Before the Activity Begins

Each child is asked to bring in an empty cereal box, or more, if possible. There should be one box for every student in the classroom.

Day 1: To get the students interested in the assignment, it is helpful to show them a video with some of the cereal commercials from Saturday morning cartoons. When the teacher does this in class, every student sees the same commercials and can discuss them as a whole group. If this is not possible, students can be asked to watch one or two commercials on their own television at home. (**Note:** This can present a problem when a child does not have a television or when a parent is not in agreement with the assignment.)

Students at this time are gearing up for preparing their own commercials that will be videotaped and evaluated later during this activity. Watching commercials will assist them in becoming better prepared to create their own.

A discussion on ways that advertisers attract someone to their product is held during class. These are called *propaganda* techniques. Some ideas that might be discussed are: emotional words, join the band wagon, testimonial, celebrity endorsement, and repetition.

Working in pairs, students now think of any brands of cereals with which they already are familiar that they would see in the grocery store. They fill out the *Cereals That Already Exist* sheet (found at the end of this section) and file it in their notebooks.

As a homework assignment, the students are asked to write a paragraph describing their favorite cereal. This is written on the form entitled *An Up Close and Personal Look at My Favorite Cereal* (found at the end of this section).

Day 2: When a classroom set of boxes is complete, the students are asked to think of ways to categorize them. The students work in teams to think of categories, such as: size, color, child-type cereals, adult-like cereals, sugary cereals, nutritious cereals, those with a character on the box, those without a character, company names, those with a gift inside, those with an activity to do on the back, generic brands, etc. An upper-grade class will come up with a lot more ideas, using the cooperative brainstorming technique. After this session is completed, the students practice the skill of categorizing by placing the boxes into the groups they have chosen.

Days 2 and 3: Each child, with a box on his/her desk, compiles a list of all the things that can be found on a cereal box (size, weight, company, ingredients, calories, nutritional value, etc.). This list is kept on the *What's on a Cereal Box?* form (found at the end of this section). It is kept in the child's notebook for future use. From this list, the class compiles notes and definitions for the words they will be seeing on the boxes. Health lessons on grams, calories, protein, fat, carbohydrates, sodium, and more can be discussed from the health book, lectures, dictionaries, and other reference materials. Having the school nurse or a nutritionist come into the class gives an added degree of importance to the assignment. Clarification of these terms and the importance to the students' health is emphasized here. Discussion and finding out what the students know about healthy choices is an essential part of these first sessions.

Day 4: Students compile a list of descriptive words they find on the cereal boxes. These words are ones that are emotional and cause us to think of eating (honey-coated, new and improved, delicious, sensational, nutritious, fat-free, sweet, healthy, kid-tested, mother-approved, no added colors, no preservatives, no sugar or salt, natural whole wheat, crispy, etc.). From this, students are encouraged to use their thesaurus to locate more words that could be used to describe their own cereal that they will be creating.

Days 5, 6 and 7: The students are ready to embark on their mission as a cerealologist (a scientist who studies cereal). They should understand that they are now scientists who need to record data in a reliable manner. Illustrations and notes are part of a scientist's search for accuracy and validity. Neatness, readability, color, and correctness should be stressed.

Depending on your students, a specific number of *Cereal Box Investigation* forms (found at the end of this section) should be assigned. For students who are more skillful, possibly 6 to 8 forms should be required. For students who are more challenged with reading and writing, possibly 3 to 5 forms may be required. The more forms filled out, the more the students will read, write about, and be able to compare.

At the same time, a large class matrix on butcher or chart paper may be used to show a comparison of the cereals and provide a discussion tool at the end of the collection of information.

Day 8: Most students will be completed with their investigation by this time. If they need more time or help, a parent or aide may need to assist them in the completion of the activity.

Today is a good day to discuss the results of the scientific investigation. In other words, what have they learned so far about cereal boxes and the information they provide? Discussing the class chart is helpful. Scientists need to write about their conclusions and findings. At this time, the students may write a paragraph to summarize their findings.

Day 9: Now that the class has become totally exposed to cereal boxes, each child will create his/her own personal cereal box. Students may work in pairs. They should be reminded about everything that is on a cereal box from the lists they compiled earlier. They need to include all the items found on a real cereal box.

Students may cover their own boxes in butcher paper, gift wrapping paper, foil, tissue, etc. We use school-provided butcher paper of different colors, and have a parent or two assist the students at school in actually covering their boxes. Some students have not learned how to wrap a gift or cover a book, so the classroom may be the first exposure they have with this type of skill. Having a student do the first step at school gets him/her off to a successful start. Although the box is wrapped in school, the actual construction of the front, back, and sides can be done at home.

After the box is wrapped, a cereal box planning sheet entitled *My Own Cereal Box Creation* (found at the end of this section) is filled out. A team of experts circulates the room and helps with spelling. When the sheet is completed, students transfer their drawing onto their covered box. Students are encouraged to recreate the illustration in pencil first, so that mistakes can be taken care of more easily. Colored pencils, marking pens, construction paper, puffy paints, cloth, etc., can be used to make the outside of the box more attractive.

Day 10: This is a great day to review the cereal commercials that have been looked at on the first day. Each child will create a 30-second to 1-minute television commercial to sell his/her cereal to the class. It will be videotaped, previewed, and evaluated by the teacher, classmates, and themselves. The students should fill out a *Cereal Commercial Planning Sheet* (found at the end of this section.)

Many students like to use other props besides their cereal box to enhance their commercials. The use of glasses, wigs, aprons, costumes, dialect, music, slogans, make-up, dance, etc., also challenge the child to use not one, but several of his/her seven intelligences. Let them be creative!

Day 11: Students will have a work period to finish their cereal boxes and pair up with another student to practice and time their commercial.

Day 12: The teacher will video all the commercials.

Day 13: The class will preview all of the videos, and each student will evaluate him-/herself and three other students' commercials and cereal boxes. (A *Cereal Commercial Evaluation Form* is found at the end of this section.)

Day 14: Put closure to this activity. The class should have a discussion about what they have learned and what they liked and disliked about the investigation and project.

Throughout this two- or three-week activity period, the teacher should set high expectations on quality, neatness, and creativity. Each student's project should be measured individually according to his/her ability level, participation, enthusiasm, as well as other pertinent criterion.

Day 15: Compile all the notes, planning sheets, investigation sheets, evaluations, and lists into a construction paper folder. Have students design a cover on their own, or have a contest for the cover, and run off the winning cover for everyone in the class.

Day 16: Have a Parent Day or invite another class in where the students can share what they have done. Make it a special performance day. Invite your principal.

CANDY WRAPPERS AND LABELS ON FOOD PRODUCTS

Students can learn a great deal from looking at other product wrappers.

Labels from cans and wrappers contain a great deal of information such as:

- cost
- weight in standard and metric measurement
- price
- grams of fat
- daily value
- date of expiration
- ingredients
- the company that creates it

Teachers and parents should take the opportunities to introduce this information to the children so that they learn to use it to become more aware of health issues in their daily lives. When reading these materials, students begin to see their value.

- At the beginning of the year, tell parents what you will be doing with can labels, and wrappers of all types, and ask for their assistance in collecting them. Start a collection of these items. Have a labeled box where the students know where to place them. As you have a good number to start with, hand out one to each child and instruct students as to why the labels are required by law to have certain information on them. Use the *Wrapper/Label Information Sheet* at the end of this section.

- Begin a *Wrapper/Label Center*. Encourage students to review the labels during their free time or during Planning/Doing/Reflecting. As students investigate and read the labels, they will be motivated to compare and contrast, to look closely at nutrition facts, and become more conscious of how food relates to them.

- Invite the school nurse or a nutritionist to the class. As an expert, he/she can fill in some of the facts that will relate to the students' lives.

- Visit a grocery store as a class field trip. Have students in cooperative groups locate foods with the best food value, least cost per ounce, best cost value, and so on.

- Have cooperative groups share their findings using a posterboard with the rest of the class and with parents.

JOKES/RIDDLE BOOKS

Jokes and riddles can be seen and heard almost everywhere. In the classroom, a good way to start each morning off is to tell a joke or riddle, or place one on the board for the class to ponder as attendance is being taken. Make sure that the jokes and riddles are age appropriate. For instance:

- What has no beginning or end and nothing in the middle? (*a doughnut*)

- How much dirt is there in a hole exactly one foot deep and one foot across? (*None. A hole is empty.*)

- Why shouldn't you keep a library book on the ground overnight? (*Because in the morning, it will be overdue [dew].*)

Riddles and jokes motivate students to listen carefully and to think. They are tools to enhance reading, writing, listening, and speaking. For the reluctant reader, the teacher might:

- Ask a student to read one or two pages from a riddle or joke book that is available in the classroom. That child must choose two riddles to present to the class in the morning on a specified day. If the child has difficulty reading the riddles, another student may be paired up to read with him/her. This gives silent reading as well as oral reading opportunities for the child, and compels the child to read carefully and clearly. This short form of reading builds self-esteem and develops confidence in oral language presentation.

- Have a riddle/joke fair where everyone contributes his/her favorites. Juice and cookies could be served.

- Have each child create a page for a classroom riddle book. The page could have five of the child's favorite riddles or jokes, and illustrations to accompany them. Children write them on the computer or print them neatly.

- Have a riddle/joke sharing experience with younger-age students.

- Have reluctant readers read to younger children from a riddle book; then they create some of their own.

- Cut photos out of newspapers and magazines and think of funny captions for them or funny things for people in the pictures to be saying.

- Have students write their own riddles and jokes, and add art work to them.

- Encourage children to tell riddles to their parents, brothers and sisters, and for the children they baby-sit.

MENUS

As soon as kids are old enough to read, they love looking at menus and choosing their own meals. So why not continue with this interest as they develop into the years of adolescence? Menus are basically free, and if you start early in the year with your "Wish List" for parents, you will receive a large supply of menus to keep in a container.

Suggestions for how teachers and parents can use menus to motivate children to read and learn other skills at the same time, include:

- Children may choose a breakfast, lunch, and/or a dinner of their choice from any menu on file. For the younger children, they may use a calculator to add the cost of each meal. Older children may figure out tax and tip also.

- They may also take orders for their family members and their friends. Writing the orders on a special receipt or tablet is more official and will motivate some children because it is more like the real-thing. Waiter / waitress order forms can be found at some office supply stores, and provide an enjoyable, educational activity for children.

- After reading several menus, children can categorize them by types of foods, alphabetize them, or compare and contrast them as to which is the best buy. Graphs can be made to show the comparisons of several food items from two or three different restaurants.

- Children may visit a restaurant and find out how food items have been selected, and how or who designed the menu.

- Students may design their own menus and create their own restaurants, describing them in detail through the writing process, or creating them artistically through drawing, or a combination of both. (See *Let's Read a Menu* at the end of this section.)

THE KID'S ADDRESS BOOK

Every classroom should have the book *The Kid's Address Book* by Michael Levine. In it, children find over 2,000 addresses of celebrities, athletes, entertainers, and other famous people. Children love to write to real people because they relate to them and are hopeful of receiving an answer. So this book gets kids reading while they select a famous person, and then it moves them to write. This book can be used at home by parents or in the classroom at a center.

ALMANACS AND WORLD RECORD BOOKS

Another type of book that really gets kids' minds working is *The Guinness Book of World Records*. In our classrooms, we have watched the most unwilling reader grab one of these books and become totally engulfed in the short factual information. There is something captivating about world records.

With a little bit of teacher direction, students also find almanacs surprisingly interesting. Once given a chance, many children feel very comfortable reading for factual information because these sections are short and manageable to read. (See the *Almanac Research Sheet and Create Your Own Almanac Questions* at the end of this section.)

TELEVISION AND MOVIE GUIDES

Keeping these guides close by presents a great reading and writing experience for children in the classroom or at home. We need to draw on the natural interest students have in movies and television programming. Activities that students may want to participate in are listed below.

- Have students highlight programs in the television guide that would be appropriate for young children, and make a list of their names and the times of day they are broadcast. Students write a paragraph explaining why these programs were chosen.

- Students use the television guide for one day and select three shows their family members agree upon and would like to watch together. As a family, discuss the programs after they're watched.

- Using a calendar, students write a list of three programs each day for a week that they would like to watch if they were allowed to watch anything on regular television. They explain their choices.

- Using the movie section, students locate a movie they and their family would like to see. They highlight the time that would be best for them to see it and find the theater that is nearest their home. How many times does it show each day? What number would students call to find out more information? What rating is the movie? (See *Let's Read a Television Guide* at the end of this section.)

POPULAR MUSIC

Since music is the universal language, why not use it more often to engage students in a reading experience? Presenting words on the overhead projector or on sheets of paper, students enjoy reading the words when they are backed up with music. Have the students keep a notebook of the most popular songs so that they can be used again when needed. (See Section 19, *Making the Most of Music in the Classroom.*)

CHILDREN'S MAGAZINES

Some students who do not like to read chapter books, find magazines an excellent form of reading. *Sport's Illustrated for Kids* is one magazine that many students find interesting because the articles are relevant to them.

Other magazines of interest to children are:

- *National Geographic World*
- *Ranger Rick*
- *Boys' Life*
- *Cricket*
- *Kid City*
- *Zillions for Kids from Consumer Reports*
- *Kids Discover*
- *American Girl*

COLLECTIONS OF SHORT STORIES

When you want someone to read, but he/she doesn't seem to be interested, try handing that student a book of short stories. Many times this does the trick. Short stories are more readable because of their brevity. Some books that might be enjoyed by upper-grade students are:

Baseball in April (Gary Soto)
Scary Stories (Alvin Schwartz)
Oxford Book of Scary Stories (Dennis Pepper)
Rites of Passage: Stories About Growing Up by Black Writers from Around the World (edited by Tonya Bolder)
The Hardy Boys Ghost Stories (Franklin)
The Book of Dragons (Michael Hague)
Short Stories from *Highlights*

"Storm's Fury and Other Horse Stories"
"The Ghostly Bell Ringer and Other Mysteries"
"In the Shadow of an Eagle and Other Adventure Stories"
"No Pets Allowed and Other Animal Stories"

CALDECOTT BOOKS

Even in the upper grades, students like to reconnect to picture books. It is an enjoyable experience for students to review Caldecott Award books that are full of exquisite illustrations and stories of substance. Whereas these books must be read to children in the primary grades, upper-graders can enjoy the reading of the text, as well as study and appreciate the depth and artistic techniques used in the illustrations. Having a Caldecott collection available can open up critical discussion on why these books have been selected for this distinguished award. (See the *Caldecott Books Recording and Information Sheet* at the end of this section.) Students might enjoy these award-winning books in big book form. After reading a few, they may want to try writing their own big book, independently or cooperatively. Here's how to start it off:

Make Big Books in the Upper Grades

1. Now that your class has just finished reading some of those great Caldecott award winners, it might be fun to borrow some of the Big Books from the primary grades.

2. Have several class periods when students can read the Big Books silently.

3. Break your class into cooperative groups and have each group present a Big Book to their classmates. They absolutely love it!

4. Discuss the reasons why little kids enjoy Big Books and other picture books.

5. Have students pair up with other children who complement their skills. In other words, encourage those who love to write to pair up with someone who is a good artist. Discuss the importance of blending the artistic and the creative writing skills.

6. Discuss subjects that are appropriate for primary children.

7. Give a review of lower- and upper-case printing. Use the language book as a model for writing while on this project.

8. In pencil and on rough draft paper, have the students sketch out their story in words and pictures. They should have one page for every page they intend to have in their final Big Book. Use peer editing and correction.

9. Use 12" × 18" white tag or white construction paper for the final draft.

10. Show students how to make a 1" frame around each page using a ruler. This gives a finalized look to the book. Frames should be drawn first on each page before any pictures or writing are done. The frame may be a solid line or a simple creative design, but should be exactly the same on all pages. One color of marker should be used.

11. Students should measure lines with a ruler at the bottom of each page for writing their text. The lines should be either 1 or 2 inches apart depending on how many words the students have on each page. This is a great math lesson and involves concentration and planning.

12. Students should write and illustrate everything in pencil on their final paper.

13. After being proofread, the students finalize the words in black marking pen (thin line) and color the pictures in markers, crayons, colored pencils, or watercolors.

14. The pages are numbered at the bottom.

15. Students create a front and back cover for the book.

16. An "About the Author" page with a picture of the author is included at the end of the book.

17. It is a good idea to double the paper or have students write only on one side if they are using markers. Some markers leak through onto the other side of the paper.

18. Each page is laminated and spiral-bound.

19. The books are shared with the younger children.

20. At our school, this project began as a sixth-grade gift to our site library. The students wanted to share a part of themselves with the school they were about to leave. They were donated to the librarian at the promotion ceremony in June. The books are favorites of the primary students when they visit the library.

CHOOSE-YOUR-OWN ADVENTURE STORIES

These short stories allow the reluctant reader to make choices. How the story ends depends on how the child wants it to. The child finds that he/she can choose the direction the story will take. If they want to, they can take the short cut through the book. They can read and reread as much as they want, or as little as they want. For students with reading difficulties, this is a manageable reading selection that fosters confidence and success.

RECIPES

How about trying recipe books? Some children can become absorbed in these books, especially if they have pictures to accompany them. (See *Let's Read a Recipe* at the end of this section.)

READING ACTIVITIES THAT EVALUATE CHILDREN'S UNDERSTANDING OF CORE LITERATURE

The ideas mentioned on the preceding pages are all ways to enhance a regular reading program. All children must be able to also take a good piece of literature and show understanding of what they have read. Children need to have a variety of ways to show what they know and what they have learned from reading literature.

The Value of a Bookmark

Every child loves to see the magic that appears on the pages of a colorful picture book. Younger, as well as older, children can be fully engrossed in a book with only a few words and illustrative images on the pages . But what happens when the child stops having the pictures to cue him/her into the story? From our experiences, it appears that at about the fourth-grade level, when the books become void of illustrations, a segment of our students become disinterested and unmotivated readers. The reading period becomes a time for daydreaming and getting lost in other thoughts. Without pictures and illustrations, some students "turn-off" to reading.

What we want the students to learn is that no book is unconquerable. Although the picture books and short stories turn into chapter books, we want children to learn the skills to make reading manageable. The art of pacing and looking at a book in smaller chunks or manageable pieces is paramount in helping all kids to conquer a book.

The first week of school is the time to start. We talk about a reading scientific investigation. We become "read-iologists." Using the same piece of literature, every student reads for fifteen minutes. On the bookmark, he/she writes the date, page started, and page ended in that 15-minute segment. That gives the student an understanding and feel for how many pages of a grade-level book he/she can read in a controlled period of time. This experimentation continues for the full five days of the week. At the end of the week, the student averages the number of pages he/she reads, and hopefully better understands how to break up a book in the future so as not to leave it until the last minute. If the students see that on the average they can read ten pages in fifteen minutes, then they can figure out that to read a 200-page book of their level, it will take 20 fifteen-minute segments to complete the book. Hopefully, they will learn that if they read for a half-hour segment, they can read that same book in ten sessions. Even in our own profession, we know that many of us have left a book until the night or weekend before the test or the book report is due, and have had to power read at the last minute. If we take the time in class to help students learn to pace their reading—not just for one week, but several times throughout the year—students will see themselves as more successful readers and realize that reading can be a journey that is fun and rewarding in itself.

It is important that you occasionally evaluate the student's bookmark and check to see if the student needs to read for a longer period of time. This bookmark also helps parents keep pace with the amount of reading their child is doing. It is also useful for library as well as in-class reading.

Our goal is to have students read on a regular basis—not just during the classtime reading period. If students start viewing upper-grade books in small bites instead of big mouthfuls, we have begun to make them see that reading is conquerable.

The bookmarks at the end of this section can be duplicated on colored paper, used regularly by the students, and filed in a child's portfolio for evaluation by the parent, an aide, or the teacher.

Reading/Writing Conferences

All students should have the opportunity to meet one-to-one with their teacher—a personalized period of time when the teacher and student can sit face-to-face and talk with one another about his/her reading and writing. Because the elementary school day is so jammed packed, finding that special one-to-one time is often difficult to schedule.

You can find out so much about your students with just a five-minute conference. The rewards of this sharing time far outweigh the difficulty with scheduling. In Section 15, *Making Oral Language Come Alive in Your Classroom*, several suggestions on how to juggle your schedule to accommodate reading/writing conferences are suggested. Parents, senior citizens, volunteers, and aides can also be used to conference with children about what they are reading, what they like to read, how they read orally, and if they are comprehending what they are reading. Writing can also be looked at, read aloud, and discussed. Many children do not have the opportunity to spend personal time with their own parents for sharing, reviewing, and reading; therefore, this brief conference can be very meaningful for the child and also for the adult.

The following ideas can be used for any type of one-to-one conference. Oftentimes a parent stops into the classroom and asks if there is anything he/she can do for a few hours to assist you in the classroom. Having a folder on file (portfolio) for each child is a convenient way to utilize the assistance of a parent when he/she just "drops in" on the spur of the moment. In the child's portfolio is placed a *Reading and Writing Conference* sheet, found at the end of this section. The person giving the conference asks a few questions or helps on writing skills, and follows up with a brief summary of the conference. These notations are helpful for the teacher to review before parent conferences.

Here is an example of a reading/writing conference conducted between teacher:student, parent:student, or student:student.

Reading

1. *Ask the student some basic questions about his/her book (approximately 3 to 5 minutes):*
   - *Who are the main characters?*
   - *Describe one of the main characters—personality, behavior, physical characteristics.*

- *What is the setting (time, place) of the story?*
- *What was your favorite part?*
- *What was the funniest part?*
- *How did the last chapter you read end?*
- *What is the main problem faced by the main character?*
- *Would you like the main character as a friend? Why or why not?*
- *What do you think was the climax or high point of the story?*
- *How do the characters work out their problems?*
- *What do you and the main character have in common? How are you different?*
- *Would you recommend this book to a classmate? Why or why not?*
- *Choose one of the pictures in the story and explain what is happening.*
- *Choose a title of one of the chapters that you have read, and tell why the chapter has that title.*
- *How might you extend this story?*
- *How would you change this story if you had a chance?*

2. **Have the student read a part of the book orally to you for 1 to 2 minutes.** *Respond favorably to the student's success. If you feel like it, read orally to the student yourself. Make this a pleasurable experience for both of you.*

Writing

1. *Select one of the most recent student compositions from a student's Language Arts Portfolio or one that the teacher has set aside for you to work on.*

2. *Have the child read the composition to you orally.*

3. *Respond in a positive way.*

   I really like the part about _____

   You made me laugh when you said_____

   One thing I really liked about what you wrote was _____

4. *Assist the student in one or two areas that he/she is experiencing difficulty with:*
   - *topic sentences*
   - *length of paragraphs—at least 5 or 6 sentences*
   - *description*
   - *spelling*
   - *fluency of thought*
   - *proper form (indenting, margins, title capitalized, spacing)*
   - *agreement of tense*
   - *use of dialogue/quotation marks*
   - *run-on sentences*
   - *other, as evaluated*

5. *Ask the writer one of the following questions:*
   - *What part do you like best in your composition?*
   - *What part gave you the most problems?*
   - *What prewriting activity did you do?*
   - *What would you change about your composition now that you have read it again?*
   - *What did you learn about your writing from having this conference?*

Organizing the Reading Program

A child feels comfortable when he/she knows what direction his/her teacher will take in the future instruction. Because each upper-grade student should have his/her own three-ring binder during the year, a list of the monthly genres of books that will be read is a helpful mental organizer. The form *Book Report Monthly Schedule* at the end of this section can be reproduced on colored ditto paper and then filed in the language arts section of the child's notebook so that it can be easily located for reference purposes. The child and the parent can stay abreast of the reading genres and projects that are expected for the entire year.

Several of the required reading book projects are laid out for you at the end of this section. See *A Biograpical Journal, Caldecott Books Recording and Information Sheet*, and *Poetry Log*.

At the end of this section, you will find several creative activities to stimulate the reluctant reader/writer to "show off" what he/she really knows about his/her reading.

Create a report card for the main character in the book

This activity can be done in pairs, small groups, or independently. It is a good idea to use this activity before a report card period. Actually having the students evaluate themselves and where they see their strengths and weaknesses on their own school's evaluation tool helps them see how a report card is designed. Children who are more independent can create their own categories for the main character in the book to be evaluated on (courage, survival skills, kindness, building skill, physical strength, to name a few). Students who have more difficulty coming up with ideas of how to evaluate the character may work more closely with you. Together you may brainstorm to make a list of possible categories for character strengths and weaknesses. Then each child can choose five or six to use for his/her own report card. (See *Let's Create a Report Card* at the end of this section.)

Create a test after reading a core literature book

Because children are very familiar with formal tests, this activity provides them with knowledge of questioning and how test makers might formulate test questions. The creation of the test works well in cooperative groups of three or four children. The option of working independently is also available. Each child is required to think up five true/false, five multiple choice, and five short-answer types of questions. It is essential that teachers model these types of questions before the students begin their work. (See *Create Your Own Test* at the end of this section.)

Develop character sketch cards

In this activity, students must be instructed on the differences between a physical characteristic and a personality trait. Children find the physical characteristics quite easy to identify, but the personality traits are more difficult. Keeping a personality trait word bank on a chart in the classroom assists those students who experience difficulty in this search. These lists can be kept on display during writing times. They may contain words such as *confident, courteous, dynamic, protective, helpless, positive, curious, humorous, unstable, sensible, humble, happy-go-lucky*. An ongoing list can always be available for students who need that little bit of extra help to get them started writing. On the back of the character card, students may draw a picture of the main character. The two sides can be pasted together, paper-punched and hung on a string, or displayed on a board. (See *Character Sketch Cards* at the end of this section.)

Use the almanac to find out where in the world the story takes place

While students are reading the book, they should have their almanacs available. They find out some basic information about the country or area they are studying and fill out the *Literature/Geography Study Guide* found at the end of this section. The students then locate the setting of the story on the world map and label it. (It is suggested that students write in pencil first and then go over it in thin black marker to make the map look like a more polished project.) Throughout the year, students keep their map in their notebook, so that it can be updated as new books are read. At the end of the year, the class has a better grasp on world geography, and should be able to locate the countries of the world that have been studied on their maps.

Compare and contrast two pieces of literature with the same theme or topic, or with the same author

To stretch the upper-graders' minds by using their higher level thinking skills, teachers should try using two different books with the same theme or ones that are by the same author. Then students should be able to discuss and write about the author's writing style and the similarity of ideas that the books contain.

In the World War ll project, students read *North to Freedom* and *Number the Stars*. With the information given in these two excellent books regarding the war and the effect it had on the people of Europe, the students begin to understand this period of history. Discussion is held in class about the fear the people had of Adolf Hitler and his soldiers, and what life was like living with this fear. By reading these two books, the students begin to feel the fear of children their age who lived during this time, and begin to understand something about what it might have been like being a child during the war.

The World War II activities are based on the seven intelligences and offer children choice by asking them to select one of the 23 activities that are provided. Students may show their understanding of this period of history by selecting their choice of the type of activity. Music, interviewing, writing, researching, drawing, reflecting, and observing are among the skills they may develop. Students do an exceptional job on this assignment because they are so involved after reading the two books. Many students choose more than one activity.

Choosing books by one author—such as *The Great Gilly Hopkins* and *Bridge to Terabithia* by Katherine Patterson, or *Hatchet* and *The River* by Gary Paulsen—provide another opportunity to compare two books. Students can see how one author's style permeates his/her books. As students enter the upper grades, they should be provided with more opportunities to use comparing and contrasting of books and styles of writing.

Because there are so many exciting types of reading materials that can "fire up" our most challenging readers, we must continue to search for the ones that inspire them to read. Although certain children may not feel comfortable with an upper-grade chapter book, we must provide a large variety of reading materials, such as the ones mentioned above, that children can pick up and read successfully. No matter how short or simple the reading material is, we know that the more a child reads, the better reader he/she becomes.

BIBLIOGRAPHY AND RECOMMENDED RESOURCES

Cole, William. *Poem Stew*. New York: HarperCollins Publishers, 1981.

Dakos, Kalli. *Don't Read This Book Whatever You Do!* New York: Four Winds Press, 1993.

Holman, Linda, and Santella-Johnson, Mary. *Teaching with Calvin and Hobbes*. (Whole language and humor for upper elementary and junior high). Fargo, ND: Playground Publishing Co., 1993.

Keller, Charles. *Tongue Twisters*. New York: Simon and Schuster Books, 1989.

Korman, Gordon and Bernice. *The D-Poems of Jeremy Bloom*. New York: Scholastic, Inc., 1992.

Levine, Michael. *The Kid's Address Book*. New York: A Perigee Book, 1994.

Moss, Jeff. *The Butterfly Jar*. New York: Bantam Books, 1989.

Prelutsky, Jack. *The New Kid on the Block*. New York: Greenwillow Books, 1990.

Prelutsky, Jack. *Something Big Has Been Here*. New York: Greenwillow Books, 1990.

The Random House Book of Poetry for Children. New York: Random House, 1983.

Rosenbloom, Joseph. *Biggest Riddle Book Ever*. New York: Sterling Publishing Co, 1976.

Schwartz, Alvin. *Scary Stories to Tell in the Dark*. New York: Harper and Row Publishers, 1991.

Schwartz, Alvin. *Scary Stories: More Tales to Chill Your Bones*. New York: HarperCollins Publishers, 1991.

Silverstein, Shel. *A Light in the Attic*. New York: Harper and Row Publishers, 1981.

ACTIVITY USING SHEL SILVERSTEIN'S *MESSY ROOM*

Investigator's Name _____

WRITING ASSIGNMENT AND DRAWING A MAP TO SCALE

1. Write a paragraph thoroughly describing your own bedroom. Include such things as color, room arrangement, carpeting, closet size and space, stuffed animals, furniture, window coverings, wallpaper, etc. Tell whether it is neat or messy and explain how and why it is that way.

2. Sit down and take a good look at your bedroom. Use a tape measure, yardstick, etc., to find the length and width of your room (perimeter). Measure your furniture, too.

    Length and Width of Bedroom   L _____   W _____
    What is its Perimeter? _____
    Length of Closet(s) _____
    Length of Windows _____
    Length and Width of Bed   L _____   W _____
    Width of Door _____
    Length and Width of Dresser   L _____   W _____
    Length and Width of Bookcase   L _____   W _____
    Length and Width of Nightstand   L _____   W _____
    Length and Width of Desk   L _____   W _____
    Other Furniture _____
    What is the area of your Bedroom (L × W) _____

3. Draw a sketch of your room and then use graph paper to draw your room to scale.

POETRY LOG

Name _____

Date _____ Today I read a poem entitled _____
by _____. It is about _____
_____
I liked/disliked the poem because _____
_____

Date _____ Today I read a poem entitled _____
by _____. It is about _____
_____
I liked/disliked the poem because _____
_____

Date _____ Today I read a poem entitled _____
by _____. It is about _____
_____
I liked/disliked the poem because _____
_____

Date _____ Today I read a poem entitled _____
by _____. It is about _____
_____
I liked/disliked the poem because _____
_____

Date _____ Today I read a poem entitled _____
by _____. It is about _____
_____
I liked/disliked the poem because _____
_____

COMIC STRIP RECORDING SHEET

"BUSTER" ———————— by Amanda Simms
Today: Buster's birthday

Name _____

DIRECTIONS:

1. Read at least 10 comic strips from the ones provided.

2. Record the necessary information.

3. Create your own characters and make a 4- to 8-frame comic strip. Add color and conversation bubbles.

Date: _____ Comic Strip Name: _____

Main Characters: _____

Summary: _____

_____

Date: _____ Comic Strip Name: _____

Main Characters: _____

Summary: _____

_____

Date: _____ Comic Strip Name: _____

Main Characters: _____

Summary: _____

_____

Date: _____ Comic Strip Name: _____

Main Characters: _____

Summary: _____

_____

CEREALS THAT ALREADY EXIST

Student's Name _____

1. _____
2. _____
3. _____
4. _____
5. _____
6. _____
7. _____
8. _____
9. _____
10. _____
11. _____
12. _____

13. _____
14. _____
15. _____
16. _____
17. _____
18. _____
19. _____
20. _____
21. _____
22. _____
23. _____
24. _____

WHAT'S ON A CEREAL BOX?

1. _____
2. _____
3. _____
4. _____
5. _____
6. _____
7. _____

8. _____
9. _____
10. _____
11. _____
12. _____
13. _____
14. _____

Name _____   Date _____

AN UP CLOSE AND PERSONAL LOOK
AT MY FAVORITE CEREAL

You have just completed a list of the brands of cereal you can find on your grocery store shelves. On the lines below, choose the one cereal that you consider your favorite. Write one paragraph about the cereal (how it looks, what it tastes like, how it smells, words to describe it, etc.). Write a second paragraph to explain why it is your favorite, how it makes you feel when you eat it, what your parents think of it, and why you think others might enjoy it, too. Don't just answer the questions. Let them guide you in your writing. The first paragraph is a **descriptive paragraph** and the second is a **feeling paragraph**.

Write in cursive, and if you need more space, attach a separate sheet of paper.

_____

_____

_____

_____

_____

_____

_____

_____

_____

_____

_____

_____

_____

_____

_____

_____

_____

_____

_____

_____

CEREAL BOX INVESTIGATION

Cerealologist _____

1. Name of Cereal_____

2. Color of box _____

3. Net weight_____

4. Size of box in inches _____

5. Character _____

6. Three major ingredients _____

7. Recipe on box? Yes _____No_____

8. Calories _____ Protein _____ Fat _____

9. Company that produces it _____

10. Special features—games, puzzles, etc. _____

11. Descriptive words _____

    _____

    Sketch a picture of
    the cereal box here:

12. Write several sentences about
    this cereal. _____

    _____

    _____

    _____

    _____

MY OWN CEREAL BOX CREATION

Your Name _____

Required Parts: Name of cereal; name of company; weight; descriptive words; a picture of the cereal; a front, back, and two side panels; ingredients

Optional Parts: A character; a recipe; a game; maze or puzzle; a coupon

Front	**Back**

Sides

Top

Bottom

CEREAL COMMERCIAL PLANNING SHEET

What **materials** will I need to present my commercial to my audience?

_____

_____

What **propaganda technique** will I use to sell my cereal?

_____

_____

What will I do to **"hook"** my audience into my commercial?

_____

_____

What **three main ideas** will I try to get across to my audience to make them want to buy my cereal?

1. _____
2. _____
3. _____

* *

My Plan for a Commercial! Write it on the back of this page.

CEREAL BOX EVALUATION FORM

Names of team members: a. _____ b._____ c. _____

1. Evaluate your cereal box in the following areas with a +, √, or −. Your teacher will evaluate you also. That is what the second line is for.

    a. Color   _____   _____

    b. Neatness   _____   _____

    c. Team Work   _____   _____

    d. Creativity   _____   _____

    e. Factual Information   _____   _____

    f. "Saleability" (Would someone actually buy it?)   _____   _____

    g. "Extras" (games, puzzles, etc.)   _____   _____

    h. Other: _____

2. Commercial Evaluation

    a. Teamwork   _____   _____

    b. Eye contact   _____   _____

    c. Loudness   _____   _____

    d. Use of visual aid   _____   _____

    e. Creativity   _____   _____

3. Write a few sentences explaining why I should give you an "A" on this project: _____

    _____

4. Tell me what I should know about your partner's work on this project: _____

    _____

WRAPPER/LABEL INFORMATION SHEET

Name _____   Due Date _____

In order to learn a little bit more about the nutrition facts in the food we eat, you are to research **three labels or wrappers.** You are to carefully look at the information on a milk carton, a bread wrapper, and a cake, cookie or candy container. Record the information so that we can compare and contrast these items in class on the date indicated above.

1. Brand of bread _____

Net weight of package _____ Cost _____

Serving Size _____ Servings per container _____

Calories _____ Calories from Fat _____

Total fat grams per serving _____ Total carbohydrate grams _____

List the first five ingredients: _____

_____

2. Brand of milk _____ % of fat_____

Net weight of package _____ Cost _____

Serving Size _____ Servings per container _____

Calories _____ Calories from Fat _____

Total fat grams per serving _____ Total carbohydrate grams _____

List the first five ingredients: _____

_____

3. Brand of candy, etc. _____ % of fat_____

Net weight of package _____ Cost _____

Serving Size _____ Servings per container _____

Calories _____ Calories from Fat _____

Total fat grams per serving _____ Total carbohydrate grams _____

List the first five ingredients: _____

_____

Name _____   Date _____

LET'S READ A MENU

You have $50.00 to spend at this restaurant. You may take as many of your friends with you as you would like, but everyone must have an appetizer, soup, or salad, a main entree, dessert, and a drink. The object is to spend as close to $50.00 as possible! (That must include sales tax and a 15% tip).

When you are completed, write a restaurant review. Name your restaurant and describe your experience at the restaurant—the atmosphere, food, and service. Attach your paragraph to this paper.

Reataurant Name: _____

Quantity	Food Item	Cost per Item	Total Cost
	Subtotal		$
	Sales Tax		$
	Food Total (+)		$
	15% Tip (x .15)		$
	Total Plus Tip		$

ALMANAC RESEARCH SHEET

Name _____   Due Date _____

Using the almanac, find the answers to the following
questions. Place the page number you found it on
next to your answer.

1. Name the three **highest dams** in the world:
    a. Name _____ Where found_____ Height_____
    b. Name _____ Where found_____ Height_____
    c. Name _____ Where found_____ Height_____

2. What is the **world's fastest aircraft**? _____

3. Where and when was the **worst hurricane** in United States history?

    _____

4. Name four areas of the world where **typhoons** take place.

    _____

5. On what day is **Canada Day**? Why is it celebrated?

    _____

6. What was the name of the top sports show watched last year on **television**?

    _____

7. What night of the week do more persons watch **television**? _____

8. Who has had the **most homeruns** in one season of baseball in the
    United States? _____

9. What is the average age for a **first-time marriage** in the United States?
    man?_____woman?_____

10. What is **lyme disease**? _____

11. Name the three **largest islands** of the world. _____

    _____

12. Name the three **highest mountains** of the world. _____

    _____

CREATE YOUR OWN ALMANAC QUESTIONS

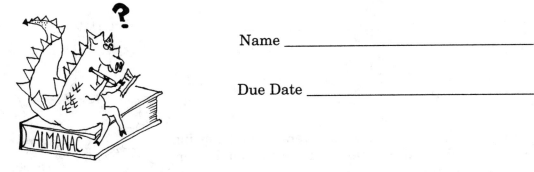

Name _____

Due Date _____

1. Use your almanac to guide you in thinking up 5 almanac questions to ask a classmate.

2. On a separate sheet of paper, write the letter of the question, the page number you found it on, and the correct answer.

3. Exchange papers with a partner. Have him/her answer your questions.

4. Check to see if your partner has answered them correctly.

QUESTION 1:

_____

_____

_____

Answer: _____ **Page Found:** _____

QUESTION 2:

_____

_____

_____

Answer: _____ **Page Found:** _____

QUESTION 3:

_____

_____

_____

Answer: _____ **Page Found:** _____

LET'S READ A TELEVISION GUIDE

Name _____   Date _____

Using the television listing, answer the
following questions.

1. What program would you be watching if you
   tuned to:

   Channel 8 at 7:00 P.M.? _____
   Channel 10 at 7:00 P.M.? _____
   Channel 39 at 7:30 P.M.? _____
   Disney at 6:30 P.M.? _____

2. On what channels would you see news at 11:00 P.M.? _____

   At 10:30 P.M.? _____ at 6:00 P.M.? _____

3. On what channel and at what time would you see *Family Matters*? _____

4. If you turned to Channel 69 at 8:00, what program would you see? _____
   _____

5. How long is the program *Unsolved Mysteries*? What time does it begin and what
   time does it end? _____

6. At what time could you tune in to see *Greystoke*? _____

7. Name three shows you might watch if you were interested in sports. Tell what
   time they are on. _____
   _____

8. Highlight in pen five programs you would be interested in watching on television
   if your parents would allow you to do so.

9. Place an X next to five programs that wouldn't interest you at all.

10. What do you think CC means in the parentheses after the name of the program?
    _____

11. Name three movies you could see on the Disney Channel between 6:00 and
    11:00. _____
    _____

FRIDAY	6:00	6:30	7:00	7:30	8:00	8:30	9:00	9:30	10:00	10:30	11:00	11:30
6 Cox 6 Dan 6 / CNC 6 CV/N 6 / SW 6 SWU 6	Fun Videos 8536	Married 9888	The Simpsons 2246	Home Imp. 8772	Sliders "Into the Mystic" (CC) 21468		The X-Files (RR) (CC) 59884		Acapulco Bay 67831		Cheers (CC) 95555	Coach (CC) 48333
8 Cox 8 Dan 8 / CNC 8 CV/N 8 / SW 8 SWU 8	CBS News 3604	News (CC) 7284	Entertainment 2082	Hard Copy 3468	Due South "We Are the Eggmen" (CC) 16536		Sergei Grinkov: Celebration of a Life (CC) 19623				News (CC) 2830915	Late Show 3014265
10 Cox 10 Dan 10 / CNC 10 CV/N 10 / SW 10 SWU 10	ABC News 4352	News (CC) 5604	Inside Edition 8062	Amer. Journal 1888	Family Matters 7710	Boy Meets ... 3517	Step by Step 38284	Hypernauts 72826	20/20 (CC) 68913		News (CC) 8564197	Nightline 5650401
12 Cox 12 CV/N 43	DOS Norteno 9420	Notivisa 762062		Rosa Angelica 9284	Movie: "Greystoke: The Legend of Tarzan, Lord of the Apes" *** (1984, Drama) (PG) 41246				Notivisa 53081		Intimamente Shanik 14888	
15 Cox 11 Dan 11 / CNC 11 CV/N 12 / SW 11 SWU 11	Travels ... 4994	Business Rpt. 5246	The NewsHour With Jim Lehrer (CC) 13082		Washington 7352	Wall St. Week 3159	Nova "Nomads of the Rain Forest" (CC) 13046		Mystery of the Senses (CC) 63523		Great Drives "A1A" (RR) (CC) 84772	
19 Cox 37 Dan 19 / CNC 19 CV/N 42 / SW 19	Noticiero 2536	Noticiero 3888	Lazos de Amor 13064		Acapulco, Cuerpo y Alma 85604		Cine Univision 88791				Noticiero 73371	Impacto 87371
33 Cox 20 CV/N 46	Prog. Comprado 75	5	TeleNoticias	María Bonita 1826	Kaina 7246		Noticiero 9739	Movie: "Perro Caliente" 43536				TeleNoticias 22371
35 SW 15	Art in Context "Jose Luis Cuevas" 13739		J. Baldessari 72710	Koto 73456	Takaezu 58130	Stuart 77265	J. Baldessari 83913	Koto 18284	Takaezu 78178	Stuart 87826	Notivisa 65178	
39 Cox 7 Dan 7 / CNC 7 CV/N 7 / SW 7 SWU 7	News (CC) 10468	H'way Patrol 94420	Wheel 74178	Jeopardy! 90604	Unsolved Mysteries (CC) 93888		Dateline NBC Contact lenses. (CC) 60492		Homicide: Life on the Street (RR) (CC) 16739		News (CC) 3662604	Tonight 3456197
45 CV/N 45	Conducido Musica Videos (3:00) 6513178						Comentarios a Caballo 391710		Música Videos 654791			
51 Cox 9 Dan 9 / CNC 9 CV/N 9 / SW 9 SWU 9	Roseanne 54826	Roseanne 45178	Seinfeld 18536	EXTRA 34062	Star Trek: Voyager "Lifesigns" (CC) 44536		Baywatch "Rubber Ducky" 24772		News Clark, Christie 34159		EXTRA 88866	Current Affair 12343
69 Cox 14 Dan 14 / CNC 14 CV/N 14 / SW 14	Step/Step 5880284	Step/Step 5871536	Movie: "King Solomon's Mines" * (1985, Action) (Violence.) 1739994		Movie: "Amityville: The Demon" ** (1983, Horror) (Adult situations, language, violence.) 6521178						Mystery Science Theater 3000 1735178	

	6:00	6:30	7:00	7:30	8:00	8:30	9:00	9:30	10:00	10:30	11:00	11:30
2	CBS News (CC) 49	Highway Patrol 71	Hard Copy 4791	Entertainment 3	Due South "We Are the Eggmen" (CC) 3420		Sergei Grinkov: Celebration of a Life (CC) 3807				News 5410994	Late Show 7576444
4 CNC 18	News (CC) 17	NBC News (CC) 7	EXTRA 6159	A Current Affair 81	Unsolved Mysteries (CC) 5888		Dateline NBC Contact lenses. (CC) 8352		Homicide: Life on the Street (RR) (CC) 8739		News (CC) 5405062	Tonight 2397492
5 Cox 5 Dan 5 / CNC 5 CV/N 5 / SW 5 SWU 15	Fam. Matters 6474	Fresh Prince 1246	Bzzz! 4604	Seinfeld (CC) 6230	Movie: "The Jerk" ** (1979, Comedy) (Adult situations, language.) 27642				News Fishman, McCormick (CC) 13449		Cheers (CC) 97913	Murphy 40791
7	News (CC) 5062	ABC News 9642	Jeopardy! 9772	Wheel Fortune 5826	Family Matters 8420	Boy Meets ... 7555	Step by Step 87536	Hypernauts 61062	20/20 (CC) 23497		News (CC) 9279943	Nightline 5036401
9	Fun Videos 6710	Fun Videos 7062	Inside Edition 4820	Amer. Journal 3246	News Kilbride, Velez-Mitchell 47420		News Harvey, Sahl 67284		News Harvey, Jackson 60371		Jerry Springer Teens and mothers at war. 21178	
11 SWU 14	Married 8178	Cops (CC) 2130	Home Imp. 2888	The Simpsons 1642	Sliders "Into the Mystic" (CC) 49888		The X-Files (RR) (CC) 52352		News Beard, Devine 62739		Married 37555	M*A*S*H 88975
13 Cox 13 Dan 13 / SW 13 SWU 13	Roseanne 9826	Roseanne 9998	Star Trek: The Next Generation (CC) 83246		Movie: "Other People's Money" *** (1991, Comedy) (Adult situations, language.) 96710				News Little, Jimenez 82517		LAPD 57333	Most Wanted 61333
28 Dan 36	Business 83352	The NewsHour With Jim Lehrer (RR) 571352		Life & Times 70888	Washington 56710	Wall St. Week 42517	American Masters (Part 1 of 2) (CC) 93826		American Masters (Part 2 of 2) (CC) 96913		"Dialogues With Madwomen" (CC) 62130	

CABLE	6:00	6:30	7:00	7:30	8:00	8:30	9:00	9:30	10:00	10:30	11:00	11:30
A&E Cox 41 Dan 34 / CNC 33 CV/N 33 / SW 25 SWU 45	Movie: "Road Games" ** (1981, Suspense) (Adult situations, violence.) 918401				Law & Order "The Reaper's Helper" 919130		Biography "Bill Gates: Tycoon" 939994		Movie: "Road Games" ** (1981, Suspense) (Adult situations, violence.) 292975			
AMC Cox 33 Dan 25 / CNC 25 CV/N 59 / SW 23 SWU 4	Movie: "Johnny Guitar" (5:00)		Movie: "All Quiet on the Western Front" **** (1930, War) Lew Ayres. Young German soldier faces WWI horrors. 661915				Movie: "Johnny Guitar" *** (1954, Western) 163284				"All ..." 712536	
BET Cox 40 CV/N 52 / SW 41 SWU 41	Video Soul Top 20 914791				Benson 472130	News 491265	Comic View Awards Jam 935284		TBA 892438	Comicview 597046	Best of Rap City 590555	
BRAV Cox 42 Dan 32 / CNC 44 CV/N 32 / SW 40 SWU 40	Movie: "Age of Consent" (5:00) ** 741230		Masters of American Music 391826		Movie: "Stairway to Heaven" **** (1946, Fantasy) 371062				South Bank Show "Miriam Makeba" 390197		Movie: "Age of Consent" ** (1969) 945081	
CNBC Cox 43 Dan 32 / CNC 46 CV/N 38 / SW 49 SWU 49	Rivera Live 33555		Charles Grodin 35826		America After Hours Pianist Billy Taylor. 11246		Rivera Live 24710		Charles Grodin 34197		Politics 42064	Paid Program 89333
CNN Cox 31 Dan 31 / CNC 36 CV/N 1 / SW 26 SWU 26	Larry King Live Alan Dershowitz. (CC) 357401		The World Today 559772		Sports 497468	Moneyline 476975	Newsnight 850913	Showbiz 369246	Politics 645178	Sports Late 654826	Larry King Live (RR) (CC) 171178	
COM Cox 48 Dan 44 / CNC 45 CV/N 58 / SW 37 SWU 37	Davidson 1365536	Comedy 1356888	Annual Young Comedians Show 3962536		M. Cho 6532623	Lounge Liz. 6511130	Comics Come Home 3951420		Davidson 3377246	D. Carey 3386994	Politically 5026710	Sat. Night 6672979
CSPN Cox 21 CV/N 2 / SW 20 SWU 20	Primetime Public Affairs (5:00) 235555				Public Policy 648371							
DIS† Cox 52 Dan 18 / CNC 32 CV/N 18 / SW 45 SWU 63	Movie (5:00) 132420	Movie: "All Dogs Go to Heaven" **. (1989, Children) (CC) 626284			Movie: "Rover Dangerfield" * (1991, Comedy) (CC) 601975		Movie: "Midnight Run" *** (1988, Comedy) (Language, violence.) 6781623				Heart 3734197	

TELEVISION WATCHING
OBSERVATION AND EVALUATION SHEET

Your Name _____

Name of television program watched: _____

Time of Day: From _____ to _____

1. Watch a television program for the full 30 minutes.

2. Use a stopwatch or a watch with a second hand. You'll probably need an extra pair of hands, so ask someone to assist you.

3. Time the actual program in minutes (do not include the commercials). How long was it? _____

4. What is the average length of a commercial? Why do you think each one is so short? _____

_____

5. Time the number of minutes used for commercial time. _____

6. Make a list of all products advertised during the commercials. _____

_____

_____

7. Write a brief summary of the program that you watched. In other words, what is it about? _____

_____

_____

_____

8. Write a short summary about one of the commercials that you watched. What will you remember about it? _____

_____

_____

CALDECOTT BOOKS
RECORDING AND INFORMATION SHEET

Student's Name _____

In the spaces below you are to preview 3 to 5 Caldecott Award-winning books. Your teacher will set your guidelines. Pay careful attention to the illustrations, the text, the story itself, and the appeal it would have for younger children. Try to decide why the book would have earned this most distinguished award. Enjoy.

Name of book:_____ Author:_____

Summary: _____

_____

_____

What do the illustrations look like? (colors, size, modern, old-fashioned, etc.) What medium was used to create them? (paper collage, block print, watercolor, pen, photographs, other) How did they relate to the story? What did they add to the appeal of the story? Do you think younger kids would appreciate these illustrations? Why or why not? _____

_____

_____

_____

_____

Name of book:_____ Author:_____

Summary: _____

_____

_____

What do the illustrations look like? (colors, size, modern, old-fashioned, etc.) What medium was used to create them? (paper collage, block print, watercolor, pen, photographs, other) How did they relate to the story? What did they add to the appeal of the story? Do you think younger kids would appreciate these illustrations? Why or why not? _____

_____

_____

_____

_____

Name of book:_____ Author:_____

Summary: _____

_____

_____

_____

Illustrations _____

_____

_____

_____

Name of book:_____ Author:_____

Summary: _____

_____

_____

_____

Illustrations _____

_____

_____

_____

Name of book:_____ Author:_____

Summary: _____

_____

_____

_____

Illustrations _____

_____

_____

_____

LET'S READ A RECIPE

ASSIGNMENT:

1. Look through several cookbooks.

2. Find a recipe that you have never tried before. Make sure it sounds delicious!

3. Read the recipe carefully and then write it in your neatest handwriting on a 3" × 5" index card.

4. Make a list of everything you would need to buy at the grocery store if you were really making this recipe.

5. Next to each item, tell what the price is. You may use the newspaper ads or you may actually go to the grocery store and price the item.

6. If possible, actually make the recipe.

7. Write a paragraph telling in your words:

      a. Who you would invite to share your recipe
      b. Why you chose the recipe
      c. How much time it will take you to prepare your recipe

Name of the recipe I chose: _____

Name of the cookbook where I found it: _____

List of the ingredients to buy and the
cost of each: _____

_____

_____

_____

_____

_____

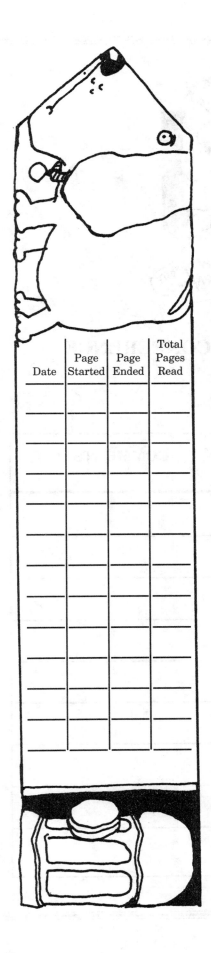

Date	Page Started	Page Ended	Total Pages Read

Date	Page Started	Page Ended	Total Pages Read

READING AND WRITING CONFERENCE

Name _____

DATE	PERSON GIVING CONFERENCE	COMMENTS

BOOKS I HAVE READ
IN ROOM _____

Name _____

Report Card Period _____

Parents Initials	Date	Book Title	Author	# of Pages	Rating 1–5

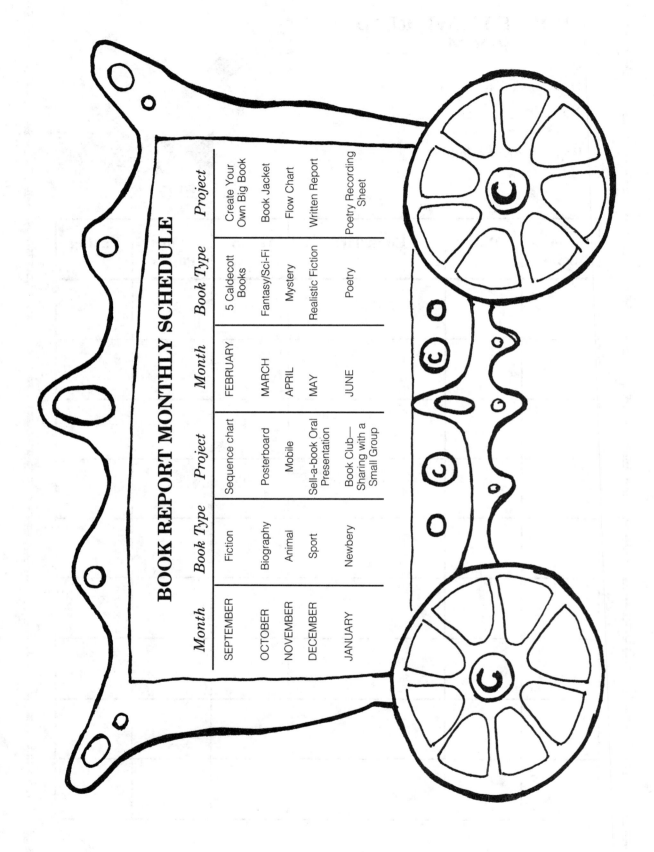

BOOK REPORT MONTHLY SCHEDULE

Month	Book Type	Project	Month	Book Type	Project
SEPTEMBER	Fiction	Sequence chart	FEBRUARY	5 Caldecott Books	Create Your Own Big Book
OCTOBER	Biography	Posterboard	MARCH	Fantasy/Sci-Fi	Book Jacket
NOVEMBER	Animal	Mobile	APRIL	Mystery	Flow Chart
DECEMBER	Sport	Sell-a-book Oral Presentation	MAY	Realistic Fiction	Written Report
JANUARY	Newbery	Book Club—Sharing with a Small Group	JUNE	Poetry	Poetry Recording Sheet

A BIOGRAPHICAL JOURNEY

You are about to embark on a biographical journey. You will be taking a trip through another person's life, either someone who lived in past history or someone who is currently living. This individual should be worthy of remembering for a contribution he or she has made to our lives or someone else's life.

HERE'S WHAT YOU'RE GOING TO DO:

1. Select a biography—that's a story of someone's life. There are so many interesting people to choose from. Here's a few to get you thinking: Bill Cosby, Elvis Presley, Harry Houdini, Judy Bloom, Alfred Hitchcock, Michael Jordan, Wyatt Earp, Clara Barton, Martin Luther King, Jr., Mark Twain.

2. In the next few weeks, read the book you have chosen. Remember to pace yourself. Don't leave it until the last minute—that's called procrastination. Use your bookmark to record your reading habits.

3. While you're reading your book, also read information about your person in the encyclopedia, an almanac, or another reference book.

4. Make a list of ten facts that tell us about this person's life. Keep that list until you are completed with the book.

5. Find five important dates from this person's life. You will be making a short timeline in class.

6. Locate a picture of your person. It should be bigger than an encyclopedia picture. Put your picture or book on my desk with a self-stick note letting me know what picture needs to be copied.

7. Select two colors of construction paper—one for the background (12" × 18") and one for the foreground color for your poster. (See the dimensions below.)

8. Select one **name card** (9" × 2 1/2") Name of Famous Person
   Select one **date card** (9" × 2") Birth and Death of Person
   Select one **fact card** (9" × 6") 6–8 Important Facts About Your Person

   These cards should all be the same color.

9. Frame the picture of your famous person on a piece of paper the same color as your cards above.

10. DO NOT GLUE ANYTHING ONTO YOUR MINI-BOARD YET. You want to make sure you have proper spacing on the board and things are not too crowded or too sparse.

11. In pencil, write the information you need for your cards.

12. Have someone proofread it.

13. Go over your words in fine-line black marker.

14. Erase your pencil marks.

15. Space your information cards on your background colored construction paper.

16. Prepare a mini-talk (2 to 3 minutes) for your classmates about your famous person. Your biography posterboard will be your visual aid. You may want to use another prop or dress as the person.

17. Also use your timeline to show some facts about your famous person.

Name Card	
Birth/Death Card	**Picture of famous person**

Fact Card

1.	6.
2.	7.
3.	8.
4.	9.
5.	10.

LET'S CREATE A REPORT CARD

Your Name: _____

Date: _____

Book Read: _____

Character Evaluated: _____

ASSIGNMENT:

1. Review a copy of your school report card. Notice that there are categories on which your teacher is required to evaluate you. You are to choose a minimum of **six** to **eight** categories on which to evaluate your character.

2. Your grading system for the academic subjects are **A**, **B**, **C**, **D**, or **F**.

3. Your grading system for effort is: **E** = Excellent, **G** = Good, **S** = Satisfactory, **N** = Needs Improvement, **U** = Unsatisfactory.

4. Evaluate the character in your book in subjects that are relevant to his/her part in the book (i.e., bravery, building, rescue skills, survival, kindness, swimming ability).

5. Make an academic as well as an effort grade for each subject you create.

6. Make a comment section for the teacher and the parent to respond.

7. Here is an example to guide you. You may make your report card similar to this, but be creative.

8. You may work alone or in partners.

Report Card

Student's Name _____ Age _____

School Name _____ Date _____

Subject	Academic Grade	Effort Grade	Grading Scale
Survival Skills			**A** - Outstanding Progress
Building			**B** - Very Good Progress
Bravery			**C** - Satisfactory Progress
Acceptance of Others			**D** - Unsatisfactory Progress
			F - Failing

Teacher Comments: _____

Signature _____

Parent Comments _____

Signature _____

Book Title _____   Your Name _____

CREATE YOUR OWN TEST

DIRECTIONS:

You have just completed a novel in class. Create a test to show how well you have read and how well others in your class have read. Make sure your work is neat and your questions are clearly stated.

Your test must include the following items:

1. 5 TRUE-FALSE questions. Ex.: This story takes place in the Caribbean.

2. 5 MULTIPLE-CHOICE questions. Ex.: Brian used which of these items as resources?

      a. Money   c. A toothbrush

      b. A very heavy jacket   d. A pocket knife

3. 5 SHORT ESSAY (ANSWER) questions. They must be more than 1- or 2-word answers. They should involve thinking. Start your questions with the following words: WHO? WHAT? WHEN? WHERE? WHY? HOW?

4. All questions will be answered on the test paper, so leave space for the answers.

5. Make an answer key on a separate sheet of paper.

6. Leave a space for the test taker's name at the top. Also include a space for the date.

7. Write your name at the bottom of the test.

CHARACTER SKETCH CARD

Book Title _____

Character's Name _____

Physical Characteristics: _____
_____
_____
_____
_____

Personality Traits:_____
_____
_____
_____
_____

Where He/She Lives: _____
_____

Your Name _____

CHARACTER SKETCH CARD

Book Title _____

Character's Name _____

Physical Characteristics: _____
_____
_____
_____
_____

Personality Traits:_____
_____
_____
_____
_____

Where He/She Lives: _____
_____

Your Name _____

CHARACTER SKETCH CARD

Book Title _____

Character's Name _____

Physical Characteristics: _____
_____
_____
_____
_____

Personality Traits:_____
_____
_____
_____
_____

Where He/She Lives: _____
_____

Your Name _____

CHARACTER SKETCH CARD

Book Title _____

Character's Name _____

Physical Characteristics: _____
_____
_____
_____
_____

Personality Traits:_____
_____
_____
_____
_____

Where He/She Lives: _____
_____

Your Name _____

Draw a picture of the main character.

Character's Name _____

I liked / disliked this character
because_____
_____
_____

Draw a picture of the main character.

Character's Name _____

I liked / disliked this character
because_____
_____
_____

Draw a picture of the main character.

Character's Name _____

I liked / disliked this character
because_____
_____
_____

Draw a picture of the main character.

Character's Name _____

I liked / disliked this character
because_____
_____
_____

LITERATURE/GEOGRAPHY STUDY GUIDE

Name _____

Country/State/Area studied: _____

Page where located in the almanac: _____

Area in miles: _____

Type of government: _____

Population: _____ Capital _____

3 largest cities: _____

Money used: _____

Major languages: _____

Major religion(s): _____

Education: _____

3 main products: _____

3 major exports: _____

What countries do they trade with? _____

Locate this area on your world map. Label it. Also label the name of the book directly under the name of the area (The Caribbean: Timothy of the Cay).

Use an encyclopedia or other reference book to locate other information about this area of the world. Write 5 to 10 new facts about the sports, foods, music, and other major concerns.

If needed, use a new sheet of paper and staple it to this sheet.

_____

_____

_____

_____

_____

_____

Name _____

WORLD WAR II PROJECT

in conjunction with the books *North to Freedom* or *Number the Stars*

You have just read a piece of core literature that dealt with World War II and the fear that the main characters had about concentration camps and the German soldiers. In order to understand this period of history better, you are to choose **at least one** of the following activities and research the topic thoroughly.

1. Interview a person who lived during WWII. Use the *Interview Plan Sheet* to plan out what you will ask. Interview your person. Find how he/she was influenced by the war and how his/her life changed during that time. Then write up a report to tell what you learned. Include a picture of the person you interviewed, if possible.

2. Who were the leaders of the major countries that were most active in the war? Tell who they were and what country they represented.

3. Write a report about the attack on Pearl Harbor and why the United States became involved in the war.

4. Draw pictures of the flags of the major countries fighting in WWII . Tell something about how and why each country became involved in the war.

5. What countries were the Axis Powers and what countries were the Ally Powers? Make a chart.

6. Draw pictures of the uniforms of the Americans in WWII. Label each and explain something important about them.

7. Locate some information about Adolf Hitler in a book or encyclopedia and tell why you think such a cruel man could become so powerful with the German people. What did he hope to accomplish by his cruelty to the Jews? Summarize your views in written form.

8. Draw pictures of the American air or sea craft used in WWII. Explain something about each of them. Label each.

9. Draw a map of Europe and show the countries that Adolf Hitler took control of during this period.

10. Read about and write a report about the role of women in WWII. Show how military women and civilian women dressed. You may want to watch the movie *A League of Their Own* to give you some ideas.

11. Research the Hitler Youth organization. Tell how the German children became part of the war.

12. Review a movie about WWII such as *The Diary of Anne Frank*; *The Sound of Music*; *Tora, Tora, Tora*; *Schindler's List*; *The Hiding Place*; *Burma Road*; *The Dirty Dozen*; *South Pacific*; *Anchor's Away*; *Midway*; *Patton*; *Enola Gay*; *Bridge Over the River Kwai*, etc. If you can think of others, check it out with your teacher first. Write a review of the movie.

13. Read a book about WWII, such as *The Diary of Anne Frank*; *Journey Back*; *Don't Fence Me In*; *Farewell to Manzanar*; *The Upstairs Room*; *Friedrick*, etc. Write a summary of the book. Bring the book into class and give an oral presentation to the class. If you find other books, let your teacher know which one you will be reading.

14. Locate some songs that were popular during WWII. Write the songs in print or on the computer. Tell how the songs were different from the songs of today. Sing or play something from that period of time for the class.

15. Create your own activity. Check it out with the teacher first.

16. Watch a documentary on television that deals with the war. Write a summary of it. For example, *Victory at Sea* has 26 episodes.

17. Research what life in your home city was like during WWII. Make a list or write a report telling about it.

18. Locate pictures dealing with the 1940–1945 era. Put the pictures together in an artful way with a brief description of each under the picture in your own words. Make sure you space things out neatly and you do not leave too much background showing. This should be no larger than 18" by 24." Neatly label it with straight lines, and remember to title the poster.

19. Watch a movie that was made during the years between 1940 and 1945. Give attention to the clothes, cars, hairstyles, makeup, etc. Make a poster to advertise the movie showing some of these things. Show a title and the names of the major stars.

20. Make a list of at least 10 important people who lived during the years between 1940 and 1945 and should be remembered for being famous. Tell why each was important to the world—film stars, politicians, people in medicine, musicians, etc.

21. If there is a place you have visited that deals with WWII, such as The Holocaust Museum, Pearl Harbor, Manzanar, etc., write a summary of your visit and share some of the items you purchased, or snapshots you took.

22. In *North to Freedom* David lived in a concentration camp and knew nothing about the world around him. Research what a concentration camp was in World War II. Write a report explaining what you find out.

23. Write a report about the Japanese Relocation in the United States after the attack on Pearl Harbor.

Due Date: _____

Requirements:

1. All projects must be neat, in pen/cursive writing, or typewritten.

2. If items are drawn with pencil first, make sure to finalize them in thin, black marker. Then erase all excess pencil marks.

3. All projects should be done on regular size paper (8 ½" × 11")

4. Maps and illustrations should be in colored pencil or marker.

WORLD WAR II PROJECT
TEACHER EVALUATION

Student's Name _____

Content	_____	Comments:
Quality	_____	_____
Neatness	_____	_____
Effort	_____	_____

* *

WORLD WAR II PROJECT
STUDENT EVALUATION

Student's Name _____

1. What did you like about doing this project? _____

   _____

2. Where did you obtain the information for this project? _____

3. Who helped you with your work?_____

4. How much time do you think this took you to finish? _____

   _____

5. What grade would you give yourself? Explain. _____

   _____

   _____

MY KINGDOM

(A Project to Accompany a Fantasy Book)

You have just completed the book *Bridge to Terabithia* where two children become king and queen of their imaginary kingdom called Terabithia. Using your own imagination, you are to create your very own kingdom, of which you are the king or queen. Have fun with this idea, but also take it seriously. We all wish we could build a perfect place to live. So for the next week and a half, you will be creating an environment where you will rule.

Before beginning, try to think! Ask for input from those around you. Let these questions guide your thinking. When you've got it together, begin writing. **Use paragraph form. Don't just answer the questions.** Be the king or queen and write about your kingdom. Be proud.

1. What would you name your kingdom?

2. Since you are the ruler, describe the kind of person you are. What qualities will make you a good ruler? Will your subjects like you? Why?

3. What does your kingdom look like? Describe it. Draw it.

4. Where is it located?

5. What rules do you have for your subjects? How will you assure that the rules are followed? Will there be rewards for those subjects who follow the rules? What will be the consequences for those who don't follow the rules?

6. What does your flag/banner look like? Describe it in words, and draw it.

7. What kinds of clothes do the people wear?

8. What kinds of games and sports do the people play?

9. If you had people from another kingdom come to visit, what would you serve them for dinner? Plan a menu.

10. Who are your enemies?

11. How is your castle protected?

12. Plan a travel brochure to show people so that they will want to visit your kingdom.

13. How is your kingdom different from the world of today?

Remember that you should incorporate some of the questions into your essay. The length of this paper should be approximately two pages—maybe more if you really get into it.

Get started thinking right now. Let your dreams be your guide!

Write it in cursive/pen or type it. Make it look snappy! No covers—you may have a title page.

THAT INCREDIBLE COOKIE

Name _____

PRE-COOKIE CLASSROOM ACTIVITIES:

1. During class, generate a list of all the cookies you could find on the shelves in the grocery stores. Work with a partner cooperatively. Your list should have at least 10 to 15 kinds of cookies.

2. Share your list with your classmates.

3. Your teacher will help you perform a simple experiment to see what your style of eating Oreo cookies is. (Eat the whole cookie; take the cookie apart and eat the frosting first; take the cookie half with frosting and eat it first, then eat the non-frosting half second; take two cookies and make a double frosting cookie; dip an Oreo cookie in milk before eating; and other ways.)

4. As a class, you will make a cookie-eating graph to show the results of your Oreo® experiment.

5. Individually, you will make your own graph to show the same information.

6. Bring in your favorite cookie recipe so that our class can compile our own cookie recipe book.

REQUIRED ACTIVITIES (Be creative!)   Due Date _____

1. Design the perfect cookie.

2. Name the perfect cookie.

3. Describe the perfect cookie thoroughly in words. (What's it made of, color, texture, etc.)

4. Great Cookie Caper:

   a. Write a mystery story in which a cookie is the main character or the main subject of the story. The cookie may be lost, stolen, or even murdered.

   b. Make sure you follow the mystery flow chart that you used during the Mystery Unit.

   c. Minimum length: 1 to 2 pages.

   d. Final drafts should be in ink or typed.

5. Make your own mini-display board with three panels on white tag board (12" × 4"). Use the following sample as your model:

> *Panel 1:* Neatly create a name for your cookie. Fill the whole space with your word.
>
> *Panel 2:* Make an illustration of your cookie. Label each part.
>
> *Panel 3:* Use 6 to 8 words to describe your cookie (mouthwatering, tasty, delicious, etc.). Print them neatly in colored markers.

Name of Cookie	Illustration of Cookie	6–8 Describing Words for Cookie

6. CHOOSE ONE OF THE FOLLOWING ACTIVITIES TO MAKE:

- A cookie collage
- A cookie cartoon
- A great cookie award
- A cookie advertisement for a magazine
- A cookie commercial for the radio or TV
- A cookie package/bag or box
- A cookie poem
- A name and design for a new cookie company
- A 3-D clay or papier-mache model of your cookie
- An activity of your own—check it out with your teacher first

Include color and use unlined paper for the above activities. Grading will be on **creativity**, **neatness**, **spelling**, **grammar**, and **quality**.

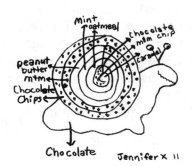

THE MYSTERY IN THE WONDER SISTER CO.

One day a factory was just opening. This factory was making a brand new cookie called The Chocolate Chip Elephant Cookie. Many people were very excited to try the new cookie.

The day the factory opened they gave a tour to the first 4 people who got there. Many people wanted to go on this tour of the factory. Finally when the factory opened the gate, everybody ran because they wanted to be the first person to go on the tour. Everybody pushed and shoved. One man was very pushy and made his way all the way to the front of the line so he was one of the four people to go on the tour. He was very excited about this.

First the tour guide told the 4 people the rules of the tour. 1) No eating the cookies. 2) No stealing the cookies. 3) No touching the first cookie because it will go in a frame. Everybody said they would obey the rules. Now it was time to start the tour.

First they had to walk through many doors. Finally they got to the cookie making part. The guy who had pushed his way all the way to the front of the line looked at every part of how the cookies were made. The tour guide told them every part of the process. Soon they were half way through and the guy who had been pushy wanted a snack, so he took one of the cookies. He sat down where nobody could see him and ate the cookie.

After the first one, he thought they were wonderful and he ate another cookie and another and another. At that point he had eaten 4 cookies. He was still hungry after that and took every cookie that came his way and ate them. Soon the people who were supposed to put the cookies in the package were not getting any cookies, so they called the people who were supposed to bake the cookies. They said the cookies were fine when they came out of the oven. So they were wondering what happened to the cookies on the way to the packaging area. They searched the machine they were supposed to end up on.

When they couldn't find the cookies they began to worry. Soon everybody in the factory knew about the problem. Everybody was worried. But the manager checked everywhere and finally found the man sleeping. Since the man was sleeping he didn't know they had found him until he woke up. Once he woke up they asked him if he knew where the cookies went. He said he didn't know. So they looked all around where he was sitting, and finally found crumbs on the man's T-shirt. He admitted he had been eating all of The Chocolate Chip Elephant Cookies as he walked by them. They called security and threw him out and said he was never allowed there ever again.

THE END!!! Breanna P

age: 11

STRATEGIES FOR HELPING STUDENTS WITH READING AND WRITING DIFFICULTIES

TEACHING READING SKILLS

In our school district, as in probably most districts throughout the country, an important goal and expectation is that by the time children have completed the third grade, they will have acquired the basic reading skills that will enable them to successfully and independently read grade-level material. Of course, we know that many children fall short of this "ideal." There are many students who have significant difficulty with various components of the reading process; and, unfortunately, have reading skills far below grade level by the time they reach the upper grades. The following material will address a wide range of strategies for helping students who struggle with decoding (word recognition and identification), fluency, recall of material read, and comprehension.

Oral Reading Strategies

Upper-grade students with reading difficulties are often in a constant state of fear that they will be asked to read aloud and, consequently, be humiliated in front of their peers. Avoid any situation that places students under such anxiety. Older students should never be forced to read in front of the class; rather, they should be allowed to volunteer. It is much less intimidating for older students to orally read with a partner or small group. Often it is helpful to give students time to read silently before the class or groups read orally.

Teachers should be reading aloud to students at all grade levels. Read-Alouds should be for students' enjoyment of literature and exposure to a variety of different genres. All students enjoy the opportunity to hear intriguing literature read to them with fluency and expression.

The following are several oral reading strategies that are alternative and preferable ways to share and involve students in reading other than round-robin strategies. Some are conducive to large group, others to small group; but all are designed to increase motivation and variety to the oral reading process in the classroom:

- **Choral reading:** Everyone in the class or group reads together at the same time. This is an excellent strategy when using a short piece to focus on at the same time. For example, make a transparency of a poem or a passage from a text and read it together in unison. A humorous poem lends itself to this strategy very well. After first modeling the oral reading of the poem, students read along with the teacher in choral reading. The lines can be numbered 1,2,1,2, with part of the class or group reading lines 1 and the others reading lines 2. One verse can be read orally by girls, the next by boys, and so forth. (See Section 13, *Hooking Reluctant Readers/Writers*, for additional strategies.)

- **Cloze reading:** The teacher reads or rereads the material, but leaves out key words. The students fill in the missing words aloud.

- **Popcorn reading:** One person begins reading and then after a few lines or paragraphs calls out "Popcorn" and names another student in the group. This student continues to read until he/she calls "Popcorn" and names someone else. (Note: It is determined in advance how few or many lines or paragraphs it is permissible to read before calling "Popcorn.")

- **Mirror (echo) reading:** The teacher reads while the students are following (in book or on overhead). The teacher reads a sentence, or part of a passage and then the student(s) repeat it. After reading a few paragraphs or pages, stop and have students orally reread certain passages. **Note:** Students should be *rereading* in a variety of situations, as well. The process of rereading passages they have heard before increases fluency and comprehension; and is particularly helpful for students with reading difficulties. Rereading can be done with partners, individually, in small groups, into a tape recorder, in chorus, to an adult (teacher, aide, parent volunteer). Have students locate information in response to teacher prompts and questioning and orally reread those passages.

- **Switch seat reading:** The teacher starts out reading with students following in their books. The teacher sits in the seat of the next reader. Oral reading continues with switching seats when another reader is to take over.

- **Shared quotations:** The teacher orally reads everything except direct quotations from the text. Whenever something is written in quotation marks, students orally read those lines.

- **Dialogue reading:** Students are assigned characters and read those parts.

- **Reader's Theater:** Students are assigned parts from scripted literature.

- **Buddy or partner reading:** Students read orally in partners, taking turns alternating (paragraphs, pages, together in unison). It is often effective for students to share one book that is placed between them. One reader can point to the words while the other is following along. Sharing one book is not, however, necessary. Partners help each other with words and suggesting strategies. They can question, discuss readings, and summarize. Teachers can assign questions that each pair of students will need to be able to answer at the end of the reading assignment to encourage focus.

Reading Methods and Approaches for Increasing Word Recognition and Fluency

- **Recorded books:** The student listens to a tape recording of the book while visually tracking the words. The student can also read aloud with the tape after listening and following. When shorter (picture books) are used for the recorded reading, it is recommended to have students listen two or three times to the same story while following along visually in their books.

- **Phonetic approach:** This approach emphasizes the teaching of letter sounds and letter sound groups, and the blending of these sounds into meaningful words. Students are taught vowel sounds and associations to help them recall those sounds, digraphs (ch, sh, th), etc. Many students in the upper grades who struggle with word recognition have not learned the sound associations for vowels or letter combinations (qu, ar, ea, ou, ai, kn). They benefit from supplementary instruction in phonics, and practicing how to break unknown words into syllables (segments) and sounding out (e.g., in-hab-it; va-ca-tion; fan-tas-tic).

- **Linguistic method:** Patterns of letters are taught and combined to form words. Words are chunked and introduced as word families. Many upper-grade students gain significantly from reading and generating lists of words in different families (rock, stock, flock; bench, wrench, quench, drench; right, might, flight, fright, bright).

- **Structural approach:** Many students are helped by directly teaching structural analysis (recognition of prefixes, suffixes, and their meanings). Focusing on the visual configuration of the word is a useful strategy for some students: "Does this word look like any other word you know?"

- **Language experience:** Students read stories they have dictated and watch while you write or type their story. The teacher (or other adult) reads the student's story orally. Then student and teacher read chorally (together at the same time). This approach emphasizes the use of key words drawn directly from sentences the students created and dictated.

- **The Fernald Method:** Beginning with the language experience method, the student traces over self-selected new words he/she can't read but wants to learn from his/her dictated writing. Teacher (or other adult) writes the selected words on cards in large letters. For each word, the key is to say the word while simultaneously tracing the word. The student traces the word with the index finger while saying the word several times until he/she can write the word correctly and automatically. This is a mildly structured whole-word approach that utilizes language experience and the tactual-kinesthetic channel. It is also referred to as a VAKT (visual, auditory, kinesthetic-tactile) method.

- **Sight word or whole word approach:** Students are taught to identify certain words as a whole unit at the automatic level. High-frequency words and non-phonetic words are generally taught this way. Frequent drill, practice, and repetition (preferably in a game format) help to 'lock these words" into the memory bank for instant recognition.

- **Neurological Impress Method (NIM):** This technique utilizes a whole word approach to the development of reading fluency, phrasing and visual-auditory channel integration. This is often effective for older students who devote excessive amounts of time to sounding out words. It helps them learn how to read material in phrases rather than as isolated words, and is most effective when used on a 1:1 basis. The student should be seated slightly in front of the teacher (or next to) so the teacher's voice is close to the student's ear. They read the same passage together orally, with the teacher or other adult model smoothly moving his/her finger along the line of the words so that it points to the words that are about to be read next. In early sessions the teacher should read a little faster and louder than the student. Together they reread the lines and paragraphs several times before going on to new material.

- **Choral Repeated Reading:** This very effective 3-step procedure developed by Candace Bos, one of the authors of *Strategies for Teaching Students with Learning and Behavior Problems*, is described in the book as follows: Together with the student select a book of interest that is one to two levels above his/her current instructional reading level. Establish a purpose for reading by introducing the book and making predictions. Read the book with the student using the following 3-step process: (1) Teacher reads a piece of text to the student ranging from several sentences to a paragraph. (Read at a normal rate and move your finger smoothly along underneath the words as the student watches, making sure that your reading matches your movement from word to word.) (2) Teacher and student read the same section together aloud while teacher continues to point to the words. Jointly reread the section once or until the student feels comfortable reading the section independently. (3) Student reads orally by him-/herself. Teacher pronounces any unknown words and notes those words student consistently has difficulty recognizing. After reading each section, discuss how it related to student's predictions and continue the procedure throughout the book. The length of each section usually increases as the book is read, as the number of rereads together typically decrease. Teacher records on word cards those words to practice for more automatic recognition. **Note:** The entire session usually lasts between fifteen to twenty minutes.

- **Uninterrupted reading:** Another very important strategy for building reading skills is to incorporate into the day a short period of time, (such as, 15 to 20 minutes, less for younger student) of uninterrupted time for everyone to be engaged in reading self-choice material at their independent reading level. In schools this has a variety of names: Sustained Silent Reading (SSR) or Sustained Uninterrupted Reading (SUR) or DEAR (Drop Everything and Read) periods. Schools will often also have all adults at the site participating and modeling in this sustained silent reading period throughout the school. **Note:** Some students have significant difficulty during silent reading time, particularly remaining focused and reading to themselves. If so, consider allowing them to be seated at a listening post and read along with a text while listening to a book on tape.

Some programs that are recommended for increasing word recognition of students deficient in this skill are: *Project Read* (decoding strand) by Victoria Greene and Mary Lee Enfield, *Simply Phonics* by Sandra Rief, and *Developing Independent Readers* by Cynthia Conway Waring. (See the bibliography and recommended resources at the end of this section.)

In the upper grades when the classroom reading material is often at the frustration level for struggling readers, provide reinforcement reading materials for independent reading at home that are high interest but lower readability level (including appropriate picture books for older students).

In order to help our struggling readers, it is important to recognize what strategies proficient readers make use of. The following are skills and strategies typically used by "good readers":

Prior to reading: They determine the purpose for reading, draw on personal experience and access prior knowledge, and build up their background knowledge on the subject.

During reading: They translate what they read into pictures and images (visualize), relate the reading to their own life and make connections, make comparisons, make predictions, and change their predictions. They also reread confusing parts, skip over parts, locate information, and use all cueing strategies for figuring out unknown vocabulary and making sense out of what they read (semantic, syntactic, and phonetic cues). In addition, "good readers" focus on major content, constantly check their comprehension and understanding through self-correcting strategies, and stay focused on the reading task.

Teaching Reading Comprehension Skills

- **Prior to reading** relate stories or reading material to prior experience and knowledge through: class discussions, brainstorming and charting prior knowledge, setting a purpose, previewing the visuals in the text and making/listing predictions, and using visuals/audiovisuals related to the topic of literature (e.g., maps, music, filmstrips).

- Have students fill out the first two parts of a three-column K-W-L chart prior to reading text of content area material.

    I already **know**—**What** I want to find out—**I learned**

- Have students look at (preview) key information (illustrations, captions, headings, chapter questions) in the text before reading through.

- Previewing can also involve students listening to passages read aloud first before independently studying and rereading.

During reading strategies to aid comprehension and stay focused on text:

- Teach students how to paraphrase a paragraph, putting into their own words the main idea and significant details. Some students find that paraphrasing each paragraph and stating into a tape recorder is a very helpful technique.

- Teach textbook structure (significance of bold and italic print, headings, subheadings).

- Teach how to find introductory paragraphs and summary paragraphs.

- Teach students how to rephrase main ideas, and headings into their own words.

- Teach how to find the subject, main ideas and sift out the key facts and important details from the irrelevant and redundant words/text. An outstanding program for teaching this skill is the comprehension component of *Project Read*. (See the Bibliography and Recommended Resources.)

- Teach students to read the questions at the end of the chapter before beginning the reading of the chapter.

- Provide students with a pad of self-stick notes. As they are reading they can jot down notes, vocabulary words to clarify, question marks by items they don't understand, and place directly on the text. The self-stick notes can be placed directly next to key points and main ideas for fast/easy reference.

- Assign shorter amounts of required reading.

- Teach story mapping: identifying the setting (time/place), characters, conflicts/problems, action/events, climax, resolution of conflicts.

- Use peer tutors, partner reading, and cooperative strategies in reading texts.

- See if a reading marker or strip helps to focus students who lose their place in reading, and have difficulty visually focusing on text.

- Teach clustering and semantic mapping.

- Utilize reciprocal teaching methods for comprehension that combine four reading comprehension strategies: predicting, clarifying, summarizing, and questioning. (See Section 11, *Effective Questioning Techniques for the Classroom*.)

- Enlarge a page of the book and make a transparency of it. Have students come to the overhead, locate certain information, and underline it.

- Photocopy pages for students and have them highlight important information.

- Provide study guides to aid in looking for important information in the text.

- Underline or circle important points in the text.

- Color-code a master textbook for lower readers. Important vocabulary can be highlighted in one color. For example: vocabulary in one color, definitions in another color, important facts and topic sentences in a third color.

- Tape-record textbooks for individual use or group listening at a listening post. Use a good quality tape and a recorder with counter numbers. For ease in following text at a listening post, have clear signals on the tape for when to turn the page, or include periodically on the recording the chapter and page number. Pages can be marked with the counter number at the beginning of each chapter.

- **Teach SQ3R technique:** This strategy for increasing comprehension and retention of textbook material involves the following steps:

  1. **Survey:** Briefly view the reading assignment, survey the titles, look at the chapter headings, skim through the assignment, and read the chapter summary and/or end of chapter questions.

  2. **Question:** Turn the headings and subheadings of the text into questions. Example: *Producing Antibodies* can become "How do our bodies produce antibodies?" *Organic motor fuels* can become "What are the different organic motor fuels?"

  3. **Reading:** Ask questions to self while in reading process (e.g., "What is the author trying to tell me?") Jot down any questions or unknown vocabulary.

  4. **Recite:** State in some form in own words what was read. Note: Restating or summarizing into a tape recorder is often very effective.

  5. **Review:** See how much you remember. Check for important information that you may have forgotten.

- **Cloze technique:** Students are presented with passages that have words deleted from them with blanks where those missing words belong. They are to use their cueing systems and context of the text to try determining the missing words. Cloze exercises are constructed by selecting passages from texts. Every seventh to tenth word should be omitted in primary-grade material. Every fifth word can be omitted from upper-grade material, although for difficult material fewer words can be deleted . The first and last sentences of the passage remain intact. This is a very effective strategy for teaching cueing strategies and building comprehension skills. Cloze procedures can be adapted to omit vocabulary terms or parts of speech (e.g., all verbs or all adverbs).

Cloze procedures are very effectively used on the overhead projector. One method is to prepare a transparency with a few typed paragraphs from the chapter in cloze format. The teacher orally reads from the chapter in the text to the students. As she/he approaches the cloze paragraph, the transparency of the cloze paragraph is projected. Specific vocabulary words are deleted rather than every *x* number of words. The teacher can provide the first letter or few letters of the missing words to help narrow choices. Students choose words that would make sense in the blank. The following is an example of a *modified cloze* technique using a paragraph from the book *Sadako and the Thousand Paper Cranes* by Eleanor Coerr.

> *With a great effort Sadako l_____ herself out of bed. Mrs. Sasaki helped her put on the k_____ and tie the s_____. Sadako was glad her swollen legs didn't show. Unsteadily she l_____ across the room and sat in her ch_____ by the window. Everyone agreed that she was like a p_____ in the kimono.*

Graphic Organizers to Aid Reading

There are numerous graphic displays to accompany reading of literature and textbook material. The following are a few that are useful in increasing comprehension of text:

- *Framed outlines:* Students are given copies of a teacher-prepared outline that contains missing information. As the student reads or through subsequent discussion, students fill in the missing information. Ideally, this can be modeled on the overhead to teach the skill.

- *Advance organizers:* Prepare study guides to help focus students on important points, present information in a logical sequence, and help direct attention to essential information.

- *Venn Diagrams* (overlapping circles): These help students in visualizing the similarities and differences between two characters, places, topics, and objects in the book.

- *Comparison charts:* Similar to a Venn Diagram, it is used to compare/contrast 2 or 3 characters, for example.

- *Cluster maps:* These are used to categorize or identify related information.

- *Storyboards:* Divide sections on a board or piece of paper and have students draw or write story events in sequence in each box/frame.

- *Story frames:* This graphic includes essential elements of a story (setting, characters, time, place, problem or conflict, resolution).

- *Timelines:* These are used to help visualize chronological text and sequence of events.
- *Plot charts:* Somebody . . . Wanted . . . But . . . And So . . . .
- *Flow charts:* See the example of the Mystery Flow Chart at the end of Section 2, *Learning Developmentally.*
- *Response logs:* Students record their thoughts, feelings, and questions about what they are reading.

TEACHING WRITTEN LANGUAGE

For many students in our classrooms, particularly those with learning disabilities and/or ADHD, writing is the most challenging and frustrating of academic tasks. Some common difficulties in written language include: spelling, mechanics, grammar and sentence structure, organization, written expression, output onto paper, neatness and legibility of product. The following material, along with Section 13 to motivate and "hook our reluctant writers," is designed to share some effective practices for helping students achieve confidence and success in writing.

Written Expression—Prewriting Strategies

The task of writing—deciding what to write about and how to express those ideas—is a struggle for all of us at times. We have many students who experience difficulties in written expression, and who find it hard to get motivated to write. They need a great deal of assistance at this prewriting stage of the writing process, with help generating ideas, organizing thoughts and planning before writing. This is often the most neglected stage of the writing process, but of critical importance in helping our students with expressive writing difficulties. When given a written assignment, our students will often be stuck at this stage, not able to generate an idea to write about or knowing how to begin. The following are some prewriting techniques/strategies designed to stimulate the production of ideas, enabling students to find a topic to write about:

- **Brainstorm:** These sessions are very short and focused (no more than 3 to 5 minutes). Given a general theme or topic students call out whatever comes to mind related to that topic, and someone records all responses. Brainstorming can be done as a whole group with the teacher recording responses, or most effectively in partners or small cooperative groups. It is very helpful to keep writing tablets or a single whiteboard with dry-erase pen readily available on students' desks for this purpose. A large-group sharing can follow partner or small-group work.

- **Quick write:** Students are given a few minutes (no more than 3 to 4) to write down everything that they can think of related to a given topic. The teacher is also modeling the same uninterrupted writing along with his/her students at this time. During a brief, focused quick write, students are told to continuously write something. They are not to worry about spelling, mechanics, complete sentences or neatness—just to write! Student volunteers can share with the class, or everyone can share what they wrote with a partner.

- **Writing topics:** Have students maintain a list or folder of possible writing topics to which they can refer. Include on individual lists hobbies, places they have visited, jobs they have done, personal interests, interesting/colorful family members, neighbors, friends, pets, favorite restaurant, favorite sport, and so forth. Provide time for partners, groups of students, or full class to share items on their lists and add to them throughout the year.

- **Personal collage writing folder:** Have students make a personal collage writing folder by using words and pictures cut out from magazines, newspapers and travel brochures, and laminating the folder when done. Students should include things they like, places they have gone, hobbies, favorite foods, cars, etc. This serves as a stimulus for writing ideas and is excellent to keep as part of a portfolio for the year with writing activities.

- **Reference books:** Pass out reference books to groups of students to look through (e.g., vehicles, antique cars, deserts, horses, motorcycles, fashion, mammals, oceans, boats, baseball, mysteries of nature, etc.). In cooperative groups, students generate lists of topics related to their book. These lists can also serve as stimuli for writing ideas.

- **Writing prompts:** Provide a stimulus such as a poem, story, picture, song, or news item to prompt writing. Keep a file of pictures from magazines, old calendars, postcards, etc. as stimuli for writing activities.

- **Vocabulary lists:** Have students generate a vocabulary list of words related to a theme or topic the teacher would like the class to write about. Assign a student to "toss a spongeball' (or beanbag) to each student in the room who must say a word that comes to mind when he/she catches the ball (beanbag). The teacher lists on the chalkboard all of the words the class generated. For example, everyone might supply a word related to: nature, climate, archaeology, words that make me shiver, words that make me hungry, soft words, angry words, and so forth.

- **Self-talk:** Teach students to self-talk through the planning stage of their writing: "Who am I writing for? Why am I writing this? What do I know? What does my reader need to know?"

- **Telling personal stories:** In cooperative groups have students orally respond to prompts by *telling* personal stories: "Can you remember a time you got sick right before something you really wanted to do?" "Can you tell about a time you got in trouble for something that is funny now when you think about it, but wasn't funny then?" After the oral telling and sharing of stories in small, cooperative groups, students write a rough draft or outline of the story they told.

- Use the picture book *Aunt Isabel Tells a Good One* by Kate Duke about a mouse who makes up a story to her niece using "the ingredients of a good story" (a heroine, hero, danger, excitement, a little romance, a villain or two, a happy ending). It can be used as a stimulus prior to writing a creative story.

- **Graphic Organizers:** One of the most effective ways to help students generate their ideas and formulate and organize their thoughts is through training and practice using *graphic organizers*. For students with written language difficulties, use of a graphic organizer of some sort is a critical intervention in helping them plan before they begin to actually write. Provide teacher modeling and guided practice in a variety of techniques with the utilization of graphic displays for writing ideas: **Note:** The graphic organizers that aid students in reading comprehension are useful in organizing thoughts prior to writing activities. Some examples of graphic organizers are:

Clustering—Write the main idea in a box or rectangle in the center of a page; surround the main idea box with bubbles containing all of the supporting ideas.

Writing frames—Fill in the blanks from a framed outline.

Mind mapping—A circle is drawn in the center of a page. The topic is written inside the center circle; on lines stemming from the circle are related ideas. (This technique is also called webbing, and the graphic is called a web.).

Diagrams—Venn Diagrams, for example, are graphics of overlapping circles used to show comparison between two or three items/topics/characters/books.

Compare/contrast charts—This is another way of depicting similarities and differences.

Story maps—These are used in planning the critical elements to be included when writing a story (setting, characters, problem, action, resolution).

Provide Models

Students who have difficulty with writing need many oral and visual models of good writing. These include:

- Read examples of written works that demonstrate the skill you are emphasizing (e.g., expanded, descriptive sentences; well-developed paragraphs; use of metaphors/similes).
- Display models and classwide standards for acceptable written work.
- Display models of proper headings, spacing, and organization of written work.
- Teach and display steps of the writing process (prewriting, composing, responding, revising, editing, publishing).
- Teach and display steps of the editing process.
- Post a cursive alphabet for reference.
- Provide many examples and display samples of pre-writing graphic organizers.
- Stop students after a few minutes of writing and ask for student volunteers to share what they have written so far.
- Provide printing or cursive reference charts to individual students.
- Make lists and charts of certain vocabulary or parts of speech, and display for reference (e.g., lists of adjectives, adverbs, transition words, etc.).
- Provide models of papers containing: introduction, body, conclusion.

Many of today's students are significantly weak in writing skills, particularly spelling, grammar, and mechanics. Students with learning disabilities and/or ADHD are generally deficient in written language, but so are many other children in the classroom, as well. Writing samples of students in any classroom will reveal weakness in: proper sentence structure and organization; grammar; capitalization; punctuation; syntax; verb tense; subject-verb agreement; incomplete and run-on sentences; and lack of sequence, coherency, and closure in story development. Students need direct instruction, guided practice, and teaching of these skills.

For Help in Spelling

See Section 12, *Motivating Techniques for Teaching Spelling and Vocabulary*.

For Help With Written Organization and Sequence

- Teach students to write sequential steps by writing "how-to" make something, or construct something, or follow a sequential recipe, steps in a task or skill, etc.

- Some students who tend to ramble in their writing—without any thought towards where their story is going, or how to end, may do better with planning and writing the ending first and then creating a story around the ending.

- Teach students to self-talk through the organization of their writing. "How can I group my ideas? Am I missing any details? How can I order my ideas?"

For Help With Grammar, Structure, and Mechanics

- Teach students parts of speech and have them practice locating nouns, verbs, adverbs, etc., in their text. Example: List 10 verbs or action words you find in the chapter. Find 5 adjectives.

- Tell students to listen for words they hear that are a certain part of speech (noun, adverb, adjective, verb). Read to students from a book, stopping after each page or two in a picture book, or every paragraph in a chapter book. Call on students as they name words they heard in the reading, and make a list on the board or transparency.

- Have students do a search for parts of speech and record in notebooks, or keep class charts of examples.

- Provide models and displays of capitalization rules and punctuation rules.

- Teach students abbreviations and contractions.

- Provide direct instruction and guided practice in the skills of mechanics (punctuation and capitalization).

- Teach sentence expansion and combining of sentences. Given a short 2- to 3-word sentence, practice expanding with detail and description to the simple sentence by adding: "where?" "how?" "when?" "why?'. Example: The girl cried. When? The girl cried throughout the night. Why? The lonely girl cried throughout the night because she missed her best friend, Amy.

- Teach the structure of a paragraph by writing paragraphs using a graphic of a hamburger. Make a graphic display of a hamburger with its two buns, hamburger pattie, and condiments to represent the parts of a paragraph. The top bun represents the topic sentence. The hamburger pattie is the meat of the paragraph, each of the condiments (lettuce, tomato, pickle) represent the details that add flavor and interest to the paragraph, and the bottom bun is for closure.

Teaching Editing Skills

- Teach students the skills of proofreading and editing. One method is by making transparencies of unedited work of anonymous students or teacher samples of writing that are lacking in capitalization, punctuation, etc. Edit as a group.

- Encourage students to circle words they think are misspelled in their writing.

- Teach students to respond to their own writing.

> *My best sentence is* _____. *My five favorite descriptive words that I used were* _____, _____, _____, _____, _____. *A simile or metaphor I used was* _____. *My ending shows the reader how my problem was resolved* _____ *(yes/no).*

- Teach students to self-talk through the editing/revising stage of their writing: "Does everything make sense? Did I include all of my ideas? Do I need to insert, delete, or move ideas?"

- Use peer editing. Have students work with a partner to read their work to each other. The partner listens and reads along as the author reads. The peer-editing partner tells what he/she liked best. Then the editor questions the author about anything that doesn't make sense; suggests where more information is needed for clarification; helps edit when he/she hears/sees run-on or incomplete sentences. The author responds to all of the editor's questions and makes notes for revisions. The partners then reverse roles for this stage of editing. Peer editors can then re-edit after revision for content, accuracy of capitalization/punctuation, can assist with spelling, and so on. **Note:** This peer-editing process can also take place in small groups of three or four students listening to each other's stories, responding and editing each other's work.

- Conduct teacher-student writing conferences. (See the *Reading and Writing Conference* sheet in Section 13, *Hooking Reluctant Readers/Writers*.) At that time the teacher provides feedback, the student reflects on his/her own work, and both share what they like about the piece of writing. The student self-evaluates improvement and skills to target for continued improvement.

> *My writing has improved in* _____ *(sentence structure, paragraphing, fluency, creativity, organization, capitalization, punctuation, spelling).*
> *I plan to work on* _____.

- Writing conferences using this format can be done parent to student, aide or parent volunteer to student, and peer to peer.

- Try providing students more time to write in class and more direct, supportive feedback.

Written Output Difficulties

Many students, particularly those with ADD and learning disabilities, have significant difficulties with their ability to produce on paper and to demonstrate their knowledge in written form. There is often a giant discrepancy between what they know, what information they have and can express verbally, and what they are able to actually put down on paper. Written output difficulties might mean production of illegible work (with fine motor and handwriting difficulties, numerous erasures, disorganization of written product, immature letter formation and spacing). Often it means students are not able to produce more than a few words or sentences, far less than is considered average output for the grade level. The speed and rate of their writing may be rushed and illegible; it is often excruciatingly slow and tedious. These students need to find ways to bypass or circumvent their writing disabilities.

TO BYPASS WRITTEN OUTPUT DIFFICULTIES

- Substitute nonwritten projects (e.g., oral reports) for written assignments.
- Give students options and choices that don't require writing, but draw on students' strengths (hands-on project-oriented assignments of: investigating, building, drawing, constructing, creating, making, doing, simulating, experimenting, researching, telling, singing, dancing, and so on).
- Provide worksheets with extra space.
- Enlarge the space for doing written work (math papers, tests).
- *Notetaking assistance:* Assign a buddy to take notes, share and compare.
- Provide NCR paper or carbon paper for multiple copies to be given to the notetaker.
- Make photocopies of teacher notes or designate students who take neat, organized notes to give to those students who can't copy from the board easily.
- Stress accuracy, not volume
- Follow written exams with oral exams and average the grades for those students.
- Allow oral exams.
- Allow oral responses for assignments/tests.
- Permit students to dictate their responses and have someone else transcribe for them.
- Do not assign large quantity of written work.
- Allow students to use a tape recorder to record thoughts, rough drafts, responses to questions, etc.
- Provide access to a computer and motivating writing programs with a variety of fonts and graphics (e.g., *Children's Publishing Center*).
- Teach proper keyboarding/typing skills and provide practice to increase skills.
- Teach word processing skills, including the use of editing options ("cut and paste") and various format options.
- Provide assistance typing/printing final drafts of papers.
- Encourage parents to invest in a word processor, computer, or typewriter for the student.
- Encourage students to utilize computer, wordprocessor, or typewriter at home.
- Accept homework that is typed instead of written by hand.
- Sit with student and help talk or prompt him/her through writing the first one or two sentences to get student started.
- Have student dictate and you write the first one or two sentences for the student to get them started.
- See Section 8, *Interventions and Adaptations for Accommodating Students with Special Needs.*

FOR HELP WITH NEATNESS AND LEGIBILITY

- Use real-life situations (job applications, filling out checks) to stress the need for legible writing.
- Stress how studies have proven that teachers tend to give students the benefit of the doubt and grade higher if their papers look good as opposed to being sloppy or hard to read; how neatness and legibility reflect attitude and caring about your work, and make a very important impression.
- Avoid the pressures of speed.
- Set realistic, mutually agreed-upon expectations for neatness.
- If student writes too heavy or too light, change the pencil type, use pencil grips, try a mechanical pencil.
- Often small-lined paper is better than large-lined paper, as it requires less execution.
- Teach placing of index finger between words (finger spacing) to help students who run their words together without spacing.
- Provide students with a strip of alphabet letters (manuscript or cursive) for a reference on their desk.
- If the student's paper is frequently sliding around and student doesn't anchor it well, provide a clipboard.
- Make sure students have sharpened pencils and erasers at their desks.
- Use writing warm-ups—physically stretching, wiggling fingers. If possible, do the warm-ups to a song, rhyme, chant or rap.
- Make an "ooze bag' by placing some hair gel in a zip-lock baggie. With permanent marker write each letter for practice on the outside of the bag. The student traces the letter, which is an interesting texture with the gel inside of the bag.
- Using the gel bag, color-code the strokes of a letter on the outside of the bag. The first phase of the stroke can be one color (purple), the second phase can be another color (yellow). Arrows can also be drawn indicating the directions of the letter formation.
- Students can practice correct letter formation by tracing sandpaper letters, or letters written on other textures.
- Many upper-grade students haven't mastered how to form cursive letters, and struggle with formation or speed. Provide guided practice for students in need by modeling on the overhead projector in color while talking through the steps.
- Use a parent volunteer or aide to work 1:1 with upper-grade students who need help mastering cursive formation. Use tactile-kinesthetic techniques of tracing in sand, on the carpet, or other textures with two fingers. Sometimes the adult needs to gently place his/her hand over the student's writing hand, to guide in the formation.
- Provide prompts for correct letter formation/directionality by placing dots indicating where to begin and arrows indicating in which direction to write the strokes of the letter(s).
- Allow for frequent practice and corrective feedback using short trace-and-copy activities.
- For upper-grade students who struggle significantly with cursive, permit them to print.
- Encourage appropriate sitting, posture, and anchoring of paper when writing.
- Alternate the size of the paper or lines.

- For motivation, add *variety*—paper size, paper shape, texture of paper, colored paper, fancy stationery.

- Use computer paper with students writing on the green lines or white lines only, so editing can be easily done in the space above.

- For variety have students write on individual chalkboards with chalk, or dry-erase boards with colored pen.

- Allow students to sometimes show their work by providing them with a blank transparency and requiring them to do their neatest writing in color to be shared on the overhead.

- Teach standards of acceptable work in your classroom, whatever those standards may be (e.g., writing on one side of paper only, rough draft papers written on every other line, math papers with two or three line spaces between problems, heading on upper right section of paper).

BIBLIOGRAPHY AND RECOMMENDED RESOURCES

Bos, Candace S., and Vaughn, Sharon. *Strategies for Teaching Students with Learning and Behavior Problems*, third edition. Needham Heights, MA: Allyn & Bacon, 1994.

Bromley, Karen, Irwin-De Vitis, Linda, and Modlo, Marcia. *Graphic Organizers—Visual Strategies for Active Learners*. New York: Scholastic Professional Books, 1995.

Duke, Kate. *Aunt Isabel Tells a Good One*. New York: Dutton Children's Books, 1992.

Greene, Victoria E., and Enfield, Mary Lee. *Project Read—Language Circle*. Bloomington, MN: Language Circle Enterprises, 1994.

Meese, Ruthlyn. "Adapting Textbooks for Children with Learning Disabilities in Mainstreamed Classrooms," *Teaching Exceptional Children*, Spring, 1992, pp 49-51. (See note below.)

MacArthur, Charles. "Peers + Word Processing + Strategies = A Powerful Combination for Revising Student Writing" *Teaching Exceptional Children*, Vol. 27, No. 1, Fall, 1994, pp 24-29.

Meier, Frieda E. *Competency-Based Instruction for Teachers of Students with Special Learning Needs*. Needham Heights, MA: Allyn & Bacon, 1992.

Murphy, Deborah, Meyers, Celia, Olesen, Sylvia, McKean, Kathy, and Custer, Susan. *Exceptions: A Handbook for Teachers of Mainstreamed Students*. Longmont, CO: Sopris West, Inc., 1988.

Prentice, Linda, and Cousin, Patricia Tefft. "Moving Beyond the Textbook to Teach Students with Learning Disabilities," *Teaching Exceptional Children*, Vol. 26, No. 1, Fall, 1993, pp 14-17.

Rief, Sandra. *Simply Phonics*. Birmingham, AL: EBSCO Curriculum Materials, 1993. For more information call: 1-800-633-8623.

Routman, Regie. *Invitations—Changing as Teachers and Learners K-12*. Portsmouth, NH: Heinemann, 1991.

Stevens, Dannelle, and Englert, Carol Sue. "Making Writing Strategies Work," *Teaching Exceptional Children*, Vol. 26, No. 1, Fall, 1993, pp 34-39.

Stires, S. With Promise: *Redefining Reading and Writing for "Special Students."* Portsmouth, NH: Heinemann, 1991.

Walker, Rena M. *Accelerating Literacy Handbook*. San Diego, CA: Walker Enterprises, 1995. (See note below).

Waring, Cynthia Conway. *Developing Independent Readers: Strategy-Oriented Reading Activities for Learners with Special Needs*. West Nyack, NY: The Center for Applied Research in Education, 1995.

- *Project Read/Language Circle*, developed by Victoria E. Greene and Dr. Mary Lee Enfield, is a mainstream alternative language arts program for the child or adolescent who needs a systematic learning experience with direct teaching of concepts through multisensory techniques. *Project Read* has three strands: decoding, comprehension, and written expression. All strands are integrated at all grade levels, but specific strands are emphasized at certain grade levels. *Project Read/Language Circle* is designed to be delivered in the regular classroom. The regular classroom teacher works in collaboration with a special education teacher. It is also used by special education, Chapter One, and reading teachers where the child or adolescent with language learning problems receives instruction. Although *Project Read* is an early intervention program for grades one through six, it can be used with adolescents and adults as well. For more information, contact: Language Circle, P.O. Box 20631, Bloomington, MN 55420; Phone: 612-884-4880.

- *Accelerating Literacy (A.L.)*, developed by Rena M. Walker, Ph.D., is a balanced, whole language approach for preschool through eighth-grade classroom instruction. This program pulls together the pieces that are basic to whole language theory and presents teachers with possibilities for planning and organizing these pieces into an instructional day. For more information, contact: Accelerating Literacy, Walker Enterprises, 650 Columbia Street #113, San Diego, CA 92101; Phone: 619-237-9836.

MAKING ORAL LANGUAGE COME ALIVE IN YOUR CLASSROOM

There is a real thrill at the utterance of a baby's first words—not only by the parents who oogle and oggle over those precious moments, but by the child herself/himself, who seems to understand that he/she is going to get a lot of positive attention by making these sounds. Babies are rewarded for "talking." It seems natural that babies want to talk because they receive a lot of verbal stimulation that motivates them to form sounds and words. Parents write baby's first spoken words in baby books, and the list grows as the baby develops.

If oral language seems to be natural, then why don't all children share the same desire to engage in oral language as they get older? In fact, some children are so hesitant to speak in class, that they rarely utter a word—prefering the 'safety' of silence rather than having to speak up in front of their peers. While we must respect the child's personality, cultural background, and learning style, we, as teachers, must strive to pull each child into actively engaging in the oral language process.

To be deficient in our ability to present ourselves orally to those around us puts us in an awkward position in our adolescent and adult lives. Since communication is comprised of both speaking and listening, children must be made aware of its importance in their lives, not only in the present, but also for their success in the future. Teenagers many times break off communication with their parents and turn more to their peers. Oral communication, no matter how small, must be kept open in these adolescent years. As teachers in the elementary and middle schools, we can do our part to keep the flow of communication open. This can be done by providing enjoyable oral language experiences to children in the classroom that will motivate them to become good communicators. These experiences include:

- videotaped presentations
- tape recordings/having children listen to themselves and evaluate

- partner oral language experiences
- cross-age oral language experience with younger as well as older people
- informal, impromptu role-playing situations
- small discussion groups dealing with reading and writing
- adult/child reading/writing conferences
- student/student reading/writing conferences
- parent/student oral language experiences
- reader's theater presentations
- puppet plays
- poetry recitation and dramatic performances of favorite poems
- interviews
- cooperative groups assistance
- a variety of purposeful, formal speeches

GETTING STUDENTS INTERESTED IN ORAL LANGUAGE PARTICIPATION

In an upper-grade classroom, often the teacher wonders if anyone is actually "out there" sitting in the seats. It seems that upper-graders progressively become less interested in telling what they know. This coincides with the child's need to blend in, instead of standing out. A teacher who feels the students aren't participating in the classroom needs to "pull the students into" the instruction. Some ideas that might be used are:

- Have more opportunities for partner sharing and responses, making sure every child is using oral language daily.
- Use seating chart tally marks. When a child responds, the teacher marks a tally mark on the seating chart to show that the child has participated.
- Use a deck of cards with students' names on each card. The teacher draws one card at a time in order to assure that every child during the day is being called on. (See Section 11, *Effective Questioning Techniques for the Classroom.*)
- Hand out pencils or other small rewards when a child responds.
- Every child is handed a part to recite of a popular poem or song. Any child who has difficulty reading that part may ask for assistance from his/her partner before the presentation time begins.
- Have a set pattern of asking for responses (Table 1, 2, 3), so that no student is left out of having the opportunity to use oral language during the day.
- Have students respond with answers to teacher questions as they are leaving the room (*Name three proper nouns. Name three ways you could use a paper clip. Pay a compliment to another person in the classroom. Tell me one thing you like about coming to school. Tell me three things you are truly thankful for.*) Simple oral exercises that "force" students to talk and think can start a year out right.

Students need many opportunities to stand in front of a group and speak. Public speaking is one of the greatest fears among adults; it is one that we can help children to conquer. It is important to provide students the opportunity to practice this skill frequently in ways that are nonintimidating and, hopefully, FUN! How fortunate for students if they are given positive training, coaching, and encouragement by their teachers, parents, and peers. Teachers must be very sensitive to the discomfort and anxiety many people experience in public speaking. They must work hard to establish classroom environments that are 'safe' and free of ridicule, criticism, and teasing.

DEVELOPING TRUST

Within a classroom, children must develop a trust of their classmates and teacher. Starting on the first day of school, students should have the opportunity to speak in front of their classmates. The following is an example of a short and effective oral language experience:

- Each child is given a set of questions to find out about his/her partner. This means that the child must speak and listen carefully to the partner.
- The partner writes out the answers.
- Throughout the day, the partners are asked to come to the front of the room and personally introduce their partner to the rest of the class.
- Although this is uncomfortable for some, it is the beginning of a process that must be established in order to assure the students that what they say is valued and that they will be listened to.

The teacher is truly the person who sets the tone of respect and trust for others. During the first week of school, the teacher might initiate a game such as: *One thing I think I'm really good at is* _____. *Something I really could improve on is* _____. When the teacher makes these statements first about himself/herself, the student sees that the teacher has strengths and weaknesses. This opens up a child's desire to share orally a little more about him-/herself. In turn, the child offers the same two statements that show his/her strengths and weaknesses.

QUICK-TALKS

Another fun way to get oral language rolling in the classroom with upper graders is to have a good morning warm-up.

- Each child is asked to speak constantly for 15, 30, or 45 seconds. This is something like a Quick-Write—only this is a *Quick-Talk*. (We usually have one or two "verbally comfortable" students model this exercise first. It usually adds a bit of comic relief, as these students mentally search for things to say nonstop!) Students must stay actively talking for the full amount of time. This works well after a vacation period. The teacher asks, *What did do you do during vacation?* Many upper-grade students would respond by saying, *Nothing.* If you asked them to write about what they did, they would say something like, *We always have to do this.* But if you make it a new experience and ask them to Quick-Talk, they have a very pleasurable experience. After that warm-up, the students seem more eager to share with the rest of the class. This also might be the springboard to a writing assignment, but now they have a foundation upon which to build. It should probably be noted to the class that most students will use one, long run-on sentence, connected, of course, with "and."

- Another idea is to have a Quick-Talk where the child cannot use the word "and" for the entire time. Now the exercise gets a little more complicated. Again, all the students want to try the activity, but it now has a purpose. Tape-recording several students and letting them listen to it again provides a memorable experience. Note: You might want to try this yourself on videotape. It's an eye-opener for teachers!

- To continue with this same idea, students might next be asked to speak for the entire number of seconds, but may not say "uh" or "um."

Each verbal adventure is difficult at first, but children build up their skill quickly. Because these exercises are enjoyable, the timid students are eager to try them, too.

TONGUE TWISTERS

Another exercise that really gets students motivated to use oral language is tongue twisters. You may want to have a weekly tongue twister on the board. Throughout the week, provide a time when students can practice the "twister" with their partner. At the end of the week, the students must either say the twister in front of the entire class, or may say it privately to another adult or a student representative. All students must participate, but the final product can be delivered in the manner chosen by the student. This opportunity provides a nonthreatening path for the limited English proficient student to also become involved. (See Section 13, *Hooking Reluctant Readers/Writers*.)

POETRY

Poetry entices students to participate more enthusiastically. As shared in the poetry material of Section 13, Shel Silverstein and Jack Prelutsky poems are wonderful poems to begin with for oral language experiences. Children who have inhibitions about orally presenting tend to lose them fairly quickly when humorous poetry is used.

The teacher might:

- Hand each child a poem that he/she must memorize and recite in front of the entire class. Be selective in giving students who have difficulty shorter poems to memorize and present.

- Each child may dress up as a character in the poem or bring a visual aid that would enhance the reciting of the poem.

- The child is given opportunities during class to recite the poem to his/her partner. Multiple practice periods are encouraged. Practice improves the presentation.

- Student presentations are videotaped and reviewed.

- Students evaluate their own oral presentation. After looking at all the presentations, the student is able to evaluate his/her product more effectively and honestly. How does the presentation compare with the other students?

- Three other students evaluate a classmate's presentation.
- The teacher evaluates the oral presentation.
- Consider having poetry parties on a regular basis. Each student is responsible for sharing a poem of his/her choice. Memorization of the poem is optional, but encouraged. If weather permits, these poetry parties are fun to do outside seated on blankets or carpet squares. Serving refreshments is always a nice touch.

FORMAL SPEECHES

The previous oral experiences provide the foundation that fosters confidence in a child's presentation skills. As the year progresses, you may want to provide information and training about how to make more formal speeches. Elements that can enhance the speech itself may also be introduced, such as:

- posture
- appearance
- voice (tone, tempo, pitch)
- diction (clarity)
- rehearsing
- gestures
- humor
- visual aids

With upper-graders, you might think about providing monthly opportunities for the children to have formal, oral language opportunities that can be videotaped. A visit to Howard Gardner's Key School gives a close-up look at what can be done in the area of oral language. To coincide with the themes that have been chosen by the teachers for the year, each child chooses a project based on one of the seven intelligences. Each child has a personal videotape, and three times a year the child performs or presents a project for the camera. Conceivably, a child who enters the Key School in kindergarten can exit the school several years later, with a full videotaped history or portfolio of all the oral language presentations he/she made throughout the elementary years. As a parent, wouldn't it be wonderful to have this taped portfolio as a keepsake? To see the full development of a child's progress over the span of time would be a special gift, indeed. The Key School is fortunate to have a full-time person to tape and organize these presentations. Not all schools are so lucky.

Some suggestions that might get your school headed on a similar path of video-production for each of your students in a modified manner would be:

- Every parent could be asked to send in his/her own blank video.
- Each child could be videotaped once during the year, instead of three times.
- A volunteer or nearby high school production class may be able to offer its assistance.
- Possibly beginning with one grade level for taping each year would be more cost effective and manageable.

HOW-TO-DO SPEECHES

One of the easiest forms of formal speech is the How-to-Do Speech, for which children are given some suggestions. (See *A How-to-Do Speech* at the end of this section.) Students should think of ideas that are of greatest interest to them. Keeping a time allotment of 1 to 2 minutes probably is best during the beginning of the year. At the end of the year, students may feel more relaxed and use a 3- to 5-minute allotment of time.

Teachers should set the desired expectations and might use the following guidelines:

- If the teacher models a good speech, the students will follow suit.
- Students should stay within the time allotment given.
- Visual aids are an important part of all speeches.
- Preparation should be evident.
- Students should have a brief written plan they will follow when delivering their speech. (See *Speech Plan Sheet* at the end of this section.)
- Notes can be used to glance at, but not to read from.
- Practicing in front of a mirror is very beneficial.
- Teachers should have a student information sheet letting the students and parents know what the expectations are for the activity.
- A list of oral language experiences for the entire year helps students plan for the future events. (See *Oral Language Presentations for the Year* at the end of this section.)

NEWSCASTING

Newcasting is another means to inspire students in oral language. You might set up the class in the following manner:

- The class should be encouraged to watch a newscast on the local news station for the week preceding the activity.
- If that is not possible for most students, you might record a newscast and let the students watch it during class time. The first fifteen minutes are the most crucial.
- Students should evaluate and note the responsibilities of the anchorperson. They should also notice how the news team works together to report the news. How do they dress? What does the background look like? How do they present the news? Is it relaxed or is it more formal?
- The students then meet in news teams that the teacher has formed. Usually heterogeneous groupings work best of about five people. As a team, they decide the responsibilities that each team person will have. Some suggestions for team members are:

Anchorpersons	Sports reporter
Weather reporter	Trouble shooter for consumers
Traffic reporter	School reporter
"Staying Healthy" reporter	Other
Restaurant reviewer	

Teams should decide on props that can be used and colors or attire that anchorpeople will wear.

- Weather reporters might want to use self-stick notes to note weather conditions in other parts of the country and world on a U.S. world map.
- This will probably take about a week of preparation time.
- The reports should be approximately 5 to 10 minutes long.
- Students should create a name for their television station, and have a logo to represent it.
- All news reports will be videotaped and watched by the class.
- Students will self-evaluate and also evaluate their classmates.

INTERVIEWING

Throughout the year, students should be given opportunities to interview another person. One that always seems successful is that of interviewing the oldest member of the student's family. Besides offering a perfect avenue for bridging the generation gap, it also helps students to be more compassionate and sensitive towards older people. Another idea is presented in the *World War II* project choices where a child can interview someone who lived during this period of history. (See *Interview Planning Sheet* at the end of this section.) Some of the most compelling reports have been written after students have interviewed a person who lived in Europe during World War II or who actually fought in the war. We can always learn from history; and when students hear it through personal contact, it seems more real.

PUPPETRY

It doesn't matter what the age, students always seem to like to get involved in puppet shows. Whether the puppets are commercially created or personally created by the children, oral language seems simple when you have a puppet in hand. Students who are hesitant to speak up in class seem to have a miraculous lack of stage fright when they can hide behind a puppet or behind a puppet theater. Even the older children have fun creating impromptu scripts. When a puppet center is set up in an upper-grade classroom during the PDR segment of the day, students seem to gravitate to it. (See *Planning, Doing, Reflecting* in Section 2, *Learning Developmentally*.) During the reflecting part of the process, the students usually are quite agreeable to performing their skits in front of the entire class.

CREATING SCRIPTS FROM LITERATURE

Students enjoy taking their favorite part of a piece of literature and performing it for their classmates. Sometimes reader's theater scripts can also be written and read aloud with dramatic intonation. Children can perform these parts from books they read in their free reading time, or from books read as a whole class. Placing students in cooperative groups assures all students of participating in some form, and gives them an opportunity to show they understand what they have read.

TEACHING A GAME

As the year progresses, students become more comfortable with orally presenting to others than just their classmates. For instance, at our school we have a Multicultural Fair in the Spring. To combine multiculturalism and math strategy, our resource teacher, Kathy Aufsesser, brought her collection of multicultural games to share with the class. After she shared some of the history of each game, the students rotated into actually playing the games. As an extension of this lesson, students were asked to share the games with their kindergarten buddies.

Each child was asked to:

- Select a game he/she wanted to teach.
- Read the instructions carefully and figure out the correct rules.
- Present the game to another group of upper-graders
- Teach the game to their "buddies."

Students were given time in class to prepare. Oral language became important because the students now became the experts. They had to share their knowledge, and make sure that correct rules were explained and followed.

We were very fortunate to have many multicultural games from which to choose. Where this is not the case, teachers could use games that the children are somewhat familiar with already (Monopoly, Checkers, Chess, Connect Four, Uno and so on). In this case, students would explain the correct rules and make sure all students in the group were following them.

Games can also be set up on a rotation basis. In other words, five games could be set up on one day. The students in charge of teaching the games would have several groups rotate into their game. Students would then have been exposed to five games.

Game Days are enjoyable for all students because it's a chance for them to take a break from the routine of the regular curriculum. Because games use mathematical strategies, once a month a Game Day could be set up in the classroom, similar to a math lab. Students could choose from the games they have been exposed. When this less formal kind of oral interaction takes place, the teacher sees the children in a different light. Some students who are reluctant to speak in class are able to open up in small groups and actively engage in conversation with their peers. The more inhibited oral language student sees this experience as less intimidating. Students who normally don't interact with one another now find a common need to converse in an informal, more relaxed manner. (See *Game Day Activity* at the end of this section.)

SCIENCE EXPERIMENTS

As part of the assigned oral language for the year, science can be introduced. Model a simple science experiment in the classroom. (Students should be pulled up closer to the center of instruction because science experiments need to be closely observed.) Because students enjoy watching science experiments, most everyone wants to have a front-row seat; therefore, let's discuss the $50, $25, and $10 seats. Students earn the privilege of sitting in the $50 seats by having exceptional behavior before the experiment is presented. Of course, the $10 seats are in the back row and students also "earn" those. By providing this challenge for the students, we make science experimentation a special period.

Students are asked to present a simple science experiment. Many books of experiments are brought into the classroom by the teacher. Students can also locate other books and choose their experiment from those. Books like *Handmade Slime and Rubber Bones* by William R. Weellnitz, Ph.D., *Amazing Science Experiments with Everyday Materials* by E. Richard Churchill, and *Simple Science Experiments With Everyday Materials* by Muriel Mandell are excellent sources to motivate students to become involved in child-centered, fun experiments. (See *Science Experiment Planning Sheet* at the end of this section.)

COMMERCIALS

Students love to create their own commercials. In the unit *On Becoming a Cerealologist* (in Section 13, *Hooking Reluctant Readers/Writers*), students devise their own cereal box and are then asked to "sell" their cereal to their classmates. The students should be asked to preview three commercials at home. If this is not possible for most of your students, you can tape commercials and bring them in for the class to review together. Oral language comes alive as students creatively promote their product. Commercials can be given in partners or alone. Of course, this is a perfect opportunity for the video camera. All students should be videotaped and then evaluated. (Note: The commericials during the Super Bowl are the most extraordinary. See the *Super Bowl Math Activity Packet* at the end of Section 16.)

TELEPHONE ROLE PLAYING

Practice telephone skills simulating different situations, such as: making reservations, requesting information, and setting up appointments. Discuss the importance of phone etiquette, speaking clearly and politely. Assignments requiring students to utilize the telephone are helpful. (Note: See *Survival Math Packet* in Section 16 for some suggestions of real-life purposes for using the telephone to obtain information.)

STUDENT:TEACHER;PARENT:STUDENT; STUDENT:STUDENT CONFERENCES

Teachers can learn a lot about a child's oral language skills by sitting with him/her on an individual basis during a reading, writing, or portfolio conference. On a one-to-one basis, children talk more freely and seem to be less inhibited. For instance, during a reading conference, a teacher or other adult can evaluate informally how well a child has read a book he/she has chosen. Basic questions such as those seen on the *Reading/Writing Conference Sheet* in Section 13 can start students talking. By asking these questions, a teacher can "pull" students into conversation.

Since children talk differently to other children than to an adult, it is also a good idea to allow students to conference with their peers. Reading/writing conferences can be set up with peer partners. The same basic lists of questions can be used, as mentioned in the preceding paragraphs.

Conferences for portfolio selections are also good opportunities for a teacher to listen to a child's oral language skill. Providing experiences where a child is verbally relaying reasons for choosing selections for a portfolio adds reflective insight into a child's ability to organize and evaluate his/her own work.

STORYTELLING

Storytelling is a very powerful means of communication, a gift that more and more teachers are recognizing the need for, and learning how to bring back into the classroom. Very few activities can captivate an audience of any size or age as completely as the *oral telling* (not reading) of a good story. Catherine Farrell, author of *Storytelling: An Evocative Approach to Literature*, describes what happens in the immediacy of a storytelling session:

> *Time seems to stop. The teller creates an environment free from distractions, maintains continuous eye contact and speaks directly to the listeners. The images from the story appear to hang in the air, and the silence in the classroom deepens. All the students become engrossed in the shared experience of literature. The heightened attention to a literary work created by storytelling has many teaching possibilities. Each teacher should try to develop a repertoire of literary pieces for storytelling. As teachers discover the compelling nature of storytelling as a teaching method, they will be greatly rewarded for their efforts.*

Many children have never heard a story told in the oral tradition. The benefits of storytelling to students are numerous. Storytelling promotes good attention, inner concentration, and invites active involvement. It encourages visualization and the active use of imagination. It develops children's sense of story and listening skills. It is an excellent vehicle for motivating students, particularly distractible, hard-to-reach students. It has been our experience that even the most inattentive, distractible child is quiet and captivated while listening to the telling of a good, short story.

Some of us have had the great fortune of taking classes on storytelling during the past few years (which were offered at one of the universities in San Diego), having the pleasure and privilege of hearing many outstanding professional storytellers from around the country perform and share their craft. Our appreciation is given to the instructor—teacher, librarian, and storyteller, Vicky Reed—for providing so many of us the opportunity to receive such a wonderful gift, the joy of storytelling. The following "pearls of wisdom" were comments and recommendations shared by some of these wonderful storytellers who were guest presenters at Vicky's classes:

- A story is like a journey. As long as there are human beings, there are stories. (*Joseph Bruchac*)
- The universality of stories is the broth of the stew; they are satisfying. (*Carol Birch*)
- Tell a story that speaks to you in your heart. (*Jane Yolen*)
- Use the text as a springboard, and then release or liberate yourself from it. (*Milbre Burch*)
- Telling of a story has to be liquid; it can't be learned by rote because it changes and shifts in the telling. (*David Novak*)

- Every story in the world is about the same thing—about how someone ran into trouble and lived through it. If you had trouble (crisis) in your life, you have a story. A crisis is anything that takes a piece of the world you have gotten comfortable with, and turned it over—so we need to change. (*Donald Davis*)

- Pick a story that has action, which is vivid and well-visualized, rising to a satisfying climax. Make sure the sequence of events is clear and easy to understand, and the conclusion is tidy and brief. Keep as much of the language of the author as you can. (*Martha Holloway*)

- Choose a story and scrutinize it. Is it a good tale? Does it move? Then take the bare bones and give it flesh and flavor. Attaching sensory memory to a story gives young people the way to learn through the skin—the way we learn best. (*Gay Ducey*)

- Storytelling pulls people into deeper associations. I'm responsible for what I say, but not for what you hear. When you listen to stories you see with your inner eye. Kids need stories everyday. When you listen you see with your inner eye. Imagination is the basis of creativity and empathy. We need to give children time to listen, to image, to reflect. As teachers, you have keys to the kingdom in your hands. Learning to be a storyteller is a process. You have to take risks, have intelligence and integrity when telling cultural stories that aren't of your culture; and not feel you'll die if you make a mistake. (*Carol Birch*)

Trying Our Hand at Storytelling . . . What to Do?

There are several ways to learn a story. Many storytellers recommend the following: *Select* a story. A picture book of a folk tale that appeals to you may be a good place to start, or choose a short story from an anthology. (See the recommended resources at the end of this section.) *Read* the story several times. *Block* the story, writing out or drawing the main points, or making a graphic organizer such as a flowchart or story map to depict the scenes and sequence of events. Then *visualize* each sensory detail, watching like a silent movie the scenes unfold. *Read the story aloud and keep practicing* until you feel confident that you know the story. It is not recommended to try learning the story word by word. Some storytellers make an outline, and list the main events in order.

- One storyteller, a very multisensory learner, tape records herself reading the story and plays it back several times. To make the story "her own" she first *flushes out* the story line in a few sentences. Then she draws the action on butcher paper to get a sense of the story's flow. She draws cartoons to help herself visualize the story, so that if in the telling she forgets where she was language-wise, she can picture the scenes. She then takes the script she has typed out and highlights some of the language in different colors to help her remember what she wants to include in the telling (e.g., yellow for descriptive vocabulary, blue for action words). As *Milbre Burch* shared, "If the story is good enough to learn, it's good enough to do your homework on."

- Another storyteller (*Carol Birch*) recommends you pick stories you like; don't memorize it, just tell it in the order of the pictures you see; and tell it with attitude. Amplify the humor and the pathos of the characters. Just get up there and do it.

- *Gay Ducey*, a historical storyteller, shares how *powerful* historical storytelling is in the classroom. First, you need a story from history that fires you, and the interest to want to tell it. We can teach the vital life force of what history is. As the storyteller, you are an emissary of the time period or person. She recommends picking a story from your favorite historical period and telling it through the lens of a more narrowed theme (e.g., one family). Choose a point of view and a voice—a smaller lens will give the story more intimacy. Ducey recommends finding the under-represented events in history. Fascinating historical stories can be found in magazines, newspapers, travel guides, and other numerous sources if you look for them.

Teachers need to be willing to take the risk of trying their hand at storytelling. It is risky to "perform" in front of an audience; yet, a good teacher does so all the time—catching the interest of students and "reeling them in." We highly recommend giving it a try. Once you have experienced it the first time, it becomes so much easier each successive time the story is told. Your students will be very appreciative of your efforts, and it is so very rewarding!

Teaching Students the Art of Storytelling

Children should also be given the opportunity to tell stories to their peers, as well. Upper-grade students can be taught to apply the same recommended techniques to learn a simple story to tell; and should be allowed to perform to a small group if they are not comfortable telling their story to the whole class. In all fairness, teachers should be modeling storytelling to students before asking students to make the effort and take the "risk."

Easier ways to elicit informal oral sharing of personal stories is to have students work in cooperative groups. In different sharing sessions throughout the week, provide prompts to the students to trigger sharing about personal experiences. For example, "Can you remember a time you were ever locked out of your house or somewhere?" "Can you remember a funny incident with a pet you ever had?" "Have any of you ever been in a car that ran out of gas or broke down on the road somewhere?" "Have you ever lost something that didn't belong to you?" "Tell about a visit from a relative to your house."

In *telling sessions* with prompts such as the above, not everyone will be able to share a story; but it is equally as beneficial to hear a story as to tell one. Some children are so bashful or uncomfortable sharing in even a small group, that after listening to the students in small group, they may wish to orally share with a partner instead of the group. By first sharing and listening to others share stories, students are better able to transfer their stories into written form. *Donald Davis*, professional storyteller, recommends this technique as an important step in helping students learn to write stories. Students briefly write some of the stories they shared in small group (story starts) and save them. After they have collected a few, they are asked to select one to work on writing into story form. Davis suggests telling students as they are writing to "fatten up" their written stories with the necessary words to recapture the story they told.

HOW TO EVALUATE ORAL LANGUAGE

Because of the complexity of oral language assessment, teachers should look for direction from their own school district's standards. In the San Diego City Schools, children are evaluated as beginning, developing, or independent learners in the area of language arts. The developmental speaking/listening language arts continuum for ages 10-12 is comprised, in part, of some of these areas of knowledge, understanding, skills, and attitudes:

- Plans and organizes an oral presentation
- Develops confidence in ability to speak formally before a small-size group
- Speaks confidently to large groups
- Relates experiences effectively, clearly, and sequentially
- Contributes comments and asks questions appropriate to class discussions and problem-solving situations
- Participates in dramatic presentation (e.g., choral reading, tableau, reader's theater, dramatizations)
- Comprehends facts, details, and ideas through discussions
- Listens and follows directions
- Recites poetry or reads aloud excerpts from literature
- Participates appropriately in group discussions (e.g., contributes, takes turns, encourages others)
- Asks questions to clarify understanding and satisfy curiosity

Because oral language is somewhat difficult to evaluate in a formal manner, teachers must assess children more informally through observation and by taking anecdotal records as the process unfolds. Since speaking/listening is only one area of the language arts program, we can modify the many skills on a continuum by:

- Starting with a small target group of students and assessing their skills at each report card period of the year
- Using only a part of the skills in the subject area and appraising a larger group of students

Students should also be involved in the process of evaluation. Through the use of the video camera or tape recorder, students can listen to themselves and see how they compare with the others. Peer evaluation of oral presentation is also helpful. When students see good modeling, they can build their own oral language skills, and grow as a successful oral communicator. In all aspects of oral language, students should use self-evaluation, peer evaluation, and teacher evaluation. Including the parents in evaluation is also important. Possibly sending a parent evaluation form while a child is practicing for one of his/her monthly oral language presentations would be beneficial. We should strive to bring parents into the evaluation process. (See *Oral Language Evaluation* forms at the end of this section.)

BIBLIOGRAPHY AND RECOMMENDED RESOURCES

Cranston, Jerneral W. *Transformations Through Drama: A Teacher's Guide to Educational Drama, K-8.* (1991) University Press of America, Inc., 4720 Boston Way, Lanham, MD 20706.

Cresci, Maureen McCurry. *Creative Dramatics for Children.* Glenview, IL: Scott, Foresman and Co., Good Year Books, 1989.

Famous Americans: 22 Short Plays for the Classroom (Gr. 4-8). New York: Scholastic Professional Books, 1994.

Farrell, Catherine. *Storytelling: An Evocative Approach to Literature* (Appendix), *Recommended Literature, Grades Nine Through Twelve* (1990), California State Board of Education, P.O. Box 271, Sacramento, CA 95802-0271.

Farrell, Catherine. *Word Weaving: A Guide to Storytelling.* San Francisco: Word Weaving, Inc., 1987.

Griffin, Barbara Budge. *Students as Storytellers, Storyteller Guidebook Series.* Barbara Griffin, P.O. Box 626, Medford, OR 97501-0042.

Kelner, Lenore Blank. *A Guide for Using Creative Drama in the Classroom.* (1990), InterAct, Inc., 11401 Encore Drive, Silver Spring, MD 20901.

MacDonald, Margaret Read. *Twenty Tellable Tales: Audience Participation Folktales for the Beginning Storyteller.* New York: H.W. Wilson, 1986.

Miller, Teresa. *Joining In: An Anthology of Audience Participation Stories and How to Tell Them.* (1988), Yellow Moon Press, P.O. Box 1316, Cambridge, MA 02238.

Novak, David. *Telling Experiences—A Learning Activities Package for Teaching Story and Story-teaching.* Telling Experiences, P.O. Box 620327, San Diego, CA 92162; Phone: 619-232-1019.

Pellowski, Anne. *The Family Storytelling Handbook.* New York: Macmillan, 1987.

Pellowski, Anne. *The Story Vine: A Source Book of Unusual and Easy-to-Tell Stories from Around the World.* New York: Macmillan, 1984.

Thomson, Greg. *Step by Step Theater: Creating Plays for Class Presentation.* Belmont, CA: Fearon Teacher Aids, 1989.

STORYTELLING NEWSLETTERS

Stories, 12600 Woodbine Street, Los Angeles, CA 90066.

The Story Bag, Harlynne Geisler, 5361 Javier Street, San Diego, CA 92117-3215.

California Storytellers Catalog, 6695 Westside Road, Healdsburg, CA 95448.

National Storytelling Association (previously called the Preservation and Perpetuation of Storytelling [NAPPS], P.O. Box 309, Jonesborough, TN 37659; Phone: 800-525-4514 or 615-753-2171.

ORAL LANGUAGE PRESENTATIONS FOR THE YEAR

Month	Presentation Type	Month	Presentation Type
SEPTEMBER	Magazine Article (1 minute, alone)	FEBRUARY	Hobby or Interest (2-3 minutes, alone)
OCTOBER	Biography Book Report (1 minute, alone)	MARCH	Research Project (2-4 minutes alone)
NOVEMBER	Demonstration Speech (1-3 minutes, alone)	APRIL	Teach a Game (10 minutes, partner)
DECEMBER	Science Experiment (1-3 minutes, partner or alone)	MAY	Persuasive Speech (2-3 minutes, alone/partner)
JANUARY	News Team (5-10 minutes, team)	JUNE	Poetry: Recite a poem (minimum 2 stanzas)

A HOW-TO-DO SPEECH

What to do:

You are to become an instructor. You are to choose a subject you are truly interested in. Remember the KIS rule (Keep it Simple). You will be expected to speak for 1-3 minutes. You may use an outline while you are in front of the class, but do not write things out word for word.

Here are a few examples that will get you started to think:

1. How to french-braid hair
2. How to set up a two-person tent
3. How to apply make-up
4. How to draw a person's face
5. How to make an origami frog
6. How to throw a football correctly
7. How to draw a cartoon character
8. How to eat an Oreo® cookie
9. How to make finger Jell-O®
10. How to make the basic knots with rope

Now, these are just a few suggestions, and knowing your talent, I'm sure you've got many more ideas. For more suggestions, ask your family for help. They like to get involved.

REQUIREMENTS:

1. Hand in your plan sheet to have it approved by the teacher.
2. Gather your materials and come prepared on your assigned day.
3. Practice your speech at home and come prepared.
4. Speak for 1-3 minutes. Extra time may be requested before your presentation. You will be timed.
5. You must have a visual aid.
6. You may have an assistant, but everyone must do his/her own speech.

GRADING:

You will be evaluated on the following things:

Your visual aid	Loudness of your voice
Eye contact	Enthusiasm
Evident preparation	Content/Information
Speed of your delivery	Posture/Poise

There will be a sign-up on the door for your presentation date and time. Sign up early. It's easier to get it over with and not have to worry.

SPEECH PLAN SHEET

Presenter _____   Date _____

Title of presentation: _____

MATERIALS AND EQUIPMENT I NEED:

1. _____
2. _____
3. _____

OUTLINE OF MY TOPIC:

1. _____
2. _____
3. _____
4. _____
5. _____
6. _____

ANSWER THE FOLLOWING QUESTIONS:

1. I practiced my speech about _____ times.

2. I practiced my speech with _____.

3. I feel prepared for my speech.   YES   NO

4. I could do better by _____

5. I really feel I have done my best.   YES   NO

6. I deserve a (an) _____ on this speech because _____

_____ .

INTERVIEW PLANNING SHEET

Sometimes when you do research, you will want to get a more personal look at your subject. For instance, if you are trying to find out something about World War II, you might find out a lot by reading a book or an article in the encyclopedia. For a more personal touch, you also might want to interview a person who lived during that period of time.

A good interview takes some thinking. Because you do not want to waste your subject's time, you should always be prepared BEFORE you do the interview.

Try to think of some meaningful questions that bring out the best in the person you are interviewing. These questions should make your subject feel comfortable. Make sure the questions are appropriate and show sensitivity. When you are finished with the interview, thank the person for helping you.

Interviewer's name _____   Date of interview _____

Person being interviewed _____   Place of interview _____

How do you know this person? _____

QUESTION 1: _____

ANSWER: _____

_____

QUESTION 2: _____

ANSWER: _____

_____

QUESTION 3: _____

ANSWER: _____

_____

QUESTION 4: _____

ANSWER: _____

_____

QUESTION 5: _____

ANSWER: _____

_____

GAME DAY ACTIVITY

Scheduled Day _____

In the next few weeks, you will be asked to sign up to explain a game to a small group of your classmates. You may select a game you already know or one you would like to learn.

Here is what you need to do:

- On your scheduled day, you will need to be the "expert" on your game.

- The game you choose should be simple enough to explain in approximately 10 minutes.

- You must obtain the game from home, a friend, a neighbor, or a relative. You can also borrow one from our game center.

- You must carefully read the game rules and possibly even highlight the most important rules.

- You should play the game before you present the game to your classmates. This will assure yourself of being prepared if your group has questions.

- On Game Day, you will present your game two times. Two different groups of your classmates will rotate into your game-teaching session. You will be the teacher.

- Learn your game well, practice, and be prepared!

SCIENCE EXPERIMENT PLANNING SHEET

Oral Presentation

Names of students: _____

Briefly describe your experiment: _____
_____
_____

What will your question be?_____
_____

Hypothesis: Predict what you think will happen.

    I think that _____
_____

Procedure:

Step 1_____
Step 2_____
Step 3_____
Step 4_____
Step 5_____

Materials Needed: _____
_____
_____

Conclusion: (Findings) _____
_____
_____
_____
_____

ORAL LANGUAGE EVALUATION

Presenter's Name _____

Evaluator _____

Time taken _____

EVALUATE THE FOLLOWING WITH A +, √, OR –

1. Visual aid   _____

2. Eye contact   _____

3. Evident preparation   _____

4. Speed of delivery   _____

5. Loudness of voice   _____

6. Enthusiasm   _____

7. Content/Information   _____

8. Posture/Poise   _____

Comments:

_____

_____

_____

_____

Preceding the presentations, the class should discuss how the presentations are to be evaluated. A list of positive comments and constructive suggestions can be formulated by the students, so that negative comments do not become overwhelming. This form can be made in numerous copies. At least five classmates should evaluate the presenter, along with the teacher. After the presentation, the evaluators' copies are given to the presenter.

ORAL LANGUAGE
PEER EVALUATION FORM

Presenter's Name _____

Evaluator:_____

Subject: _____

Time: _____

Evaluate with +, √, −

1. Visual aid _____
2. Eye contact _____
3. Preparation shown _____
4. Speed of delivery _____
5. Loudness of voice _____
6. Enthusiasm for subject _____
7. Content/Information _____
8. Posture/Poise _____

ORAL LANGUAGE
PEER EVALUATION FORM

Presenter's Name _____

Evaluator:_____

Subject: _____

Time: _____

Evaluate with +, √, −

1. Visual aid _____
2. Eye contact _____
3. Preparation shown _____
4. Speed of delivery _____
5. Loudness of voice _____
6. Enthusiasm for subject _____
7. Content/Information _____
8. Posture/Poise _____

ORAL LANGUAGE
PEER EVALUATION FORM

Presenter's Name _____

Evaluator:_____

Subject: _____

Time: _____

Evaluate with +, √, −

1. Visual aid _____
2. Eye contact _____
3. Preparation shown _____
4. Speed of delivery _____
5. Loudness of voice _____
6. Enthusiasm for subject _____
7. Content/Information _____
8. Posture/Poise _____

ORAL LANGUAGE
PEER EVALUATION FORM

Presenter's Name _____

Evaluator:_____

Subject: _____

Time: _____

Evaluate with +, √, −

1. Visual aid _____
2. Eye contact _____
3. Preparation shown _____
4. Speed of delivery _____
5. Loudness of voice _____
6. Enthusiasm for subject _____
7. Content/Information _____
8. Posture/Poise _____

MOTIVATING STUDENTS TO BE SUCCESSFUL MATHEMATICIANS

By the time students reach the upper elementary grades, many have established their basic attitude toward learning mathematics, their perception of what mathematics is, and how it can be used. Unfortunately, high numbers of students have a *negative* attitude toward math, feel incompetent in their skills; and sadly, are unable to see the relevance or connection of the curriculum to their lives. With this realization, the teaching of mathematics in the upper-grade classroom has been modified slowly over the past few years to include a more meaningful, hands-on approach. More and more emphasis is being placed on students' understanding of the concept (rather than just finding the "right answer"), and a far greater emphasis is placed on application of skills to the real world. Children are in need of grasping the *connections* of how math in the classroom relates to math used daily in our everyday lives.

Many teachers feel uncomfortable teaching without the aid of their textbook, and rarely deviate from the routine of teaching directly from the text, assigning all computational and word problems straight from the book. There is a reluctance among many teachers to try different teaching approaches, in spite of some dismal statistics regarding how our students are performing functionally across the nation. In September, 1993 the U.S. Department of Education released the following statistics based on its National Center for Education Statistics from nearly 250,000 students attending 10,000 schools in every state: . . . "only 16 percent of fourth-graders, 8 percent of eighth-graders and 9 percent of high school seniors correctly answered mathematics questions requiring problem-solving skills in 1992 testing."

Upper-grade teachers have the difficult task of bridging the hands-on math program of the primary classrooms with that more traditional viewpoint and curriculum of secondary schools. It is our responsibility to build a strong, solid foundation for our students that includes math literacy skills of "the basics," as well as to challenge their thinking processes and help them to become active problem-solvers. The upper-grade teacher must prepare students for the use of a textbook and copying from it, and taking more formal, standardized tests. This will be expected of the students in most middle schools and junior high schools. At the secondary level, as well, many teachers are beginning to incorporate more hands-on, active learning into the program. It is essential that at all levels the mathematics program promotes the understanding and enjoyment of math and provides a high degree of motivation. Hopefully, by the time students reach the secondary level, they will have an awareness, appreciation, and understanding of the importance of math in their own lives.

We must show our students that math is everywhere in our world and that to be deficient in math makes our lives more difficult. This section will provide numerous suggestions and activities to challenge and motivate our students through real-life problem-solving opportunities. As we enable children to see math work in their own world, engaging them in useful and relevant problem solving, students "buy into" the math program and increase their motivation.

It is also important that we *integrate* the teaching of mathematics with other subject areas to show our students the connections that math has with science, social studies, music, art, P.E., health, and so on. Again, making the curriculum have meaning in the lives of older students helps them to see math as a tool to be used on a daily basis, not as a separate subject area that is only used while they are in math class. When we begin to show the connections between math and sports, cooking, reading music, working on cars, purchasing items, taking medicine, and viewing the artistic world, our students will become more interested in understanding math as it pertains to them. We must develop in each child the understanding that math is essential to them and their *survival* in the real world. Very few students ever grasp math's relevancy to their lives through the use of a textbook.

The National Council of Teachers of Mathematics (NCTM) Curriculum and Evaluation Standards for School Mathematics, a major spearhead of the national call for change, states that elementary math instruction should incorporate the following:

- a problem-solving approach to teaching math
- active learning in the classroom
- the use of concrete materials
- cooperative work in small groups
- discussion of ideas
- justification of thinking
- writing in class lessons
- ongoing assessment

Teachers need to seek out new, interesting, and meaningful ways to approach math both in and out of the classroom. For problem solving, the students should be given opportunities to work cooperatively, as well as individually. Math seems to have more meaning when two or three students can approach a task together. Children should have the opportunities to create their own problems, and be able to talk about how they approach and solve them in different ways. We, as teachers, need to provide opportunities to allow students to write about their understanding, and talk about different ways to dissect a problem.

WHAT ABOUT MASTERY OF BASIC MATH FACTS AND COMPUTATION SKILLS?

Children still need to have a very solid foundation in the basic facts and skills. When children get into the upper grades and have not developed some rudimentary understanding or memory of the basics, math in the classroom and in the world around them is a puzzle. It is very difficult to have success with more advanced mathematical concepts and skills without the basics. Lacking the basics, students struggle to apply the skills of estimation; to approach problems involving fractions, decimals, percentage; or to apply math in the real world (e.g., tax, tips, buying, banking, and so forth).

There are a certain percentage of our students in the classroom—particularly those with learning disabilities—who have significant difficulty memorizing basic math facts. These children need the understanding of their teachers, and should be allowed to proceed with the rest of the class with the use of tools or aids to help them compensate for their disability. Other children have not acquired these skills for other reasons, with some students taking an apathetic approach. It is our contention that regular drill and practice in a variety of formats to acquire mastery of basic skills needs to be built into the program, although this portion of the math lesson must be *brief.*

USING CONCRETE EXAMPLES AND ANALOGIES TO CONNECT MEANING WITH ABSTRACT CONCEPTS

Children relate well to dramatic, creative teaching styles. A teacher can readily hook students into a lesson on reducing fractions, for example, through the comparison of a fraction in need of being reduced to an overweight person who needs to lose weight. A teacher might bring to class an advertisement from a weight-reduction program. The discussion might start out about why people go on diets, how they go about losing weight, and who can assist them in their weight-loss program. Ultimately, the students bring up the weight-reduction program. The teacher might say, "Just like a weight-reduction success story, a fraction can also be reduced. Here is how that happens . . . "

When the concept of equivalent fractions is introduced, demonstrate that concept by using a student as a model in class. Placing one layer of jackets or sweatshirts on at a time (about five layers altogether), the student appears to look like he/she is becoming larger, although he/she is still the same person underneath all of the layers. This building of layers of coats to simulate the idea that the person appears larger than he/she started out to be, gets the idea across to students that a fraction can look larger although it is really the same size/value. Through this type of demonstration, an abstract concept becomes very visual and memorable.

Another mathematical concept that can be better grasped through analogy is comparing "finding a common denominator" to marriage. When a man and woman decide to get married, usually the woman changes her last name to become the same as her husband's. So, if Miss Five marries Mr. Ten, they become the Ten family. Once again, when students associate finding a common denominator with "marrying" of fractions, most children will find it more understandable and will remember the concept for a long period of time.

Learning styles research shows that we tend to remember ideas better when we use them in creative ways. You need to continue to strive for ways to make math appear fun, challenging, and meaningful.

ASSESSMENT

Typically teachers use formal testing to assess students' understanding of math. From experience we all know that not all children test well, especially when there is only one right answer. It is strongly suggested that students have additional means of demonstrating their understanding of math concepts. Keeping *math journals* and writing about how they approach a problem is very much an eye-opener for the teacher. Giving students an opportunity to be the *teacher of the minute* and to demonstrate and explain to their classmates how they solved a problem is always well received. We give students the opportunity to take control of the teaching process at the overhead projector. Students feel empowered with an overhead pen in their hand. Providing this opportunity also communicates to students that their individual way of doing things and solving problems is listened to and valued.

PROBLEM-SOLVING STRATEGIES

With regard to *problem solving* within the mathematical curriculum, it is important that we teach the skills of problem formulation, analysis, selection of strategies, solution techniques, and interpretation of solutions. We need to model problem-solving behavior whenever possible, exploring and experimenting along with students. It is also very important to ask appropriate questions that encourage critical thinking and the discovery approach:

"How did you solve the problem?"
"Why did that approach work (or not work)?"
"What is another way to solve the problem?"

We must take the time to *teach* students specific steps for problem solving:

1. Restate the problem in their own words, trying to simplify the language.
2. Find the question or statement that tells what they are being asked to find.
3. Summarize the important information given.
4. Plan the strategies for solving the problem.
5. Utilize strategies as appropriate (e.g., making a model, drawing a picture, acting it out, looking for patterns).
6. Check for the "reasonableness" of the answer.

Teaching problem solving in cooperative group settings is very beneficial. It allows students the opportunity to interact with other students in a setting conducive to speculating, questioning, and explaining concepts. Students feel more comfortable trying out ideas in small groups rather than in front of the whole class. Students can more easily explain and show their thinking processes and problem-solving strategies with partners or small groups.

PROVIDING EXTRA HELP DURING MATH

There are many ways to provide extra assistance to students within the math class. Some of these ways include the use of "student experts" and parent volunteers in the classroom. In our classrooms students have had exposure to Howard Gardner's theory of multiple intelligences and are familiar with the idea of "math smart." (See Section 1, *Reaching All Students Through Their Multiple Intelligences and Learning Styles.*) We always utilize students who have strengths in various areas to be the class "experts" whenever appropriate. Math class is a perfect time to do so. Sometimes during work times the teacher selects a team of "math experts" to assist other students. When a new concept is introduced, the teacher is only one of several people who helps students with trying to learn and understand the concept. "Experts" roam around the room and check students in the way they are approaching the problem or answer questions as needed. These "experts" know their skills are valued and their assistance is greatly appreciated.

A recent example of a self-esteem building experience for us was when one of our resource students had completed all of his math assignments with a strong degree of success before anyone else in the classroom. We gave him the title of "expert" and he went around the room helping the rest of the students. For those students who were feeling a little smug about a "resource" student helping them, it was a humbling experience. For the "expert," he was given the chance to shine. The positive experience gave him a reason to be proud, and to stay focused in math in the future.

At our school we are very fortunate to have one or two parents who volunteer in the classroom on a regular basis. Sometimes parents drop in on a more informal basis and want to help out. There are three areas in which we think parents or volunteers can assist greatly in the math classroom: helping students with clock skills, measurement, and money. Every child in our fifth/sixth grade classrooms is assessed in his/her understanding of measurement to one sixteenth of an inch, telling time on a traditional clock, and counting back change. These concepts are assessed by the volunteer with a plus or minus on a recording sheet. From there, the teacher can teach the concept to a small group as the group forms out of the individual assessment. A class list is provided where the volunteer records the results. It is attached to a clipboard, and the volunteer always knows where to find it when he/she enters the rooms. It doesn't matter when the volunteer comes into the classroom because the process is ongoing. Other math skills (such as use of a compass and protractor) can also be assessed in this manner by volunteers.

It is amazing how often we, as teachers, just assume that children in the upper grades have mastered such functional skills as counting money or knowing how to tell time. However, there are many students at this level who cannot do so. Since digital clocks have become so popular, many children cannot tell time on a regular clockface. It is very helpful to assess these functional survival skills on a one-to-one basis. Students should not be made to feel foolish if they are weak in these skills. One-to-one assistance with a volunteer helper is a perfect avenue for students who are lacking these skills to learn in a more private, personal way.

We are fortunate to have students from the neighborhood high school who work at our school as part of their elective class. We utilize these students by having them work directly with our children who need assistance in the academic areas. Our upper elementary students relate well to teenage tutors, and, therefore, greatly benefit and enjoy working on their math with these high school students.

Collaborative teaching (regular and special educators co-teaching and working together) is also very effective for providing intensive assistance to students during math instruction. Both authors are working together in such a collaborative teaching model. (See Section 10, *Team Efforts.*)

As is the case in all aspects of life, math needs to be approached in a balanced way. For the older students, the hands-on approach and the more directed textbook-drill-and-test approach must reach a happy medium so that students are exposed to a little of each.

It is important that, if students are working from a textbook, they are given clear direction as to their assignments. At our school, students in the upper grades are given assignment sheets on a weekly basis. The daily assignments, project assignments, dates of tests and quizzes, problems of the day and week, extra credit, family math activities, and other math puzzlers are placed on this sheet. Students keep records on this sheet indicating what they have done and how well they have done it. This gives them input into their daily math activities and helps them pace their day and week. Parents seem to really appreciate knowing what their children are actually doing and what the teacher's expectations are.

MODIFICATIONS AND ACCOMMODATIONS FOR STUDENTS WHO STRUGGLE IN MATH

There are students in our classrooms who do poorly in math computation because of difficulties they have with copying and organization of math problems. They may be deficient in visual-motor integration skills—causing them significant difficulty aligning numbers, writing within the minimal amount of given space on the page, remembering which number gets carried up when regrouping, and so forth. Some students have a disability in their memory skills; no matter how hard they try, they may be unable to commit math facts to memory. Many students with learning disabilities and/or ADD make numerous careless errors in their computation, but are often quite strong in mathematical reasoning and math aptitude.

These students should be provided with accommodations to help them bypass these disabilities so that they can be successful with their classroom math:

- Provide many kinds of manipulatives to help visualize and work out problems.
- Allow and encourage use of calculators.
- Give students a choice of computing with a calculator, paper/pencil, or mentally.
- Allow extra time on math tests so students aren't rushed to make careless errors.
- Encourage students to write and solve their computation problems on graph paper rather than notebook paper. Experiment with graph paper of varying square sizes.
- Allow students to write and solve their problems on notebook paper held sideways (with lines running vertically rather than horizontally). This makes it much easier for students with difficulty to align numbers, reducing careless errors.
- Reduce the number of problems assigned (half-page, evens only, odds only).
- Reduce the amount of copying required by photocopying the page or writing out the problems on paper for certain students.
- Color-highlight processing signs for students who are inattentive to change in operational signs on a page.
- Provide a large work space on tests. If necessary, rewrite test items on other paper with lots of room for computation.
- List steps clearly.
- Provide models of sample problems.
- Provide a chart of multiplication facts/tables for student reference.

- When testing long division or multiplication problems that involve using several digits and regrouping, give problems with numbers for which most all students know the math facts (e.g., $6274 \times 52 =$; most students know the ×5s and ×2s). This way they are tested on their understanding of the process, and aren't penalized because they have poor memory skills.

- For students who haven't mastered multiplication facts, try using mnemonic devices to help. There are a variety of rhymes, raps, and songs to help students memorize the multiplication tables. There are also different "finger tricks" for learning ×6, ×7, ×8, and ×9 tables. Some mnemonic programs are available that use picture associations and clever stories to help master multiplication facts, as well. One such program is *Time Tables the Fun Way—A Picture Method of Learning the Multiplication Facts*. (See the recommended resources at the end of this section.)

LIFE SKILLS MATH: MAKING THE CURRICULUM RELEVANT AND FUN

There is so much that students can learn from in the real world. We, as upper-grade teachers, need to bring the real world into the classroom, but also take the students out into the real world to face the challenges of being consumers.

In the following material you will find ways that students at our school have been exposed to math in other ways besides a textbook—ways that make math more enjoyable and meaningful. Students are given the chance to interact with their environment and try to make practical use out of what the textbooks are trying to get across (often with little success or understanding of concepts).

"MONEYWORKS"

Our school is fortunate to have Union Bank as one of its business partners; therefore, our students learn first-hand about banking and currency. A field trip to the bank is very instrumental in giving students a close-up look at occupations in the banking business, security, ATM, loans, checking, etc. Students begin to feel more knowledgeable about the challenges their parents encounter in their lives.

As an extension of this real experience, students in San Diego are given the opportunity to participate in a wonderful program called *MoneyWorks*, a Children's Museum simulation of real-life working and consuming skills. *MoneyWorks* is a traveling, interactive exhibit where children manage money in real-life situations. There are six modules: a Bank, an ATM, a General Store, a Payroll Office, a Restaurant, and four Billing Offices (Telephone, Housing, Auto, and Utilities). Students in grades kindergarten through six act out the roles of customers, shopkeepers, clerks, bankers, and bill collectors as they learn to make choices, exchange money, and balance a checking account. This program is offered to schools for a nominal fee. Each class is given a time frame of 1 to 2 hours, depending on the grade level. Students feel very connected to the real world and discover a greater appreciation of their parents' lives as they progress through the simulation.

As part of the simulation, classes can also pursue the world of money. Students can talk about currency *vs.* coins, how and where coins are minted, foreign currency and its value compared to the dollar, counterfeiting, and so on. Students can learn what is printed on the dollar and what purpose it serves, then create their own currency to be used during the *MoneyWorks* exhibit. Learning to look closely at what a piece of currency contains and then reproducing those elements creatively, can give the students an up close view of money in the real world. Most children do not ever thoroughly inspect a piece of currency. By asking children to use a real dollar as a model, the students quickly learn the basic parts that their own personal currency must contain. Children will remember these parts because they have designed their own in a creative way. After the money is produced, the students choose their favorites from the class, and that is the money used during the simulation. Using generic play money doesn't have the same impact that student-created money has for upper graders.

CONSUMER MATH FIELD TRIP

Another experience students are given at our school is a buying trip to a variety store. A field trip to a store like Pic and Save, Kmart, The 99 Cent Store, Woolworth's, or Wal-Mart can be an eye-opener to upper-grade students. When the students are asked to shop with a team and follow certain guidelines as presented in the letter to parents, they find themselves in the real world of currency and consumerism. It is always a good idea to preface this trip by giving the store a call and making sure the manager knows exactly what the purpose of the trip is. The employees then become part of the process and students must ask questions of the employees instead of relying on their teacher or the parents who have provided transportation.

Before the trip is taken, the classroom teacher must teach the skills of tax, addition and subtraction of decimals, use of the calculator, and working cooperatively. Three elements are added to the process to make things even more tightly formed: the time factor (30 minutes of shopping time), a ceiling of $4.00 per group, and the necessity of buying an agreed-upon number of items (5 to 7 items must be purchased). These restraints give more structure to the process, and make the students work together to problem solve. Although students complain about the restrictions, the time, number of items, and the $4.00 ceiling work out very well. More time, money, or items just complicates the situation.

Although most children really work well as a team, the groups do have a few things of which they are not aware, such as the additional charge on plastic bottles of soda and on cans of soda (CRV). Sales tax also causes a problem.

The goal of this assignment is to get as close to spending the full $4.00 without going over. (One group got as close as $3.99.) If the group goes over the allotted amount, they are disqualified from the grand prize (usually ice cream treats). The students get so charged up in this whole process that they don't seem to bicker about what they actually buy, although they are encouraged to buy items that are useful to the entire group.

When the students return to school, they are asked to fill out a form to show how they spent their money, and display their purchases for the rest of the class to see. The other teams evaluate each other's purchases, and the items are divided among the team members. Each person receives a plastic zip-lock bag to place his/her portion of the purchases. At this point, the class decides which group got the most for its money. There is usually one group that really makes astonishing purchases and everyone is envious of its wealth of items!

The last part of this exercise comes when students are asked to summarize and evaluate their experience. Self-evaluation reveals many important ideas for the teacher to see. Students are asked to write three paragraphs showing their understanding of the importance of this adventure.

Students' comments in past years about this experience are listed below. A fifth-grader reflects on his adventure in the accompanying letter.

- *I thought it was fun racing around choosing things you wanted. The only problem was that we always didn't agree on some items, but after the half hour shopping spree, we had to come to some agreement, and fast.*
- *My classmates are a lot different when they are not in school. I liked getting to see them in a different light.*
- *I liked the fact that no adults helped us because it made the "adventure" more fun. I think this was a very creative way to get us to learn math.*
- *I liked this project because it was adventurous and exciting. I thought we could have had more time to shop and more money. Nevertheless, this was much better than a boring math lesson.*
- *On my team we weren't very organized, but we wouldn't get an item unless the whole group agreed on getting it. I learned that there is no sales tax on food. There is only sales tax on stuff you can't eat. But there is CRV on beverages that come in plastic containers and aluminum cans.*
- *You get to learn different things about your classmates that you normally wouldn't in school.*

The parents who accompanied the classes on this trip gave the experience rave reviews. They were very pleased to see what the children were actually doing. Their comments were very positive. By the time students are in the upper grades, many times the available field trips become redundant. Students are not receptive to taking the same field trip several years in a row. This type of experience was worthwhile and unique. The children, parents, and teachers were thrilled with the experience and what the children actually learned. (See the parent letter regarding this activity at the end of this section.)

LOW- OR NO-COST MATH MATERIALS FROM NEWSPAPERS AND PAMPHLETS

As teachers, we should be looking for materials that are not too costly for enhancing our math programs. Just by looking through the newspaper we can see math abounds—and ideas for math centers or activities are readily found. The television and movie guides can generate many questions and activities for students. For instance, children in cooperative groups can plan a one-day schedule for a primary student's television viewing. They should write out a chart with the time of day, the channel, and the program listed. Another group may want to plan a television-viewing schedule for students of their own age, using only appropriate programs to which all their parents would agree.

In most grocery stores, *AutoTrader* magazines and *Home-Buying Guides* can be found for no cost. These guides can also be used in the classroom. Students may be asked to locate a car they would like to buy between the cost of $3,000 and $7,000. The idea that most young people cannot afford a new car can generate discussion. The issue of insurance and the difference between boys' and girls' insurance premiums can be discussed, and the reason why boys' insurance is more costly should be brought out. The concept of sales tax, registration and licensing fees, tires, maintenance, and gasoline prices enlighten the students as to the high cost of owning a car.

Writing can be drawn into this math lesson with a composition about Car Ownership. Students can write about why they chose a certain car, how they would earn money to buy and maintain the car, the responsibilities of being a driver, and the reasons why there are age restrictions on drivers. Students can also make graphs and charts to show comparisons of car prices. Having the children cut out the car they choose from the book and pasting it to a piece of paper, special accessories their car has, the great deal they got, and the excitement of being an "owner" takes the outside purchasing power into the classroom math setting. Some students who do not own a family car now have gone through the experience of "buying" a car. This gives them the opportunity to dream a little.

The same holds true for buying a home. Through the *Home-Buying Guides*, students develop a sense of how costly homes really are. Special features such as fireplaces, swimming pools, large pieces of property, location, etc., all become not only a practical reading lesson, but also a practical math experience that students really enjoy. Comparing and contrasting home prices through charts and graphs makes children appreciate how costly a home is. For some whose families do not own their own homes, this may offer them an understanding of why their parents cannot afford a home; and for those who do own a home, they may develop a greater appreciation for what they have. As in the car-buying activity, students can write about "their home" by telling why they chose it, what they will do to pay for it, how they will maintain it, and what other costs owning a home will entail.

Real estate offices are usually very helpful in giving out their extra or old flyers about homes that are or were on the market. Having an entire class set can be valuable for whole class instruction. You may want to place one of the flyers on a transparency and decode the abbreviated description of some of the information with the whole class. This gives the children a reference point when they are deciphering their own flyer. A real find is a used *multiple listing catalog*. (Realtors are more reluctant to give these out for public use.) For the middle school students these are very complete, and the students are extended in their math abilities by the more complicated listing of information.

CLASSROOM MATH CENTERS

To vary the math program and expose students to the use of their math skills in a more informal way, you may provide a *Center Day* where students choose or rotate into math-related centers. This may also be called a *Math Lab*. Depending on your schedule, this special math day may be once a month, or even once a week for a 30- to 40-minute session. This is the time where students will pull all of their skills out of their memory bank and use them to approach math in a different way. Suggestions for centers might include the following:

The Graphing Center. Students find a large number of graphing pictures to create from numbered pairs. All developmental levels of graphing skills are stimulated by easy to more complicated pictures, including positive and negative integers.

The Math Manipulative Center: Students explore such math manipulatives as geoboards, pattern blocks, pentominoes, and tangrams.

The Math Game Center: These games teach math skills. You might use Othello®, Sorry®, SMath®, Trouble®, Mastermind®, Pente®, 50 in One®, Uno-Dominos®, HI-Q®, Qubic®, Math Pentathlon®.

The Restaurant Center: Students choose from a variety of menus and order a meal, and figure tax and tip. Actual order receipts may be used to make the center more real for the students.

The Card Center: Students play a variety of card games to enhance their mathematical strategies and skills, such as Concentration, Crazy Eight, Rummy.

The Computer Center: Students use a variety of math programs to build their skills in math ranging from easy to more difficult math games and activities. Examples are *Math Blasters* and *Number Munchers*.

The Calculator Center: Students have a variety of calculator activity cards, puzzles, and games to explore.

The Math Art Center: Students have a variety of art/math activities to create using geometry, tessellations, perspective drawing, number pictures, line and angle drawings, etc.

The Measurement Center: Students use a variety of measuring tools—including liquid and linear, metric and standard—to measure the world around them. Include rulers, yard-sticks, metric sticks, containers, measuring cups and spoons, tape measures, and so forth.

Note: See Section 2, Learning Developmentally, *for more information about the use and creation of centers in the classroom.*

MATH IS EVERYWHERE YOU LOOK

At the very beginning of the school year, students are asked to look around their environment and find examples of how math is used. In class the students generate a list of at least 25 items that would involve the use of math. Examples from students' lists include music, clocks, putting wallpaper and flooring into your house, playing games, sewing, shoe sizes, cooking, tools, the microwave, sports, coupons, labels on cereal boxes, bus schedules, medicines, mileage for traveling, etc. The assignment is extended to the home where students are to add more ideas with the help of their parents. Getting the parents involved in their child's math experience is very worthwhile. (See the *Math Is Everywhere You Look* forms at the end of this section.)

After the students have generated their lists, they are asked to elaborate in writing form about 8 to 10 of those items. The students cut pictures out of magazines or newspapers, draw their own pictures, take snapshots, or use graphics from the computer. A variety of these types of illustrations adds the element of balance, and allows each child to approach the project in his/her own individual style. Here is an example of what one student did:

> *Katie drew a picture of a measuring cup. She wrote underneath her picture, "I need to know how to use a measuring cup so I can measure ingredients in a recipe. Knowing fractions and how to add them in case I want to double a recipe is also important. I need to know liquid measurements, too. Some recipes have you measure liquids in ounces. I need to know how many ounces are in a cup in order to do that."*

The "Math Is Everywhere" project stretches students' thinking by building upon experiences and knowledge they already have. Aaron, a sixth grader, approaches the project using baseball team standings. (See his sample.)

> *Aaron wrote the following about sports from the newspaper: "These are the Baseball Standings from the Sports section in the newspaper. There are records, number and percentages listed on it. For example, our San Diego Padres have a 60 (w) and 63 (l) record. Their percentage is .488 and they are 4 ¹/₂ games behind (GB) the 1st place Colorado Rockies. The use of Math gives us the knowledge to understand percentages, read numbers, etc."*

It should be impressed upon students that a due date is when the project must be handed in. A discussion of the real world of work and how a boss would not tolerate it if a major project was not prepared by its due date, is helpful in getting this point across. We do a great disservice to students by not enforcing a due date. On the due date of this project, students share and evaluate their project with the other students in their classroom. An important part of any student project should be self-evaluation. This is when the children look at other students' projects and constructively assess their own work. Seeing how other students approached their activity assists all students in seeing how they might approach their project in a different way next time.

GRAPHING

Teaching graphing skills and how to make a "homemade" graph of their own is essential in the middle- and upper-grade years. Finding examples of easy-to-read graphs from the newspaper and magazines and placing them on overheads for the entire class to see is a good starting point. Students start to understand that graphs show comparisons and let us see things in a visual way that unlocks categories of ideas. Students tend to comprehend bar graphs more readily than other forms of graphs and tend to make them more often when given a choice. On the first day of school a teacher may quickly assess some pertinent information about the students in the classroom. This is done by handing the children several self-stick notes upon which to write their individual names. Then the children post their names under the heading *Girl* or *Boy* on the chart paper. This immediately lets students see the difference in numbers according to gender. In a combination classroom, the heading may be *5th Grader, 6th Grader*. The children can easily see what the make-up of the class is. Other headings such as *What School Did You Attend Last Year?* and a list of schools where the class may have originated from the previous year also makes the class quickly make connections that would otherwise take more time.

With younger students *What is your favorite kind of ice cream?* might be a good starting point. Again, each student would be given a self-stick note to write his/her name on. The categories would be: *Chocolate Chip Cookie Dough, Jamaica Almond Fudge, Cookies and Cream, Marble Fudge, Neapolitan*, or any other favorites the teacher can think up. Students can then place their notes with their names under the favorite category. This bar graph then becomes the basis for discussion, comparison, and contrast.

Math tends to make more sense when relationships begin to take shape. Students are able to verbalize or write about what they can actually see. For instance, a third grader may say, "I see that more students in our classroom like chocolate chip cookie dough ice cream than cookies and cream." An upper-grade student may write, "Twenty out of 32 fifth graders in Room 8 prefer chocolate chip cookie dough ice cream. This is a 20:32 ratio. Restated in percentage, 63% of our class prefers chocolate chip cookie dough to the other kinds of ice cream." A more skillful and thorough approach is given as the children developmentally learn new math concepts.

Younger children might be given more opportunities to use pictographs and bar graphs, whereas older children may be encouraged to use circle and line graphs. Graphs with positive and negative integers also need to be introduced as the students become more skillful. (See the *Graphing Can Be Fun* project, *List of Questions for Graphing Projects*, and *Graphing Project Design Form* at the end of this section.)

SURVIVAL MATH

This project is an outgrowth of many years of searching for how to teach math more meaningfully, and letting students begin to realize the concerns their parents have when they say, "We can't afford that this month" or "We don't have the money." Those comments by parents don't seem to make sense when students don't see the connections. Most children think you can simply write a check for anything at anytime. They don't realize parents have to have money to cover their purchases. With the wide use of credit cards, students just think you can say "Charge it" and that covers everything.

Through the activities suggested in the *Survival Math* packet, students begin to feel a part of their world by opening bank accounts, practicing check writing, using the telephone to check out prices of airfare and bus fare, reading schedules, going grocery shopping, and watching the rise and fall of gasoline prices during the month. These monthly activities provide the opportunity for students and parents to work together in the discovery of math in our world. Parents begin to feel a sense of importance in helping their children to responsibly understand the money world of adulthood. Children and their parents interact and participate in relevant and meaningful activities to let students know why they have to understand key concepts in the textbook; if they don't, survival in the real world is significantly more difficult.

Ten activities are required by the end of the school year. Students may hand them in any time before the end of the month. Each child has a math portfolio and the student's monthly activities are placed in the folder after they are evaluated by the teacher and the students. The teacher showcases on a regular basis a number of student projects that have been turned in during the month. These examples serve as models for the other students, and motivate them to complete their own quality activities.

These activities also provide excellent problem-solving opportunities. The beginning of every math period can start out with the use of one of these personalized activities. For instance, Jennifer brought in a list of coupons she and her mother cut out and used when they went shopping for groceries. They saved $13.13 by using the coupons. She told the class that the store she shopped at doubled the coupons. The teacher now had an opportunity to capitalize on the personal activity and teach the entire class some problem-solving strategies. She asked the students to take out their calculators and figure out how much savings there was when the coupons were doubled. She further stretched the student's minds by asking them, "If Jennifer saved this much money for one week, how much could she and her family save over a year's time?" In this group of sixth graders, it was immediately discovered that very few students knew how many weeks were in a year. After establishing that fact, the students discovered that Jennifer's family could save $682.76 per year. That seemed to make a real impression on them. The class then tried to think of what they would buy if they actually had that much more money to spend on other things besides groceries.

Another activity done by the same student, Jennifer, was filling out order forms for magazines she would like to have. One of the orders she placed was for *Cricket*, a child's magazine of literature and poetry. The cost of the subscription for one year was $26.79. The teacher asked the class, "If Jennifer purchased *Cricket* for one year at $26.79, how much does it cost per month?" In the fifth-grade class, the students truly were perplexed by the question. One of the students thought she had the correct answer when she decided to multiply the price per year by 12. The entire class agreed with her, until through questioning by the teacher, she herself realized that that would be the cost for 12 years of subscriptions, not one month. The students finally realized that the operation to be used would be division, but the idea didn't come easily.

We must train students through problem-solving strategies to look at word problems as puzzles to be put together. We take each part and find how it fits. We must also train students to look for reasonable answers. The fifth grader above knew after some teacher direction that her answer wasn't reasonable and didn't make sense.

In this process of showing students the faults in their process of deduction, we, as teachers, must be careful not to make students feel incompetent because they make mistakes. We must carefully show students that through mistakes they will learn to think more thoroughly and reasonably. This same type of questioning could have been set up in the classroom in cooperative groups or in partners, giving students the opportunity to talk through the problem together. This allows students to feel less afraid of failure.

Another strategy that could be used with the survival math activities would be to give students the basic foundation of the problem, such as *Cricket magazine subscription, $26.79 per year, 12 issues, Jennifer's order*, and have the students come up with a word problem for their classmates using the information. This process of working with the facts and generating their own questions gives the students a chance to see the parts and feel secure in putting together the whole. Knowing how testmakers create the questions is helpful in understanding word problems. We should provide opportunities throughout the year to have students problem solve, but also to create their own problems for others to solve. (See *Survival Math Parent Letter, Survival Math Packet, Survival Math Record Sheet*, and *Survival Math Evaluation Form* at the end of this section.) Included here is a sample of one student's survival math activity.

Andy
Age 10
Survival Math

Question # 36--Oil Change

    I had to find out how much an oil change would be for our family car, so I called the places below and found the best and cheapest place.

    At the Chevron station at the corner of Navajo and Lake Murray in San Carlos, the manager told me that he would change our oil for $21.00--on sale. He said that oil change usually costs $26.00.

    At the Firestone center in La Mesa, that same oil change costs 16.04, with tax included.

    At the Instant Oil Change in La Mesa, the manager told me the oil change would cost $26.29.

    If we were to change our own oil, we wouldn't have to pay as much.
    It would cost $5.90 for 5 bottles of oil, at $1.18 a bottle.
    It would cost $3.69 for an oil filter.
    It would cost $2.00 to get rid of the old oil.
    That is $11.59, but we would need tools, we would get dirty, and it would take a lot of time.

    When you have a car, you should change the oil every 3000 miles. The cost of changing the oil can be very high, if you don't shop around for the best price. If you change the oil yourself, you can save as much as $14.70, every time you change the oil.

SUPER BOWL MATH

It is important that we capitalize on a mathematical moment. Since the Super Bowl is the single most watched event in America, and has the highest rate for advertising, why not use it to enhance our students' math ability? Although we can't get everybody to be interested in sports, the Super Bowl does motivate not only some of our more reluctant math students, but also helps to extend math understanding to some of our higher achieving students. This project's intent is to inspire children to get involved in an activity, and find out how money, scores, advertising, attendance, roman numerals, height, weight, time, weather, statistics, and other math skills are used in the event. Parents tend to enjoy this project because it gives their child a focus during the Super Bowl, and when parents get involved in their child's education, the child feels it is important.

Although much of this packet is math-oriented, there are other skills that can also be developed or extended: writing, mapping, geography, interviewing, illustrating, vocabulary development, oral language, and spelling. (See the *Super Bowl Math Activity Packet* at the end of this section.)

One 5th grader summarizes a Super Bowl commercial for one of her required activities in the following way:

Pepsi Can Commercial

The Pepsi commercial is about a person who works for the Coke company. He is delivering the coke cans and putting them on the rack. When he is done, he looks over and sees the Pepsi rack right next to the coke rack. Then he looks around to make sure no one is looking. Then he opens the door to the Pepsi rack, grabs one, but all the Pepsi cans fall out, and land on the floor. They make a loud sound. Then everybody looks at him, and he has an embarrassed face.

I think this commercial was worth a million dollars because it will interest more people to buy Pepsi.

Laura
1-28-96
Age 11

CREATING A CHILDREN'S COUNTING BOOK

All students need a little break from the routine of computational math. One way to do this is to elicit from your children where and how they began to understand math ideas. In a class discussion the students will fondly remember their days of watching *Sesame Street* and other children's television programs that helped to teach them numbers. The students also remember the importance of counting books in helping them learn numbers.

As the students reflect on the past, they are given the assignment to create their own counting books that will be shared with their primary-grade buddies upon their completion. We look at this project as a philanthropic service project to motivate young children (kindergarten and first graders) to read and write numbers.

First, you must gather a number of counting books so that students can be instructed to look for important elements that these books contain. Having a class collection, with one book for every child, is most desirable. The supply of these books may be gathered from a variety of sources:

- public library
- school library
- primary teachers at the school site and other schools
- students' personal books from home
- purchased books

Then choose several counting books to read and discuss with the class. Key features found in these books are discovered by the students as the books are presented. A list is developed to use for discussion, and is visible on a chart throughout the unit. These features include:

- use of bright colors
- rhyme
- repetition
- simplicity
- simple storylines
- different languages from around the world
- cultural diversity
- uniqueness of customs and values
- variety of counting methods (1-10, 1-20, counting forward, counting backwards, counting by 2's, 5's, 10's, etc.)
- use of animals, shapes, symbols (e.g., dots throughout the book, wheels, footprints)
- cut-outs for certain parts of the illustrations (e.g., fish eyes, caterpillars)
- different textures

After you show examples of these elements in the selected books, ask the students to fill out the sheet *Looking More Closely at Counting Books* found at the end of this section. Students are asked to look carefully at three to five counting books as research for creating their own book. You may have more capable readers/writers evaluate five books, while the student who is more challenged in reading/writing may be asked to look at only three. The books are circulated around the class during two to three 20- to 30-minute sessions.

Examples of Counting Books:

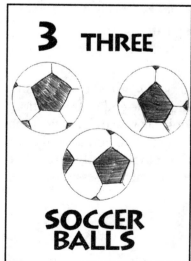

Counting With
Joel and the Pets
in His
Pet Shop

Counting   1...2...3...
With Joel
and the Pets in His
Pet Shop!

Joel loves pets as you
Can see from
The sign on his
Front door

Come on in and count
with him with the
animals in his pet store

1

One green turtle sitting
in his bowl

Hoping that you will
buy him from the pet
keeper Joel.

3

Three very small mice

with hair as white as rice.

4

Four tweety birds sitting
on a twig

trying to stay away from
the guinea pig.

6

Six little kittens begging
for love and care

hoping that kitty
shopping is why you
are there.

8

Eight fluffy bunnies
hopping about

Their mother is sleeping,
so please don't shout.

Now you see how easy
counting can be.

Now by yourself you
will count your

1...2...3's

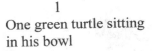

Numbers of the City

By James Kornweibel

2 Two
Big Trucks

3 Three
Basket balls.

4 Four
Nice flower pots.

6 Six
Beautiful Flowers.

7 Seven
Children playing.

8 Eight
Cool Surfboards.

9 Nine
colorful umbrellas.

This is what I saw on my walk today and I hope you enjoyed it as much as I did!

As the students complete the forms, they will then begin thinking about their own book. Each child should receive a piece of 12″ × 18″ newsprint. This can be folded into eight equal parts, giving a total of eight parts on the front and eight parts on the back. The students can use each section as a page of their book. This is a rough draft and should be drawn in pencil and in sketch form.

The parts of the books that each child should have are:

- cover
- dedication
- storyline
- special features
- illustrations
- about the author
- rough draft
- self evaluation

The students take their writing through the entire writing process to completion of a quality product. Peer and adult editing is used. As rough drafts are edited, students receive final pieces of white construction paper (9″ x 12″). They then finalize their story and add color. Many students like to write their stories on the computer and then draw their illustrations. If students do not have access to computers, you should review the skill of printing. All students can use large pieces of primary-lined paper to practice their printing. Many of them forget the difference between lower- and upper-case letters.

Students can finalize their illustrations and pencil writing in black, thin marker. All excess pencil marks should be erased. A final copy should eliminate all pencil marks. Books are laminated and spiral bound. They are then donated to the school library for students' enjoyment for years to come. The final step to this project is that the students practice reading the stories to their classmates, and then take their show on the road to their primary buddies. This is a rewarding experience for both ages of students. This simple math/writing assignment establishes within the students a sense of completion, pride, and self-esteem. (See *A Children's Counting Book*, *Looking More Closely at Counting Books*, *Counting Book Self-Evaluation*, and *Counting Book Teacher Evaluation* at the end of this section.)

BIBLIOGRAPHY AND RECOMMENDED RESOURCES

Baretta-Lorton, Robert. *Patterns & Connections in Mathematics*. Saratoga, CA: Center for Innovation in Education, 1993.

Baretta-Lorton, Robert. *Mathematics: A Way of Thinking*. Menlo Park, CA: Addison-Wesley Publishing Co., 1977.

Burns, Marilyn. *A Collection of Math Lessons for Grades 3-6*. Sausalito, CA: Math Solutions Publication Co, 1987. (Distributed by Cuisenaire Co. of America)

Burns, Marilyn. *About Teaching Mathematics*. Sausalito, CA: Math Solutions Publications, 1992. (Distributed by Cuisenaire Co. of America)

Jennison, Christopher. *Baseball Math—Grandslam Activities & Projects for Grades 4-8.* Glenview, IL: Good Year Books, Scott Foresman, 1995.

"Kids Stumped by Problems on Math Test," *San Diego Union Tribune,* September 3, 1993, page A-1.

Miller, Marcia, and Lee, Martin. *Estimation Investigations.* Scholastic Professional Books, 1994.

Stenmark, J., Thompson, V., and Cossey, R. *Family Math.* Berkeley, CA: Lawrence Hall of Science, University of California, 1986.

Time Tables the Easy Way. Key Publishers, Inc., 6 Sunwood Lane, Sandy, Utah 84092.

Touch Math, Innovative Learning Concepts, Inc., 6760 Corporate Dr., Colorado Springs, CO 80919-1999, Phone: 1-800-888-9191.

ADDRESSES

Marilyn Burns Education Associates, 150 Gate 5 Road, Suite 101, Sausalito, CA 94965. Math Solutions Workshops—Gr. K-12. Phone: 415-332-4181.

Patterns & Connections in Mathematics Workshop, Center for Innovation in Education, 20665 Fourth Street, Saratoga, CA 95070-5878. Phone: 1-800-395-6088.

PUBLISHERS

Addison-Wesley Publishing Co., Jacob Way, Reading MA 01867-9984.

Creative Publications, 5040 W. 111th Street, Oak Lawn, IL 60453.

Cuisenaire Co. of America, 12 Church Street, Box D, New Rochelle, NY 10802.

Dale Seymour Publications, P.O. Box 10888, Palo Alto, CA 94303-0879.

N.C.T.M. (National Council of Teachers of Mathematics), 1906 Association Drive, Reston, VA 22091.

Project AIMS, 1717 South Chestnut Avenue, Fresno, CA 93702.

Dear Parents,

   Next week as part of the math program, our class will be participating in a field trip to better acquaint us with real-life math survival skills. Hopefully, at the end of the trip, the students will feel more confident in their ability to spend money meaningfully. On the date of _____ from the time of _____ to _____ , the class will participate in a shopping adventure.

   Here's how the experience will work:

1. Each child will bring $1.00 to pool with the other three members of his/her team.

2. The team will have one half hour to shop together.

3. The team will make decisions as to what to buy.

4. The team must purchase between 5 and 7 items, with no multiple items being allowed. All purchases should be appropriate. No guns or weapons may be bought. When shopping, consideration should be given to how the items can be divided in four ways fairly.

5. The team must use a calculator to keep a tally of its desired purchases. A notepad and pencil may be used. The store manager has been contacted, and the employees are aware of this project. They should be asked politely for assistance, if needed. Parents accompanying the students may help to clarify questions that arise, but should not offer extensive help. The students should be problem-solving as a team.

6. The team must figure out the cost of the items, plus the sales tax and other charges, before going to the register. After checking out, the team may not reenter the shopping area to take back or repurchase items. The total must be as close to $4.00 as possible without going over. Teams that go over their allotted amount of money are disqualified from receiving the grand prize.

7. When the team returns to school, they will compile a report describing why they purchased the items, how much each item cost, and how they will divide the purchases. They will make a display of what they purchased and show how the sales tax was figured out. The class will then vote on the team that got the most value for its dollar. Adult judges will assist in the evaluation for the grand prize.

   Through this experience, I hope the students learn to figure out sales tax correctly, use a calculator, work as a team, and how to purchase items in an intelligent way. As they will be representing _____ School in the public view, I hope they will also learn to be courteous shoppers.

   We will need drivers to help us with the experience. Please let us know if you might be available for the one hour period of time.

                                        Thank you, _____

                                                    teacher

THE SHOPPING ADVENTURE
TEAM RECORDING SHEET

Names of Buyers: _____

Items Purchased	Cost of Item	Ratio (Cost of item over $4.00)	% of total (Cost divided by 4)
Ex. _____			
1. _____			
2. _____			
3. _____			
4. _____			
5. _____			
6. _____			
7. _____			

Place a * next to the items that are taxable.

What item do you regard as your best buy? Explain.

Total cost of taxable items _____

State sales tax _____

Total cost of nontaxable items _____

Extra charges (cans, bottles, etc.)

Grand Total _____

What % of $4.00 did you spend? _____ (Total cost divided by $4.00)

MATH IS EVERYWHERE YOU LOOK

Your Name _____

Due Date _____

Assignment:

1. This week you will become a math detective.

2. Look around you carefully every day.

3. Keep a list of things you see in your life that involve math (clocks, scales, radios, gasoline pumps, mileage signs, medicine bottles, etc.).

4. List at least 25 items.

5. Look for pictures in magazines, newspapers, catalogs, cookbooks, and other such resources. Find pictures of televisions, telephones, watches, menus, rulers, etc.

6. You may draw your pictures or take snapshots of these things.

7. Glue the pictures of 8 to 10 items on separate sheets of 8-1/2" × 11" notebook paper. Under each picture, write 3 to 5 sentences telling why you selected this picture and how it ties into math.

OR

You may make a collage on 12" × 18" construction paper, and write a 1- to 2-page summary explaining your collage choices.

8. Add an interesting match cover sheet, or put these pages into a folder with a catchy math title and an illustration.

MATH IS EVERYWHERE YOU LOOK:
EVALUATION FORM

Name _____

1. I spent about _____ hours/minutes on this project.

2. I think I did a/an _____ on this assignment.

3. I think my grade should be a/an _____ because _____

   _____

4. Compared to the rest of the class, I feel _____

   _____

5. I asked for help from _____

6. I'd like my teacher to know this about the Math Is Everywhere
   assignment: _____

   _____

MATH IS EVERYWHERE YOU LOOK:
EVALUATION FORM

Name _____

1. I spent about _____ hours/minutes on this project.

2. I think I did a/an _____ on this assignment.

3. I think my grade should be a/an _____ because _____

   _____

4. Compared to the rest of the class, I feel _____

   _____

5. I asked for help from _____

6. I'd like my teacher to know this about the Math Is Everywhere
   assignment: _____

   _____

GRAPHING CAN BE FUN

A MATH PROJECT

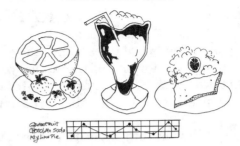

WHAT WILL I BE DOING?

1. Choose a topic from the *List of Questions* sheet. Each person will select a different question. If you think of another question that you would like to investigate, ask your teacher for approval.

2. You will make a *Prediction Card* on a 3" × 5" inch index card. Make sure you print neatly. Have a spelling expert check your work before you finalize it with a black thin marker.

3. You will receive a class list with everyone's name on it. So that your research is valid, after you survey one classmate, you need to cross his/her name off your list. Only survey the people who are available to you. Some students may be absent or out of the classroom at the time of the survey. Make sure you approach as many classmates as possible during the time allotted.

4. You will need four other index cards for *Question/Problem, Procedure, Research (The Survey), Findings,* for your graphing project. Your writing should fill up each card. Don't leave wasted space. Each card should be neatly printed and spell-checked. If you handwrite the cards, start with pencil first, and after everything has been spell-checked, write over the pencil with a black thin marker. If any pencil is still showing, erase it thoroughly. If you use a computer, make the font large enough to fill a space the size of a 3" × 5" index card. Be sure to include percentages and ratios for your findings. Also, let the observer know if your prediction was correct or incorrect.

5. You may make a line, picto, bar, or circle graph to show your results. You will first make a rough draft in pencil making sure you have a **horizontal axis** (lines moving from right to left on the grid) and a **vertical axis** (lines moving from top to bottom on the grid), and **headings** for each. Check their correctness with your teacher.

6. You are now ready to make a final draft. Use only one color from your colored pencils to make your lines, pictures, bars, or sections on your graph. All words must be in black thin marker.

7. You will receive a colored file folder to display all your work. On the right-hand side of your file folder will be your *Question, Prediction, Procedure, Research,* and *Findings* cards. On the left-hand side of the folder will be your graph; you may take a smaller piece of paper to write your name and a key for your graph. Make sure your graph has two headings, one for the horizontal axis and one for the vertical axis.

8. Make sure your materials are securely glued onto the file folder and your work is top quality.

LIST OF QUESTIONS FOR
GRAPHING PROJECTS

Look at the list of questions below. Highlight five of them that interest you most. You will sign-up for one of the topics you have chosen. You will be given the opportunity to take a survey of your classmates during the math period. As a good mathematician and scientist, you must be sure that your findings are valid.

1. What is your favorite **color**?
2. What kind of **pet** do you have at home?
3. What is your favorite **fast-food restaurant**?
4. What is your favorite **sports car**?
5. What is your favorite **amusement park**?
6. What is your favorite kind of **ice cream**?
7. How many **people** live in your house or apartment?
8. What **color cars** do the students have in our class?
9. What is your favorite **sport to watch**?
10. What time of day do you watch the most **television**?
11. What **topping** do you like on your **pizza**?
12. What is your favorite **department store**?
13. What **grocery store** do your parents shop at most often?
14. What kind of **books** do you prefer to read?
15. What is your favorite **hair color**?
16. What color **eyes** do you have?
17. What color **hair** do you have?
18. What is your favorite brand of **cereal**?
19. How often do you brush your **teeth** each day?
20. What is your favorite way to **relax**?
21. Where would your favorite **place to travel** be?
22. Who is your favorite **music group**?
23. In what month is your **birthday**?
24. What time is your **bedtime**?
25. How many **hours of sleep** do you usually get on a school night?
26. What is your favorite type of **dessert**?
27. What is your favorite **professional baseball team**?
28. What is your favorite **professional football team**?
29. How many years have you gone to the **school** you now attend?
30. Which **junior high** will you attend?
31. Can you **roll your tongue**?
32. Which kind of **earlobe** do you have?
33. What **section of the United States** were you born in?

34. What **country** did your ancestors come from?
35. How many **brothers and sisters** do you have?
36. What is your favorite kind of **music to listen to**?
37. How many inches **tall** are you?
38. What is your favorite **radio station**?
39. What is your favorite **video game**?
40. Which is your favorite **kid's movie**?
41. Which is your favorite **television program**?
42. What is your favorite **vegetable**?
43. What is your favorite **kind of food**?
44. Are you **right or left handed**?
45. What size **shoe** do you wear?
46. What is your **favorite thing to do**?
47. What is your favorite **kind of candy**?
48. What **time** do you **arrive home** from school?
49. What **chores** do you do around the house most often?
50. How much **allowance** do you get each week?
51. How many **cars** do you have in your family?
52. What is your favorite **tourist spot**?
53. What is your biggest **pet peeve**?
54. What is your favorite **sport to play**?
55. What **time** do you get up in the morning on school days?
56. What is your favorite **holiday**?
57. Who is your favorite **male celebrity**?
58. Who is your favorite **female celebrity**?
59. Who is your **hero**?
60. What is your favorite **brand of shoe**?
61. What is your favorite **magazine**?
62. What is your favorite **time of day**?
63. What is your favorite kind of **fruit**?
64. Who is your favorite **cartoon character**?
65. What is your favorite kind of **soda**?
66. What is your favorite **brand of clothing**?
67. What is your favorite **sports utility vehicle**?
68. Who is your favorite **female vocalist**?
69. Who is your favorite **male vocalist**?
70. Which is your favorite **mall** to shop?
71. What **language** would you most like to learn?
72. What is your favorite **musical instrument**?

GRAPHING PROJECT DESIGN FORM

Name _____

QUESTION/PROBLEM: _____

PREDICTION/HYPOTHESIS: (What do you think you will find out?)

_____

_____

HORIZONTAL AXIS HEADING: (The squares on the grid from right to left.)

_____

VERTICAL AXIS HEADING: (The squares on the grid from top to bottom.)

_____

WHAT WILL YOUR CATEGORIES BE?

_____

_____

MATERIALS: _____

FINDINGS: (Use tally marks to show your survey results.)

CATEGORY 1 _____

CATEGORY 2 _____

CATEGORY 3 _____

CATEGORY 4 _____

CATEGORY 5 _____

OTHER _____

FINDINGS: (A written statement using ratios and percentages.)

_____

_____

_____

_____

CONCLUSIONS: (Was your prediction correct? Explain why or why not.)

_____

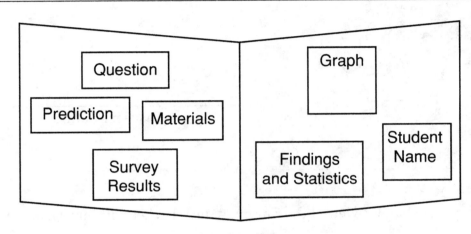

File Folder

REQUIREMENTS:

1. Completely fill out the Project Design Form.

2. Have all of your work checked by a "spelling expert."

3. All written work should be done in pen, preferably black thin marker **OR** typed in an appropriate sized font that is large enough to read from a distance.

4. All graphs should be drawn on graph paper using a picto, line, bar, or circle graph.

5. Index cards may be framed with colored construction paper **OR** borders may be drawn around the cards with felt-tip markers.

6. When you glue your work into the folder, **remember: Less is better.**

7. You will be responsible for orally sharing your results with your classmates.

8. Free-standing graphing folders will be displayed on desks for peer observation.

Dear Parents,

Please look over the Math Survival Packet with your son or daughter. Help him/her to select ten activities for the year. Find some things you think you and your child can do together, if possible, and some things your child must do alone. The purpose of this packet is to make your child an active math participant in his/her own world. It also will hopefully teach him/her responsibility and organization.

Thank you.

_____

Teacher's Name

- -

I have received and reviewed the Survival Math Packet with my son/daughter.

We have selected the following ten activities to participate in during the school year: _____

_____

_____

Child's Signature _____

Parent's Signature _____

SURVIVAL MATH

(Experiencing Math in Your Everyday Life)

Your Name _____

Due Date: _____

WHAT WILL YOU BE DOING?

Each month you will be responsible for doing one of these mini-math projects. There are over sixty to choose from, and you only need to choose **ten** of them. Of course, some of you will be so motivated, you'll want to do more, but the minimum requirement is **one per month**. By doing more quality activities than required, you can improve your math grade.

SPECIFIC DIRECTIONS:

1. All activities should be neatly written.

2. Each activity should have either a chart, a list of important data, or a copy and/or original form attached to it. Some proof of how you obtained the information should be included in the activity.

3. Where you get your information should be plainly cited on the activity.

4. The activity number and a heading should introduce each activity.

5. Some activities are more difficult to research and will take more time to do. They are worth more. You should get started on the activity early in the month.

6. You will be graded on a 10-point system by your teacher. Each activity is worth from 1 to 10 points. The highest score is a "10." Receiving a "10" on an activity means that you have gone well beyond what someone your age usually would do. It means that you have put out extra effort and have done more than your teacher might expect someone in your grade to do. It means you have extended the activity to its fullest and have gone beyond the limits of the activity. Of course, it also means that your work is the neatest and the most thorough.

SURVIVAL MATH PACKET

Directions, continued

7. If you can think of some other math life skills activities that will give you a better understanding of your place in the math world, feel free to create your own. Just check it out with your teacher first.

8. Stars (*****) indicate the amount of involvement you must have to complete an activity. The following chart shows the involvement scale:

***	**Minimum involvement necessary**	Usually can be done with very little adult help, time, or extra materials.
****	**Extra involvement necessary**	Usually takes some extra materials, transportation, communication by phone, and/or some extra time.
*****	**Maximum effort needed**	Usually takes research, transportation, parent involvement, and/or additional time and effort.

9. You will be keeping all of your activities in a special folder throughout the year so that everyone will be able to see how well you have progressed and the effort that you have put into these math activities.

10. Keep a record of your activities on the *Survival Math Record Sheet*.

SURVIVAL MATH PACKET

MINI-MATH ACTIVITIES

1. The next time your parent goes to the **grocery store**, you are to tag along. Using a grocery list that your parent and you have prepared, select 5 items for which you will do a comparative price check. In other words, if you are going to buy spaghetti, compare its price with two other brands. Make sure the weight on the package is exactly the same, and that the item is a very close match. Tell the name of the grocery store you shopped at in the title of the chart. Use a chart similar to the one below to show the comparison. ****

XYZ MARKET COMPARISON	
Spaghetti Prices	
Anthony's Spaghetti	$1.19
American Beauty Spaghetti	.99
Lady Lee Spaghetti	.79

2. Select any ten **grocery items** you normally use in your family. Make a comparison chart showing the difference in price at three different grocery stores. *****

	Von's	*Ralph's*	*Lucky*
1 gallon Dreyer's vanilla ice cream	$3.50	$4.59	$4.89

3. While you are driving in your neighborhood, look at the **price of gasoline** on the service station signs. (You may observe the prices at any three stations, not just those listed below.) Compare the price for unleaded, unleaded plus, and super unleaded at three different service stations over a three-week period. Compare the rise and fall of gas during this time. Make a chart similar to the one below, or draw a graph to show your comparisons.

Price of Gasoline at Three Different Gas Stations

STATION	*Shell*			*Chevron*			*Union 76*		
Week	1	2	3	1	2	3	1	2	3
Unleaded									
Unleaded Plus									
Super Unleaded									

SURVIVAL MATH PACKET

Activities, continued

4. Go to the bank with your parent. **Open a savings account**. Find out how much interest the bank will pay you for having your money in your account. Make a copy of your application or paper work, or fill out a deposit slip to show you know how to fill it out correctly. What is the minimum amount you must have in order to open a new account? Try to put a small amount of money away in your account each month. ****

5. If you already have a bank account, **make a real deposit** or a pretend deposit. Fill out a deposit form at the bank. If you can, fill out a duplicate form and hand it in to your teacher. Also fill out a withdrawal slip to show that you know how to fill out that form. Include the slips in your final project. Discuss with your parents how the bank teller assisted you, and if you think he/she was a courteous employee of the bank. ****

6. Keep a record of how many miles your parents' car or cars travel in a three-week period of time. Record the **mileage** at the end of each week. Find the average number of miles the cars traveled per week. Make a chart to show your findings. ***

7. Go to a **restaurant** with your family. This should *not* be a fast-food restaurant. Check to see if the waiter or waitress has added the bill correctly. Check to see if there is sales tax added to it. Ask for a copy of the bill. How much of a tip should be given to the waiter or waitress? Actually pay the bill for your parents. Did you get the right change back? Get a menu, if possible. Keep a record of what the dinners were and how much each cost. Figure out the average cost of each person's dinner. ****

8. Help your parent fill out a **catalog order** form from a store like Sears or JC Penney. Include a picture of what you are ordering. If you don't really buy anything, hand in that form. If you are placing a real order, make a copy to hand in to your teacher. Don't forget sales tax and shipping costs. ***

9. Go to a **travel agency**. Find out how much a trip to a place you would like to travel would cost for you and your family. Include a brochure from your dream trip or make up a brochure of your own to advertise the place. Write a paragraph telling why you would like to travel there. ****

10. Go to two **car agencies** and price the cost of a brand-new car that you and your family would like to have. Give a range of prices from the least expensive to the most expensive model. Include a brochure about each of the cars that you look at. List the special options that are on the car. Write a paragraph about your favorite car and what you like about it, or make a collage of cars that you would like to have. *****

SURVIVAL MATH PACKET

Activities, continued

11. If your parents are willing to share the information with you, find out how much money your monthly **gas and electric bill** is. Look over the bill and find out if you pay more for the gas or more for the electricity. Divide the bill by the number of days in the month, and find the average cost for use each day. You may want to compare your consumption last year with what you used this year. Make a list of six more things you can do to cut down on the cost of your bill. ****

12. If your parents are willing to share the information with you, find out how much your monthly **water bill** cost. See how many gallons of water you actually used during the billing period. How often is your family billed? Write it down. Divide it by the number of days of use, and find out how much an average day of water usage is for your household. Find out how much difference there is between the amount of water you used this year compared with last year in the same time frame. Write a paragraph or make a list (5 to 7 items) of things you can do to conserve water. ****

13. If your parents are willing to share the information with you, find out how much the basic service is for your **telephone** per month. Also find out the amount you pay for long distance calls. Divide those amounts by the number of days in the month and find out how much your average phone bill is per day. ***

14. Call the airlines or talk with a travel agent. Find out how much **airfare** is to a place you and your family would like to go. Compare the price with one other airline. Find out if each airline offers any special deals. What is the best deal you can find, and how much would it cost your family to make this trip? Write a short summary about your findings. ****

15. Go to a store like Target, Wal-Mart, Woolworth's, or Kmart. Go on a **shopping spree**. Select five items you would like to buy. (You do not really need to buy anything.) List the items you have selected, how much they cost, and figure out how much tax you would have to pay on the total. ****

16. Go to a **fabric store**. From a pattern catalog, choose a dress, costume, or outfit that could be made for you. How much fabric would you need? Select some fabric and calculate how much the outfit would cost you to make. Don't forget buttons, zipper, pattern, thread, and any other finishing items you will need. If you can, actually make the item. Compare the price of the item with one you can find in the store. Show the price of each of the items, how much fabric you got and its cost, and how much the sales tax was. ****

SURVIVAL MATH PACKET
Activities, continued

17. Look in the newspaper for the last five game scores of your favorite professional **baseball team**. List each of the games by who they played and the score of that game. Figure out the average number of points the team actually scored during these five games overall. ****

18. Go to an **open house**—one where a house is for sale. Get a sheet that shows how much that house costs and how much the monthly payments would be. Highlight those amounts. Hand in that sheet. Write a paragraph telling what you liked and disliked about the house. Did you think it was a good buy? Why? ****

19. Find out how much season tickets for a local, state, or national professional **baseball** team cost for the year. Find the cost for the most expensive seats and the least expensive seats. Figure out how much both kinds of tickets will cost for your entire family. Show your calculations. ****

20. Go to the **public library**. Ask about its rates for overdue books for both children and adults. Figure out how much an adult would have to pay if the book was overdue for 5, 10, 15, and 20 days. Figure out the cost of a children's book for the same period of time. ****

21. Find how much **minimum wage** is in the United States. Considering that an average adult works 40 hours per week, calculate how much a person making minimum wage would make in one week, in one month (4 weeks), and in one year (52 weeks). Remember, this does not really show the actual amount a person would take home because the government takes its share, but it is an approximation. ****

22. Figure out the differences among the costs of admission to the **major theme parks** in your state or city. Make a list to show the amount you would pay to get into each of the parks—no discounts—just the admission price. List the parks and the costs of admissions. Try to think of at least five parks. After you have the correct prices, figure out how much admission to each of the parks would be for your entire family. *****

23. Compare the price of a regular hamburger, a regular order of French fries, and a medium soda from three **fast-food restaurants**. List the restaurant and the cost of each. Figure out the price of these items for you and your family at each place. Second, find a coupon for one of the restaurants, and compare the individual item price with the coupon price. How much do you actually save? Include the coupon and, if possible, a menu or advertisement from the restaurant. *****

SURVIVAL MATH PACKET

Activities, continued

24. Compare the price of a **trip** from your city to another major city in your state by car, plane, train, and bus. You will need some help from your parents. Show your information on a chart and tell how or where you got the information about the prices. *****

25. Obtain a schedule for the **subway, trolley, and/or bus** in your city. Tell how close to your home the pick-up point is and the exact place you can catch the ride. How much is the fare for each mode of transportation? Find out how far it is to the main part of your city. Also tell the time involved in making those trips. If you want to, actually ride the trolley, subway, or bus and write a paragraph about the experience. Include a schedule if you can. ****

26. Go to the **post office** and ask for the least expensive way to send a package to New York City from your city. Ask what the rate is. Figure out how much packages weighing 2 pounds, 5 pounds, and 7.5 pounds would cost to send. Find out what the differences are in the service you will get. Write the information in paragraph form. ****

27. Find out how much an **18-hole round of golf** would cost at two local golf courses. See which one is the better deal. Also compare the cost of using a golf cart at both courses. Find out the best time of day when the prices are the least expensive and figure out how much money it would cost for your entire family to spend the day golfing and using a golf cart. Can you tell why most families do not take up golfing as a family sport? ****

28. Research two **bowling alleys**. Find out which one has the better value for playing two lanes of bowling for each member of your birthday party group. Your party will consist of ten 11- and 12-year-olds. Remember that you also need to include the price of bowling shoes for each party-goer. Tell the name of the bowling alley, where it is located, and the charges you would acquire. ****

29. You are researching the best price for taking 5 of your friends to the movie for a party. Find the best price for three **movie theaters** close to your own house and the best time of day to go. Also include the price of one small box of popcorn and one small soda for each of your five friends, plus yourself. *****

30. For your birthday party your mom has said that you may take seven friends and yourself to the **skating rink** (roller or ice). Find out how much money it will cost the eight of you to go skating. Also include the price of one hot dog and one medium soda for each member of your party. You may want to compare the price of two skating rinks in order to get the best deal. Show your mathematical figures on paper. **** **or** *****

31. Cut out **coupons** for your parents using the Sunday newspaper for two weeks. Keep them in a shoebox. Have your parents go through them with you and select the ones they will actually use. Keep a list of the name brand, item and amount of the coupon, how much money will they actually save on their grocery bill for that two-week period of time? If you saved that much every two weeks, how much would that be for a month? A year? ****

32. Find out the cost of season tickets for the next season for your favorite professional or local college **football team**. Compare the price of the most expensive seats and the least expensive seats for your own family. How much does parking cost at the stadium of this team? How much is that in all for an evening at a sports event? ****

33. Figure out the cost of feeding your family for **dinner** (your choice of food) at your local stadium. It may be a college, professional, or high school stadium. Tell what stadium you are attending. List each food item and its cost. Make sure you have the actual cost of the food items at this year's prices. ****

34. Find out how much it costs to rent a **limo** for four hours and for eight hours. Find out how many people you can take with you according to the limo rules. If you had the maximum number of people in the limo, how much would it cost per person? Write a paragraph telling what you would actually do if you took a limo ride for four hours. *****

SURVIVAL MATH PACKET

Activities, continued

35. Find out the actual amount of **sales tax** you would pay in each of five states. You will need to research how much sales tax is in each state, including your own state. Figure out the difference in price for items amounting to $10; $100; $1,000; $5,000; and $10,000 if you purchased the item in each of the five states. *****

36. Compare the cost of an **oil change** for your car at three different locations. Make a chart to show the comparison. Name each of the businesses you check out. If someone in your family changes his/her own oil, find out how much difference there is. ****

37. Find out the difference in cost of **car insurance** for a 16-year-old boy and a 16-year-old girl. You may want to check out more than one insurance company. List all the companies you check and how much the cost of insurance is for the teenage girl and boy. *****

38. What is the cost of a **fishing license** in your city and county for an adult for a day and for a year in both fresh water and in salt water? What is the age by which you must obtain a fishing license? Draw a chart to show your findings. Write a paragraph telling where you would fish and for what kind of fish. ****

39. Make an investigation into your **kitchen**. Look for items that show measurements. List them. Write a paragraph telling how measurement is used in the kitchen and what it would be like if we didn't have measuring spoons and cups. ***

40. Preview a book of **recipes** from your kitchen. Actually prepare a food item where measuring cups and spoons are used. Write your recipe on a notecard. If you can, share the food item with your classmates. Make a list of ingredients you needed to prepare the food. ****

41. Find out how much it would cost to have your local **newspaper** delivered to your house for a month. Compare it with what you would pay if you purchased it daily at a newsstand. ****

42. Find out what the cost of renting an economy, mid-size, and luxury **car** is at a local **rental agency**. Compare it with another agency's prices. What are the extra charges for mileage and gas consumption? *****

43. If you have a sports arena in your city, find out how much **season tickets** are for a team that plays there, or for three other events that take place there during the year. Also find out how much it costs to park in the parking lot at the arena. ****

SURVIVAL MATH PACKET

Activities, continued

44. How much is a **season ticket** for one of your **local college teams** for a student and for a non-student? How many home games will there be? Divide the number of home games into the price of the season ticket. What is the average cost per game? ****

45. If you live in a large city, find out the cost for **season tickets for the ballet, opera and symphony** for the most expensive and least expensive seats. Also find out how many performances there are of each and the name of each. Actually attend one of the performances, and write a paragraph describing the experience. Don't forget to share the program guide with your teacher. *****

46. If you have a **junior theater** in your city, find out how much season tickets are for you and your family to attend. Is there a difference between the adult price and the child's price? What are the names of the performances and what dates will they be held? ****

47. Choose three of your favorite **magazines**. Fill out three subscription forms by yourself. What is the cost of each for a year? Either make a copy of the forms or hand in the forms for your teacher to see. ***

48. **Interview** a person who works in a job where mostly numbers are used. Get a detailed description of the job, why math is important to the job, what education the person needed, how much math the person had to take, and what the person likes or dislikes about his/her job. Write a summary of the interview. ****

49. Ask your parents to show you the correct way to **write out a check**. If your parents have an extra check, write a pretend one and hand it in to your teacher. If you can't use a real check, copy one, or make up a check of your own to prove that you know how to write one correctly. Hand in at least three checks to different businesses and for different amounts. ***

50. **Interview your parents**. Ask why they think math is important to them in their lives. Ask them to tell you how they use math everyday, in their jobs, at home, and in their personal lives. Also ask them why they think you should do your best in math at school. Make a list of 5 to 7 reasons math is important to them. ***

51. Ask your parents to assist you in looking through the **tools in your garage or basement**. Find out how the tools involve measurement. Look for the metric numbers. Write a paragraph telling how items in the garage or basement are involved in math and what parts of math you need to know before you can use them effectively. ****

SURVIVAL MATH PACKET
Activities, continued

52. Take 6 to 8 **photographs** of math in your world. Write captions underneath each photo to show its math importance. ****

53. Compare the **values of money** from 8 to 10 different countries. Tell what it is called, from what country it comes from, and how much it is worth in U.S. dollars. Share the information with your class. *****

54. Look through the **weather** section of the newspaper for ten days. Compare the high and low temperatures of your city in graph form. Locate the highest temperature and the lowest temperature in the United States for those ten days also. Put them on a separate chart. ****

55. Make a chart of the **metric system** of measurement compared with the U.S. and Britain system of measurement. How are they different? Write a paragraph explaining why the whole world should or should not be using the metric system of measurement. *****

56. You are looking for the best price on your favorite CDs. List the five CDs you want to purchase. Compare the price of these CDs at three different **music stores**. Show your comparison in chart form. *****

57. Find out how much it costs to **camp** overnight for your family at one of our county or state parks. Also, how much does it cost at a local, favorite tourist spot **hotel** in your city? Figure out the difference for a week of vacation at both places. *****

58. Spend part of the day with a **person who works in a mathematics field**. Write a summary of what you learned while you were observing the job.*****

59. How much is the fare for a **taxi** in your city per mile? Is there a difference between taxi companies? If so, tell the difference in prices of three taxi companies. What other charges is a person responsible for if he/she rides a cab? Figure out how far it is from your house to the airport and how much it will cost for that ride. *****

60. **Save cans or bottles** for a determined period of time. Decide how you will spend the money you earn (out for dinner, to an amusement park, a movie, or a sports event). At the end of the time, add up the amount you earned and see if you have enough money to do what you wanted to do. Show your calculations on paper. *****

61. **Make up your own activity**. Check out your idea with the teacher before you get started. *** to ****

SURVIVAL MATH RECORD SHEET

Student's Name _____

Month	Activity #	Approximate time spent	Self-evaluation
September			
October			
November			
December			
January			
February			
March			
April			
May			
June			

SURVIVAL MATH EVALUATION FORM

Evaluator: _____

Name of person whose paper I am

evaluating: _____

How many points would you give this
paper? 1-10

_____

Why did you give it that many points?

_____

_____

Is the paper neat? _____

Is there a title on the paper that tells you
what activity has been done?

_____

Is there a number of the

activity? _____

What do you like about what has been

done on this activity? _____

_____

How would you improve on this activity?

_____

_____

My Name _____

Activity Numbers that I did _____

The things I liked about what I did

were _____

_____

_____

I think I could have improved by

_____

_____

Compared with the other activities I have
seen, I think my activities are

_____

_____

I think I deserve _____ points on my
activities.

Which activity was the best?

_____ Why? _____

_____

How much time did I spend on these

activities altogether? _____

_____

I learned _____

_____

_____

by doing these activities.

SUPER BOWL _____
MATH ACTIVITY PACKET

Your Name _____

Due Date:_____

Since this is Super Bowl Week, you will be asked to keep your eyes and ears open so that you can see how heavily influenced this game is with math facts and statistics. You have been given some pertinent information in class having to do with statistics from *The Guinness Book of World Records*, and your notes can be helpful to you for some of the information below.

You may find the answers to these questions by **watching the television**, **listening to the radio**, **looking at the newspapers and magazines**, or just **by asking people who already have the information**. Of course, many things may be learned by just **looking at the Super Bowl itself on Sunday**.

Everyone is to answer as many questions as possible. Some questions can be answered right now, while others will need to wait until during, or even after, the game ends. Don't get stressed if you can't find an answer. Just do your best. Try to make this a fun, fact-finding mission and get everyone looking for answers. We'll discuss our findings when we return to school the day after the Super Bowl.

You will be evaluated on how many activities you have completed independently, the neatness of your work, the effort you put into your activities, and the quality of your work.

SUPER BOWL MATH PACKET
PRE-GAME ACTIVITIES

Score Prediction:

NFC Champions _____

AFC Champions _____

1. How many Super Bowls have there been? _____

2. What was the *point spread* predicted before the game began? _____

3. How much is airfare from your city to the Super Bowl city? _____

4. How many miles is it from your city to the Super Bowl? _____

5. How many miles are between the two Super Bowl Champions' cities?____

6. If an average hotel room in the Super Bowl city is $200.00 per night, how much would it cost two families, each with its own room, to spend three days and nights there? _____

7. If it cost a person on the average $30.00 a day for food in the Super Bowl city, how much would it cost two adults to eat three meals a day for three days? Show your calculations. _____

    _____

    _____

8. Give the names, numbers, and positions of two offensive players and two defensive players of your favorite superbowl team. _____

    _____

9. How much money does the Super Bowl ring cost that every player receives for his participation in this game? _____

10. How much money will a Super Bowl player earn if he is on the winning team? _____

11. If 50,000 people each by one soda ($2.50) and one hot dog ($3.00) at the Super Bowl, what is the total amount spent by all of these people for food?

    _____

SUPER BOWL MATH PACKET, *continued*

12. How many feet high is the goal post? _____

13. Using the facts given to you in class or by looking them up in the ency-clopedia under *football*, find the perimeter and area of the football field. Perimeter: _____ Area: _____

14. Write the first 50 Roman Numerals: _____

    _____

    _____

    _____

    _____

15. What is the number in Roman Numerals of this Super Bowl? _____

16. What is the width and length of the football? _____

17. What geometric shape is a football? _____

18. What is the name of the Super Bowl stadium? _____

19. What is the face value of a Super Bowl ticket? _____

20. How are Super Bowl tickets distributed? _____

21. How many tickets is each player allocated? _____

22. How much is the airfare from the home city of the NFC champions to the home city of the AFC champions? _____

23. Take a survey of 10 to 15 friends and family members of all ages before the game to find out who they predict to win. Make a chart to show the results.

24. Find out the height and weight of five football players in this Super Bowl. Write their names and their vital statistics.

SUPER BOWL MATH PACKET, *continued*

25. Create three math questions for your classmates using information about the Super Bowl that you have acquired through your pre-game research. At the end of each question, write the correct answer upside-down. _____

_____

_____

_____

_____

_____

_____

_____

_____

_____

_____

_____

DURING-THE-GAME ACTIVITIES

1. What is the score of the Super Bowl game at the end of each of the following times?

   Quarter 1: _____

   Quarter 2: _____

   Quarter 3: _____

   Quarter 4: _____

2. What is the temperature (Fahrenheit and Centigrade) at game time in the city where the Super Bowl is being held? _____

   In your city? _____

   In the home city of the NFC Champs? _____

   In the home city of the AFC Champs? _____

3. How many people actually are in attendance at this year's Super Bowl?

   _____

SUPER BOWL MATH PACKET, *continued*

4. How many people will the Super Bowl stadium actually hold? _____

5. How much did it cost to advertise for one minute of time during the Super Bowl? _____

6. What companies did the most advertising during the game? _____

7. What was the face value of the Super Bowl ticket? _____

8. How many touchdowns were made by each team?_____

   NFC Champs: _____   AFC Champs: _____

9. What was the aggregate score of this year's Super Bowl? _____

10. Did the score of this game make any records as far as the greatest or narrowest *victory margin*? _____

11. Give the name and team name of the *heaviest person* mentioned during the game. _____

    The *tallest person.* _____

12. Listen to the ages of the players mentioned. Who is the oldest and what position does he play?_____

13. Which AFC and NFC player has played in the most Super Bowls counting this one? _____

14. What time does the Super Bowl begin in Super Bowl city? _____

    In your city? _____

    In the home cities of both the NFC and AFC Champs? _____

15. Which professional team has won the Super Bowl the most times? ____

    How many times? _____

16. Using a stopwatch or second hand on your watch, time one commercial break. List each advertiser, and the number of seconds each used for commercial time. Using the amount of one million dollars per minute, figure out how much each commercial segment cost the advertiser.____

    _____

    _____

    _____

SUPER BOWL MATH PACKET, *continued*

Compare the two teams in the categories below:

	AFC Champs	**NFC Champs**
Yards Rushing		
Yards Passing		
Yards Penalized		
Sacks		
Pass Completions		
Time of Possession		

POST-GAME ACTIVITIES
(Two required)

1. Create a collage (9 inches by 12 inches) on construction paper showing how math is used in the Super Bowl.

2. Write a paragraph ($\frac{1}{2}$ to 1 full page) telling how math has been used in the Super Bowl. Attach it to your collage.

3. Make a list of at least five other math-related facts you have learned about having watched the Super Bowl, or from reading or listening to news programs.

4. Plan a menu for a Super Bowl Party. Tell what you would buy and how much it would cost totally. You may want to use the food section of the newspaper to help you out. Show a picture of what you want and how much it will cost.

5. Draw a map of the United States. Locate your city of residence, and the city where the Super Bowl is being played, and the two cities where the championship teams are located. Label them.

6. Write a paragraph describing one of your favorite commercials you saw during the Super Bowl. Tell why you think it was worth the company's money to run it.

7. Write a paragraph telling why so many people have Super Bowl parties and what the benefits are to the people who attend.

8. Interview a person who went to the Super Bowl. Tell what he/she thought were the high points of the trip and get an estimate of how much the trip cost. Ask questions about the Super Bowl city, the fans, the stadium, the weather, traffic, etc.

9. Write a paragraph telling which Super Bowl team is your favorite and why you like it.

10. Draw illustrations of each team's football jerseys. Use color.

11. Write a paragraph about the halftime show. Be complete in your detail.

12. Make up a word search with the teams in the NFL. Have someone try to locate each with a highlighter.

13. Scramble up to 15 Super Bowl words (for example: rtreuaackqb = quarterback). Have a partner unscramble them.

14. On a map of the United States locate 15 pro football team cities. Show where they are and label them.

15. Make up your own idea to show how math is important to the Super Bowl.

SUPER BOWL MATH PACKET
SELF-EVALUATION

Finish your answers on the back of this sheet if you run out of space.

1. What did you enjoy most about this Super Bowl math project? _____
   _____
   _____

2. What did you learn by doing it? _____
   _____
   _____

3. How did you go about finding the answers to these questions? _____
   _____
   _____

4. Did anyone help you find answers? _____
   Who? _____
   How did that person(s) help? _____
   _____
   _____

5. How much time do you think you put into completing this packet? ____
   _____
   _____

6. What was the most difficult part of this activity? _____
   _____
   _____

7. How would you improve this math activity? _____
   _____
   _____

8. If you were going to give yourself a grade on this packet, what would
   you give yourself? Explain your answer for your teacher. _____
   _____
   _____

A CHILDREN'S COUNTING BOOK

(The reading/writing/math/art connection)

In the next week, your teacher will be showing you a variety of counting books that help little kids learn their numbers. You need to look closely at the illustrations and words, so that you will be able to successfully create a picture counting book for our primary students at this school.

You may have some counting books at home that you enjoyed as you were learning to count. Please bring them in to share with your classmates. The more books we review, the better our own books will be.

HERE'S WHAT YOU NEED TO DO:

1. Look at a variety of counting books. There is a full set of these books in the classroom.

2. Decide what language you would like to use for writing your book (French, Spanish, Italian, Vietnamese, Hebrew, etc.).

3. Choose the numbers you want to use (1 through 10, even numbers, counting by 10's, counting by 5's, and so on).

4. Use a piece of 12" by 18" white construction paper. Fold it into eighths. Sketch your word/picture/number plan onto the paper, using one square for each page of your book. Use pencil. This is a rough draft. Your teacher will proofread it for you and offer suggestions.

5. Decide on the size, shape, and color of your book. You may want to create pages that are shaped like animals, objects, foods, and other items that refer to your theme.

6. Decide on what kinds of materials you will use (construction paper, watercolor, cloth, wallpaper, markers, puffy paint, pencil, tempera paint, snapshots, magazine pictures, coloring book pictures, newspaper pictures, etc.).

7. Create a simple storyline that connects your numbers to a central theme, such as. . .

    One day I was cleaning out my closet and I was surprised to find. . . one (1) wool mitten, two (2) white boots, three (3) plastic puzzle pieces, and so on.

8. If you are using unlined construction paper to create your book, make sure you draw the lines for your words with a ruler. If you are unsure how to do this correctly, ask your teacher for help. Since you are an upper-grader, this is a skill you should acquire to assure you of quality.

9. Lightly draw and write your words/pictures/numbers onto your final paper.

10. Design a cover with some reference to counting in the title.

11. Design a *Dedication* page.

12. Design an *About the Author* page and include a picture of yourself.

MORE PARTICULARS:

1. The book should be **no larger than** 9" by 12". It may be a shape.

2. All writing should be neat and in **printing** or **typed**. Your teacher will provide you with opportunities to practice your printing, just in case you have forgotten exactly how the little kids learn how to print. If you use the computer, use a large size font because little kids need to see the letters larger than you do.

3. You may work independently or with one other partner.

4. All materials should be kept in the manila envelope or construction paper folder that you receive from your teacher, so that you do not lose any of your work.

5. All materials that you are working on should be at school each day. You will have some time in class to work on this project. Your teacher will help you to evaluate your work as it is being done in class.

6. All writing should be edited by an adult or an in-class *Writing Expert* before it is rewritten in final form.

DUE DATES:

_____Rough Draft

_____Cover/Title page

_____Dedication page

_____About the Author page

_____Final Book

LOOKING MORE CLOSELY AT COUNTING BOOKS

Student's Name _____

You are to take a long, hard look at 3 to 5 picture books that appeal to you, or that you think little kids would want to pick up and read. On the lines below, write a brief summary of the book, tell how the author made the book appealing, how the illustrations are drawn, how many numbers the book explains, and why you think kids would or would not enjoy the book. There may be some other ideas you'll want to explore. Use sentences to explain your answers. If you run out of paper, use a piece of notebook paper to finish your thoughts.

    Your teacher has shown and discussed with you some of the common elements found in counting books. Here is a reminder list, in case you have forgotten.

- Use of bright colors
- Rhyme
- Cultural diversity
- Different languages
- Repetition
- Use of animals/symbols
- Large illustrations/few words
- Storyline to tie the numbers together
- Cut-out spaces for parts to pictures
- Variety of ways to count

Name of the Book:_____

Author: _____ Illustrator _____

# of Pages: _____ # of Numbers Used:_____

Special Features: _____

_____

_____

Summary: _____

_____

_____

_____

_____

Name of the Book: _____

Author: _____ Illustrator _____

# of Pages: _____ # of Numbers Used:_____

Special Features: _____

_____

_____

Summary: _____

_____

_____

_____

_____

- -

Name of the Book: _____

Author: _____ Illustrator _____

# of Pages: _____ # of Numbers Used:_____

Special Features: _____

_____

_____

Summary: _____

_____

_____

_____

COUNTING BOOK SELF-EVALUATION

Name _____

1. I liked, disliked (circle one) doing this project because _____
_____

2. By creating this book, I learned _____
_____

3. What do I think I did well? _____
_____

4. What could I do to improve my book if I were to do it again? _____
_____

5. I think I spent about _____ hours working on this book.

6. I'd like my teacher to know _____
_____

7. Did I procrastinate (leave this project until the last minute) or did I pace myself
when I was working? How did I spend my time? _____
_____

8. Who checked the final draft of my book? _____
_____

9. I really liked _____ 's book because _____
_____

10. Grade myself with a +, √, or – for the following areas:
    Storyline _____
    Creativity _____
    Color _____
    Neatness _____
    Cover _____
    Special features: _____
    Effort _____
    Illustrations/Pictures _____

11. I think I deserve a (an) (A B C D F) on this project because _____
_____
_____

COUNTING BOOK TEACHER EVALUATION

Student's Name _____

Storyline _____

Creativity _____

Color _____

Neatness _____

Cover _____

Special Features _____

Effort _____

Illustrations/Pictures _____

Comments/Suggestions: _____

_____

_____

_____

_____

_____

_____

REVVING UP THOSE RESEARCH SKILLS

There are probably thousands of parents across the country today pulling their hair out because their child has uttered those words, "I have a research paper to do." Many times these dreaded words cause havoc in the family environment because often a child's research paper becomes a *parent's* research paper. Recently a group of our teacher friends was socializing and one mother said, "Can you believe it? Mrs. _____ assigned my child a two-page research paper, and he is only in second grade!" The mothers all gathered around to retell their own horror stories about their children's research assignments.

The common thread that frustrated the women was not the fact that the project was assigned, but that no formal instruction had been given to assist the children in actually knowing what to do. Most research was usually handed out for homework, and most of the time the children had no idea where to begin. It is important for parents to be involved in their child's education, but it is also essential that the children acquire skills as they get older so that they can work independently or with minimal assistance from their parents.

Fundamental research skills need to be taught to all children, beginning in the primary grades with the organization of simple facts. Probably one of the most important skills our students will need in order to be successful in the 21st century is the ability to access and utilize the abundance of information and resources available. As students need to acquire research skills throughout their educational pursuit, a school should look at building a comprehensive research program that develops students' skills to a higher degree of sophistication each school year.

The important thing for teachers to remember is that research is a skill that needs to have direction and instruction, just like teaching a new mathematics concept. It is also necessary for teachers to realize that research must be appropriate to the age level.

TEACHER-DIRECTED RESEARCH INSTRUCTION: THE MINI-RESEARCH PROJECT

In the upper grades, students should be given basic instruction in research skills. For instance, before the thematic mystery unit begins, the teacher might take the entire class through a mini-research project to make sure that when they need to do their own independent research, they know the correct way to do so. Students would have clearly structured, guided instruction and modeling of the procedures and steps involved, as well as clarification of the teacher's expectations and standards before beginning their own independent work.

In October, students are always captivated with scary or mysterious-sounding places of the world. So why not capitalize on their curiosity and excitement? Here's an approach you might take:

- Hand each child three different articles about Bigfoot (one from an encyclopedia, one from a book, and another from a magazine or periodical). Each child should have exactly the same materials.

- Each article is placed in a different colored folder with a label indicating what source it came from.

red construction paper folder	yellow construction paper folder	blue construction paper folder
Bigfoot Article from a book	Bigfoot article from a magazine	Bigfoot article from an encyclopedia

- Impress upon the students that different facts can be discovered if three different sources are used. Not all writers' facts agree with one another.

- One of the articles should be read aloud as a class or in small groups. For instance, the Bigfoot article from a magazine could be read aloud by the teacher. It is helpful if a transparency is made of the article and projected on an overhead projector. This is an excellent opportunity to model to students how to highlight important information on which they will take notes. The students must be aware that most times they will not be able to highlight information found in a book. Therefore, they must take notes and keep them in an organized manner.

- After the article is read, instruct the students on notetaking. Explain that when notetaking, everyone must keep their notes organized. It is essential that any material that is read needs to be referenced. That means students need to record the name of the book or article, the author, and the page where the information was found. That is probably enough for the intermediate grade levels or for those children who have learning difficulties. As the child progresses into the middle school, more complete referencing may be required.

- In this mini-research project, the students are asked to color code their notes and bibliographical information. For instance, because the magazine article on Bigfoot is in a yellow folder, a yellow dot is used to identify notes taken from that magazine. The bibliographical information taken from the material is also color coded with a yellow dot. The intent of this system is that the students will begin to see the connection between the materials they use and the information they keep.

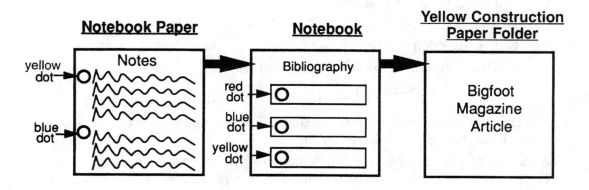

- All students receive a Research Notetaking Sheet. (See the end of this section.) Throughout the Bigfoot study, these notes become their guide for writing the research paper.
- All students receive an Information About Bibliographies sheet. (See the end of this section.) On this sheet, students find the correct form to use for referencing their papers. This should be kept in their three-ring binders. Students are again reminded to use the color-coding dot to show the book they are using.

The students continue the process by repeating the steps for the encyclopedia and the book articles:

- Highlight the important facts.
- Take notes from the source using the color-coding method. A red dot on the notetaking sheet is used to indicate that the information has been taken from the book, and a red dot is used on the bibliography page to connect the reference information, the book itself, and the notetaking.
- Blue dots are used to connect the notetaking with the bibliography reference and the encyclopedia.
- Three index cards are handed out to each child. The bibliographical information is written on each card (for the book, magazine, and encyclopedia).
- These cards are glued down by author's last name in alphabetical order on a 8-1/2" × 11" piece of colored construction paper. This will be labeled Bibliography and included with the rest of the mini-research paper.

As highlighting and notetaking are completed, structure a simple topic outline for students to use while formatting their paragraphs for their paper. Here is an example:

I. Bigfoot
    A. Introduction—Hook your reader
    B. What is it?
    C. Physical characteristics
    D. Location where it is found
    E. Evidence that has been found
    F. Other interesting information about Bigfoot
    G. Concluding paragraph

- The children use this basic format because all of the information can be found in the materials that have been selected by the teacher.

- A sample introductory paragraph is written for the students by the teacher. This modeling helps the students to see how an introductory paragraph will hook the reader and make him/her want to read more. Now the children are asked to write their own introductory paragraphs. The teacher should have students volunteer to share their paragraphs. It is very helpful to have student samples read to the entire class so that those students who are having difficulty initiating their own, may hear more ideas. Some students may need to basically copy the teacher's example or one of their classmates.

- The second paragraph is written together as a class. Students create a topic sentence and then the class adds details and ideas that complete the paragraph.

- The third paragraph is written in pairs or triads. One child records, while the other two review their notes and find the information that would complete the topic. Having the children write this paragraph on a large piece of lined tagboard or lined newsprint gives more examples for the rest of the class to review together. These cooperative research groups work together and then read these paragraphs to the class.

- The fourth paragraph can also be written cooperatively and reviewed as a class. The more examples the students have, the easier the process is for all students.

- The last two paragraphs can be written independently by the students. By now the students should have the idea of how to develop their own paragraph writing by using their notes. Pair sharing of the paragraphs, or oral reading by individuals for the rest of the class, can be used to assure the students that what they have written is factual and sufficient.

- Because all the students have exactly the same materials to use for this mini-research project, the students can see how their peers used the information differently to make more detailed or complete paragraphs. All students should be able to write a "barebones" paper with the notes they have taken. Some students will be able to extend their writing because they are able to look through all three references and draw that information together to make very thorough paragraphs. Each child is writing at his/her own developmental level.

- Since this is a rough draft, students are encouraged to write on every other line of the paper. Corrections and additions can be made more easily.

- When they have finished their rough drafts, all students read their paper to a partner.
- Peer editing is done with the same partner.
- Rough drafts are reviewed by the teacher.
- Rough drafts are rewritten in neat handwriting or typed.
- The suggested length is 1 to 2 pages. Think carefully about what your goal is in teaching research skills. It is important that you do not encourage your students to copy information. Long research papers *do* encourage copying of material. When a report is kept short, students are more likely to write the paper in their own words; and in essence, that is what we want to teach children to do. The word plagiarism should be discussed with students, and some of the consequences for plagiarizing in the academic and business worlds might be noted.
- After the paper is officially completed, instruct the students on ways they can embellish or extend their paper by adding little "extras." Some of these embellishments that may be added to this research paper are:

  1. a hand-drawn map of where Bigfoot has been seen
  2. a newspaper or magazine article giving more information
  3. an illustration of or picture of Bigfoot (drawn or copied)
  4. a diorama or model of Bigfoot
  5. other (to be checked out with the teacher before proceeding)

Other *required* parts of the research project are:

- Cover
- Title page
- Basic outline
- Research paper itself
- An "extra"
- Pages numbered
- Bibliography

This mini-research project establishes some necessary groundwork and structuring for students. Because they have received guided instruction and modeling of the process, they are now more skillful in writing their own research papers. While this is fresh in their minds, you should capitalize on the moment and remind students that they will be participating in a Learning Fair later in the year, and that the information they have just learned will be helpful in the near future.

WHAT IS A LEARNING FAIR?

A learning fair is a developmental process in which students become totally emerged in the excitement of research. They choose a topic that is of interest to them, and then they actively pursue their subject. By the end of the research period, children have the tools to explain information about their topic to others—and through their growth of research skills—to become an "expert" who motivates other students to learn more about their subject. The process encourages active participation by all students, and allows them to become more skillful at researching at their own developmental level of understanding. The goal in a Learning Fair project is to spread excitement about the wonderful world we live in, and introduce the resources that are available to pursue through research.

HOW MUCH TIME SHOULD A LEARNING FAIR TAKE?

This is an individual choice. You should plan on a period of about four to six weeks. Depending on how much skill the students have to begin with, and how much time you will actually spend using class time, the time can be extended or shortened accordingly. Class work periods should be built into the project so that you may observe how the students are progressing and who needs help. Twenty- to 30-minute periods of class time several times a week usually works well with older students. As the end of the project nears, longer work periods may be needed. Some work will need to be done as homework.

HOW DO YOU GET STARTED WITH THE LEARNING FAIR PROJECT?

- To begin with, *inform the parents and students about the project early in the year.* Most schools have a Back-to-School Night, where the teachers explain their program for the year. This is a perfect opportunity to broach the topic. This gives everyone a stretch of time to be thinking about what subjects are interesting to the students. As students take trips or visit monuments, parks and museums, they can be searching for topics of interest.

- About a month before the project begins, hand out *a parent letter* so that parents are informed again about the project. A tear-off sheet for the parent to sign and return to school assures you that all families have been informed.

- *A bulletin board* should be created by the students and the teacher with suggestions for research projects. Students can look through National Geographic, encyclopedias, library books, magazines, newspapers, etc., to generate interesting topics.

- *Brainstorming sessions* also are good opportunities for students to hear of topics they might want to become involved with. With partners, the students can create a list of possible topics. Topics can be written on large charts or can be placed on sentence strips and added to the bulletin board.

- The more time you spend at the beginning of this project by helping students to think of subjects for their research, the easier the whole process will be. If students have a topic in which they are genuinely interested, they will be motivated to continue seeking information.

- Because students self-select their own topics, they have ownership in the project. The opportunity for choice should be built into assignments for older students. When they "buy into" their work, they are much more enthused about it.

- The decision must be made if students will work in partners or independently. This decision may be made by you for the whole class or by the students themselves. With the older children, working independently may be the preferred way. In other classrooms, you may want to give some choice, but then assign others into partners. It is your knowledge of the classroom that will set this choice in motion.

- Since the students have already been taken through a mini-research project as a class, they have a solid foundation to begin with. The groundwork has been laid out, and the process is ready to begin.

WHAT MATERIALS AND RESOURCES SHOULD THE STUDENT HAVE AVAILABLE?

- A class trip to the library is always a good starting point. Contact the librarian at your school and also at a nearby public library. Students can take a field trip and learn how to locate materials for their reports.

- Most school districts have a *central media center* to order materials. Students can look through the catalogs to see what is available. They may learn how to order these materials and preview them for their classmates. Films, videos, study prints, and other audio-visual materials can be ordered and the students can become skillful in this aspect of research.

- Parents should be asked to volunteer their time for helping students who do not have very much parental assistance from home. Research is difficult in the initial stages, and some students need individual attention to get started. All students are not self-starters. *Parent volunteers* can work on a one-to-one basis with those students who require extra help at any stage of the research. Peer tutoring can also be arranged, such as a sixth-grade student helping a fourth grader in developing a research idea.

Setting Deadlines

The students should be aware of the importance of deadlines. As you fill out the *Learning Fair Due Date Schedule* (at the end of this section), be sure all students are given ample time to complete each part of the project. You also need to make consequences for students who do not meet the deadline due date. The importance of a due date should be emphasized. Monitoring these due dates can be time consuming; therefore, ask for assistance from a student monitor, an aide, or a parent volunteer. A chart might be set up in the room, and, as students complete an activity, they may receive a dot, a star, a check mark, or a sticker.

The Learning Fair Packet

All students should receive their own copy of the entire *Learning Fair Packet*, which is kept inside their three-ring binder for use throughout the project. Punch holes in the packet so that the pages are firmly attached to a section of their notebook. Each child then has all of the information at his/her fingertips so that there are no misunderstandings about what the expectations are between the school, the home, and the child. If all students do not have a binder, construction paper folders can be used.

Reviewing the Student/Teacher Evaluation Form

Before the project begins, the students should review the *Student/Teacher Evaluation Form* (at the end of this section). By going through the three parts of the project and making sure the students know what is being asked, many questions will be answered. The students can always refer back to this form when they are not sure of the guidelines.

WHAT ABOUT THOSE EXTRAS?

Students need to be shown what a graph, chart, map, illustration, etc., should look like. Therefore, you must model some examples. Save samples of student projects from previous school years to provide excellent examples of what students can do to enhance their project. You might make a copy of student work so that they may be used the next year. (Five cents is a real good bargain at the copy store!) These student sample copies may be filed for future use.

WHY SHOULD THE STUDENTS KEEP A DAILY LOG?

During the first few weeks of research, the students receive a 20- to 30-minute period of class time to work on their projects. This allows you to observe who is having difficulty and who is "off and running." Students really motivate each other. There always seems to be someone who is "out in the front of the pack." These are the students who provide motivation for the rest of the class. Daily updates, reviews, and sharing opportunities give eager students an intrinsic reward for their hard work. Those students who are lagging behind are given a little encouragement and assistance in getting started. Filling out the *Daily Log* (see the end of this section) at the end of each work period helps students to reflect on what they have actually accomplished, and focuses them on the time it has taken to accomplish that task. The *Daily Log* can be collected by the teacher at the end of the week and evaluated.

THE DISPLAY BOARD

- The size of this display board may be determined by the teacher. 12" × 18" chipboard works well for upper graders. Sometimes two panels provide a large enough area to "tell the story" of their research. Some students may require a larger surface provided by three panels. You should help determine what size is needed by the student(s). The display board is the visual representation and culmination activity for the research. Since a report is usually not read by too many others besides the teacher, the display board becomes the student's visual expression of his/her topic.

- The display board consists of two or three pieces of chipboard that are taped together on the back side. The boards may be covered with either butcher paper or wrapping paper. Some students like to purchase their own boards. At our school, we recycle the boards each year. The students take home their butcher paper with their display of materials, but the chipboard remains at school for use by other students the following year.

- As the students are researching, they can also be working on preparing materials for their display boards. During the class work periods, the students can make their maps, graphs, charts, and other "extras."

- Many students like to use the computer to type their written information for the display board. Since the display board is a larger surface area and needs to be seen from a distance, students usually use a larger font than used on their research paper. If the students do not type their written work for the board, they may print the material on 5" × 7" notecards.

- All work is in rough draft form until it is glued onto the display board. Pencil written notecards and typed material must be peer corrected and approved by a teacher. All written work must be redone in a black thin marker, so that it is readable from a distance.

- Students are not allowed to glue any materials onto the display board until all parts are completed. This is because many students don't have the eye for filling in space. Spacing of materials is very important. There should be a minimum of background space showing.

- The children choose the background color paper and two foreground colors of construction paper.

- To enhance the eye appeal, each item that is going to be placed on the board is framed or backed with a piece of colored construction paper. Some students double-mount their items. For the older students, the use of the paper cutter may be taught. Therefore, students create even borders for the items they use.

- After all parts are self-corrected, peer corrected, and adult corrected, students arrange the items on their board. No gluing is allowed until an "expert spacer" gives final judgment. This person helps the student make sure the materials that are being used are spaced evenly on the board, and very little background is showing.

- Gluing down of materials is now permitted. Students need to be reminded that "less is more" in the case of glue. Even upper-graders don't always have the concept that gluing can ruin a perfectly good project. Since rubber cement is not allowed in many schools because of its toxicity, glue sticks are preferred over white glue.

- All gluing is done in class. This project is to be the student's work, not his/her parents. Since a Learning Fair ends with a presentation to parents, the unveiling of these projects is not done until the night of Open House or Parent Night. It is important that the final product be done in class so that it is a surprise to the students' parents.

The Oral Presentation

As a culmination of this entire process, the students need an audience to demonstrate their knowledge and accomplishments through presentation to their peers. As the students complete their research and display boards, time must be built into the program to practice the oral presentation.

- All students should practice with a partner.

- All students should deliver their presentation to the entire class. The peers should have the opportunity to evaluate their classmates. (A peer evaluation form is included at the end of Chapter 15, *Making Oral Language Come Alive in the Classroom*.) It is a good idea to have at least three students evaluate each presenter. The presenter receives these evaluations. Teachers should review the standards and model constructive praise and criticism of presentations.

- Use of the video camera is an excellent evaluation tool. Students should have the opportunity to see themselves in action as they present.

- Another classroom can be invited to rotate through the Learning Fair.

- Parents are invited to walk through informal presentations of the topics. Cookies and juice can be served. This is a perfect way to get all parents to visit the classroom.

HOW WILL THIS PROJECT BE EVALUATED?

All students received an evaluation form before the project actually began. This let the students know what they needed to do and the number of points each part was worth. As the project develops, the student should continue to refer to the evaluation form to assure his/her understanding of the guidelines and standards that are expected of him/her.

On the evaluation sheet the point values are added up and the individual teacher may grade the project as he/she sees fit (e.g., 90% to 100% is an "A," and so on). The teacher evaluates each paper, display board, and oral presentation.

The students are taught how to evaluate themselves, making a comparison with the other students' projects. The video camera puts things into perspective. Students are able to observe how theirs is unique or different from their classmates. Some students are really hard on themselves, while others are overly boastful. Through peer, self, and teacher evaluation, the student should begin to see a realistic view of how his/her project compares with those of other class members. A final grade is given and comments are made by the teacher.

LEARNING FAIR ESSENTIALS

1. This project consists of 3 parts: the *Research Paper*, the *Display Board*, and the *Oral Presentation*.

2. All parts should be neatly written in cursive writing or typed.

3. *The Research Paper* should be ____ to ____ pages in length. It should be written in your own words. It should include the following things:

    a. An attractive cover

    b. A title page

    c. A topic outline

    d. A bibliography (at least 3 references should be used)

    e. "Extras" (see the attached "Extras" sheet)

    f. Numbered pages

4. *The Display Board* will consist of 3 panels. The total size is ____ by ____ . You may design items for the board at home, but the final placement of materials will be done in class. ***NO GLUING* WILL BE DONE BEFORE THE BOARD HAS BEEN CHECKED BY THE TEACHER**. Try to limit the number of "copied" pictures that you use. Make your own materials such as maps, charts, graphs, etc. A combination of written descriptions and graphics should be used. Tell the story of your subject in words and pictures.

5. *The Oral Presentation:* See the *Student/Teacher Evaluation Form* to see what items you will be graded on.

LEARNING FAIR DUE DATE SCHEDULE

DUE DATE   RESEARCH ACTIVITY

_____   Make a list of all subjects you are interested in.

_____   Narrow your choices to one subject.

_____   Visit the library to find books on your subject.

_____   Notetaking—1st check.

_____   Notetaking—2nd check.

_____   Notetaking—final check.

_____   Topic Outline—main topics.

_____   Topic Outline—main topics and subtopics.

_____   Bibliography index cards.

_____   Final form of bibliography.

_____   Rough draft check—1st three paragraphs.

_____   Rough draft check—2nd three paragraphs.

_____   Rough draft check—3rd three paragraphs.

_____   Rough draft check—last paragraphs.

_____   Title page.

_____   Research paper cover.

_____   Display board sketch.

_____   Final research paper (cover, title page, outline, research paper, bibliography, and "extras").

_____   Lettering for display board.

_____   Pictures, graphs, maps, etc., framed on construction paper.

JUST A FEW TOPIC SUGGESTIONS
FOR YOU TO THINK ABOUT . . .

1. Optical Illusions

2. The Honey Bee and Its Life Cycle

3. U.F.O.'s

4. Orthodontics—How It Works

5. All You Want to Know About Ice Cream and More

6. The Poisonous Snake and How It Affects Us

7. The Great Houdini—Why Does His Fame Live On?

8. Earthquakes—Nature Shakes the Earth

9. Police Dogs and Their Training

10. How Does a Person Become a U.S. President?

11. A Close Up Look at the Game of Soccer

12. The History of Rock-and-Roll

13. Dreams and What They Mean

14. Dyslexia and How It Affects a Person

15. Right Brain/Left Brain—What Are the Characteristics?

16. I Want to Be an Astronaut—Here's the Real Scoop

17. The Life Story of an Ant—Why Do We Need Them, Anyway?

18. The Black Hole

19. The Story of Elvis Presley and His Impact on the Music World

20. Henry Ford and His Contributions to the People

21. Twins: The Tale of the Two of Us

22. What is ADD?

23. Mummification and Why the Egyptians Used It

24. The Development of Women's Rights in U.S. History

25. Japanese Relocation in the U.S.A. During World War II

ADD SOME OF THOSE "EXTRAS"

You may want to add some of the following things to your project to make it "come alive." Try to make them "homegrown." In other words, make them yourself—don't just use photocopies from books. Add those personal touches that show your reader more about your subject. Here are some things you can add to make your research paper more interesting:

1. Make your own map of the area you are researching.

2. Add a chart that tells more about your subject.

3. Take a survey/Make a graph showing your results.

4. Interview an expert.

5. Invite a guest speaker expert to talk with your class about your subject.

6. Find a newspaper or magazine article about your subject.

7. Preview films, videos, or soundstrips from the library or other school supply or materials center.

8. Add music to your presentation.

9. Dress in costume to get more "into" your topic.

10. Make a diorama or model.

11. Make a special food that is associated with your subject.

12. Take snapshots of some aspects of your report.

13. Make a slide show to enhance your research.

14. Draw an illustration or picture of some aspect of your research.

15. Make a timeline to show the progression of time for your subject.

RESEARCH NOTETAKING SHEET

Student's Name _____

On this sheet you should begin to record information that will be included in your report. While you are reading, jot down some important facts you want to remember when you actually start to write. In the column on the left, write the author's last name and the page number you found it on. If you need more space, staple this sheet to any other pieces of notebook paper where you take notes. You'll use these notes to assist you in writing your research paper.

Author's Last Name	Page Where Found	Notes

INFORMATION ABOUT YOUR REPORT

Student's Name _____

1. To write this report, you will need to use three references or sources. You should have at least one encyclopedia and one book. You might also have a magazine or pamphlet.

2. As you start to take notes, jot down the important information about the book or encyclopedia that you are using.

3. Make a list of the information in the spaces below.

* *

BOOK

Title of book _____

Author _____

Publishing company _____

Where published _____

Date published _____

Pages used _____

* *

ENCYCLOPEDIA

Title of article_____

Name of encyclopedia _____

Volume # _____

Year of publication _____

Pages used _____

PERIODICAL/MAGAZINE/PAMPHLET

Title of article _____

Author _____

Title of magazine _____

Volume # _____

Month and year of publication _____

Pages used _____

* *

If you have other books, encyclopedias, or pamphlets, list them below in the same manner as shown in the examples.

_____

_____

_____

_____

_____

_____

_____

_____

_____

_____

_____

INFORMATION ABOUT BIBLIOGRAPHIES

1. A bibliography is a list of the books, encyclopedias, pamphlets, magazines and other reference materials you use to form your ideas for your research paper.

2. While you are taking notes about your subject, you should also make a list of the materials you are using.

3. There is a particular way you must list your materials in your bibliography:

   a. Alphabetize items in your bibliography according to the last names of the authors, or, where there is no author, by the first important word in the title.

   b. When an entry takes more than one line, indent all the lines after the first.

   c. See the examples below to help you with your bibliography order.

PERIODICAL

Duncan, Todd. "The Newest in Tennis," *Journal of Active Sporting,* Vol. 3 (Apr. 1979) p. 30.

ENCYCLOPEDIA

Smith, John. "Football," *World Book Encyclopedia,* Vol. 7 (1979), pp 312–320.

BOOK

Kelley, Brent P. *100 Greatest Pitcher*s, New York: Bison Book Corp., 1988, pp 15–20.

RESEARCH DAILY LOG SHEET

Name _____

Research Topic _____

Keep a Daily Record of the time you spend working on your research project. Keep an accurate account of what you accomplish during your work time. Your teacher will be reviewing this with you occasionally.

Date	Time Begun	Time Ended	Tasks/Accomplishments

STUDENT/TEACHER EVALUATION FORM RESEARCH PROJECT

Student's Name _____

WRITTEN REPORT

Title _____ (+5)

Cover _____ (+5)

Neatness _____ (+10)

Information _____ (+20)

Introduction _____ (+5)

Conclusion _____ (+5)

Bibliography _____ (+5)

Outline _____ (+5)

Spelling/Grammar _____ (+10)

On Time _____ (+10)

Pages Numbered _____ (+5)

"Extras" _____ (+10)

Ink/Typed _____ (+5)

Total Points _____ (+100)

ORAL PRESENTATION

Total time taken _____

Knew information well _____ (+10)

Well prepared _____ (+10)

Looked at audience _____ (+5)

Spoke loudly _____ (+5)

Used notes well _____ (+5)

Posture of delivery _____ (+5)

Answered questions well _____ (+5)

Stayed within time limit _____ (+5)

Total Points _____ (+50)

DISPLAY BOARD

Good use of color _____ (+5)

Straight positioning of lettering _____ (+5)

Pictures/graphics well framed _____ (+5)

Neatness of written and drawn materials _____ (+10)

Good spacing of items _____ (+5)

Personally created materials _____ (+5)

Spelling/grammar/punctuation _____ (+5)

Lettering, gluing, erasing _____ (+5)

Use of preparation time in class _____ (+5)

Total Points _____ (+50)

FINAL GRADE

WRITTEN REPORT _____

DISPLAY BOARD _____

ORAL PRESENTATION _____

IN-CLASS WORK HABITS _____

TEACHER'S COMMENTS:

_____

_____

_____

_____

GETTING THE MOST OUT OF STUDENTS THROUGH SCIENTIFIC INVESTIGATION

Teachers always have a captive audience when they are demonstrating a scientific principle through a simple experiment. Many students view science as a magic trick. They question how the "trick" really worked. Building scientific investigation skills is really very simple because all life is one big investigation. We must teach students the importance of being observers in the world around them. As children become better observers, they are actually becoming more keen in scientific observation skills.

Although many school districts have adopted science curriculum with kits that include numerous hands-on activities, other districts have to rely on more teacher-created materials that take children through the wonderful world of science. Below are listed some basic principles and ideas to keep in mind for developing a science program with a minimum amount of expense:

- Science should be fun. Children should enjoy investigating the world around them because from the time they were babies, they have been naturally inquisitive.

- Children should see that science is related to other areas of the curriculum such as art, math, and social studies. Helping children to see that there are different branches of science that connect the world to each of them is an important process.

- Science materials should be easily accessible.

- If we want students to investigate, then we should have science experiments based on common household items and easily acquired materials.

- *A science station* can be made available for students during the day. Simple materials can be laid out on a table, possibly one new experiment per week. When students complete their work, or during free choice time, or before or after school, the children can experiment with the materials and learn to follow easy-to-read instructions that explain fundamental principles of biology, chemistry, and physics. Since science experiments involve step-by-step instructions, those students who have difficulty with more complicated reading assignments find these instructions less threatening. Many children who have learning disabilities are perfectly comfortable with hands-on experimentation. Because many of the experiments are also illustrated, these challenged students can find a greater degree of success.

- Schools where science materials are not abundant can request assistance and materials from parents. These inexpensive materials—such as plastic cups, spoons, measuring spoons and cups, jars, washers, corks, food coloring, balloons, tongue depressors, baking soda, small bowls, cornstarch, etc.—can be stored in shoeboxes or plastic containers in the classroom. A parent letter ("Wish List") requesting donations of supplies early in the school year can get any classroom started.

- A science cart can be accessible for all teachers to use. A parent may be interested in volunteering time to gather together and replenish simple materials for science. The cart may be used by all teachers on a check-out basis. Having the cart housed in an area where teachers see it frequently will remind teachers of the materials that are available. Old microscope kits are also very valued in the elementary setting.

- Inviting guests into the classroom who have expertise in science is always helpful. Many parents are really excited about sharing their field with the students. If you are somewhat limited in science knowledge, asking for assistance from a parent is a step in becoming more confident. Some of our best science lessons have been offered by parents in the area of dissection. Having a person who is willing to share this expertise with the students is a real bonus.

- Students love to conduct science experiments. As mentioned in Section 15, *Making Oral Language Come Alive in the Classroom*, children can make a science experiment into a presentation. For instance, during one month, all students could be required to present an experiment for their oral language experience. Students can work alone or with partners. The presentation can be videotaped by the teacher.

- Fun and simple science experiment books should be available for students within the classroom. Books such as *Homemade Slime and Rubber Bones* by William R. Wellnitz, Ph.D., *Amazing Science Experiments with Everyday Materials* by E. Richard Churchill, and *Simple Science Experiments with Everyday Materials* by Muriel Mandell are inexpensive and at an appropriate level for all elementary grades. The procedures are easy to follow and provide many experiences that students will enjoy.

As the students reach the middle and upper grades, it is important that teachers give them the opportunity to develop a science experiment that is more sophisticated and complex. Many students enjoy the behavioral sciences. Watching and observing the actions of people is fairly easy to do. As students generate their list of interests, you can assist them in forming an experiment. Students can be guided in their discovery that almost anything can be turned into a science project, and that science can be fun!

One teacher had his students list all the things in which they were interested. Several girls stated that they liked to "hang out" at the mall. The teacher then suggested they design a science project that allowed them to spend time at the mall as a threesome. They came up with the idea that they would like to observe what age group of people would bend down to pick up certain denominations of coins. They used pennies, nickels, dimes, and quarters. As you can well imagine, the girls did have an initial cost and they knew that they would not see the money again. They each placed seven dollars into the experimental pot. At the mall they observed people and found out that older people bent down most often for all denominations of money, while younger people bent down most often only for the quarters. The girls enjoyed the company of each other, and the idea that they were at their favorite location. They were able to observe over 100 subjects in a four-hour session that was an enjoyable and educational experience.

Another experiment at the mall involved a mother and her daughter watching shoppers as they exited the mall. They kept a tally of each shopping bag that was carried out of the mall. At the end of the two-hour period of time, they had observed over 150 people and were able to see what store had been visited most often. A third experiment at the shopping mall was designed by two boys who wanted to find out who (male or female) carried the bag when couples were shopping. They observed 125 couples.

What about the boy who said that he didn't like to do *anything*? The teacher asked him if he would just like to sit in a lawn chair and watch the traffic on his street. He agreed that was just about like doing nothing. He sat by a stop sign in his neighborhood and observed cars to see who made complete stops, who stopped but went over the crosswalk lines, and who didn't stop at all. This boy was involved in science even though he liked the "lazy" form of participation.

When kids feel they can put together an experiment that is enjoyable and relevant to the world around them, then they become more interested in pursuing a finished product. Not all science experiments require huge amounts of apparatus. Many students view science as a complicated subject that requires extensive research, documenting, observation, and equipment. When students start seeing that the principles they learned in the primary grades can be examined more extensively in the upper grades, then the task becomes easier. Creating behavioral science experiments can be one choice for students while others might want to engage themselves in the more traditional topics.

As in the case of the *Learning Fair* described in Section 17, some teachers may want to give their students the experience of a Science Fair involving research, scientific investigation, a display board, and an oral presentation. The entire class may concentrate on science. Other teachers may want to give the students choice where they may pursue science, but other students may choose to participate in the research of other areas of the curriculum. A true Learning Fair takes in the interests and choices of each child. Therefore, a child might investigate the topic of earthquakes or weather phenomena, while another child may study politics (*What Does It Take to Be a U.S. President?*), or history (*Was the Boston Tea Party Really a Party?*), or music (*A Look at Music Through the 1950s*).

Involving students in enjoyable science experiences, and capitalizing on that natural curiosity of investigation and observation in the upper grades, will establish some fundamentals of a lifelong interest in scientific pursuit.

BIBLIOGRAPHY AND RECOMMENDED RESOURCES

Churchill, E. Richard. *Amazing Science Experiments with Everyday Materials*. New York: Sterling Publishing Co., Inc., 1992.

Mandell, Muriel. *Simple Science Experiments with Everyday Materials*. New York: Sterling Publishing Co., 1992.

Richards, Roy. *101 Science Tricks*. New York: Sterling Publishing Co., 1992.

Strongin, Herb. *Science on a Shoestring*. Menlo Park, CA: Addison-Wesley Publishing Co., 1985.

Wellnitz, William R. *Homemade Slime and Rubber Bones!* New York, NY: Tab Books, 1993.

SCIENCE PROJECT DUE DATE _____

    This is a more complicated experiment than the oral experiment you did earlier this year. You will need time to actually do it. I won't be handing you a lot of homework during the next two and a half weeks, so use the time you are given. Don't leave it until the last minute. You may do this project at school, at home, or in the field (the mall, grocery store, gas station, intersection, etc.).

    The focus will be on *observation*. The ideas I have given you are what I call BEHAVIORAL—that means we are observing the way people act in certain situations.

    Here are a few of the experiments we talked about in class . . .

1. At the mall:

    a. Watch couples at the mall. Design an experiment to see who (male or female) carries the bag while shopping.

    b. Observe the bags people carry at the mall. Design an experiment to see which is the favorite store.

    c. Leave coins (penny, nickel, dime, quarter in an open area). What is the speed for picking up these coins?

    d. What age group is most likely to pick up a coin at the mall?

    e. What kinds of foods do people eat at the mall? Observe those walking around or go to the food court area.

2. At the intersection:

    a. What kinds of cars (vans, pickups, or other) tend to use a turn signal when turning?

    b. At a crosswalk, how many cars stop behind/in front of a crosswalk?

    c. What is the most popular car type or color within the intersection?

    d. What is the most popular state license plate?

3. At the grocery store/gas station:

    a. What store has the lowest prices on 15 selected foods?

    b. What is the decrease/increase of gasoline prices at 3 different stations over a two-week period of time?

    c. Do more women than men put their own gas in their cars? (If you live in a full-serve state, who comes to the gas station more often—men or women?)

4. At the school:

    a. Give 50 students a taste test to see which drink, cookie, etc., is preferable.

    b. Show students pictures from magazines of different foods on cards to determine what food they would select as their favorite.

    c. Show students pictures of faces of people. Ask them which one they would prefer as a friend or neighbor.

    d. Color cookie dough (blue, red, green, etc.). Which color cookie is preferred?

    e. Take a generic cookie/product vs. another brand of cookie. See which is preferred by certain ages of children.

    f. Take a non-fat product, and compare it to a "fat" product. See which is preferred by students at your school.

These are just a few ideas. Try to create something of your own. Have fun with this!

REQUIREMENTS:

1. Use a Large Sample of Subjects (Between 25 and 50).

2. Try not to do all your observation in one day. Break it down so it is manageable.

3. Create a question that you want to answer.

4. Make a prediction of what you think will happen (*Hypothesis*).

5. Make a list of materials you need.

6. Make a list of the procedure you will use so you are prepared. (Explain exactly what you will be doing.)

7. Write your conclusions and findings after you have completed your observations. Show your findings in words, pictures, and graphs.

8. Take snapshots of your experiment as you are working. These will be real assets when you are done. If you are working at school, I will be happy to take them for you. Just ask.

STUDENT INTEREST SURVEY
FOR SCIENTIFIC INVESTIGATION

Your Name _____

Answer the questions below. By doing so, you will begin to gather your thoughts on what interests you. This may help you to create a science question that you would like to pursue.

1. If you weren't at school today, what would you be doing right now?

   _____

   _____

   _____

2. When you get home today, list two things you will probably do.

   _____

   _____

   _____

3. If you could write one question right now about anything in the world, what would you ask?

   _____

   _____

   _____

4. Pick one of the things you are interested in and write two questions about it.

   _____

   _____

   _____

PARENT PERMISSION FORM SCIENCE PROJECT

Student's Name _____

Your child has expressed an interest in working on a science project entitled _____

_____

_____

    We will be working with your child in class to ensure that he/she knows the responsibilities involved in this project. Of greatest importance to me is for your child to be aware that whether working at home, in school, or in the field, he/she must represent our school in an appropriate manner. Since some of the experiments/observations involve being around cars, at intersections, at shopping malls and grocery stores, I would appreciate your support in providing some form of supervision in keeping your child safe and on-task during this observation time.

    I have set high standards for the observations, and have discussed at length the responsibility of each student in this scientific process. I would appreciate your reinforcement of high standards while the experimentation process is taking place.

    Thank you!

    I am aware of what my child will be doing for his/her science project and give my permission for him/her to pursue the project. I am willing to assist in helping him/her in this process.

_____
Parent Signature

I will act responsibly at all times during the scientific investigation.

_____
Student Signature

SCIENCE PROJECT INFORMATION SHEET

Name _____

1. State your **question**: _____

   _____

2. What is your **prediction/hypothesis**? _____

   _____

   _____

   _____

3. Make a list of the **materials** you will need to carry out your experiment.

   _____

   _____

   _____

4. List the steps you will take in order to carry out the experiment. (**procedure**)

   _____

   _____

   _____

5. Write in summary form what you find out. What conclusions can you make? Use
   the back of this paper. (**conclusions/findings**) _____

   _____

   _____

   _____

   _____

   _____

MAKING THE MOST OF MUSIC IN THE CLASSROOM

Music makes the world a happier place to be—and that includes the school. Unfortunately, as children approach the upper levels of the elementary school, music in the classroom diminishes. Some teachers, not having music backgrounds, do not feel comfortable teaching music; therefore, this part of the curriculum is left out. Music has a place in the primary classroom, but what about in the middle and upper grades in the elementary school or middle school?

BACKGROUND MUSIC

A very easy way to introduce music, one of the seven intelligences, into the classroom is to have it as background music. Learning-style research shows that many students perform better at their work if there is baroque or classical music playing during work periods. The introduction of music does tend to add the dimension of relaxation to the classroom.

A MUSIC CENTER

A music center may also be available to students with a variety of activities. (See the Plan-Do-Review section in Chapter 2, *Learning Developmentally*.) Having a keyboard for students to play is also fun. With guidelines, students can play and work out simple tunes as time permits.

MUSIC PERFORMANCES

Opportunities for students who possess musical talent should be made available. Once or twice a year, small performances for their peer group can be informally made. Those children who want to perform a song on the piano, trumpet, guitar, flute, etc., should be encouraged to participate. Students who want to sing should also have the chance. It is important for the teacher to draw out these students who might be apprehensive to "show off" their talent. We need to showcase our students for their strengths. Some of our students who are musical are not confident in other areas of the curriculum. As we prepare to plan for these special occasions, you must call attention to the specialness these students possess. The poise and ability to stand in front of others to perform is something to be commended.

On a larger scale, every year our school presents a talent show where students perform to the delight of the audience. The talent show is coordinated by a group of parent volunteers. After-school practice sessions are held to polish the acts. Any child who wants to participate can. Through gentle guidance, children are sometimes combined into groups so that everyone can be successful. Sometimes "canned" acts are suggested by the volunteers so that those who want to participate, but don't have an act of their own, will be able to perform. Because the talent show lasts for about two hours, the management of this endeavor is a tremendous task. Every year, though, our parents make the show better and more spectacular. The performances run like clockwork because of the outstanding direction of the parent volunteers. At our school, the performing arts are valued and the children's success and enjoyment is given top billing. That is why this talent show is such a popular event.

CONTEMPORARY MUSIC IN THE CLASSROOM

Singing is an enjoyable part of any day. Many of the records for older children are too high pitched for students to relate to. We must compete with the students' out-of-school experiences with music. Bringing appropriate songs into the classroom that students listen to on the radio and CD is one way of relating to their interests. Most children, by the middle and upper grades, like to sing with the songs on the radio. They know the words and are able to repeat them verbatim. It is essential that we provide some opportunities for children to sing on a regular basis in school. Contemporary songs delight the children, especially if they already know them from the radio. The following is a list of some popular songs that children seem to enjoy:

"The Yellow Submarine" (The Beatles)

"Kokomo" (The Beach Boys)

"Somewhere Out There" (*An American Tale*)

"This Used to Be My Playground" (Madonna)

"Surfin' USA" (The Beach Boys)

"Can You Feel the Love Tonight" (Elton John)

"The River of Dreams" (Billy Joel)

"Hero" (Mariah Carey)

"America" (Neil Diamond)

"Anytime You Need a Friend" (Mariah Carey)

"La Bamba" (Richie Valens)

"A Whole New World" (*Aladdin*'s Theme)

"Under the Sea" (*The Little Mermaid*)

"Part of Your World" (*The Little Mermaid*)

"We Are the World" (Michael Jackson)

"Heal the World" (Michael Jackson)

"It's So Hard to Say Good-bye to Yesterday" (Boys II Men)

"Wind Beneath My Wings" (From *Beaches*, Bette Middler)

"Circle of Life" (*The Lion King*, Elton John)

"That's What Friends Are For" (Dionne Warwick)

"Black or White" (Michael Jackson)

RHYTHM INSTRUMENTS

The older children also enjoy playing the rhythm instruments that they used in the younger grades. Occasionally provide these for experimenting with rhythm to contemporary songs. Children love the experience. Simple rhythm instruments can also be constructed by the older children. Giving them the chance to share their newly made instruments with younger children is also a very rewarding experience.

LISTENING TO THE RADIO

As a reward, students may earn the privilege of listening to their favorite radio station occasionally during more informal times of the day. Many students do perform quite well in class while their favorite music is playing. In our class a simple experiment was done during the math period. Students were given two computational tests, each of equal difficulty. One test was given while classical music was played, and the other was done while a local, popular radio station was played. Overwhelmingly, the class did better when they were listening to the popular music! After the results were in, the students who performed better with the popular music said they did so because they already knew the music, and it was less distracting. It seems that the classical music diverted their attention because it was unfamiliar, and may have caused them to focus less on the test and more on the unfamiliar sound of the "new" music. Although this finding is not particularly scientific, every year when the experiment is done, a greater number of students do better on this particular test with the popular music playing in the background. As teachers, we need to assess our children in many ways, and provide opportunities for them to interact with music of all kinds.

SHARING MUSIC OF DIFFERENT GENERATIONS

One of the most rewarding experiences in music for our students was when one of the classes was paired with a nearby senior citizens group. Once a month the students in the class and the seniors participated in an exchange. The seniors were paired with small groups of children, sharing their interests, hobbies, family life, pictures, jobs, etc., with the students.

On one day the seniors brought the music from their generation, and shared it with the students. Together the seniors and the students enjoyed the simplicity and "silliness" of the songs of the 1920s, 1930s, and 1940s. In our own way we were bridging the gap between the generations in a language that was very understandable. On another day the students traveled to the senior center and again the music was shared. The final outcome of this program was an appreciation and respect for the music of other eras. Music does tend to bring people closer together in enjoyable, nonthreatening experiences.

CROSS-AGE SINGING

Likewise, most of our upper-grade classes are buddy paired with a primary-grade class. The positive value of this exchange is long lasting. Part of these programs is the interaction of the children through musical experiences. The older students sing with the kindergarten and first-grade children. This gives the upper-graders a lot of enjoyment, bringing back fond memories as they reconnect to the songs that made their primary years so musically rich.

THE SCHOOL CHORUS

Having a school chorus can also be a way to build musical intelligence of a large population of children. Meeting once or twice a week with a teacher who is especially interested in music, children experience a wide variety of music. Special performances that allow children to express their love of music are appreciated by the community. If this large of an endeavor is not available to your school, possibly the formation of smaller afternoon or at-lunchtime music clubs is an option. The use of parents, volunteers, and other school personnel may be utilized.

INTEREST CLASSES

To tap the musical intelligence of the school community, "wheel" or "interest classes" can be set up. Children can either choose music as an option for a period of time, or all children can be rotated at some point into that group. Teachers who have a strong interest in music can, therefore, share their talent with many students, whereas another teacher who is uncomfortable teaching music can share his/her interest with another group of children. This team-teaching approach of using everyone's special talents and strengths makes everyone a winner.

MULTICULTURAL MUSIC

In many of our schools, a very diverse multicultural population is serviced. There is no better way to bridge the cultures together than through music. Teachers may center their music program around the music of the different cultures represented in their classroom or in the school at large. Having children bring in and share the music of their culture should be encouraged, and the children in the classroom should begin to appreciate and respect the shared music experiences that bring our cultures closer together.

The Multicultural Fair at our school is held to honor our diversity. Dances, songs, and games of our representative populations are performed by the individual classrooms. The upper-graders research each country being represented, and then go to the primary classrooms to share their knowledge. Each upper-grade group makes a flag and locates samples of authentic money for their country. Multicultural food is provided by the parents. Each child uses his/her three pieces of money (copies of the real thing) to choose the food from the country of his/her choice. Building good relationships among cultures and taking pride in our diversity begins with the simple elements of music and dance. The world looks smaller and less complicated when music is added to our school lives.

At whatever level our music ability is, we, as classroom teachers, must continue to provide experiences for children in music. To leave this important enjoyable relaxation experience out of the lives of our students is to neglect one of the seven basic intelligences. To enhance and balance a highly academic day, music may be the much-needed element that gives a challenging or unmotivated student a short reprieve so that he/she can regroup, take a breath, and go on.

BIBLIOGRAPHY AND RECOMMENDED RESOURCES

Carratello, John, and Carratello, Patty. *Focus on Composers.* (1994), Teacher Created Materials, Inc., P.O. Box 1040, Huntington Beach, CA 92647.

Krull, Kathleen. *Gonna Sing My Head Off—American Folksongs for Children.* New York: Alfred A. Knopf, 1992.

Rief, Sandra. *How to Reach and Teach ADD/ADHD Children* (chapter on music for transitions, calming, and visualization). West Nyack, NY: The Center for Applied Research in Education, 1993.

Vernon, Roland. *Introducing* (series of famous musicians such as Beethoven, Bach, etc.) Parsippany, NJ: Silver Burdett Press, 1995.

Walters, Connie. *Multi-Cultural Music—Lyrics to Familiar Melodies and Native Songs.* Minneapolis: T.S. Denison and Co., 1995.

REACHING STUDENTS THROUGH THE ARTS

When we take a look at Howard Gardner's Seven Intelligences, we realize that all of us are not equal in our ability to present ourselves artistically to the world around us. It doesn't take much effort for a child in the elementary school to look around the room and see that Johnny sees things differently from the other children. Johnny draws things the way they really look. The Johnnys of the world have natural ability or talent. They possess a high percentage of art smartness or spatial intelligence. These are the people who are able to perceive, manipulate, and recreate forms in the world around them. The question of whether art ability is inherent or is learned has been discussed and rehashed. Whatever the answer, the fact is that some people just are better at art than others. This is the case with both students and teachers.

Some people who are not naturally artistic must be exposed to many experiences in art so that they can become better at expressing themselves in this form. Yes, everyone can grow in their spatial intelligence by participating, focusing, and putting out some effort. Everything in life is difficult to someone—to what degree of difficulty is dependent on the person. Learning to visualize the world around us takes a lot of practice for some people. As we develop an eye for detail, the world becomes less complicated and comes together in meaningful ways. A child who is asked to draw something from memory many times is lost and frustrated because he/she has not learned to carefully observe the world in detail. Much of what we can do is dependent on the personalities we possess. Some people have a more global view of life and detail is more difficult to comprehend, whereas other people have keener observational skill and readily see detail around them.

Those of us who are more global see the world in a broader, more general way. We learn to interpret what we see in our own fashion. If we all looked at the world and interpreted it in the same manner, there would be no unique style.

451

In a typical classroom, we have a small percentage of students on both ends of the spectrum—artistically talented and artistically frustrated or challenged. The majority of the students fall within the middle range. It is your goal to assure each child a sense of success in his/her art development. Each and every child deserves the privilege of growing in the ability to express themselves creatively through drawing or other art form. You need to provide appealing and exciting lessons that encourage children's growth in their art development. All students may not be equal in their ability, but everyone can learn to enjoy their own success in art.

PROVIDING DRAWING OPPORTUNITIES

In education today there is a lot of emphasis placed on the importance of teaching children to draw. Most children love to draw. Too often, though, this form of art is limiting and constrained. Children want to make things look exactly the way someone else made it without thinking of how to modify or change it to become their very own idea. When children can't make theirs look like the model, some children become very frustrated and give up. Children who are perfectionists also become frustrated because they think their art can never be as good as what they are looking at. If we, as adults, are asked to draw a house, my house probably would look very similar to what the person next to me draws. That is the way we learned to draw a house from our own teachers when we were in elementary school. It is our hope that students today will have a foundation to see that all houses do not look the same, and that there are an infinite number of ways to draw different objects. We want children to learn some basic ideas of drawing, plus be given the freedom to modify and enhance their drawing skill. We should encourage children to reflect their own unique awareness and view of the world (not someone else's) in their pictures.

Since students love to draw, there should be many opportunities for them to do so. Setting up a center with art drawing books is an excellent idea so that students may choose what they want to learn to draw. No pressure is put on them to draw things exactly as the book has them. This center should be filled with materials that they may use to draw from, such as *How to Draw Monsters, How to Draw Horses, How to Draw People*, etc. The public library is a great source to use for these types of materials. Children need many opportunities to follow steps and put together parts to understand relationships in the world. When asked to draw a horse from memory, many students have no idea where or how to start. They have limited relational memory. How long is the tail of a horse? Is it longer or shorter than the neck? Is the body wider than the legs are long? Children need to have experiences that build understanding of size, shape, and relationships of body parts. A good idea is to have numerous pictures of what you are having the students draw. You should accumulate a myriad of illustrations and keep them in a file, so that when you ask students to draw certain things, there are examples to use. So that students do not copy, these pictures should be handed out to look at before the drawing begins, allowing time to observe what the object looks like, and then collected. This gives children a feeling of comfort because now they have something to recharge their detail memory of the object.

USING AVAILABLE RESOURCES

Developing a collection of art prints and pictures is easier than you think. Just call upon parents to save calendars, nature magazines and old greeting cards, and let them know what you are looking for. Over the course of a few years, your collection will be bulging and you'll have them to use to the children's delight.

Enlisting the assistance of volunteers who are willing to share their art expertise in small groups throughout the year is always a good idea. Teachers should be seeking out ways to pool the skills of parents and community members who can bring their talents to share with the children into the classroom. (See Section 3, *Increasing Home/School Communication and Parent Involvement.*)

The public libraries should be used extensively to access books to demonstrate the style and art forms prevalent in the works of famous artists and in periods of art history. Librarians usually are eager to assist teachers in finding materials to extend the basic curriculum that will be used in the classroom.

At our school, we are fortunate to have a wonderful art teacher, Pat John. Three of her lessons are provided for each classroom through the PTA funds. Individual teachers also use additional school funds that are available to them, or personal funds to hire her for classroom art projects. Her method is to center a lesson around the uniqueness of a famous artist and his/her personal art techniques such as Georges Seurat (dots), Georgia O'Keeffe (enlarging an item and making it bigger than life), and Grandma Moses (folk snow scenes). Study prints and samples are used to focus the students on each artist's styles. Books and art prints from the library, personal files, and the instructional media center are also used as visual aids to enhance the lesson. Built into each session is the success of each child.

Teachers should exhaust their resources and use creative funding to assure their students of extending their art skills to the fullest potential.

ILLUSTRATIVE AND EXPRESSIVE ART

Teachers need to give children opportunities to use their illustrative capabilities in all areas of the curriculum, not just during an art period. With whole language, children should be given many experiences in drawing their images of the characters, the setting, and the plot. During the social studies, science, and math periods of the day, drawing should be encouraged to provide better comprehension of the material being taught. Many children show their understanding of ideas through drawing, and teachers need to allow this form of informal assessment in the classroom. A child who may not be able to explain things intelligently in words may show his/her capabilities in drawing or picture form. (See Section 1, *Reaching All Students Through Their Multiple Intelligences and Learning Styles.*)

The upper-grade teacher should have a balanced art program between illustrative art (drawing) and expressive (creative) art. In expressive art, students develop a sense of originality. The *process* of the piece of work is far more meaningful than the final product. Children need experiences where ownership is sought because they pursue their own personal style stemming from their own heart, not from the teacher's direction. They need to be confident in knowing that their work is cherished and valued. They should desire to take credit for the idea they have truly created.

You can provide experiences in art where samples are shown, but where the children know that they can modify, adapt, investigate, and explore new approaches or directions within the guidelines of the desired project. You must instill a feeling that risk taking, originality, and uniqueness are valued and appreciated. When this idea manifests itself, students do feel successful knowing that what they have done is worthwhile and enjoyable.

Let's take a look at a project presented by Pat John to fifth and sixth graders that allowed a great deal of individual expression, gave children choice, was open-ended, and everyone was successful. The lesson was based on the unique style and technique of the artist, Georgia O'Keeffe. Because O'Keeffe herself chose to explore flowers, an imperfect part of nature, she looked closely at a small subject, placed it under a personal microscope, and enlarged it.

- First allow children to look through pictures of numerous flowers with their keen eyes. This helps them to recall what flowers in nature really look like.
- After perusing through the pictures, students were given a 12" × 12" piece of white paper and a piece of chalk. Looking carefully at the picture, they are asked to draw the flower in chalk from their own perspective. Allowing adaptation and modification from the child's eye is valued by the teachers. Most students do not get frustrated with this process because the subject matter is recognizable and easily designed for success.
- As the preliminary chalk drawing is appraised, children may make changes at any point.
- From this, the children are given limited direction on how to use color pastels and some simple shading techniques. It is up to the child to choose the colors he/she likes, even if the picture presents the flower in one particular color. Experimentation is part of this expression. There is no wrong way to feature this flower. The flower does not have to be whole. It could flow off the page.
- After this, the background is painted in a mixture of white and turquoise blue tempera paint.
- After drying, the flower is outlined with a mixture of half black tempera paint and half white glue that is gently squeezed out of an applicator bottle with a pointed nozzle.

Students, parents, and teachers were amazed at how lovely each and every one of the products turned out. The project allowed and encouraged the children to creatively observe, explore, experiment, and express a simple idea.

GRADING AND ASSESSMENT

Since many teachers are not formally trained in the area of art, it is difficult to grade or evaluate a finished product. A very simple form of evaluation might be for the teacher to use two simple statements on the back of the project or on a self-stick note.

"Something I really liked about your picture is _____ ." "A suggestion I would like to make is _____ ."

A system of plus (+) or minus (–) might also be used to let children know how they applied the skill they were being taught. Formal grading of art in the elementary school seems to discourage students in their ability to be expressive and creative. They can become more concerned about pleasing the teacher than in pleasing themselves. Since evaluating art is very subjective, teachers must be very careful in "grading" art because it can be the discouraging factor that squelches a child's enjoyment and confidence in a very relaxing pastime.

For assessment purposes, you are encouraged to start a student art portfolio. Keep the students' work on file so that the students and parents can see a development of art ability throughout the year. (Due to lack of space, schoolwide art portfolios have not gained a lot of momentum.) Can you imagine the excitement children would feel if when they exited the school as fifth or sixth graders, they were handed a history of their development in art since their kindergarten year? Only one or two pieces of work each year could be saved, much of it chosen by the child him-/herself. What a delight!

The importance in art should be placed on the *process* of the art and not the product. Too often we forget that our focus should be on the enjoyment of art. Children should be evaluated on their effort and participation, not on the product itself. As long as children stay within the guidelines of the skill being taught, students should be allowed to make choices, so as not to be too restricted by the teacher's control.

YOUR ROLE DURING THE ART PERIOD

Let's face it, some of us are not artists and this time of the day is a challenge for us as teachers. We need to seek out classes, guided sequential art lessons in manual or books, and ask for suggestions and ideas from our fellow teachers. Before presenting any lesson to our classes, it is imperative that teachers "try out" the lesson themselves. This will give a better sense of the pitfalls of the lesson and where the children might falter. For a novice artist, this will help to gain understanding about how the children are going to feel who are less than eager to try art. This also gives the teacher an additional sample for the children to look at. It is always a good idea to have more than one sample to present to children before the lesson begins. Since our goal is to give children ideas without them feeling the need to copy our sample, three samples is a good number to use. As children begin to feel more confident and feel free to express themselves and take risks within the guidelines of the lesson, they will not feel the need to copy the sample. This usually takes place as the children develop and mature naturally.

WHERE CAN TEACHERS GET OTHER SAMPLES TO SHOW THE CHILDREN?

- Ask a child who finishes early to make a second project—that really makes a child feel good about him-/herself. The fact that you will use his/her sample to show other children in the years to come is a real positive charge.
- Make color copies of your best student works for use for the next year. Few children like you to keep their work forever. The cost of one dollar at the copy store assures you have a wonderful example to use in the future. (You can do the same for samples that other teachers may lend you.)
- Borrow samples from other teachers.

It is a good idea to use student samples. The kids relate to their own peer group's ideas better than to an adult's. An adult perspective of art is more difficult for a child to connect with.

During the working period, you should be observing, assisting, asking questions to refocus students on their process, making constructive suggestions, and checking to see if students have followed the basic parameters of the technique or skill being taught. Since one of our goals should be to see students becoming progressively more skillful at their developmental level, you should set standards and strongly encourage students who are frustrated or have a slump on the project to complete their work.

Children love to see their teachers involved in the lesson also. It is fun and enjoyable for teachers to try the lesson again with their students. Sitting with the students and making another sample of the lesson gives credibility to the project, and lets kids see that even though the teacher might not be the best artist, he/she is putting in effort and enjoying what is being done.

Your role in the art process should also be to encourage students throughout the lesson. Praising a child's work is usually well received if the child believes that you are being honest. While you are observing the work period, you will probably want to offer some suggestions to those students who are experiencing difficulty or who have not really understood the assignment. Questions such as "What do you think would happen if you tried?" "If you were to add another color, what would it be?" "What could you add to make your project more complete?" might direct students to be more successful in their end result.

CLASSROOM ENVIRONMENT

It is important that students do not feel too restricted by the time allotted for the art project. Your objective should be that students enjoy the art so much that they want to complete what they have started. Too often teachers put constraints on the students because there is only a 40- or 50-minute time frame for art. Special consideration should be given to students who do not finish their project during the class time. Extra time may be required or the project may be taken home so that the student gets a feeling of completion.

You also need to treat each child's work as something of value. If you say at the end of the period, "Fold your picture in half and place it in your backpack," the child never sees the work as valued or important. As often as possible, children's work should be displayed on a bulletin board. Every child should sign his/her name to the picture to show pride of ownership. It is also preferred that children's work be framed in construction paper, again to enhance that child's sense of worth as an artist.

Sometimes during art, teachers and the students view the period as a socialization activity. In some classrooms, the art period becomes a social buzz session where children spend more time chatting with their friends than actually focusing on the project they are working on. The art period should be a relaxing time for everyone. Research shows that people who work quietly as they delve into an art project are more focused; less distraction also gives the person a greater feeling of success and pride at the end of the project. When soft (not over stimulating) music is added, relaxation and focusing are intensified. The element of music tends to also eliminate some of the self-consciousness that students feel when they are around their peers. Some children are uptight and restricted in their ability to express themselves freely, but music tends to lift these concerns and allows relaxation to set in. Those people who find art challenging know those feelings of frustration and concern. When someone feels incompetent in an area, feelings are intensified, and fear sets in because no one wants to be laughed at for being unskillful.

An example of a student who typifies a success story in art is Jeff. At the beginning of the year, he had no interest in art and was frustrated at any type of art lesson that was presented. He became angry and frustrated when he could not create anything to his satisfaction. Quiet guidance by the teacher also did not work. Something destructive would always happen to his project before it was finished (it got torn, mashed up in his desk, stepped on, etc.). He said he hated art and he didn't want to be forced to do it. Around January, all of a sudden, he started gaining confidence. The turning point was a project of a large-scale bug all done in black thin marker, the inside being textured with many different forms. Somehow he was able to identify with this idea, gain confidence, and appreciate his originality. Voila! An artist was born. From that day forth, every project was completed with excellent effort and participation. His Georgia O'Keeffe flower was a real favorite. The icing on the cake was when the World War II project came about and he actually chose to do the drawing part (WW II planes and ships). What pride he took in knowing it was appreciated and praised by his teacher and classmates! (See the World War II lesson at the end of Section 13, *Hooking Reluctant Readers/Writers*.)

We must look at art as an integral part of a child's education, not as a frill that can be left out. Art continues to play an important role in a child's development. We must see art as one of the seven intelligences that must be cultivated in order to form a well-balanced child.

BIBLIOGRAPHY AND RECOMMENDED RESOURCES

Baer, Gene. *Paste, Pencils, Scissors & Crayons*. West Nyack, NY: Parker Publishing Co., 1992.

Bloom, Dwila. *Multicultural Art Activities Kit*. West Nyack, NY: The Center for Applied Research in Education, 1994.

Brooke, Sandy. *Hooked on Drawing! Illustrated Lessons & Exercises for Grades 4 and Up*. West Nyack, NY: Prentice Hall, 1996.

Gomez, Aurelia. *Crafts for Many Cultures*. (gr. 1–6). New York: Scholastic Professional Books, 1992.

Rabott, Ernest. *Art for Children Series*. New York: Harper Trophy Publishers, 1993.

Romberg, Jenean. *Arts and Crafts Discovery Units*. (Series that includes books on crayon, paper, mobiles, tempera, tissue, watercolor, weaving). West Nyack, NY: The Center for Applied Research in Education, 1973.

Ryder, Willet. *Celebrating Diversity with Art (Thematic Projects for Every Month of the Year)*. Glenview, IL: Good Year Books, 1995.

Schue, Lori Van Kirk. *Art Works for Kids*. (Series includes books on printing, painting, weaving, clay, nature, and recyclables for grades 1–6). (1995) Evan-Moor Educational Publishers, 18 Lower Ragsdale Drive, Monterey, CA 93940-5746.

Schuman, Jo Miles. *Art from Many Hands*. Worcester, MA: Davis Publishing Co., 1981.

Tejada, Irene. *Brown Bag Ideas from Many Cultures*. Worcester, MA: Davis Publishing Co., 1993.

Venezia, Mike. *Getting to Know the World's Greatest Artists Series* (Including Da Vinci, Michelangelo, Picasso, and Rembrandt). Chicago: Children's Press, Inc.

Wachowiak, Frank. *Emphasis Art*. New York: Harper and Row, 1977.

— Section 21 —

A FEW FINAL WORDS

As we reflect on the writing of this book, we find that there are some common threads and key factors necessary for effectively reaching and teaching all of the children in our classrooms:

- Teamwork and collaboration among the school staff, parents and community
- Dedicated educators who motivate and inspire their students to be the best that they can be:

  —Teachers who are flexible, enthusiastic, and positive role models

  —Teachers who provide nurturing and encouragement to their students

  —Teachers who are willing to grow, extend themselves, and aren't afraid of change

  —Teachers who are committed to meeting the individual academic and emotional needs of their students

- Providing *balance, options, variety,* and *choices*
- More encompassing assessment and accountability
- Respect, appreciation for each others' differences, and positive attitudes
- Strong efforts to welcome and involve parents in a partnership with the school
- Relevant, *motivating* lessons, activities, and curriculum that taps the interests and strengths of all students
- Adaptations and accommodations that will allow students with special needs and varying developmental levels to achieve success

- Active learning and participation of all students
- Avoiding complacency or silence when it comes to the welfare and best interests of our children
- Setting and maintaining high expectations for educators and students by not tolerating mediocrity
- Close communication between the home and school
- Strong support systems within the school

With more and more children who have significant special needs being placed in the general classroom, it is essential that we provide the necessary supports that will allow them to experience success in inclusive settings. Classroom teachers need help and support—they cannot and should not be expected to do it alone. All efforts to give personalized attention to address the diverse, individual needs of students, and to make special accommodations/ modifications as appropriate takes *time* (and training).

Administrators must seek ways to support teachers in this effort. Through strong leadership, creative means can be found for teachers to:

- Be provided some time for planning and collaboration
- Be kept updated about effective strategies and to participate in useful, meaningful professional growth opportunities
- Be given extra assistance in order to lower the adult-student ratio within the classroom (e.g., parent volunteers, cross-age tutors, aide time).

We need to find effective and creative ways, as well, to provide special education and support services to the maximum benefit of students without watering down or eliminating critical programs and services to our children. In our attempts to provide inclusive opportunities to children eligible for special education, we must take great care not to deprive those students of the services, materials, and supports to which they are entitled.